Corporate Reputation

Psychological and Behavioral Aspects of Risk Series

Series Editors: Professor Cary L. Cooper and Professor Ronald J. Burke

Risk management is an ongoing concern for modern organizations in terms of their finance, their people, their assets, their projects and their reputation. The majority of the processes and systems adopted are very financially oriented or fundamentally mechanistic; often better suited to codifying and recording risk, rather than understanding and working with it. Risk is fundamentally a human construct; how we perceive and manage it is dictated by our attitude, behavior and the environment or culture within which we work. Organizations that seek to mitigate, manage, transfer or exploit risk need to understand the psychological factors that dictate the response and behaviors of their employees, their high-flyers, their customers and their stakeholders.

This series, edited by two of the most influential writers and researchers on organizational behavior and human psychology explores the psychological and behavioral aspects of risk; the factors that:

- define our attitudes and response to risk,
- are important in understanding and managing 'risk managers', and
- dictate risky behavior in individuals at all levels.

Titles Currently in the Series Include:
New Directions in Organisational Psychology and Behavioural Medicine
Edited by Alexander-Stamatios Antoniou and Cary Cooper

Risky Business
Psychological, Physical and Financial Costs of High Risk Behavior in Organizations
Edited by Ronald J. Burke and Cary L. Cooper

Safety Culture
Assessing and Changing the Behaviour of Organizations
John Bernard Taylor

Corporate Reputation

Managing Opportunities and Threats

Edited by

RONALD J. BURKE,
GRAEME MARTIN
and
CARY L. COOPER

GOWER

Gower Applied Business Research
Our programme provides leaders, practitioners, scholars and researchers with thought provoking, cutting edge books that combine conceptual insights, interdisciplinary rigour and practical relevance in key areas of business and management.

Published by
Gower Publishing Limited
Wey Court East
Union Road
Farnham
Surrey, GU9 7PT
England

Ashgate Publishing Company
Suite 420
101 Cherry Street
Burlington,
VT 05401-4405
USA

www.gowerpublishing.com

British Library Cataloguing in Publication Data
Corporate reputation : managing opportunities and threats.
-- (Psychological and behavioural aspects of risk)
1. Corporate image. 2. Public relations. 3. Issues
management.
I. Series II. Burke, Ronald J. III. Martin, Graeme, 1949-
IV. Cooper, Cary L.
659.2-dc22

ISBN: 978-0-566-09205-3 (hbk)
ISBN: 978-1-4094-2327-0 (ebk)

Library of Congress Cataloging-in-Publication Data
Corporate reputation : managing opportunities and threats / Ronald J. Burke, Graeme Martin and Cary L. Cooper.
    p. cm.
Includes index.
ISBN 978-0-566-09205-3 (hardback) -- ISBN 978-1-4094-2327-0
(ebook) 1. Corporate image. 2. Brand name products--Management. 3. Corporations--Public relations. 4. Organizational effectiveness. 5. Performance--Management. I. Burke, Ronald J. II. Martin, Graeme. III. Cooper, Cary L.
HD59.2.C685 2011
659.2--dc22

2010038060

Printed and bound in Great Britain by the
MPG Books Group, UK

Contents

List of Figures

List of Tables

List of Contributors

Kristin Backhaus is an associate professor in the School of Business at the State University of New York at New Paltz. She teaches courses in management, leadership and human resources, and was awarded the SUNY Chancellor's Award for Excellence in Teaching in 2009. She has published research in the areas of corporate social responsibility, organizational attractiveness, employer branding and cognitive styles. Her articles have appeared in journals including *Business and Society*, the *Journal of Business Communication*, *Career Development International* and the *Journal of Management Education*. She serves as an associate editor for *Organizational Management Journal*. Backhaus conducts corporate training in supervision and is a consultant in the area of employer branding.

Ronald J. Burke is Professor of Organizational Behavior, Schulich School of Business, York University, Toronto, Canada. He is the editor or co-editor of 31 books and has published over 500 journal articles. He was the founding editor of the *Canadian Journal of Administrative Sciences*, and has served on the editorial boards of over 20 journals. His current research interests include work and health, crime and corruption in organizations, occupational health and safety, corporate reputation, and women in management. He has participated in numerous management development courses and consulted with both private and public sector organizations on human resource management issues.

Craig E. Carroll (PhD, University of Texas at Austin, 2004) is an assistant professor in the School of Journalism and Mass Communication at the University of North Carolina at Chapel Hill. His research has been published in *Communication Research*, *Corporate Reputation Review*, *Journalism and Communication Monographs* [Chinese], *Journal of Organizational Change Management*, *Management Learning* and *Public Relations Review*. He serves on the editorial boards of *Corporate Communications*, *Corporate Reputation Review*, *Journal of Communication*, *Journal of Public Relations Research* and *Public Relations Review*. Carroll serves as the Chair of the International Communication Association's public relations division.

Professor Thomas Clarke is Director of the University of Technology Sydney Centre for Corporate Governance which is engaged in research and policy development in international corporate governance. Formerly he was a professor at the China Europe International Business School (CEIBS) in Shanghai. In the UK he was a member of the Royal Society of Arts Tomorrow's Company Inquiry. Among his publications are *Theories of Corporate Governance* (2004); *International Corporate Governance: A Comparative Approach* (2007) and *European Corporate Governance* (2009) all published in London and New York by Routledge. His most recent publication is the *Handbook of Corporate Governance* (London: Sage) edited with Professor Douglas Branson of Pittsburgh Law School.

Cary L. Cooper is Distinguished Professor of Organizational Psychology and Health at Lancaster University Management School. He is the author of over 100 books (on occupational stress, women at work and industrial and organizational psychology), has written over 400 scholarly articles and is a frequent contributor to national newspapers, TV and radio. Professor Cooper is a Fellow of the British Academy of Management and also of the Academy of Management (having also won the 1998 Distinguished Service Award). In 2001 he was awarded a CBE in the Queen's Birthday Honours List for his contribution to organizational health. He was also the lead scientist to the UK Government Office for Science on their Foresight programme on Mental Capital and Well Being (2007–2008), and was appointed a member of the expert group on establishing guidance for the National Institute for Health and Clinical Excellence on 'promoting mental wellbeing through productive and healthy working conditions', 2009. Professor Cooper is Chair of the UK's Academy of Social Sciences.

Gary Davies is Professor of Corporate Reputation at Manchester Business School in England where he is also head of the Reputation Brand and Competitiveness research group. He has published inter alia in the *Strategic Management Journal*, the *Journal of the Academy of Marketing Science*, *Harvard Business Review*, the *Journal of International Business*, *Industrial Marketing Management*, *Journal of Business Research*, *Journal of Advertising Research*, *British Journal of Management* and the *European Journal of Marketing*. His current research is into the relationships between human and brand personality, employer branding and the influence of reputation on investors.

Dr Helen Francis is Director of the newly established Edinburgh Institute of Leadership and People Management and Reader at Edinburgh Napier University. She has played key roles in research, teaching and commercial developments, and published extensively in leading management, organization and HR journals. She has also presented at a wide range of national and international conferences, and her contribution to the HR profession was recognized at the HR Network (Scotland) National Awards in 2007. As a Chartered Fellow Member of the CIPD, Helen has developed strong links with the institute and local business communities and been very active in supporting the development of closer alliances between academics and HR practitioners, reflected in her spearheading of a Research Consultancy Framework © with Dr Martin Reddington.

Associate Professor Paul J. Gollan holds an MSc (Econ) and PhD from the London School of Economics and is currently an associate professor and research director in the Department of Business at Macquarie University. He is also Visiting Professor in the Employment Relations and Organisational Behaviour Group in the Department of Management at the London School of Economics and Adjunct Professor at the Macquarie Graduate School of Management, and Visiting Senior Fellow at the Australian School of Business at the University of New South Wales. Previously he was a lecturer in the Department of Industrial Relations at the London School of Economics. He has authored, co-authored and co-edited a number of books in the fields of human resources and industrial relations. In 2002 he won an Award for Excellence for his paper 'Tunnel vision: non-union employee representation at Eurotunnel', published in *Employee Relations*. In 2003 he was a winner in the Advances in Industrial and Labor Relations (AILR)/Industrial Relations Research Association (IRRA) Best Paper Competition. In 2008 he was named in the most influential list for 'The ones to watch' in *Human Resources Magazine* Most Influential HR People in the UK. He has consulted for a number leading private and public sector organisations.

Kerry Grigg (BCom, MCom) is currently researching employee perceptions of work–life balance policies and practices as part of her PhD candidature at Monash University. Her other research interests include employer branding, psychological contracts and talent management. Kerry has disseminated her research at Australian and international management conferences and has presented workshops to industry and professional groups including the Australian Institute of Police Management and the National Local Government HR Association of Australia. Kerry has worked as a consultant to a diverse range of organizations from industry sectors including local government, fast-moving consumer goods and professional services.

Robin Hadwick is currently pursuing his PhD in international management at the Shidler College of Business at the University of Hawai'i at Manoa. He has 30 years of management experience in the restaurant and airline industries and draws heavily on this background in his current research, which include cross-cultural aspects of reputation and customer service. He studied economics at the University of Michigan and was a winner of the Inaugural Shidler College Business Plan competition while earning his MBA at the University of Hawai'i.

Celia Virginia (C.V.) Harquail is a consultant, independent scholar and blogger at www.AuthenticOrganizations.com. She has her PhD in organizational behavior from the Ross School of Business, University of Michigan, and was on the Leadership and Organizations Faculty of the Darden School at University of Virginia. Prior to earning her PhD, she worked at Procter & Gamble. Dr Harquail's research and consulting address issues of organizational identity, image, reputation, branding and authenticity. She has published her research in journals such as *Administrative Science Quarterly*, *Academy of Management Journal*, *Organization Studies* and *Journal of Management Inquiry*. She serves on the editorial board of *Academy of Management Review*.

Dr Julie Hodges, MA, PhD is Director of the MBA at Durham University Business School and a senior teaching fellow in organizational behaviour. Julie joined the business school in 2006. Prior to this she worked as a development and management consultant for over 20 years in a number of organizations in the profit and non-profit sector.

Julie has carried out a wide range of consultancy and workshop-based assignments in leadership development, change management, skills development and business and team transformations.

Julie has a PhD in organizational change and stress management. Her research interests are leadership branding; leadership and narcissism; sustaining change in organizations; the careers of mid-life women and the transformation of HR.

Graeme Martin is Professor and Director of the Centre for Reputation Management through People (CRMP) at the University of Glasgow in Scotland. He also holds visiting appointments at Macquarie University and Peking University, where he is researching into the links between human resources management and corporate reputations. He has written or edited six books, including *Corporate Reputations, Branding and People Management: A Strategic Approach to HR* with Susan Hetrick and numerous articles and book chapters on HRM, leadership, corporate reputations, technology and HRM with other contributors to this volume, including Thomas Clarke, Helen Francis, Paul Gollan, Kerry Grigg, Julie Hodges and Martin Reddington. Graeme is currently working on the links between HRM, governance and strategy and on employer branding as a researcher and consultant with a number of international firms.

Charles J. McMillan, Professor of Strategic Management, is the author of nine books, including *The Japanese Industrial System*, published in English, Japanese, Malaysian and Russian editions, and *The Strategic Challenge: From Surfdom to Surfing in the Global Village*; papers in journals like *McGill Law Review, Academy of Management Journal, Sociology, Journal of Business Strategy, International Organization, Organizational Studies, Canadian Public Policy, California Management Review* and *Policy Options*, as well as *The New York Times, Nihon Keizai Shimbun, The Globe and Mail* and *The Toronto Star*. He has served as Senior Policy Advisor to the Prime Minister of Canada and consulted widely to governments, multinationals and international organizations. His latest book, now in a second printing, *Eminent Islanders*, received a Heritage Foundation of Prince Edward Island award.

Professor Bill Merrilees PhD (Toronto) MA BCom (Hons) has research interests encompassing branding (including corporate rebranding and brand morphing) and innovation in a variety of contexts including firms, cities, communities, retailing and franchising. His research has been published internationally including in the *European Journal of Marketing, Journal of Business Research, Industrial Marketing Management* and *Journal of Strategic Marketing*. Based in Griffith University Queensland, he is also Visiting Professor at the DeGroote School of Business, McMaster University Canada, and invited guest speaker at University of Guelph, Brunel University and Glasgow Caledonian University. He is an invited keynote speaker at the 6th International Conference, Academy of Marketing Branding SIG.

Dr Dale Miller PhD (Newcastle) MBA BAppSc (OccThy) has research interests spanning branding in various domains including corporate rebranding, corporate branding, cities, communities, retailing and not-for-profit branding, as well as retail innovation and sustainable business. She has published widely, including in the *Journal of Business Research, European Journal of Marketing, Long Range Planning, International Journal of Retail and Distribution Management* and *Journal of Retailing and Consumer Services*. Her publications also include book chapters and the book *Retail Marketing: a Branding and Innovation Approach* (TUP). Based in Griffith University Queensland, she is a visiting researcher at the University of Western Ontario. She also lectures in Hong Kong.

Philip Mirvis is an organizational psychologist and senior research fellow at the Boston College Center for Corporate Citizenship. His studies and private practice concerns large-scale organizational change, the character of the workforce and workplace, and business leadership in society. An advisor to businesses and NGOs in the US, Europe, Asia, and Australia, he has authored 10 books on his studies including *The Cynical Americans* (social trends), *Building the Competitive Workforce* (human capital), *Joining Forces* (the human dynamics of mergers) and *To the Desert and Back* (a business transformation case). His most recent is *Beyond Good Company: Next Generation Corporate Citizenship*. Mirvis is a fellow of the Work/Family Roundtable, a board member of the Citizens Development Corporation and formerly a Trustee of the Foundation for Community Encouragement and Society for Organization Learning.

Mirvis has a BA from Yale University and a PhD in organizational psychology from the University of Michigan. He has taught at Boston University, Jiao Tong University, Shanghai, China and the London Business School.

Sascha Raithel is research assistant at the Institute for Market-based Management at the Ludwig-Maximilians-University of Munich. His scientific work is focused on linking market-based assets to financial performance. His paper 'Value-relevance of Customer Satisfaction: Empirical Evidence for Global Automobile Industry' (together with Sebastian Scharf and Manfred Schwaiger) won the overall best paper award at the 5th EIASM Workshop on Visualising, Measuring and Managing Intangibles and Intellectual Capital in 2009. He has five years' experience as analytics consultant at Pepper GmbH, an international marketing and communications agency.

Dr Martin Reddington runs his own consultancy, Martin Reddington Associates. He is a visiting research fellow at Roffey Park and the University of Glasgow, and an associate of Edinburgh Napier University. Martin was formerly Global Programme Director, HR Transformation, at Cable & Wireless. His doctoral thesis examined the perceptions of managers towards web-based HR and how these perceptions can affect future HR-led investment decisions. He is a member of the CIPD's national advisory group on technology and HR, and an expert advisor on HR transformation to the Public Sector People Managers' Association (PPMA). He is also a member of a working group set up by the Department for Business Innovation and Skills, tasked with examining the role of ICT in supporting UK businesses over the next 10 years.

He recently co-authored a CIPD Research Report which examines the impact of Web 2.0 in organizations and offers guidance to the HR profession on how best to utilize these new technologies. His new book, *HR Transformation: Creating Value through People* (2nd edition), has just been published.

Mooweon Rhee is Shidler College Distinguished Associate Professor, Associate Professor of Management and Cooperating Graduate Faculty of Sociology at the University of Hawai'i. His ongoing research interests revolve around organizational learning, corporate reputation, social networks and Asia-based theories of organizations. His publications have appeared in the *Academy of Management Learning and Education*, *Academy of Management Review*, *Corporate Governance: An International Review*, *Development and Society*, *Journal of Management Studies*, *Management and Organization Review*, *Management Science*, *Organization Science*, *Rationality and Society* and *Strategic Organization*. He received his PhD from the Stanford Graduate School of Business.

Richard Rinkenburger is a research assistant at the Institute for Market-based Management at the Ludwig-Maximilians-University of Munich. He studied business administration with majors in empirical research and corporate planning as well as production and controlling at the Munich School of Management and Copenhagen

Business School. His scientific work is focused on linking CEO reputation to corporate reputation.

Prof. Dr. Manfred Schwaiger is full professor of business administration at the Munich School of Management within Ludwig-Maximilians-University of Munich (LMU), for which he has been serving as a dean and dean of studies for many years. He is head of the Institute of Market-Based Management (IMM) at LMU, member of the board of the German Academic Association for Business Research (VHB) and editorial review board member of the *Journal for Public Policy and Marketing*, the *Journal of Advertising* and the *International Journal of Advertising*. Current research interests cover corporate reputation, communications management, market and trend research and exploratory data analysis.

Matthias Schloderer is a research assistant at the Institute for Market-based Management at the Ludwig-Maximilians-University of Munich. He studied business administration with focus on empirical research and corporate planning, marketing, and market psychology at Munich School of Management. His scientific work is focused on antecedents and consequences of corporate reputation in the recruiting market as well as scale development and PLS path modelling. In 2010, his paper 'Developing a Measurement Approach for Reputation of Non-profit Organizations', co-authored by Marko Sarstedt, was published in the *International Journal of Nonprofit and Voluntary Sector Marketing*.

Importance of Corporate Reputation

CHAPTER 1

Corporate Reputations: Development, Maintenance, Change and Repair[1]

RONALD J. BURKE

Corporate reputation has become a "hot" topic in the past few years given the evidence linking a favorable corporate reputation and various intangible and tangible benefits, the high profile corporate scandals that have come to dominate the media, and the generally low opinion the general public has of corporations and business (Backhaus and Tikoo, 2004; Balmer and Greyser, 2003; Davies and Miles, 1997; Davies et al., 2003; Dowling, 2001). Recent financial crises have juxtaposed "Wall Street" and "Main Street." Entire industries have suffered reputation loss (e.g., automotive, financial services) and the misadventures of one firm has spilled over to affect the reputations of other firms, termed "reputation spill-over" (Schwartz and Gibb, 1999; Williams and Barrett, 2000).

According to Ernst and Young, the investment community believes that between 30 and 50 percent of a company's value is intangible, based mostly on corporate reputation. Others have placed the value of such intangibles at 70 percent.

What is a corporate reputation? A corporate reputation is a function of the perceptions and attitudes toward it held by individual members of a particular stakeholder group. A corporate reputation rests on assessments made by individuals outside the organization (Highhouse et al., 2009; Schwaiger, 2004; Wartwick, 2002).

Fombrun (1996, p.37) defines corporate reputation as "the overall estimation in which a particular company is held by its various constituents". Zyglidoupoulos (2001, p.418) defines it "as the set of knowledge and emotions held by various stakeholder groups concerning aspect of a firm and its activities." Corporate reputations have many aspects (e.g., are multidimensional) and vary with different stakeholder groups (e.g., are stakeholder specific). Corporate identity results from assessments by insiders to an organization, though insiders can be aware of how outsiders perceive their organization and the attitudes outsiders hold towards it (Bartel et al., 2007; Bouchikhi and Kimberly,.2008; Deephouse and Carter, 2005). A corporate reputation is the composite or overall assessment by groups of individuals of an organization that goes beyond assessments of particular

---

1   Preparation of this chapter was supported in part by York University.

features or qualities (Shenkar and Yuchtman-Yaar, 1997). Corporate reputations also make it possible to compare organizations (Dowling, 2004). While very useful, assessments of corporate reputation and corporate identity are still imperfect.

Earle (2009) draws a distinction between trust in an organization and confidence in an organization. Trust is based on shared values such as morality, benevolence, integrity, inferred traits and intentions, fairness and caring. Trust is relational. Confidence is based on past performance and experience with an organization. Competence, ability, experience and standards.

Does corporate reputation matter? Studies of the Fortune 500 companies have shown that the most "admired" companies have much higher price:earnings ratios (about 12 percent higher) than do the less "admired" companies, a $5 billion increase in market capitalization for the typical Fortune 500 company. Thus company reputation is associated with a company's financial performance (Dube, 2009;.Preston and O'Bannon, 1997; Fombrun, 2001; Roberts and Dowling, 1997, 2002; Schuler and Cording, 2006; Tadelis, 1999; Waddock and Graves, 1997). People also prefer to do business with companies they "like" (Bromiley, 2000; Dollinger et al., 1999; Carmeli et al., 2006; Pollock and Rindova, 2003; Shapiro, 1983; Yoon et al., 1993). Employees stay longer and work harder for companies that are liked. Individuals prefer to work in firms having good reputations (Greening and Turban, 2000; Lievens and Highhouse, 2003; Lievens et al., 2001; Martin, 2009a, 2009b; Turban and Greening, 1997). Seventy-three percent of MBA graduates indicated that a company's reputation was "extremely import" or "very important" in their selection of potential employers. Corporate branding helps an organization attract qualified people in "the war for talent" and retain them (Backhaus et al., 2002; Martin and Hetrick, 2006; Martin et al., 2005) Corporate reputation has become one of a company's most valuable assets.

Corporate reputation may also be a critical factor in responding to a crisis (Schnietz and Epstein, 2005).

A survey of senior managers in the US by the Economist Intelligence Unit on how they choose professional services firms found that the firm's reputation was the most important factor followed by personal contact with firms' representatives. Financial advisors and high net-worth investors allocate ore market value to reputation than to board quality.

Hill and Knowlton (2006) reported a study of the role of corporate reputation in the decisions of financial analysts when assessing a firm's performance. Quality of management (a strong leadership team, keeping promises, a sound corporate strategy) emerged as the most significant factor in corporate reputation, when financial performance was excluded. CEO reputation was the next most important factor in their decision to recommend a firm for investment. The analysts strongly believed that a CEO should be terminated if his/her behavior negatively influenced the firm's reputation. Financial analysts also saw clear firm communication with all stakeholders as an important factor in their financial assessment of a firm.

Hall (1992, 1993) surveyed 847 CEOs in the UK from a number of different industries and found that they estimated it would take them, on average, almost 11 years to rebuild their firm's reputation if they had to start from the beginning. A 2004 Burson-Marsteller survey of 685 business leaders from Fortune 1000 firms found that they believed it would take more than four years to recover from a crisis that damaged an organization's reputation and three years for a crisis to fade from the memory of most stakeholders. But 90 percent believed that a company could restore a tarnished reputation

A 2005 Burson-Marsteller survey of business leaders from around the world reported that 81 percent reported more threats to corporate reputation today than two years ago. The top five early warning signs indicating that corporate reputation is falling were: low employee morale, internal politics were more important than doing the job well, the departure of top executives, CEO celebrity displaced CEO credibility, and employees spoke of customers and clients as nuisances.

McKinsey, using an index of Topple Rate, a measure of market leading companies that lose status during the next five years, found that the Topple Rate in the period 1997–2002 was 14 percent as opposed to only 8 percent in the 1970s. It has been estimated that a firm can lose 30 percent of its share value as a result of a highly publicized crisis.

More than 82 percent of major companies are making a substantial effort to manage reputation risk, and 81 percent have increased their efforts over the past three years, according to a survey of 148 risk management executives at US and European corporations reported by the Conference Board. Though social media are gaining influence among customers and investors evaluating companies, only 34 percent of the executives surveyed said they regularly monitor social networking sites for information about their companies, and only 10 percent participate in them.

A study recently conducted by the New York Stock Exchange (NYSE) of 205 CEOs whose firms were listed on the NYSE reported that almost 100 percent said their jobs have more personal legal risk than three years earlier, 75 percent reported tracking their firm's reputations through surveys, 44 percent indicated that their firm reputation was more important now than three years ago, and 84 percent though they were taking adequate actions to protect their firm's reputations, typically through informal discussions with stakeholders. Over 80 percent undertook informal discussions with relevant stakeholders, about 70 percent undertook discussions with or surveys of employees, and about 65 percent reviewed published rankings within their industries.

There are two broad outcomes of a favorable corporate reputation: employer benefits-employees and customers love the company and spread the word (Kumar, Peterson and Leone, 2007), and reputational capital – the firm differentiates itself from others and develops legitimacy. Both of these benefits contribute to short and long term performance.

A good corporate reputation is enhanced by the tangible things that it does—not by advertising (e.g., by delivering better products and services, being seen as a good place to work, and the building of trust with internal and external stakeholders).This leads to a distinction between well-known celebrity firms and firms having a solid corporate reputation (Rindova, Pollock et al., 2006; Rindova, Williamson et al., 2005) A corporate reputation is an investment. Although different stakeholders have different perceptions of a company's reputation, customer and employee perceptions are the key.

A favorable corporate reputation rests on competing successfully in the market place, achieving a familiar and positive image, building an ethical and high performance work culture, and communicating widely with various stakeholders (Deephouse, 2000; Fombrun and Van Riel, 2004). And more companies are seeing the value of company reputation in an increasingly competitive global business environment.

A positive organization reputation will increasingly influence purchase decisions when there is little difference in price, quality design and product. There is even more competition, lack of differentiation, and pricing concerns in the service sector. Thus building a highly regarded corporate reputation or corporate brand had become even more important.

Interestingly, most people have a low opinion of corporations in general. So being admired offers an even more substantial benefit. In addition, there are more threats to a company's reputation today than previously.

Corporate reputation has two components: sympathy—emotional identification and liking—and competence—the quality of services and products delivered (MacMillan et al., 2005). Corporate reputation has the following building blocks: emotional appeal, vision, leadership and integrity, social responsibility, and a workplace environment supporting performance. Reputation comes from direct experiences with an organization, word of mouth, advertising and media coverage. It takes considerable time to develop an outstanding reputation; yet reputations can be damaged in an instant.

Corporate reputation can be damaged quickly given increasing media scrutiny and global coverage and communication via the internet. The evidence indicates significant financial costs to organizations from damaged reputations resulting from misconduct or faulty products. For example, companies guilty of "cooking the books" generally suffer almost ten times the financial loss from damaged reputations than from whatever fines may be imposed.

Reputation Stickiness

Reputations, positive or negative, become embedded in the minds of stakeholders (Rao, 1994). I bought my first Japanese-made automobile about 25 years ago when the Big Three automakers started getting a bad rap about the lower quality of their vehicles in consumer reports. The advertisements now talk about the quality of the Big Three being equal to or superior to Japanese-made cars but I am skeptical about these ads.

Reputation Spillover

The reputation of an organization can spill over to affect other organizations in the same industry or sector or even the industry or sector as a whole (Yu and Lester, 2008). For example, a few banks in various countries (e.g., RBS and HBCS in the UK, and Bank of America and Lehman Brothers in the US) have suffered damage to their reputations which has then spread to all/many other banks or financial institutions in these countries. Banks and financial institutions that were functioning fine were affected by the negative comments by the media, which then reflected badly on all managers in that sector or industry.

Few companies have the expertise and resources to manage a threat to reputation or a crisis effectively. As a result they commonly rely on external consultants for such assistance. Threats include rumors, innuendos, lies, lawsuits, disgruntled employees or ex-employees, theft of data, cyberattacks, errors and accidents, defective products, product recalls, and misbehavior of key corporate officers (drunkenness, sexual harassment, a messy divorce).

Organizations experiencing such crises have a high "stumble rate" (Gaines-Ross, 2008). Most have not done well in addressing such "failures" or crises. In fact, 79 percent of organizations experiencing damaged corporate reputations in the past decade have "fallen" in reputation indicators. Failing to successfully address challenges to corporate reputation has consequences (e.g., witness Enron, Arthur Andersen, Société Generale).

But organizations can regain lost reputations through appropriate actions (e.g., the Tylenol case involving Johnson & Johnson, the introduction of New Coke in 1985). But recovery also takes a long time, estimated by executives at three to four years. So recognizing potential threats or anticipating potential risks emerges as a critical organizational competence. In Canada, in the summer of 2008, a plant of McCain Foods in Toronto was found to be the source of listeria, a bacteria on tainted meat products that caused 22 deaths. The firm recalled much of its product and lost sales for months but is now slowly bounding back. The CEO, Michael McCain, is credited with responding to this crisis in ways that minimized the damage to their "brand". It will take another year at least for McCain Foods to fully recover.

What constitutes an effective strategy to proactively develop and sustain a favorable corporate reputation at such trying times? Effective dealing with such crises requires taking full responsibility for it, offering a sincere apology, quickly disclosing details of the crisis, making progress or recovery visible, and analyzing what went wrong so it will not happen again.

Caring or Good PR?

A good deed, corporate givebacks, or more PR? Companies in a few countries have made recent efforts to help individuals who have lost their jobs and their savings in the recent economic downturn. Americans who have lost their jobs, savings and health care coverage have been offered free drugs and medications for up to one year (e.g., Viagra) by Pfizer upon proof that they had been already purchasing these Pfizer products. General Motors (GM) has indicated that individuals who bought their products and then lost their jobs could have a grace period of up to nine months in paying for their vehicles. GM has also indicated that if you bought their products and then concluded that you did not like the vehicle, you could return in within a specified time period. Jet-Blue Airways will refund air fares for people losing their jobs after purchasing a ticket. Hyundai allows individuals to return leased vehicles with no fee. Clothier Jos. A. Bank will refund the money but let anyone who had lost their job keep their suit. Some restaurants allow patrons to pay what they can for what they have eaten. Caring or good PR?

This collection deals with the development of corporate reputation, managing corporate reputation, risks or threats to corporate reputation, changing a corporate reputation, and recovering from a damaged corporate reputation. A corporate reputation is harder to build than to destroy.

This introductory chapter has two objectives. The first is to highlight the importance of corporate reputation, identify some of its antecedents, illustrate the benefits of developing a favorable corporate reputation, indicate some of the challenges to building and maintaining a favorable reputation and some of the threats to doing so which then requires rebuilding of a damaged reputation (Alsop, 2004; Bernstein, 2009). This content serves as an introduction to the topic and the chapters that follow. Material on the development, maintenance and rebuilding of individual reputations will be included where relevant. This collection covers why corporate reputation matters, the increase in reputation loss, threats to corporate reputation, monitoring reputation threats online and offline, the key role of leadership in reputation recovery, and making corporate reputation immune from threats. The second objective of this chapter is to briefly summarize the chapters that are included in the remainder of the collection.

Sources of Corporate Reputation

The early work on corporate reputation was dominated by the fields of marketing and communication. But today these have been integrated with human resource management (HRM) and corporate strategy (Barrow and Mosely, 2005; Fombron, 2005; Fombrun and Shanley, 1990; Friedman, 2009). The reputation of an organization was conveyed to outsiders by managers in the organization. It is now widely accepted that corporate reputations start from the inside out (Martin, 2009a, 2009b).

Fombrun (1996) observed that organizations doing a good job managing their corporate reputations stressed the following factors:

1. Distinctiveness—firms occupied a distinct place in the views of stakeholders.
2. Focus—firms emphasized a core them.
3. Consistency—firms were consistent in their communications with all stakeholders.
4. Identity—firms were seen as genuine by stakeholders.
5. Transparency—firms were seen as open and forthright in going about their business.

A corporate reputation differentiates an organization from its competitors while still remaining legitimate in its sector and the wider market place. A favorable corporate reputation gives significant advantages in industries predicated on intangible assets such as innovation, creativity, intellectual capital, and high levels of service to customers.

Where do corporate reputations come from? On what are they based? There are at least three schools of thought on these questions (Davies, 2008):

1. There is a corporate character explanation. People value organizational personality traits such as trustworthiness and reliability.
2. Firms become similar over time, termed institutional isomorphism by organizational theorists. People value behaviors and actions that fit the cultural norms of an industry or society.
3. Firms develop reputations—favorable or unfavorable—based on benefits that the organization has recently provided to the individual.

A firm develops a positive/favorable corporate reputation based on internal HRM practices. These include the presence of sound and well-developed and articulated HRM strategies, initiatives to increase employee engagement, and efforts to attract, retain and develop talented employees (talent management).

Research conducted by Weber Shandwick and the Reputation Institute identified six elements in building a favorable corporate reputations. These were:

1. Responsibility—supporting worthy causes, demonstrating environmental responsibility, and community/societal responsibility.
2. Communications—marked by transparency, full disclosure and open dialogue.
3. Products and services—offers high quality, innovative, customer satisfaction, and positive word of mouth.
4. Talent—rewards employees fairly, retains talent, attracts talent, promotes diversity. Jack and Suzy Welch refer to these organizations as "talent magnets".
5. Financial measures—does better than competitors, stable, has a high investment value.
6. Leadership—the CEO and senior team are sound, solid leaders, and implement good governance.

Chun (2005) found different views on the nature of corporate reputation in various literatures. Thus reputation was seen as an intangible assed having financial worth, as traits or signals that influence perceptions of the organization by external stakeholders, as perceived by customers and clients, as perceptions of the organization held by internal stakeholders (employees), and as an overall perception of an organization's performance relative to societal expectations and norms. Perceptions of corporate reputation can be internal (employees, managers), external (customers, shareholders), or both. And different stakeholders can have different perceptions of company reputation.

Chun draws a distinction between image, identity, and desired identity. Image refers to "how others see us," identity is "how we see ourselves," and desired image is "how we want others to see ourselves." There are also various measures of corporate reputation. Some of the common dimensions of these measures include emotional appeal, quality of products and services, quality of management, vision and leadership, workplace environment, social responsibility, financial soundness, and long-term investment value.

Building a Favorable Corporate Reputation

The Four Seasons Hotel chain is noted for its exemplary customer service. Sharp (2009), its long time CEO, lays out the chain's business philosophy. Four qualities distinguish the Four Seasons from some of its competitors: service, quality, culture, and brand. Sharpe outlines the countless efforts, big and small, that the Four Seasons makes every day to achieve these four elements.

Smith (2009) tells the interesting story of how the sports network ESPN started, survived, faced challenges, and grew over the 30 years of its existence. When Americans think sports they think of ESPN. Smith attributes much of its success to branding and reputation. ESPN developed a tight culture and leadership from the bottom up and has maintained its values from its beginning to the present day. ESPN created product and employee brand awareness by being consistently focused.

These two case studies or stories indicate the importance of senior executives speaking with one voice. Voss et al. (2006) show what happens when leadership disagrees on "who we are."

Davies (2008), in a study of 859 managers form 17 organizations, investigated the association of their employer brand with four outcomes (perceived differentiation, affinity, identification, and loyalty). Five dimensions of employer brand were included:

agreeableness, enterprise, chic, competence, and ruthlessness. All four outcomes were predicted by aspects of employer brand. Agreeableness had the strongest predictor of outcomes. Surprisingly, competence was not related to any of the four outcomes.

Ulrich and Smallwood (2005, 2007a, 2007b) illustrate the benefits from developing a leadership brand. Organizations with a favorable leadership brand have a reputation for developing exceptional managers with a distinct set of talents that fit the expectations of customers, clients, and investors. They outline five stages in the development of a strong leadership brand. These stages are:

1. A focus on the fundamentals of leadership (e.g., setting strategy, grooming talent) and differentiating this focus from that of others.
2. Connect these leadership fundamentals with expectations of customers and clients and the desired leadership brand.
3. Evaluating leaders based on these criteria using internal and external perspectives.
4. Invest in broad-based leadership development having both customers and investors provide feedback and guidance.
5. Evaluate the progress of these leaders over the long term on building the leadership brand.

Fulmer et al. (2003) found that companies on the "100 best places to work" list had both highly positive workforce attitudes and a higher financial performance. The authors attribute this to the link between positive employee relations contributing to better financial performance.

A company reputation differs in the eyes of various stakeholders. One might conclude that there is no single company reputation. Employees, customers or clients, shareholders, the media, and investors form perceptions of a company reputation, and these various stakeholders use different factors and criteria.

Yet company reputations are fairly stable—all things being equal—and raters generally agree. Highhouse et al. (2009) had university professors in various areas make repeated judgments about corporate reputations of highly visible US corporations. There was considerable agreement on overall ratings and how they weighed different dimensions of corporate performance in making their global judgments. They conclude that stable estimates of global reputation can be achieved with a small number of items and raters.

Mangold and Miles (2007) focus on internal corporate reputation. This reputation is the extent to which employees know and understand the organization's mission, values and desired brand image and the degree to which their psychological contract is being fulfilled. They divide efforts to create a favorable internal reputation into external and internal and formal versus informal. Informal efforts outside the organization involve word of mouth; formal efforts outside the organization include advertising aimed at external stakeholders, and PR directed at external stakeholders. Informal efforts inside the organization include customer feedback, co-worker influences, organizational culture values, and organizational leadership actions; formal efforts insider the organization include HR management strategies such as recruitment and staffing, training and development, compensation, performance management, PR directed to employees, and advertising directed to employees.

Steps to Building a Favorable Corporate Reputation

1. Formulate a corporate reputation strategy and key factors in business sustainability.
2. Integrate the communication and social responsibilities into the company's corporate reputation strategy.
3. Develop a crisis management strategy to defend against threats to reputation.
4. Communicate the corporate story to internal and external stakeholders (Wartick, 1992, 2002).
5. Build a corporate culture that attracts and retains talent.

The building blocks of corporate reputation: emotional appeal, vision and leadership, social responsibility, workplace environment, financial performance, and quality of products and services.

How does one measure corporate reputation? Recognition, trust, stock price or financial performance, employee recruitment and retention. Trust may the most important factor.

Collins and Han (2004), in a study of 99 organizations, found that corporate advertising and firm reputation had direct effects on applicant pool quantity and quality.

The construction of a company reputation includes both objective factors (financial performance, financial stability, growth) and emotional factors (trust, liking, faith in, first-hand experience with its products and services). Reputations are also based on cognitive factors (e.g., facts, data, information) and affective factors (emotions, reactions).

It takes quite a long time to build a company reputation. Strong brands would include Coca-Cola, Microsoft, IBM and GE. Reputation building involves media coverage, sponsorship of events, public relations, publicity, offering high quality products and services, and most of all, "walking the talk"—behaving in the market place in accordance with stated values and principles. Organizations need to continually monitor their reputations in order to self-correct. Building and maintaining a favorable corporate reputation require considerable investment of resources.

Familiarity and visibility can cut both ways (Brooks et al., 2003). Highly familiar and visible organizations provide information that fits with both admiring and condemning than less familiar organizations. In addition, organizations need to decide whether they want to create an overall corporate brand or whether to let separate units maintain their own brands (Dev, 2008).

The reputation of corporations, and business in general, has taken a hit over the past few years. Seventy-one percent of consumers say that the reputation of Corporate America is poor (HarrisInteractive, 2008). There were several reasons for this. Company behavior has fallen short in regard to public expectations. Poorer company behavior has decreased the credibility of company executives and organizations themselves as public confidence in them also fell. The gap between what executives and organizations promise in terms of their own behavior and what happens increased public cynicism and disappointment. It has also been suggested that, given the low levels of trust some stakeholders have in particular firms or industries, the value of communication programs has decreased.

There has been an increase in the number of companies that offer consulting services to organizations interested in developing and maintaining a favorable reputation, and companies that have encountered a threat to their reputation and want to better manage the fall-out and rebound from the damage inflicted.

Corporate Reputations—Local, National or International?

Some organizations face an important decision whether to keep their organizational brand at a local level or extend it to a national and/or international level (Dev, 2008). Creating national or international brands sends out a consistent message. But spreading an organizational brand throughout a country or across counties faces the challenge of having the message "fit" the local conditions.

Building Reputations in New Firms

Fischer and Reuber (2007) tackle the intriguing question of how new firms develop a reputation. Most of the research and writing on corporate reputation deals with established firms. How can a new firm develop an initial reputation when its history is short and information about it may be/is mixed? Useful information is provided by the founder's track record, quality of partners, certifications achieved or obtained, quality of members of the boards of directors, logos, stories in the popular press, focused communications to stakeholders, ratio of "good" to "bad" information, and comparisons with and differentiation from, other firms. Clegg et al. (2007) discuss the need for organizations in emerging industries to also establish their legitimacy.

Corporate Reputation and "Legitimacy Lies"

Rutherford et al. (2009) suggest that founders and managers of start-up firms engage in:"legitimacy lies"; they "gild the lily" when discussing their firms, intentionally misrepresent the facts of their situation. There is little information available to external stakeholders about new firms. Thus managers lie about the size of their firms (number of employees), number of clients, length of existence, types of resources, and ability to deliver on projects.

Individual Reputations

Individual managers have images or reputations. Consider Jack Welch, Steve Jobs, Bill Gates, Richard Branson, Warren Buffett, and Martha Stewart. In many cases the person becomes synonymous with their company. The image and reputation of the CEO becomes the image and reputation of the company. With the passage of time the luster of some of these individuals has begun to fade. But are the days of the celebrity CEO coming to an end? Some writers think so. Instead effective CEOs build their reputations through having integrity, communicating, team building, planning for the long haul and possessing a vision.

Individuals, similar to corporations, can have damaged reputations. Late-night TV host David Letterman announced on the air that he had sexual relationships with several female staff members of his show while single in response to an alleged extortion plot. He spoke about the extortion plot and his sexual relationships on at least the next two shows (the first on October 1, 2009). He apologized for his actions. Reputation commentators said he handles this incident well. Letterman was criticized by some women's groups for his actions in creating a "hostile work environment" in which women with less power may have felt coerced into these liaisons. The network did not believe that Letterman violated their policies. His viewing audience has not fallen off nor have his advertising sponsors left.

American golfer, Tiger Woods, has been a public figure since he was three years old, has a squeaky clean image, and earns hundreds of millions of dollars annually, perhaps billions to date, in endorsement fees. On early Sunday morning (2:25 am), November 29, 2009, Woods drove out of his Florida mansion and hit a fire hydrant and a tree, the car sustaining US$5,000–$8,000 in damages. He went to hospital where he received treatment for minor injuries, mostly to his face. Liquor was not involved. Neither Woods nor his wife, Elin Nordegren, who arrived at the crash site following the accident talked with police and Woods was given a $164 fine and 4 demerit points on his driver's license. On the day of the accident two of Woods's spokespeople (one his agent, Mark Steinberg) gave brief statements to the media indicating that Woods received only minor injuries. Woods took full responsibility for the incident. And a few sponsors indicated that they were remaining with Woods. Since then, Woods admitted to having multiple affairs, his marriage has ended, other sponsors have left , and his golf game has deteriorated.

Later on the same day that the above paragraph was written, e-mails and voice recordings of Woods talking with one of his mistresses became public. Woods then apologized to his family and fans on his website for causing pain to his family, asked for privacy, and committed to being a better father and husband. He referred to this liaison as a "transgression." Stonewalling, weak denying, and offering vague admissions failed to work. Lawyers, agents and bodyguards could not control or contain the story. Tiger Woods cheated on his wife. His reputation has been tarnished. More recent news reports (December 7, 2009) link Woods to at least 10 women, and a poll by CNN and *USA Today* found that Woods' approval rating had dropped dramatically since June. Some sponsors have dropped Woods (Accenture, AT&T), a third is not showing Woods in any advertisements for the moment (Gillette), and a fourth (GM) has taken away his Cadillac. It has been estimated that the Woods scandal has cost sponsors US$12 billion in lost market value according to Professors Victor Stango and Christopher Knittel of the University of California at Davis. Stango and Knittel looked at stock market returns on the 13 trading days after the accident and compared returns of sponsoring companies with non-sponsoring companies. Woods has become the butt of jokes and skits. Woods has not appeared in any TV commercials since November 29, two days after the incident, and sponsors appear to be backing away from him. Experts believe Woods needs to publicly appear on TV and honestly indicate his transgressions. My sense is that he can never fully recover from his actions and it is not clear that his marriage will be saved. Some have speculate that the Woods situation likely will lead to a decline of celebrity endorsements. Ethical misconduct on the part of celebrity CEOs has led to a decline in the cult of the celebrity CEO, leading to the decline in the value of celebrity of any kind. In fact, Hansen et al. (2010) have shown that the best performing CEOs in the world are typically people that no one has heard of. Agents of celebrities are now more likely to take out insurance against any losses resulting from a transgression on the part of their celebrity clients.

In August 2009, Rick Pitino, famed basketball coach at the University of Louisville, admitted having sex with a woman in a restaurant. Pitino, a devout Catholic, is married with children. Pitino gave her US$3,000 when the woman said she was going to have an abortion. Pitino's contract includes dishonesty and moral depravity as grounds for firing. Pitino apologized for his "indiscretions." The university president expressed disappointment in Pitino's "errors in judgment." The president said "As we try to teach our students, when you make a mistake, admit it and right it as fast as you can, coach has done that today."

UK MP Iris Robinson resigned her seat, and her husband, Peter Robinson, Ireland's First Minister, stepped down from his job after it was revealed that his wife had an affair with a boy who was 19 at the time, managed to get the young man money to start a restaurant from the government, and had the young man give her some of the money back (January 2010).

A top executive at the UK firm, Nomos Capital, Mark Lowe, is being sued (November, 2009) by a Canadian female employee, Jordan Wimmer after her employment was terminated. Lowe is accused of bringing prostitutes to meetings, repeatedly calling Wimmer a "stupid blonde," and, during a business trip to Paris, taking Wimmer and another female employee to a strip club where he attempted to persuade them to have a lap dance.

Canadian MP, Ruby Dhalla, was criticized in the press by three foreign workers for their treatment by Dhalla and her family. A survey conducted by Angus Reid of Canadians found that about three times as many believed the employees/workers as believed Dhalla, and about one third now thought less of Dhalla. The damage to Dhalla was short-lived however; many months later this story has faded well into the background. Michael Vick, a professional football player in the US, lost product endorsements and salary when convicted of bankrolling a dog-fighting ring and spending two years in jail. Michael Phelps, winner of eight gold medals at the Beijing Olympics, lost a few endorsements when a photograph of him smoking marijuana appeared in the media.

Robert Mugabe, President of Zimbabwe, has a legacy of widespread corruption. He has terrorized his citizens, created an economy characterized by hyper-inflation and a country that endured a cholera epidemic, police brutality, food shortages, limited health care and education, rigged elections, and introduced "taking" land productively farmed away from whites. A report titled "Electing to Rape" published by Aids-Free World, a New York-based advocacy group (December 10, 2009), indicated that the Mugabe regime used rape and torture as strategic weapons against their opposition.

Industry-wide Reputations

Industries and industrial sectors have images and reputations. The banking and financial services sectors have taken a beating over the past two years. Winn et al. (2008) show the dynamic tension between organizations in the same industry that compete with one another but also must develop a collective reputation to protect against external threats to industry legitimacy.

The image of the pharmaceutical industry in some countries (Canada, US, UK) has suffered over the past decade. Pharmaceutical companies spending on ads has grown at an annual rate of 14.3 percent a year since the US Food and Drug Administration (FDA) allowed companies to expand direct-to-consumer marketing in 1992. But when pharmaceutical companies are charged with deceptive marketing, they lose 1 percent of market value on average.

Another study concluded that pharmaceutical companies would be better off (more viable and profitable over the long term) if they spent more money on innovation (coming up with new treatments) than on marketing.

Since 2000, pharmaceutical firms have paid a total of almost US$4 billion in settlements and fines. The pharmaceutical industry has historically been highly regarded for its commitment to improving human health. But there has been an increasing number of product recalls in the past decade. The general public now sees pharmaceutical companies more interested in profits. Less than half of US consumers have a favorable view of the pharmaceutical industry—only tobacco companies were viewed lower.

Pfizer agreed to pay the largest fine in US history—US$1.2 billion—for promoting a pain killer (Bextra, since taken off the market) and other drugs for uses not approved by the FDA.

An overemphasis on marketing coupled with the withdrawal of high profile drugs (e.g., arthritis drug Vioxx) have produced an increasing distrust of pharmaceutical manufacturers. Researchers have suggested that the negative effects of Vioxx could have been detected three years earlier if Pfizer had made their data public. Although the court case is still in process at the time of writing, Johnson & Johnson has been charged by US prosecutors with paying tens of millions of dollars in kickbacks to nursing homes to use its products.

At least two other industries have become concerned about their reputations. First, Canada and a few other countries, obtain oil and gas from tar sands operations which unfortunately emit greenhouse gases, putting the industry at odds with the "green" movement. Investing in tar sands projects will help Canada's ailing economy, provide jobs and money to petroleum workers and producers, and might even keep gas and oil prices to consumers lower than they might otherwise be. But the tar sands are Canada's largest producer of greenhouse gases.

Second, the reputation of the mining industry has taken a recent hit. Canada and several other countries have developed mines in various countries around the world (e.g., Mexico, El Salvador, Ecuador, Congo, Papua New Guinea). Increasingly, Canadian mining firms in these countries have had clashes with anti-mining activists. These clashes have involved beatings, shootings and gang rapes of women encountered nearby by guards patrolling the mines. Not surprisingly, the mining industry (November 2009) denied allegations that they engaged in human rights and health and safety violations and claimed that government legislation aimed at controlling the mining industry would lead them to ruin, making them uncompetitive with their foreign rivals. A Canadian mining company, Blackfire Exploration Ltd., under investigation for the death of an anti-mining activist, had their Chiapas Mexico mine closed due to environmental infractions (December 2009). Three Blackfire employees were arrested over the November 27, 2009 slaying of Mariano Abarca Roblero, who had publicly protested against the mining operation. The environmental violations included pollution and creating toxic emissions. Blackfire has also been accused of bribery and threatening anti-mining activists.

There are currently over 230 Canadian mining companies working in Mexico, 200 in exploration and over 40 in running mines. These events give a "black eye" to Canadian mining organizations and the mining industry as a whole.

Country Reputations

Countries also have images or reputations. My country apparently needs to change its image. At a recent Economic Edge Conference held in Toronto (Wednesday, October 21, 2009) Ms. Trish Wheaton, chief marketing officer of the global marketing agency, Wunderman, and chairwoman of its Canadian unit, noted that Canada needed to improve its overseas image if it wanted to emerge from the global economic recession stronger. Investors were looking to emerging markets and Canada's image of friendly, unaggressive people, beavers, and clean wilderness, while favorable, was not the right country brand to attract business investments. In addition, the tourism image of Canada also needed to change to reflect an intelligent and business awareness that distinguished it from other countries, according to business leaders present.

Yet country reputations can change and change quickly. Canada hosted the 2010 Winter Olympic Games in Vancouver. Despite some early problems with too warm weather, and the death of a Georgian luger, these games came off relatively well. As a result, not only did Canadians come together with a increased spirit of pride, visitors and athletes from various countries commented on the good job that Canada did.

Israel is another country with an image problem. Israel is seen as a land of conflict. The Israeli image wasn't help much when soldiers and snipers from the Israeli Defense Force, following attacks in the West Bank and the Gaza strip, wore T-shirts having a picture of a gun sight targeting a pregnant woman with the slogan "1 shot, 2 kills" on it and in another case, a gun-toting child with the slogan "The smaller they are, the harder it is". This suggests that relying on Israel for goods and services can be problematic. But since Israel has produced reliable products and services historically, its biggest strength being innovation, Israel needs to show to the world what it has contributed.

Although South Africa had the image of a country racked with crime, it was awarded and held the World Cup in 2010, the first time the World Cup was held in Africa. There was concern that violence in South Africa would keep the numbers of visitors down and this in fact happened. Its image was not helped in Canada, when two Canadians who were born in South Africa and returned annually to visit family and friends were beaten and stabbed outside Cape Town, known as a relatively safe South African city (December 2009). Earlier in December a Canadian priest was killed and another Canadian priest narrowly survived an armed assault near Johannesburg. Four Catholic priests have been killed in South Africa in 2009.

Islamic militants killed more than 50 tourists in Luxor Egypt in 1997, and bombings in Sharm el-Sheik killed 120 people between 2004 and 2006. Tourism figures for Egypt indicated only a small drop in 2007.

Celebrity versus Credibility?

Several CEOs have become celebrity pitchmen and women for their companies, including Lee Iacocca (Chrysler), Dave Thomas (Wendy's), Orville Redenbacher (Redenbacher popcorn), Victor Kiam (Remington Products), Richard Branson (various companies), Martha Stewart (Martha Stewart Enterprises), Oprah Winfrey (Harpo Enterprises), and Harland "Colonel" Sanders (Kentucky Fried Chicken). These individuals were their companies to outsiders.

The cult of celebrity has emerged in several countries. CEOs have become as well known as national leaders, actors and rock stars. Wade et al. (2008), based on Fombrun's use of the phrase "the burdens of celebrity," consider whether CEO celebrity is a benefit or a burden. They note first that some celebrity CEOs fall from grace, some rapidly, others slowly. They identify both pluses and minuses. The pluses include: signaling to stakeholders that the CEO is of high quality and will increase the value of the firm; increased ability to attract higher quality staff, get financial resources at lower rates, and work out more favorable arrangements with suppliers; and more power in dealing with other internal and external stakeholders. The burdens include: hubris and overconfidence in decision-making, self-enhancement at the expense of the organization, and reduced morale among other executives. Using data from CEO of the Year contests run by *Financial World Magazine* Wade et al. address the question of whether star CEOs add value to their organizations, and issues of compensation. Firms with award-winning CEOs were more highly evaluated by the stock market in the three days following the announcement but in the longer term firm performance became more negative. Award-winning CEOs received a salary premium immediately after winning the award but salary over the longer term was a function of how well the organization performed. Wade et al. draw the following conclusions: First, do not become dazzled by CEO celebrities. Second, if the CEO is a celebrity (a star) or the firm wants to hire a celebrity CEO, time pay levels clearly to organizational performance. They caution celebrity CEOs not to be excited at their fame, accept it modestly, and be leery of the burdens and pitfalls.

Malmendier and Tate (2009) studied the impact of CEOs achieving celebrity status, in this case the receipt of prestigious business awards, on the performance of their firms. The found that award-winning CEOs subsequently under-perform, both relative to their prior performance and relative to a matched sample of now-winning CEOs. Yet these celebrity CEOs get higher levels of compensation from their firms, both in absolute amounts and relative to other top executives in their firms. They also spend more time on public and private activities outside their firms (e.g., sitting on corporate boards, writing books).

CELEBRITY CEOS—THE PROS AND THE CONS

- the benefits: increased personal visibility, personal reputation, firm visibility, firm reputation; credit for firm's success; signal to investors that CEO is of high quality; ability to attract higher quality employees, get capital at lower cost, and make more favorable deals with suppliers; advantage in dealing with others; more power over board of directors; adds values to firm in the short term.
- the burdens: a rapid fall from grace is possible; hubris and over-confidence are dangers; over-paying for acquisitions (risky decisions); overestimating results; belief in self as infallible; too many self-promotion activities mean taking one's eye off company issues; undermining executive teamwork; negative impact on morale of other executives, particularly if overly rewarded; no long-term value added to the firm, particularly if not performing well; and higher performance expectations.

Corporate Re-branding

Even successful global companies need to rebrand. GE has been a successful company previously led by a celebrity CEO (Jack Welch) that grew through acquisitions. The current CEO (Jeff Immelt) concluded that it needed a new brand and vision. GE is now focusing on R&D and creating new products and services becoming an innovation and environmental leader. It changed its vision from "We bring good things to life" to "Imagination at work" to reflect this rebranding. GE aimed to be a cleaner, greener and more profitable firm going forward. To achieve this change in brand, GE used television, print and online ads beginning in 2003. GE also tailors its message to the various countries in which it operates.

Some Canadian universities have hired marketing consultants and used focus groups to reach potential students by projecting a "new" and "different" image of their universities, in other words, refining their brand identities... This involved redesigning their websites, sending out information via cell-phones, and focusing on the emotional essence of their brand.

Rebranding involves the same steps a new company would take to develop its brand. But given the internet, firms need to move more quickly. These steps include:

1. Developing a unique brand essence. Who are you and how do you differ from your competitors?
2. Creating a guiding framework and philosophy for moving the rebranding forward using various forms of communication.
3. Delivering the message consistently.

Merrilees and Miller (2007) examine change between an initially formulated company brand and a new formulation. Key issues involve the extent of the change, justifying the change in terms of costs and benefits, internal resistance to the change, and alerting all stakeholders to the new brand. They distilled six principles in the rebranding process:

1. The need to balance the old with moving forward with the new.
2. The possible need to keep some of the core concepts from the new and revised brand.
3. The need to meet the needs of the new market segment.
4. The need for communication training and internal marketing.
5. The need to integrate and coordinate all aspects of the communication and marketing strategy.
6. Promotions to make all stakeholders aware of the revised brand.

Some changes don't work out all that well. In April 1985, Coca-Cola introduced New Coke, changing its secret formula developed in 1886. Customers hated the change. Coca-Cola returned to the original formula three months later also retaining the new version. New Coke was later discontinued.

Countries also engage in rebranding. During the eight years of the presidency of George W. Bush, the US developed a particular reputation. Current President Barack Obama has devoted considerable time and energy to rebranding the US. He has visited more countries in his first year as president than any previous president, generally taking a more conciliatory and open stand that did his predecessor. In fact, one might argue that Obama is the best known brand in the world at present.

Threats to Corporate Reputation

These include "bad behavior" by executives, unsafe or defective products, customer complaints, employee complaints, poor treatment of employees, poor handling of layoffs and/or terminations,
Consider the following:

- Only 40 percent of consumers say companies frequently or always meet their service expectations according to Accenture's 2009 Global Consumer Satisfaction Survey of more than 5000 people in 12 countries. This is down from 45 percent in 2008 and 53 percent in 2007.
- Zyglidopoulos (2001) found that organizations doing environmental damage as a result of accidents (e.g., Exxon Valdez) suffered a drop in reputation scores for social performance while damage to individuals (e.g., Union Carbide's Bhopal disaster) had no effects. Interestingly, industry executive and analysts differed in their reputational re-evaluations. Features of the accident such as severity, complexity, media attention, and company responsibility were hypothesized to have an effect on accidents on loss of reputation.
- News that a Tim Horton's Inc. franchise owner in Warwick, R.I., US was sponsoring an anti-gay event resulted in thousands of responses quickly appearing on Twitter. Twitter responses advocated that Tim Horton's cancel their sponsorship, while others accused the company of homophobia and would boycott the company. Tim Horton's (Monday, August 10, 2009) announced that its sponsorship of the event had been cancelled as it violated company policy. Rather than have the story appear for two or three days, it should have immediately found out about it by searching the internet for its brand name and when the news was detected, immediately indicate it was looking at this.
- Dave Carroll, a Canadian folksinger, had his guitar and guitar case broken on a United Airlines flight in the summer of 2009. He contacted United for compensation and was rebuffed. United treated the problem badly. He then created a song about his plight and placed it on YouTube where it was watched by millions, bringing negative publicity to United. Faced with this world-wide bad publicity, United had a change of heart, agreed to compensate Carroll for his broken guitar and apologized. United has used Carroll's videos as training tools for its employees. Then, on a flight from Regina to Denver on October 28, 2009, United lost Carroll's luggage. He was told to remain in the international baggage claim area as his luggage was delayed not lost. The luggage arrived three days later. Ironically, Carroll was to speak to a group of customer service representatives in Colorado. Carroll says he tries to avoid United whenever he can.
- Three airlines (Continental, Expressjet, Mesaba) were fined US$175,000 for their role in stranding 47 passengers overnight on a plane in Rochester Minnesota on August 8, 2009. The plan landed at 12.30 am after forced to divert to Rochester because of a thunderstorm. The only airline employees working at that time refused to open the

terminal for the stranded passengers. The passengers were kept waiting nearly six hours in the cramped regional airplane, with crying babies, no food, and a smelly toilet, though they were only 50 yards from the terminal. The pilot pleaded to allow the passengers to deplane to no avail. When they deplaned, they then waited almost three hours in the terminal before reboarding the same plane to continue their flight.

- WestJet, a Canadian airline, noted for low fares and high levels of customer service, built its reputation over almost two decades. It recently changed its computerized customer reservations system (October 17, 2009) which unfortunately failed to recognize over 500,000 bookings made before October 16, the changeover date. Disgruntled customers had to wait hours on the phone to get information. Apologies were offered by WestJet and some customers received discount flights. It was announced a few days later by WestJet that it would take several more weeks to address problems with its new computer reservations system. WestJet will also suffer a financial decline as a result.

- Marks and Spencer received bad press in the UK (May, 2009) when it announced it would now charge US$3.50 more for bras that were size DD or larger. It backed down after 14,000 women gave their names to a Facebook campaign to eliminate this surcharge. In newspaper ads, the company apologized and offered a 25 percent reduction on bras of all sizes for the next two weeks. The group of women also threatened to challenge Marks and Spencer's executives at the company annual meeting. Marks and Spencer's sales fell off sharply during this time. The media also supported this group of women protesters.

- It has been known for some time that some Catholic priests abused young boys and girls. Investigations, some as recent as 2009, have indicated that the Church hierarchy knew this was going on and shielded priests from prosecution while most priests turned a "blind eye" to the behaviors of their colleagues. Public acknowledgements of such abuses have been made in the US, Canada, Australia, Austria, Britain and Ireland. Files on at least 100 priests were developed but never made public. One priest admitted to abusing over 100 children. Few priests were punished and a few known child-abusers are still working. The Catholic Church has faced several threats to its reputation including sexual abuse of young boys and girls by priests, supposedly celibate priests having children and later marrying, and Pope Benedict making reference to a passage in the Koran that angered Islam. It is difficult to determine the costs of these, and other incidents and events, to the Church's success however.

- York University in Canada, my employer over the past 43 years, has a major reputation problem. The university just celebrated its fiftieth birthday. A recent Canadian University Report published by the *Globe and Mail* (October 22, 2009), based on surveys of 38,000 students across Canada rated 53 universities according to size (York is large—in the category of 22,000 students or more) on 19 factors (e.g., quality of education, teaching, student services, food services, buildings and facilities, and libraries, among others) There were 16 large universities. York ranked in the bottom three on all but one factor and was dead last on nine. Not surprisingly it ranked last on academic reputation. Sadly, York University has ranked at or near the bottom on similar surveys carried out over the past decade or more. The university has created a committee a few months ago to examine its reputation. The evidence suggests it will take some time to turn York's reputation around.

It was ironic that on the same day as the *Globe and Mail's* ratings of universities appeared, another paper (*Toronto Star*) carried a full page add paid for by York touting its vision for the future (improving in the 19 areas was not among them).

York university has had more strikes (by faculty, support staff, teaching assistants and part-time faculty, maintenance workers) than any other university in Canada. I have lived through eight of them. The last strike, by teaching assistants and part-time faculty, occurred in late 2008 and early 2009 and lasted several months. The strike inconvenienced all stakeholders, particularly students. The strike resulted in students transferring to other universities when the academic year was over, a dramatic drop in new students applying to York, and a significant number of students dropping courses affected by the strike and getting their tuition refunded. A colleague at another university located one or two hours away from Toronto, in the smaller category, thanked me—really my university—since her university has had a surge in new applicants.

Research on the effects of university strikes at York (Greenglass et al. 2002; Wickens et al. 2006) indicated that students interrupted their academic studies and worsened their financial situations, but increased their recreation and social activities.

Now, in 2010, York University is being sued by students seeking US$250 million in damages for failure by the university to fulfil its required duties and for any financial losses that students may have assumed.

- Coca-Cola launched its new brand of so-called "pure" Dasani bottled water in the UK in March 2004. But glitches occurred. Dasani was reported in UK media to be nothing more than London tap water taken from the city system. Then it noted that what the organization termed its "highly sophisticated purification process" based on NASA spacecraft technology was just the same processes used in most domestic water purifiers. The UA$13 million dollar launch was stopped when it was noted that a cancer-causing chemical was found in the samples.
- In October 2007, a young man from Poland, Robert Dziekanski, arrived at Vancouver airport to spend time in Canada with his mother. He knew almost no English. He became disoriented following the long flight to Canada. He apparently was acting in a strange way wandering around the terminal building unable to find anyone to help him. Four members of the Royal Canadian Mounted Police (RCMP) intervened, and during a scuffle, Dziekanski was tasered five times, and died from cardiac arrest shortly thereafter. A survey of Canadians indicated that 60 percent thought that the RCMP has used excessive force. The four RCMP officers gave testimony at odds with video surveillance evidence, offered conflicting stories, changed their stories over time, and apologized for the incident but denied lying or suppressing information. An RCMP media officer admitted that levels of public trust are below levels they would like to see. The RCMP acknowledged that this incident had tarnished their image in the eyes of the Canadian public. As often happens, the RCMP investigated the incident (investigated itself) having what they termed an "unwinnable image" problem. The RCMP has since announced that tasers will no longer be aimed at an individual's head In addition, Vancouver airport has made many changes such as having translators available 24/7, better trained (more friendly) and helpful staff, and a redesigned, more open visitor arrival areas. The Commission for Public complaints about the RCMP released a report of this incident concluding that RCMP officers acted inappropriately, lacking the necessary training and experience (December 8,

2009), and was critical of the RCMP explanations of the event (distortions in their stories, deceptive answers). It indicated that the reputation of the RCMP had fallen in the eyes of Canadians. It probably did not help when it was revealed that the RCMP tasered a 15-year-old girl who was lying face down and handcuffed (March 13, 2007). Individual reputations, and that of the RCMP, have been damaged but as of yet no individual has been fired. In February 2010 the Superintendent of the RCMP announced that the RCMP would no longer be investigating itself. Instead "outsiders" would take part in these inquiries. It was not stated who these outsiders would be, how they would work, or whether greater transparency would be the result.

- In a related story, the RCMP has decided to replace its current watchdog Paul Kennedy. Kennedy has been overseeing the RCMP for the past four years and has criticized their use of tasers, and argued with the Canadian government about the size of his budget.

- Toronto, the city in which I live, has a public transportation service that provides bus and subway services to about 1.5 million riders each day. The Toronto Transit Commission (TTC) is responsible for managing the delivery of this service and employs about 12,000 workers. In early February 2010 a man working at a subway booth asleep at his workplace was captured by a rider using a cell-phone. This image then appeared on YouTube and elsewhere being seen by millions. A bus rider captured a bus driver stopping his vehicle outside a donut shop, going in to use the bathroom, then buying a coffee and donut, before boarding his bus and proceeding. This story also made the news media. The upshot of these postings was an uproar against the shoddy service provided to Torontonians by the TTC. The TTC received a black eye in the media. It was revealed that the TTC received about 31,000 complaints in the first 11 months of 2009, up from 26,000 over the same period in 2008. An employee of the TTC wrote an anonymous letter to the media agreeing with the poor service and describing a workplace culture that did not value quality service. The union head then responded by defending his staff (phone user should have tapped the sleeping token taker to see that he wasn't suffering from a heart attack), highlighting the rudeness of transit users, and encouraging his members to take pictures of the mess left in their buses and subway cars by transit users. The head of the TTC sent an e-mail message to his employees telling them to "shape up or ship out." He followed it up with an apology to riders of the transit system. The upshot of this "war of words" and "war of pictures" was an acknowledgment that the TTC was providing shoddy service to the taxpaying users of the service. A constructive dialogue might emerge from these events that ultimately improves the service of the TTC but that would be a major long-term undertaking.

- Minorities in Toronto have developed more negative views of police officers over the past 15 years, with Canadian-born children of immigrants holding the most negative opinions.

- Some Starbuck's employees charged rescue workers at the World Trade Center (on 9/11) for bottled water.

- The Burger King fast-food chain has a policy requiring all customers to be wearing a shirt and shoes. Employees at one of their franchises asked a young mother and her six-month-old baby, who was in a stroller, to leave because the baby was not wearing any shoes. When this became known, the franchise apologized to the woman.

Common Sense Anyone?

Karpoff et al. (2006), in a study of 585 companies that were disciplined by the US Securities and Exchange Commission (SEC) for financial misrepresentation from 1978 through 2002, and which were tracked to 2005, found that the SEC penalties imposed on each firm averaged US$23.5 million, the penalties imposed by the market from the damage done to the firms reputations was significantly greater, estimate by the researchers to be 7.5 times greater.

According to Gaines-Ross (2008), the corporate reputation "stumble rate" is continuing to rise. She states that over three quarters of the world's number one most admired companies lost their standing in their respective industries over the past five years. Crisis events inside and outside of organizations have shown that a company's reputation can be damaged in seconds. Fraudulent actions, recalled products, product tampering, the necessity of financial restatement disclosures, and poor responses to a crisis can damage a respected reputation instantly.

Social networking technology has come to play a larger role in both creating and maintaining corporate reputations and damaging them (Beal and Strauss, 2008). Pope Benedict told priests that they must learn to use new forms of communication and new technologies to spread the gospel.

But the new technology can prove damaging. The private diary of a Chinese Communist Party official, Han Feng, a sales director of a state-owned tobacco company, indicating a daily schedule of sex, drinking and bribe taking, was leaked on the internet (February 2010) by the husband of a woman Han was sleeping with. Han's daily diary indicated that he also did very little work. Han has since been suspended from his job.

Several members of France's government have been shown in online videos acting inappropriately (e.g., Nadine Morano, Secretary of State for the Family, apparently drunk, bumping and grinding with male supporters; Eric Besson, Immigration Minister, making an obscene gesture to a cameraman). The zone of privacy previously afforded politicians seems to have disappeared. But individuals lying about politicians may still be subject to legal action. Online chatter and conversation can have an influence on making or breaking a product or a service. These technologies include Twitter, Facebook, blogs, interactive websites and Web 2.0. Social media seem to have shifted control of an organization's reputation away from the organization and to users of the Internet. It is therefore important to monitor these sites since there is no guarantee that information on them is accurate and truthful. Beal and Strauss (2008) offer guidance for building, managing, monitoring, and repairing your corporate reputation online. It should also be remembered that three quarters of US adults still read printed news on a weekly basis according to the Nielsen Company.

Reputations can be damaged very quickly. Organizations therefore need to attempt to preempt threats to their reputations, and respond both quickly and appropriately when their reputations have been attacked or damaged.

Insensitive terminations can also damage a company's reputation, damage morale, future recruiting, and the morale of the fired employee. Employees have been terminated while on a business trip, via e-mail; some have been asked to call a 1-800 number and hear a voicemail recording, with no explanation, and others have been asked to come to a meeting and then fired.

Instead, terminations should be done in person in private, at the end of the work day. The employee should be offered a reason for the termination. Policies should be available to guide the termination process, and the employee should be offered assistance in finding a new job. It is possible for even terminated employees to become alumni of an organization forever if done right.

Making a "tough" decision and announcing it.

1. Get to the point quickly.
2. Talk straight, plainly simply.
3. Be honest and trustworthy; use authentic behaviors.

It is also likely that a firm that has developed an outstanding reputation (e.g., for timely and outstanding service) will have their reputations damaged more severely by a mishap than firms that have not put themselves on a "service pedestal."

Events that lead to a damaged corporate reputation at one point in time may not have this effect at another point in time. Love and Kraatz (2009) studied the effect of organizational downsizings in the financial services sector, collecting data from Fortune 500 companies between 1985 to 1994. The reputation of these firms were obtained from both financial analysts and organizational peers. They found that organizational downsizings were associated with negative effects on reputational change (i.e., financial firms that downsized dropped in reputation). Downsizings violated commitments made to employees in terms of secure employment. But this effect only occurred early in the study time frame. Firms that downsized later fit with analysts' and financial executives' views of legitimate and necessary actions, especially when the downsizing benefited them. Thus violating commitments made to employees in terms of secure employment.

There seems to be a "band-wagon effect" operating. Staw and Epstein (2000) found that organizations making greater and more visible use of the latest (more popular) management techniques had a reputational advantage.

Competitors may do things to undermine a corporate reputation. Competitors may spread rumors, innuendos, and leaks that appear in chat rooms and on internet message boards. Competitors may post opinion, company employees may air opinions and gripes. Companies should view these sites and take immediate corrective action if necessary. Employees have been terminated for bad-mouthing their bosses and companies on their blogs. Suggestions to help companies in this regard might include the following:

1. Identify risks to your corporate reputation so you can be prepared. Several potential risks exist: management, financial operational government intervention, environmental impact, legal, international.
2. Build and improve a corporate reputation: communicate people, values and ethics to critical audiences.
3. Develop a crisis response plan. What you will do if an unforeseen event occurs.

With Friends Like These

The head of Danish airline Cimber Sterling had to apologize to the CEO of rival Norwegian Air Shuttle for making fake bookings of cut-rate Norwegian tickets "bought" by Cimber employees (January 2010). Cimber employees sabotaged Norwegian by reserving hundreds (over 650) of cheap Norwegian tickets under fake names, one employee "buying" 458 tickets. The CEO of Cimber said that his employees did this on their own initiative.

Several French firms were upset by humorous ads satirizing their firms appearing on video-sharing web-sites such as YouTube (January 2010). Most French firms are still responding to satirical video spoofs instead of proactively using this media to market their brand. Common targets included France Telecom for their high rates of employee suicide, supermarket chain Carrefour for implying that their discount food contained human remains, and French bank Société Generale SA, victim of a huge financial fraud, for their "helping hand" campaign.

Product Recalls

- Mattel Inc. agreed to pay US$12 million to 39 states to settle claims that it shipped toys tainted with lead paint (December, 15, 2008). Various Mattel dolls made in China were involved, but fortunately these toys never made it to the store shelves.
- Toyota indicated on September 29, 2009, that it would recall at least 4.2 million Toyota and Lexus cars to fix a potential safety problem caused by a floor mat affecting the accelerator. Later (January 21, 2010) Toyota recalled another 2.3 million cars in the US and Canada to fix accelerator pedals that can become stuck and have resulted in accidents and deaths. Toyota has recalled significantly more cars in the last year than a decade earlier. Since this early recall, Toyota has recalled significantly more vehicles and is under investigation in the US. It is estimated that Toyota's stock value has fallen by US$23 billion. The company is expected to spend between US$2 and US$3 billion in making the necessary product repairs. Competitors of Toyota have undertaken initiatives to attract potential Toyota buyers by offering cash incentives. Others have suggested that Toyota is likely to fall to number 3 in size given current projections. Toyota has stopped selling particular products and some car rental services have removed Toyotas from their fleets. It has been speculated that Toyota's push to become the largest car manufacturer may have handicapped their famous engineering and quality control processes.
  - Toyota has taken out full page ads in Canadian newspapers on at least two occasions during February 2010 and has changed its advertising on television. These efforts apologize to consumers, attempt to reassure them that Toyota products are safe, and that steps are being taken to fix whatever defects have been identified. The President of Toyota, residing in Japan, has been criticized for being invisible during the first week of this crisis. He has since made a television appearance basically repeating what has appeared in the newspapers. At this point (February 2010) it is not clear whether Toyota has contained a major problem or is facing a full-blown crisis. February sales reported by Toyota indicated a drop. Data in March 2010 showed however that the Toyota brand still remained strong. Toyoto mounted a vigorous ad campaign in February and March as well as offering incentives to purchase their cars prompting other automakers to do the same.
- Johnson & Johnson, a firm that received kudos for its handling of the recall of Tylenol several years ago, issued another recall of up to 50 million bottles of Tylenol products (January 2010) from the Americas, Fiji and the United Arab Emirates. The Food and

Drug Administration was critical of the time allowed to elapse between concerns being first raised and the announced recall.

- Fairbank Farms, located in Ashville, NY, recalled 450,000 pounds of ground beef products that might be contaminated with E.coli (Tuesday, November 3, 2009). People in at least three states became sick after eating these meat products. The Peanut Corporation of America distributed tainted peanut products to countless firms leading to the largest food recall in US history. More than 2,100 processed and packaged foods were linked to a salmonella outbreak which led to nine deaths and made 660 people sick.

- Deaths by at least four infants in baby cribs resulted in a recall of over two million cribs on November 23, 2009. Parents were to immediately stop using the cribs and contact Stork Craft Manufacturing to receive a repair kit that addresses the problem (a drop side is to be changed to a fixed side).

- More recently (January 2010), Dorel Industries Inc. recalled 642,000 baby cribs in the US and Canada. Dorel framed its recall as reputation management and steps taken by the organization were part of a crisis plan that included adding staff to call centers, getting legal advice, and accelerating child-proofing education programs.

There is evidence that the number of product recalls is increasing. Laird (2009) estimates that 17 million lead-contaminated retail products were called in 2007 alone. Product recalls can range from small to large scale. These include tainted food products such as meat and vegetables, and defective products. And product recalls put company reputations at risk. Individuals, potential consumers and current owners, will have concerns about product quality and the competence and motivations of the firm's management. Negative comments about the recalled products begin to circulate. Product recalls also have negative performance consequences (Bromiley and Marcus, 1989; Hoffer et al., 1988) particularly for firms having exceptionally positive reputations (Rhee and Haunschild, 2006). Firms having highly visible reputations receive more scrutiny from the media and consumers. Firms whose products are recalled act to defend their reputations. Firms having highly favorable reputations are more likely to respond quickly following a product recall. Firms that have had previous product recalls are likely to move more slowly in defending their reputations (Laplume et al. 2008). In addition the indirect costs from reputation loss are likely to be larger than the direct costs (Rupp, 2004).

Product recalls are going to increase. The globalization of business has required greater vigilance by government officials, more proactive monitoring by some organizations, and more activist consumers have increased scrutiny of products. In addition more organizations have made efforts to cut costs, shifting production to less developed countries. These countries may have lower quality standards, and in many cases organizations do not closely supervise activities in them. In addition, there is increasing pressure to deliver products first and quickly. Organizations need to monitor the total product life cycle from design to safety testing to outsource suppliers to protect themselves for recalls. Companies facing product recalls must be ready to respond immediately, that is, within a three-day window.

Here are some tips for handling product recalls:

1. Act promptly in recognizing a problem and taking corrective action. All this needs to be done within three days or less.

2. To reduce liability, products and production must be supervised from inception (design), safety testing and outsourcing suppliers.
3. Undertake a thorough inspection and auditing of outsourced suppliers.
4. Carrying out a recall promptly will reduce later liability.
5. Use social network media (e.g., YouTube) to get your recall message out.

The timing of a reputation defense is important. A too hasty recall may signal admission of mistakes with potential litigation costs; but delaying a recall signals confusion and uncertainty, more negative consumer/customer perceptions, and the chance that the problem may become even larger if not dealt with promptly. The prompt response by Johnson & Johnson to the Tylenol poisoning event which led to a recall of 31 million bottles at a cost of over US$100 million (Shrivastava et al. 1988) turned around a highly negative situation and led to the design of a tamper-proof bottle. Tylenol quickly regained market share which fell dramatically following the initial event.

Recovering from a Damaged Corporate Reputation

- In the mid-1990s, Nike received negative publicity by being portrayed as a company that exploited its labor in its overseas plants (Burns and Spar, 2000). Nike at first denied the charges stating it had no control over the business practices of the independent contractors that made their products. Human rights activists continued to keep the pressure on Nike however. Nike then required its suppliers to pay a "fair or living" wage. Nike has rebounded from this adverse event.
- The Dow Corning Corporation suffered a dramatic fall from grace in the early 1990s when it was revealed that its silicone breast implants leaked on some occasions and were a health hazard to women receiving them. Dow Corning had claimed that these implants would last a lifetime. Between 1.5 and 2 million women received them. It was alleged that Dow Corning had information about the leaking and its potential problems but failed to act. Prior to this point Dow Corning was regarded as a well-managed, ethical and successful organization. Dow Corning faced over 10,000 lawsuits and talked of settling these claims for US$4.25 billion. It stopped the production of these implants in 1992. The CEO was demoted, and Dow Corning lost US$287 million in 1993. Dow Corning employees remained loyal to the organization. A new CEO was brought in. Today, Dow Corning is a successful organization producing silicone-based products, and was named by *Fortune Magazine* (2007) as one of the "100 Best Companies to Work for".
- On August 7, 2008, Maple Leaf Foods was informed by distributors that there was a public health inquiry into some of its meat products. On August 12, the Canadian Food Inspection Agency began an investigation into three products from a Toronto plant. Positive tests over the next few days found listeria monocytogenes in two of its sliced meat products. On August 23, a recall of 191 products was begun and the Toronto plant closed. Michael McCain, CEO of McCain Foods, addressed the media on that date. McCain was credited by the pundits with doing a good job of handling the crisis. He communicated an apology, believing he and the company were accountable. The company responded as soon as the tests were positive. McCain attempted to teach the public about listeria. The company cleaned the plant and

continued to monitor food safety, establishing a food safety board, and vowed to work with the government and other companies to increase food safety. McCain was genuine and concerned. Consumption of food products dropped. McCain Foods estimated the cost of the recall at US$20 million and compensation to victims to settle claims against the company at $27 million. Investors sold their stock as the crisis continued and deaths increased. The value of its market capitalization dropped dramatically.

- Maple Leaf Foods Inc. reported (October 28, 2009) that it is now selling almost as much packaged meat as it did before the listeria outbreak in one of its Toronto plants in the summer of 2008. This outbreak killed 22 people and made several more sick. Sales of its packaged meats fell about 50 percent after the outbreak.
- On December 16, 2009, McCain and Maple Leaf Foods took out a full page ad in Canada's major newspapers acknowledging the challenging year it and many Canadians had, and on behalf of their 24,000 employees and loyal customers, donated over 100,000 meals to food banks and shelters this holiday season. He also thanked their millions of customers for their support during the year. A nice touch and a class act.

Individuals at high levels in organizations sometimes fail in a very public and high profile way. Most fallen executives never recover after their failure. Sonnenfeld and Ward (2007a, 2007b) examined cases of successful recovery of executives from a career catastrophe. These included Bernie Markus, Jamie Dimon, President Jimmy Carter, Martha Stewart, Michael Milken, and Mickey Drexler. They identified five important factors: deciding how to fight back, recruiting others to support them in their battles, clearing their reputations and restoring their status, proving their competence by doing a great job, and rediscovering their heroic mission which reignites their passion and gives meaning to their lives.

Although agents for Tiger Woods made short media statements, and Woods commented on his accident on his website, Woods has chosen not to appear personally and clear the air on what happened, and he may have good reasons for not doing so. But this has only fueled rumors, many of which are unfavorable to him and speculations of a cover-up. Experts believe that immediate response work best, and they offer the actions of David Letterman in support of this claim. Taking too long to respond, lying, or engaging in a cover-up almost always end up being worse than immediately telling the truth.

Dealing with a Crisis or Scandal

It is inevitable that things will always go wrong for organizations (Anheier, 1999). Organizations and their managers will have to deal with a crisis situation.

The actions of NYC Mayor Rudy Giuiliani on 9/11 were often described as effective. These included: frequent communication, being seen and visible, act promptly, boldly and sensitively, indicating what was known "now," using "experts" on some issues, controling the message, being certain and confident, and behaving empathically.

Other experts have offered the following advice: forthrightness and even offering admissions, being visible, taking responsibility, providing information, making an extensive recall of products (if relevant), apologizing, indicating how the situation will be fixed, and doing what you say you will do.

US President Barack Obama is seen as a good crisis manager. Obama is calm and patient, visible, and a good communicator; he has momentum, uses consistent messages, instills confidence, is pragmatic and realistic, and has changed the feeling and tone of the country when the country was ready for such a change.

Tybout and Roehm (2009) suggest the organizational response to a scandal should fit the scandal. Not all scandals are alike. Tybout and Roehm believe that scandals vary in terms of responsibility for the wrongdoing (e.g., accidental, negligent, intentional) and a common approach to all scandals won't work. They suggest a consideration of characteristics of the brand, the nature of the scandalous event, and the company's degree of responsibility for it. They developed a four-step framework for managing scandals.

Step 1. Assess the incident from the customer's viewpoint not managements. An incident becomes more serious when it is surprising, vivid, emotional or relevant to a central feature of the company or brand. Not all incidents are serious.

Step 2. Acknowledge the problem, express concern for whoever might have been harmed, indicate how it will be investigated, and how future damage will be prevented.

Step 3. Craft a response which will differ if allegations are false or true, the incident was accidental, the result of negligence or intentional.

Step 4. Undertake responses to the incident, often involving communications, marketing and executive expertise. Decisions must be made on the issues that need attention, what level of detail, who should deliver the response, and with what kind of tone.

Margolis and Stoltz (2010) suggest that managers respond best to a crisis when the move quickly from over-analyzing the crisis event to looking forward, figuring out the best course of action given the new situational realities, understand the size and scope of the crisis as well as the levels of control they can exert, and what impact they may have on their crisis situation. The offer some questions to help managers facing a crisis sort out their negative feelings and replace them with forward looking, creative responses in the face of real or imagined challenges.

Weiner (2006) focuses on crisis communication. A company's reputation is severely tested during a crisis. A crisis, whether short of long lived, affects individuals inside and outside the organization. The first job for the organization is to recognize when a crisis has occurred and the risks involved (crisis prevention). Some crises cannot be controlled; others can be foreseen. Many crises can be anticipated. The organization needs to identify the critical issues and prioritize them in terms of magnitude and probability of occurrence. The organization then needs to develop a communications plan. Who are the contact people? What is the level of crisis? Who is to be contacted? The second stage is crisis management. Weiner lists 10 rules for crisis management (e.g., communicate, take responsibility, centralize information).The last stage is crisis recovery, the regaining of trust.

McCarthy (in Schacter, 2008) offers these tips:

1. Don't speculate about what happened or what could happen.
2. Don't cover up, lie or hedge.
3. Don't hedge sympathy with a "but."
4. Don't assign blame, instead try to resolve the crisis. Finding fault will come later.
5. Don't promise anything you can't deliver.
6. Be prepared before giving interviews.
7. Get all the facts as quickly as you can.
8. Be present at all sessions, you are the leader.
9. Give the facts.
10. Be honest about what you know and don't know.
11. Acknowledge and be sympathetic to human suffering.
12. Accept responsibility for handling the crisis but not causing it.
13. Give all the bad news at once, not in dribs and drabs.
14. Set up a rumor control hotline or website.
15. Prepare yourself with answers to a few "difficult" questions since you will be asked these.

Dealing with Lawsuits

Garcia and Ewing (2008) offer advice on how organizations should deal with lawsuits.

1. Understand the context of the fight.
2. Identify the likely issues and adversaries.
3. Pre-empt your adversaries.
4. Act quickly.
5. Communicate forcefully.

Too Many Apologies?

Individuals and organizations that "fall from grace" typically offer an apology and we are beginning to understand when and why apologies work (Kim et al., 2004).

After being criticized for letting a few months pass before making any statements, Tiger Woods held a press conference on Friday, February 19, 2010. He read a prepared speech, had friends and family in the audience, and took no questions in this highly scripted and rehearsed performance. While admitting that he cheated, few details were provided. He was undergoing treatment for "sexual addiction" and was attempting to rebuild his relationship with his wife. Since he provided so little information, most viewers thought he avoided critical issues and were left with unanswered questions and skepticism. This performance though likely represented a first step in his comeback.

GM took out a full page ad (December 2008) in which they apologized for betraying their customers. A senior official in the Vatican apologized after Pope Benedict lifted the ban on a formerly excommunicated bishop, Michael Williamson, who was acknowledged to be a Holocaust denier. They attributed this mistake to management errors made by Vatican staff and sloppiness it their decision. The Catholic School Board in Toronto apologized in a letter published in the press for using board monies for personal expenses. The Provincial Government in Newfoundland apologized to female patients for mishandling their breast cancer examination results (March 2008), promising compensation. About 386 patients received incorrect breast cancer results between 1997 and 2005. The Christian Brothers, a teaching order affiliated with the Catholic Church in Rome, apologized for sexually abusing their wards in schools and orphanages. Microsoft apologized for altering a photo in its website that changed the race of one of the people shown. A black man was replaced by a white man's hand and face in its Polish business units website. The President of Toyota. Akio Toyoda, went on an around the world apology tour (February and March 2010), and the President of Toyota Canada apologized to Canadians.

The Canadian RCMP Chief, William Elliott, apologized (June 1, 2009) for the death of Polish immigrant Robert Dziekanski, who died after he was tasered at Vancouver International Airport in October 2007. I know that all the facts need to be obtained, but should it have taken almost two years?

Given the relatively low levels of trust various stakeholders have of CEOs, business in general, and government, the old public relations strategies and spin no longer work. Instead, organizational leaders need to be open and honest and commit themselves and their organizations to socially responsible activities working with their constituencies.

Are Some Organizations and Individuals Impervious to Reputation Damage?

It seems that even though some organizations face threats or events that damage their reputations things continue for these organizations pretty much the same. Toyota recalls millions of cars, yet Toyotas continue to sell and receive high ratings. Banks and credit card companies get negative publicity for how they mishandle a client yet they continue to prosper. The RCMP suffer a drop in their credibility yet they continue to do well in attracting new recruits (offering a very good pay and benefit package). The Catholic Church continues to receive criticism for its handling of priests involved in the sexual abuse of boys and girls (MacIntyre, 2009) with little sign of crisis. Are these organizations and institutions "too big to fail" as was the case with the US banking and financial services sector that received massive government bailouts? Is it a matter of every car company gets involved in recalls of their products so what choice do consumers have? In Canada we only have five banks and if they all mistreat clients there is no choice.

On the individual level, there are only a few late-night shows, so if David Letterman falls from grace, he still gets his audience. If Louisville coach Rick Pitino, though a married Catholic who gives speeches on family values, has an affair, he still is the coach of a winning basketball program. In addition, many societies believe in second chances and redemption. Are damaged individuals and damaged organizations also given a second chance?

Silvio Berlusconi, billionaire prime minister of Italy, has put his foot in his mouth in situations too numerous to count (Obama has a nice tan), commented favorably on the beauty of women and appointed attractive women to his government, had extra-marital affairs, and been charged with corruption (but Italian law until recently prevented legal action against the prime minister). Yet he continues to get re-elected and has high levels of Italian citizen support. His fortunes may be changing however. His current wife has filed for divorce and asked for the largest settlement in recorded history. And the Italian government changed the laws so that they can bring fraud and corruption charges against him.

Events more at a rapid pace. On Saturday, December 9, 2009, about 90,000 people marched in Rome protesting at Berlusconi's leadership and citing, among other things, his sex scandals and repeated allegations of corruption. Berlusconi may not be "to big to fail" after all.

After this was written I came across a note written by Gill Corkindale (December 2009, Harvard Business Review blog) titled "Does your company's reputation really matter?" She wrote it in response to the way that Eurostar mishandled a crisis when five of their trains broke down in the cross-Channel tunnel between England and France in late December. Eurostar's CEO apologized for the fiasco. Corkindale wondered whether this event would damage Eurostar's performance and concluded that it likely would not since Eurostar provides a convenient and reasonably priced service and is the only such alternative. And when customers have no other options (e.g., with banks, airlines, government agencies, oil, gas and electrical utilities) company reputation may not matter. As a result there is little incentive for these monopolies to improve.

Apple revealed March (2010) that child labor was used at three factories that build its computers, iPods and mobile phones. They indicated that child labor is no longer being used in any of their overseas plants. This story received little publicity and it is unlikely that Apple will suffer from this revelation.

Conclusions and Implications

Corporate reputations matter. Tangible benefits accrue to organizations having favorable reputations. It takes several years to develop a favorable corporate reputation. While a favorable reputation relies on communication and marketing, it is more than that. A favorable corporate reputation is built on sound HRM practices and a viable business model and strategy. Organizations having favorable reputations are credible, they "walk the talk."

We know a lot about building, maintaining and repairing reputations (Decotiis, 2008).

Favorable corporate reputations result from effective leadership, committed employees, superior service and products, high ethical standards and high levels of socially responsible actions (Garcia, 2007; Greyser, 1999).

Companies sometimes need to rebrand themselves to better adapt and fit changing times.

There are considerable threats to corporate reputations. These include the behavior of executives, dissatisfied employees, disgruntled customers and clients, low quality products or services, rumors, innuendos, and lies spread by dissatisfied employees, customers or competitors. Organizations can monitor events, anticipate potential threats, quickly respond to real or phony threats, take responsibility for real crises, and work to ensure they never happen again. Leadership, communication and candor are vital here.

While it takes several years to build a favorable corporate reputation, it can be quickly damaged.

It is possible, however, to recover from a damaged reputation as shown by Johnson & Johnson (the Tylenol event) and McCain Foods (tainted meat products). Some organizations seem to be little affected from damaged reputations (e.g., the Catholic Church, Toyota) while other organizations fail (e.g., Enron, Arthur Andersen).

Overview of the Contents

The chapters that follow will examine these areas in some depth, and in keeping with the objectives of this volume, research findings and practical applications will be reviewed.

The first section addresses the importance of corporate reputation. Ronald Burke lays the groundwork for the chapters that follow. He considers the following content: what is corporate reputation, does corporate reputation matter, what factors influence a corporate reputation, the development of corporate reputation, the management of corporate reputation, reputation spillover, the stickiness of corporate reputation, threats to corporate reputation, monitoring and addressing threats to corporate reputation, product recalls, and recovering from a damaged corporate reputation. He makes reference to individual, industry and country reputation as relevant. Examples form the news media are offered to illustrate particular points. Burke provides suggestions at various places in the chapter offering guidance to individuals and organizations interested in applying the content to address corporate reputation needs and challenges.

In Chapter 2 Gary Davies addresses the meaning and measurement of corporate reputation. He distinguishes corporate reputation from related terms such as character, image, corporate brand, and identity. Each view of corporate reputation is associated with its own approach to measurement. Davies defines corporate reputation as "the impression stakeholders have of that organization, accumulated from a range of sources including actual experience, media comments and content, sponsored communication and word or mouth. It shapes stakeholder expectations of that organization's future behavior and their own future behavior towards that organization." Corporate reputation is subjective in nature. Reputation can be measured by asking people to rate the reputation of an organization. Such measures include cognitive factors or emotive factors, or both. Davies provides examples of both cognitive and emotive measures. He then reviews findings from his own work using his Corporate Character scale. He identifies issues in the measurement of corporate reputation and the need for more work on using measures of corporate reputation to improve the reputations (and performance) of organizations.

Manfred Schwaiger, Sascha Raithal, Richard Rinkenburger and Matthias Schloderer review recent research findings on the impact of corporate reputation on stakeholder behavior in Chapter 3. Three stakeholder groups are considered: customers, investors, and potential employees. More than two thirds of a firm's market value derives from such intangible assets. They define reputation as having both objective (cognitive) and affective (likeability) components. They first review various measures of corporate reputation. Using Schwaiger's measure, four factors of reputation emerge: quality, performance, responsibility, and attractiveness. Based on their review of the literature, they find corporate reputation has links with various stakeholder group outcomes: access to capital, more satisfied customers, volume of customer purchases, higher return on assets, and higher attractiveness among potential recruits. They conclude with managerial implications. Firms need to first decide which outcomes are of high priority. Firms then need to measure their reputation, and outcomes, within relevant stakeholder groups. Drivers of levels of reputation that are important to various stakeholder groups are then identified. Finally managers need to focus on the reputation drivers associated with important stakeholder outcomes.

The second section, containing two chapters, deals with the development of corporate reputations. Most CEOs believe that corporate social responsibility (CSR) contributes to a firm's reputation and that reputational benefits provide performance advantages. Yet trust in both business and CEOs have fallen and is now low. Phil Mirvis considers how dimensions of CSR influence company reputation on a global scale. More organizations today are globalizing their CSR programs but they must take into account country features. Both global and local trends affect CSR. CSR itself is in flux. He first lays out various dimensions of CSR. The public has high expectations of business but their ratings of its social responsibility have been falling. Mirvis uses data on individual views of companies in several countries to examine some propositions. He reports that the strongest predictor of reputation is ratings of products and services, followed by ratings of its citizenship. He presents ratings of about 600 organizations in various countries. Scandinavian firms are ranked highest overall. CSR ratings vary in predicting company reputation across countries. But CSR ratings and organizational reputation are positively related but with some noteworthy gaps. Mirvis concludes with suggestions for managing reputation and CSR globally. These include: identifying and recognizing all relevant stakeholders, understanding their expectations of business, considering company vision and values, identifying performance gaps between CSR and reputation, taking action to close these gaps, communicating honestly with stakeholders, and collecting data to assess progress and take further informed action.

The third section, containing seven chapters, looks at the managing of corporate reputations. The study of corporate reputation is still relatively young. Concepts such as image, reputation, and identity are used sometimes in ways that overlap. In Chapter 5 Kristin Backhaus presents a framework for understanding the relationships among organizational identity, corporate social performance, corporate reputation and organizational attractiveness. Organizational identity is the self-defined description of the organization held by employees. Senior management can shape this perception. Organizational identity influences corporate social performance (CSP), the latter encompassing social relationships with individuals outside the organization. CSP shapes perceptions of an organization's legitimacy and corporate reputation. Backaus focuses on organizational attractiveness as a key outcome variable. Corporate reputations across the board have fallen over the past few years. She suggests that organizations communicate more aggressively about their CSP as one avenue for increasing corporate reputations. The human resource function has an important role to play in supporting corporate reputation development.

Kerry Grigg makes the point that employer branding is now a widely used HR, communications and marketing tool worldwide to attract, retain and engage talented staff. Organizations develop their employer brand around a combination of symbolic (e.g., caring, innovative) and/or instrumental (pay, benefits) employer attributes to establish the identity of the organization as a "great place to work" above and beyond other organizations by promoting a clear view of what makes the organization different and desirable as an employer. But little is known about how or if these activities shape expectations about the employment relationship in the minds of those employees employer branding messages are designed to reach. The psychological contract concept provides a useful lens to examine the making and keeping of employer brand promises and the corresponding antecedents and consequences of psychological contract breach or fulfillment. Grigg uses the psychological contract concept to explore how employer branding activities promote the organization's unique employee value proposition and how this promotion makes explicit and.implicit promises and forms expectations in the minds of current and prospective employees, the antecedents and consequences of psychological contract breach or fulfillment as they relate to employer branding, and implications for employer branding practitioners.

As has already been noted, human resource management, human and social capital play an important role in corporate reputation. In Chapter 7 Graeme Martin, Paul Gollan and Kerry Griggs consider two competing approaches to strategic human resource management (SHRM) that emphasize distinctiveness or legitimacy for the management of corporate reputation. They advocate a strategy-in-action approach to address the negative capabilities of being simultaneously similar and different. SHRM has not played a major role yet in corporate reputation research although this is slowly changing. Distinctiveness has a internal focus whereas legitimacy has an external focus. For example, multinational organizations face a tension between being locally responsive as well as applying corporate-wide standards of legitimacy. This shows up in tension between, global and local values, inclusive and exclusive HR strategies, and between human and social capital and innovation. They illustrate these tensions through a case study of the financial services sector and their use of bonuses. They conclude with a somewhat detailed presentation of a model for reconciling difference and similarity. This model emphasizes strategists, the practice of strategy, and strategic practice—a tall but necessary order.

Charles McMillan deals with the links between corporate reputation and corporate governance. He provides a conceptual model of corporate reputation, what sustains it, and what damages it. He pays particular attention to the roles corporate governance structures and processes along with appropriate levels of risk assessment in his analysis. McMillan suggests five elements of corporate reputation: morality, legality, consistency, coherence, and inclusiveness. Reputation comes from stakeholders' recognition of special organizational qualities or attributes. Branding, brokers, competence and performance become central to building corporate reputations in his thinking. The current worldwide financial meltdown, anger at the levels of executive pay and bonuses for executives of failed or bailed out firms, and public knowledge of corporate crime, fraud, corruption and greed have damaged many corporate reputations and put a spotlight on boards of directors. New rules of corporate governance are being contemplated or already introduced to address these concerns and potentially increase the damaged reputations of entire industries. Corporate boards of directors have a key role in helping firms preserve or regain their reputations.

Julie Hodges then in Chapter 9 considers the role of the CEO and leadership branding. The reputation of many CEOs has taken a hit during the current economic crises. Yet leadership branding is a critical variable for differentiating their companies from others. CEO celebrity has both positive (e.g., reassure stakeholders, attract high quality staff) and negative (e.g., hubris, downplay team contributions) consequences. She reviews the notions of leadership as a brand in some detail. Leadership branding focuses more on leadership than leaders. Leadership branding connects the inside of the organization with the outside and helps build future leaders, and strengthens the organization. Leadership is spread throughout the organization rather than invested in one person. Effective branding requires a leader with vision. These leaders role model the reputation they expect from their organization. Multinational organizations face a unique challenge in featuring a leadership brand but encouraging local tailoring of the brand to fir their circumstances. A central message here is that leadership branding focuses on the organization not just the leader.

The news media has a great deal of influence on corporate reputation. Craig Carroll considers the role of the media in managing corporate reputation. He notes that both news coverage and corporate reputations are multidimensional concepts. News coverage has many types, forms and topics of coverage and news coverage addresses components of corporate reputation rather than its totality. He then moves to the development of a media relations program for reputation management. An effective media relations program must address both the organization's needs and the media. The organization needs to identify the key messages that it wants to convey and the most effective way to tap into its key publics. If successful, the agendas of the organization, the public, and the media come together. Media coverage is more likely to develop a favorable picture of an organization; more media coverage tells the public who to think about more than what to think about. But there is also "bad publicity." Negative visibility diminishes reputations, and media visibility affects some aspects of reputation more than others. Carroll suggests some characteristics of a noteworthy news story. He believes that organizations should generally work with/through the media rather than circumvent it; the media can provide a valuable third-party endorsement. Carroll concludes his chapter a summary of useful ways to segment the media (e.g., lead time, their competitive edge).

Martin Reddington and Helen Francis consider the role of social media technologies (Web 2.0 and Enterprise 2.0) on corporate reputation in Chapter 11. These technologies build and improve communication and engagement within the organization and a stronger employer brand and identification. But there are some concerns stemming from use of these technologies. Inaccurate and unflattering information can be communicated. They examine in some detail, using their research in the private and public sector, how use of Enterprise 2.0 has influenced corporate reputation. They first look at how HR strategies can be used to improve employee work experiences and outcomes. They also indicate how use of Enterprise 2.0 can change an organization's business model. They offer concrete examples of how use of Web 2.0 can contribute to more effective people management. In addition, intensive case studies of organizational use of Web 2.0 are provided. It appears that use of social media technologies can positively influence employee engagement and identity, firm performance, and corporate reputation in the eyes of various stakeholders.

Celia Harquail positions authenticity as the centerpiece of hoer thinking about corporate. She sees social media tools as having a major role in the way communication occurs between individuals and organizations and in making organizations more human. It is harder to dislike an organization you can get close to. Social media tools permit interaction , a wide range of information, and easy access. She uses the term "re-creating" to capture the fact that an organization's reputation is constantly being re-created with each new and unique experience a stakeholder has with an organization. She then indicated technological features that support this two-way communication. She shows how authenticity, or humanness, of communication can be achieved to produce positive effects. Given the generally low level of trust individuals today have in organizations, being authentic can have tangible benefits. She concludes with a discussion of the externally focused and internally focused challenges that organizations must face to make best use of social media.

The final section, containing three chapters, focuses on recovery from a damaged reputation. In Chapter 13 Thomas Clarke examines how a disaster in corporate governance can tarnish corporate reputations. Corporate governance has increasingly come under scrutiny for a variety of reasons including the major role corporations play in society and the emphasis on increasing organizational transparency. He begins by reviewing attempts to reform corporate governance and those interested in monitoring and reporting on corporate governance. Corporate crises have generally led to calls for better regulation of corporate governance. It has however proven difficult to regulate corporate governance practices. Some corporate boards have been passive, ill prepared, and lacking the requisite skills to provide guidance and oversight. He then reviews specific corporate boards (Enron, Worldcom) and how their failures contributed to corporate crises, tarnished reputations, and eventual failure. The current financial crisis is then considered. These events have led to diminished corporate reputations of financial institutions in many countries, along with calls for higher levels of regulation. Clarke believes it will take a long time for these firms to reestablish their reputations.

Dale Miller and Bill Merrilees examine corporate rebranding. Corporate rebranding is contrasted with corporate branding, the former refers to a change in an initially formulated corporate brand and a new formulate, the latter to the initial statement of a corporate brand. Rebranding is usually undertaken to address under-performance. Corporate rebranding appears in three major areas; organizations, cities, and not-for-profits. They propose a three-stage mode of rebranding, with six principles embedded in their model. Stage 1 involves revisioning the corporate brand; Stage 2, obtaining stakeholder buy-in of the revised brand; and Stage 3, implementing the rebranding strategy. Corporate rebranding is obviously a complex undertaking. Stage 1 principles include brand revision, retaining core brand values, and identifying possible new market segments; the Stage 2 principle involves brand reorientation, and Stage 3 principles include the alignment of brand elements and making stakeholders aware of the revised brand. They review some corporate rebranding in each of the three areas (organizations, cities, not-for-profits). They identify challenges in revitalizing declining, neglected and damaged brands. Organizations can also undertake rebranding in a proactive way, the most common current examples involve the introduction of sustainability features. They conclude with a practical list of "lessons learned."

Finally, Mooweon Rhee and Robin Hedwick consider how contextual factors impact the effects of a damaged corporate reputation and steps to repair the damage. These factors include the positive versus negative dimensions of reputation, the relevance of positive reputation to a damaging event, organization age, the diversity of markets served by the organization, and the impact of third parties such as the media and watchdog agencies. They integrate trust management and crisis management literatures and extend their earlier reputation repair thinking. Important concepts include: crisis type, time phases, organizational systems and critical stakeholders. Crises pass through phases of preparation, response, recovery, to organizational learning. They offer concrete examples of specific recovery actions undertaken by some organizations. Not surprisingly, communication is important here. Sadly, organizational learning from a crisis has typically been limited.

References

Alsop, R. J. (2004) *The 18 immutable laws of corporate reputation: Creating, protecting and repairing your most valuable asset*. New York: Wall Street Journal Books.

Anheier, H. K. (1999) *When things go wrong: Organizational failures and breakdowns*. Thousand Oaks, CA: Sage Publications.

Backhaus, K., and Tikoo, S. (2004) Conceptualizing and researching employer branding. *Career Development International*, 9, 501–17.

Backhaus, K., Stone, B. A., and Heiner, K. (2002) Exploring the relationship between corporate social performance and employer attractiveness. *Business and Society*, 41, 292–318.

Balmer, J. T., and Greyser, S. A. (2003) *Revealing the corporation: Perspectives on identity, image, reputation, corporate branding and corporate-level marketing*. London: Routledge

Barrow, S., and Mosely, R. (2005) *The employer brand: Bringing the best of brand management to people at work*. London: Wiley.

Bartel, C. A., Blader, S., and Wrzesniewski, A. (2007) *Identity and the modern organization*. Mahwah, NJ: Lawrence Erlbaum.

Beal, A., and Strauss, J. (2008) *Radically transparent: Monitoring and managing reputations online*. New York: Wiley.

Bernstein, J. (2009) *Keeping the wolves at bay: A media training manual*. Version 3.0., Sierra Madre, CA: Bernstein Crisis Management.

Bouchikhi, H., and Kimberley, J. R. (2008) *The soul of the corporation: How to manage the identity of your company*. Upper Saddle, NJ: Wharton School Publishing.

Bromiley, D. B. (2000) Psychological aspects of corporate identity, image and reputation. *Corporate Reputation Review*, 3, 240–52.

Bromiley, P. and Marcus, A. (1989) The deterrent to dubious corporate behavior: Profitability, probability and safety recalls. *Strategic Management Journal*, 10, 233–50.

Brooks, M. E., Highhouse, S., Russell, S. S., and Mohr, D. C. (2003) Familiarity, ambivalence and firm reputation: Is corporate fame a double-edged sword? *Journal of Applied Psychology*, 88, 904-914.

Browning, J. (19923) Union Carbide: Disaster at Bhopal. In J. Gottschalk (ed.) *Crisis: Inside stories of managing image under siege*. Detroit: Visible Ink.

Burns, J., and Spar, D. L., (2000) *Hitting the Wall: Nike and international labor practices*. Case study, Harvard Business School. Boston, MA: Harvard Business School.

Carmeli, A., Gilat, G., and Weisberg, J. (2006) Perceived external prestige, organizational identification and affective commitment: A stakeholder approach. *Corporate Reputation Review*, 9, 92–104.

Carter, S., and Dukerich, J. M (1998) Corporate responses to changes in reputation. *Corporate Reputation Review*, 1, 250–70.

Chun, R. (2005) Corporate reputation: Meaning and measurement. *International Journal of Management Reviews*, 7, 91–109.

Clegg, S. R., Rhodes, C., and Kornberger, M. (2007) Desperately seeking legitimacy: Organizational identity and emerging industries. *Organizational Studies*, 28, 495–513.

Collins, C. J., and Han, J. (2004) Exploring applicant pool quantity and quality: The effects of early recruitment practice strategies, corporate advertising and firm reputation. *Personnel Psychology*, 57, 685–717.

Davies, G. (2008) Employer branding and its influence on managers. *European Journal of Marketing*, 42, 667–81.

Davies, G., Chun, R., da Silva, R. V., and Roper, S. (2003) *Corporate reputation and competitiveness*. London: Routledge.

Davies, G., and Miles, L. (1997) *What price reputation?* London: Haymarket Business Publications.

Decotiis, T. (2008) *Make it glow: How to build a company reputation for human goodness, flawless execution and being best in class*. Austin, TX: Greenleaf Book Group Press.

Deephouse, D. L. (2000) Media reputation as a strategic resource. *Journal of Management*, 26, 1091–112.

Deephouse, D. L. (1976) The effect of financial and media reputations on performance. *Corporate Reputation Review*, 1, 68–72.

Deephouse, D. L., and Carter, S. M. (2005) An examination of differences between organizational legitimacy and reputation. *Journal of Management Studies*, 42, 329–60.

Dev, C. S. (2008) The corporate brand: Help or hindrance? *Harvard Business Review*, February, 49–58.

Dollinger, M. J., Golden, P. A., and Saxton, T. (1999) The effect of reputation on the decision to joint venture. *Strategic Management Journal*, 18, 127–42.

Dowling, G. R. (2004) Corporate reputations: Should you compete on yours? *California Management Review*, 46, 19–36.

Dowling, G. R. (2001) *Creating corporate reputations: Identity, image and performance*. New York: Oxford University Press.

Dowling, G. R. (1988) Measuring corporate images: A review of alternative approaches. *Journal of Business Research*, 17, 27–34.

Dube, S. C. (2009) Good management, sound finances, and social responsibility: Two decades of US corporate insider perspectives on reputation and the bottom line. *Public Relations Review*, 35, 77–8.

Earle, T.C. (2009) Trust, confidence, and the 2008 global financial crisis. *Risk Analysis*, 29, 785–92.

Fiol, C. M., and Kovoor-Misra, S. (1997) Two-way mirroring: Identity and reputation when things go wrong. *Corporate Reputation Review*, 1, 147–51

Fischer, E., and Reuber, R. (2007) The good, the bad, and the unfamiliar: The challenges of reputation formation facing new firms. *Entrepreneurship: Theory and Practice*, 32, 53–75.

Fombrun, C. J. (2005) Building corporate reputation through CSR initiatives: Evolving standards. *Corporate Reputation Review*, 8, 7–11.

Fombrun, C. J. (2001) Corporate reputations as economic assets. In M. Hitt, R. Freeman and J. Harrison (eds.) *Handbook of strategic management*. Oxford: Blackwell.

Fombrun, C. J. (1996) *Reputation: Realizing value from the corporate image*. Boston, MA: Harvard Business School Press.

Fombrun, C. J. and Van Riel, C. B. M. (2004) *Fame and fortune: How successful companies build winning reputations*. Englewood Cliffs, NJ: Prentice-Hall.

Fombrun, C. and Shanley, M. (1990) What's in a name? Reputation building and corporate strategy. *Academy of Management Journal*, 33, 233–58.

Friedman, B. (2009) Human resource management role: Implications for corporate reputation. *Corporate Reputation Review*, 12, 229–44.

Fulmer, I. S., Gerhart, B., and Scott, K. S. (2003) Are the 100 "best" better? An empirical investigation of the relationship between being "a great place to work" and firm performance. *Personnel Psychology*, 56, 965–93.

Gaines-Ross, L. (2008) *Corporate reputation: 12 steps to safeguarding and recovering reputation*. New York: John Wiley.

Gaines-Ross, L. (2002) *CEO capital: A guide to building CEO reputation and company success*. New York: John Wiley.

Garcia, H. F. (2007) *Reputation management: The key to successful public relations and corporate communication*. London: Routledge.

Garcia, H. F., and Ewing, A. (2008) Defending corporate reputation from litigation. *Strategy and Leadership*, 36, 41–5.

Gillespie, N., and Dietz, G. (2009) Trust repair after an organizational-level failure. *Academy of Management Review*, 34, 127–45.

Gottschalk, J. (1993) *Crisis: Inside stories of managing image under siege*. Detroit, MI: Visible Ink.

Greenglass, E. R., Fiksenbaum, L., Goldstein, L., and Desiato, C. (2002) Stressful effects of a university faculty strike on students: Implications for coping. *Interchange*, 33, 261–79.

Greening, D. and Turban, D. (2000) Corporate social performance as a competitive advantage in attracting a quality workforce. *Business and Society*, 39, 254–89.

Greyser, S. A. (1999) Advancing and enhancing corporate reputations. *Corporate Reputations: An International Journal*, 4, 177–91.

Hall, R. (1993) A framework linking intangible resources and capabilities to sustainable competitive advantage. *Strategic Management Journal*, 14, 607–618.

Hall, R. (1992) The strategic analysis of intangible resources. *Strategic Management Journal*, 13, 135–44.

Hannington, T. (2004) *How to measure and manage your corporate reputation*. Aldershot: Gower.

Hansen, M. T., Ibarra, H., and Peyer, U. (2010) The best performing CEOs in the world. *Harvard Business Review*, January, 104–113.

HarrisInteractive (2008) *The reputations of the most visible companies*. New York: HarrisInteractive.

Highhouse, S., Broadfoot, A., Yugo, J. E. and Devendorf, S. A. (2009) Examining corporate reputation judgments with generalizability theory. *Journal of Applied Psychology*, 94, 782–9.

Highhouse, S., and Zickar, M. J.,, Thorsteinson, T. J., Stierwald, S. L., and Slaughter, J. E. (1999) Assessing company employment image: An example in the fast food industry. *Personnel Psychology*, 52, 151–72.

Hill and Knowlton (2006) Intangibles directly influence financial analyst opinions according to Global Hill and Knowlton "Return on reputation" study. Press release, March 13. Available at: http://www.hillandknowlton.ca/index.php/news/press_releases/28.html, last accessed 16 December 2009.

Hoffer, G., Pruitt, S., and Reilly, R. (1988) The impact of product recalls on the wealth of sellers: A re-examination. *Journal of Political Economy*, 96, 663–70.

Karpoff, J., Lee, D. S., and Martin, G. (2006) The cost to firms of cooking the books. *Journal of Corporate Finance*, 12, 536–59.

Kim, P. H., Ferrin, D. L., Cooper, C. D., and Dirks, K. T. (2004) Removing the shadow of suspicion: The effects of apology versus denial for repairing competence- versus integrity-based trust violations. *Journal of Applied Psychology*, 89, 104–18.

Kumar, V., Peterson, J. A., and Leone, R. P. (2007) How valuable is word of mouth? *Harvard Business Review*, 85, 139–46.

Laird, G. (2009) *The price of a bargain: The quest for cheap and the death of globalization*. Toronto: McClelland and Stewart.

Laplume, A., Bapuji, H., Dewar, N., and Walker, K. (2008) Sooner or later: Product recalls and firm reputation. Paper presented at the 68th Annual Meeting of the Academy of Management, August, Anaheim, CA.

Lievens, F., and Highhouse, S. (2003) The relationship of instrumental and symbolic attributes to a company's attractiveness as an employer. *Personnel Psychology*, 56, 75–102.

Lievens, F., Decaesteker, C., Coetsier, P., and Geirnnert, J. (2001) Organizational attractiveness for prospective applicants: A person-organization fit perspective. *Applied Psychology: An International Review*, 50, 30–51.

Love, E. G., and Kraatz, M. (2009) Character, conformity, or the bottom line? How and why downsizing affected corporate reputation. *Academy of Management Journal*, 52, 314–35.

MacIntyre, L. (2009) *The bishop's man*. Toronto: Random House.

MacMillan, K., Money, K., Downing, S., and Hillenbrand, C. (2005) Reputations in relationships: Measuring experiences, emotions and behaviors. *Corporate Reputation Review*, 8, 214–32.

Malmendier, U., and Tate, G. (2009) Superstar CEOs. *Quarterly Journal of Economics*, 124, 1593–638.

Mangold, W. G., and Miles, S. J. (2007) The employer brand: Is yours an all-star? *Business Horizons*, 50, 423-433.

Margolis, J. D., and Stoltz, P. G. (2010) How to bounce back from adversity. *Harvard Business Review*, January, 86–92.

Martin, G. (2009a) Driving corporate reputations from the inside: A strategic role and strategic dilemmas for HR. *Asia Pacific Journal of Human Resource Management*, 47, 219–35.

Martin, G. (2009b) Employer branding and corporate reputation management: A model and some evidence. In R. J. Burke and C. L. Cooper (eds.) *The peak performing organization*. London: Routledge.

Martin, G., and Hetrick, S. (2006) *Corporate reputations, branding and people management: A strategic approach to HR*. Oxford: Butterworth Heinemann.

Martin, G., Beaumont, P. B., Doig, R., and Pate, J. M. (2005) Branding: A new performance discourse for HR. *European Management Journal*, 23, 76–88.

McGuire, J. B. Sundgren, A., and Schneeweiss, T. (1988) Corporate social responsibility and firm financial performance. *Academy of Management Journal*, 31, 854–72.

Merrilees, B., and Miller, D. (2007) Principles of corporate rebranding. *European Journal of Marketing*, 42, 537–52.

Morehouse, W., and Subramanyam, A. (1986) *The Bhopal tragedy: What really happened and what it means for American workers and communities at risk*. New York: Council on International Public Affairs.

Pollock, T. G., and Rindova, V. P. (2003) Media legitimation effects in the market for initial public offerings. *Academy of Management Journal*, 46, 631–42.

Preston, L. E., and O'Bannon, D. P. (1997) The corporate social-financial performance relationship: A typology and analysis. *Business and Society*, 36, 418–30.

Rao, H. (1994) The social construction of reputation=certification contests, legitimation, and the survival of organizations in the American automobile industry, 1895–1912. *Strategic Management Journal*, 15, 29–44.

Rhee, M., and Valdez, M. E. (2009) Contextual factors surrounding reputation damage with potential implications for reputation repair. *Academy of Management Review*, 34, 146–68.

Rhee, M., and Haunschild, P. B. (2006) The liability of good reputation: A study of product recalls in the U.S. automobile industry. *Organization Science*, 117, 101–17.

Rindova, V. P., Pollock, T. G., and Hayward, M. L. A. (2006) Celebrity firms: The social construction of market popularity. *Academy of Management Review*, 31, 60–71.

Rindova, V. P., Williamson, I. O., Petkova, A. P., and Sever, J. M. (2005) Being good or being known: An empirical examination of the dimensions, antecedents, and consequences of organizational reputation. *Academy of Management Journal*, 48, 1033–49.

Roberts, P. W., and Dowling, G. R. (2002) Corporate reputation and sustained superior financial performance. *Strategic Management Journal*, 23, 1077–93.

Roberts, P. W., and Dowling, G. R. (1997) The value of a firm's corporate reputation: How reputation helps attain and sustain superior profitability. *Corporate Reputation Review*, 1, 72–5.

Rupp, N. G. (2004) The attributes of a costly recall: Evidence from the automotive industry. *Review of Industrial Organization*, 25, 21–44.

Rutherford, M. W., Buller, P. F., and Stebbins, J. M. (2009) Ethical considerations of the legitimacy lie. *Entrepreneurship: Theory and Practice*, 34, 949–64.

Schacter, H. (2008) Report on business, *Globe and Mail*. Monday, September 1.

Schnietz, K. E., and Epstein, M. J. (2005) Exploring the financial value of a reputation for corporate social responsibility during a crisis. *Corporate Reputation Review*, 7, 327–45.

Schuler, D. A., and Cording, M. (2006) A corporate social performance-corporate financial performance behavior model for consumers. *Academy of Management Review*, 31, 540–58.

Schwaiger, M. (2004) Components and parameters of corporate reputation – an empirical study. *Schmalenbach Business Review*, 56, 46–71.

Schwartz, P., and Gibb, B. (1999) *When good companies do bad things: Responsibility and risk in an age of globalization*. New York: Wiley.

Shapiro, C. (1983) Premiums for high quality products as returns to reputations. *Quarterly Journal of Economics*, 98, 659–79.

Sharp, I. (2009) *Four Seasons: The story of a business philosophy*. Toronto: Four Seasons Hotels Limited.

Shenkar, O., and Yuchtman-Yaar, E. (1997) Reputation, image, prestige, and good will: An interdisciplinary approach to organizational standing. *Human Relations*, 50, 1361–87.

Shrivastava, P. (1987) *Bhopal: Anatomy of a crisis*. Cambridge, MA: Ballinger.

Shrivastava, P., Mitroff, I. I., Miller, D., and Migliani, A. (1988) Understanding industrial crises. *Journal of Management Studies*, 25, 285–303.

Smith, A. T. (2009) *ESPN: The company, the story land lessons behind the most fanatical brand in sports*. New York: John Wiley.

Sonnenfeld, J. A., and Ward, A. J. (2007a) Firing back: How great leaders rebound after disaster. *Harvard Business Review*, 85, 76–84.

Sonnenfeld, J. A., and Ward, A. J. (2007b) *Firing back: How great leaders rebound after disaster*. Boston, MA: Harvard Business School Press.

Staw, B. M., and Epstein, L. D. (2000) What bandwagons bring: Effects of popular management techniques on corporate performance, reputation, and CEO pay. *Administrative Science Quarterly*, 45, 523–56.

Sutton, R., and Callalhan, A. L. (1987) The stigma of bankruptcy: Spoiled organizational image and its management. *Academy of Management Journal*, 30, 405–36.

Tadelis, S. (1999) What's in a name? Reputation as a tradeable asset. *American Economic Review*, 89, 548–63.

Turban, D. B., and Cable, D. M. (2003) Firm reputation and applicant pool characteristics. *Journal of Organizational Behavior*, 24, 733–53.

Turban, D. B., Forret, M. L., and Hendrickson, C. I. (1998) Applicant attraction to firms: Influences of organizational reputation, job and organizational attributes, and recruiter behaviors. *Journal of Vocational Behavior*, 52, 24–44.

Turban, D. B., and Greening, D. W. (1997) Corporate social performance and organizational attractiveness to prospective employees. *Academy of Management Journal*, 40, 658–72.

Tybout, A. M., and Roehm, M. (2009) Let the response fit the scandal. *Harvard Business Review*, 87, 82–8.

Ulrich, D., and Smallwood, N., (2007a) Building a leadership brand. *Harvard Business Review*, July–August, 93–100.

Ulrich, D., and Smallwood, N. (2007b) *Leadership brand: Developing customer-focused leaders to drive performance and build lasting value*. Boston, MA: Harvard Business School Press.

Ulrich, D., and Smallwood, N. (2005) HR's new ROI: Return on intangibles. *Human Resources Management*, 44, 137–42.

Voss, Z. G., Cable, D. M., and Voss, G. B. (2006) Organizational identity and firm performance: What happens when leaders disagree about "Who we are"? *Organization Science*, 17. 741–55.

Waddock, S. A., and Graves, S. B. (1997) The corporate social performance-financial performance link. *Strategic Management Journal*, 18, 303–29.

Wade, J. B., Porac, J. E., Pollack, T. G., and Graffin, S. D (2008) Star CEOs: Benefit or burden? *Organizational Dynamics*, 37, 203–10.

Wartick, S. L. (2002) Measuring corporate reputation. *Business and Society*, 41, 371–92.

Wartick, S. L. (1992) The relationship between media exposure and changes in corporate reputation. *Business and Society*, 31, 33–47.

Weiner, D. (2006) Crisis communication: Managing corporate reputation in the court of public opinion. *Ivey Business Journal*, March/April, 1–8.

Wickens, C., M., Fiksenbaum, L. M., Greenglass, E. R., and Weisenthal, D. (2006) Student stress and coping following a university strike in Canada. *Journal of Collective Negotiations*, 31, 1–19.

Williams, R. J., and Barrett, J. D. (2000) Corporate philanthropy, criminal activity, and firm reputation: Is there a link? *Journal of Business Ethics*, 26, 341–50.

Winn, M. I., MacDonald, P., and Zeitsma, C. (2008) Managing industry reputation: The dynamic tension between collective and competitive reputation management strategies. *Corporate Reputation Review*, 11, 35–55.

Yoon, E., Guffey, H. J., and Kijewski, V. (1993) The effects of information and company reputation on intention to buy a business service. *Journal of Business Research*, 27, 215–28.

Yu, T., and Lester, R. H. (2008) Moving beyond the boundaries: A social network perspective on reputation spillover. *Corporate Reputation Review*, 11, 94–108.

Zyglidopoulos, S. C. (2001) The impact of accidents on firms' reputation for social performance. *Business and Society*, 40, 416–41.

Zyglidopoulos, S. C., and Phillips, N. (1999) Responding to reputational crises: A stakeholder perspective. *Corporate Reputation Review*, 2, 333–50.

2 *The Meaning and Measurement of Corporate Reputation*

GARY DAVIES

In this chapter the aim is to examine the different schools of thought within the study of corporate reputation, to identify how reputation is variously defined, and then to discuss the different approaches to the measures of reputation that are associated with each perspective.

Just What is Reputation?

The word 'reputation' conjures up more than one picture in our minds and is taken to mean more than one thing in both business practice and business theory. Dictionary definitions tend to emphasise the idea of what someone or something is known for, which is quite sterile as a perspective as it fails to capture the quite fundamental differences between what the term means compared with other similar terms such as character, image, corporate brand and identity. The subtle differences in what we can mean to communicate when using the term reputation is better illustrated in some relevant quotations from history. In *Othello*, Shakespeare has the character of Iago explaining to Cassio (who is complaining about losing his reputation: 'the immortal part of myself') that, 'Reputation is an idle and most false imposition, oft got without merit and lost without deserving'. Two sides then to the same coin from the bard himself. Somewhat later and from the other side of the Atlantic, Abraham Lincoln advises that 'Character is like a tree and reputation like a shadow. The shadow is what we think of it, the tree is the real thing.' Reputation, let's face it, has gotten itself a bad reputation with many luminaries. Even today it is often seen as synonymous with spin, the art of projecting a superficial, positive association for something that is actually flawed or undeserving. Yet reputation can be the most valuable asset a company possesses. So why the confusion?

In academe the term has certainly been used in a positive sense. But the problem here is that the area is relatively new as a topic, has no single base in a traditional discipline and (worse) many disciplines can claim ownership of the term. The outcome was probably inevitable, the growth in interest in the study of corporate reputation has been bedevilled by terminological confusion, not helped by some academics' insisting that reputation means 'this' and only 'this', particularly when it comes to what is measured as reputation. Frankly reputation means whatever the writer and audience take it to mean, which behoves authors to define carefully what they mean by the term and the allied labels of brand, image and identity.

Fombrun and van Riel (1997) were one of the first to point to the reasons underpinning the confusion in terms and the number of different ways of looking at what reputation represents. Accountants see it as an intangible asset, one that is given a value in the accounts of many companies but usually in the context of a value for product brands and rarely for that of the corporate brand, to which corporate reputation tends to be equated. Marketing tends to focus on the customer view of reputation and according to Fombrun and van Riel (1997) to be concerned with how reputation is created. Organisational theorists tend to focus more on an internal view of reputation. However at issue is whether an employee view of reputation means the same as 'organisational identity', something discussed later in this chapter. Reputation to an economist can mean something totally different again, a market signal, while in strategy there is an emphasis on mobility barriers.

Chun (2005) took a different approach to categorising these differences in conceptualisation, one based on what she referred to as 'three schools of thought'. In the 'evaluative' school reputation is assessed from its financial value or from the short-term financial performance of the firm. The 'impressional school' and the 'relational school' are similar in that they both recognise the more affective associations that are made with an organisation. The first focuses on a single stakeholder view while the second considers the views of more than one stakeholder group simultaneously. Much of the work at Manchester Business School in the field has adopted this last approach. Hence our focus has been on differentiating between in particular the employee and customer views of the organisation. More about our own work later.

HOW ABOUT IDENTITY?

If there are issues surrounding the use of the word reputation as a term, then there are even more fundamental problems around the use of the term 'identity'. It seemed in our own work useful to use the word identity to refer to the employee view of corporate reputation. But this has caused no end of problems! To an organisational scientist the term identity can have quite a specific meaning and one rather different from what we intended to communicate. What we refer to as 'organisational identity' to distinguish it from the identity component of reputation has been very precisely defined as the shared perceptions an organisation's members hold, in particular those central, distinctive and enduring qualities that guide behaviour (Albert and Whetten, 1985). Where then the conceptualisation of identity used in work at Manchester and elsewhere in reputation differs (and is closer to the view of organisational identity of Gioia and Thomas, 1996) is that we argue that both the employee and customer views of corporate reputation are tractable (rather than enduring) and therefore malleable.

Certain aspects of an organisation's identity are clearly enduring, such as its history, the products and services it offers, and its country of origin. But whether for example a company is seen as trustworthy can change in the eyes of its employees and other stakeholders. There have been various attempts to build bridges between the two views, identity as seen as the employee view of reputation and organisational identity, in defining terms such as 'perceived organizational identity' (Dutton et al., 1994) or 'organizational identity orientation' (Brickson, 2007), the former being quite similar in definition to what we used to refer to as identity. However, to try to avoid the problems that our use of the term identity has caused the writer now prefers to use the rather more long-winded expression 'employee views of the corporate reputation' to label exactly the same idea.

Unfortunately just when everyone thought it was safe to ignore the issue of terminology, another expression, the 'employee' or 'employer' brand, was introduced into both the marketing and HR literatures. Yes, the obvious distinction here is that 'employer brand' refers to what attracts applicants, what retains employees and what motivates them, which is somewhat different from both identity and organisational identity. But this does not help particularly the new researcher trying to understand what has been achieved thus far in the field as the topics overlap considerably and insights from one can be missed if a literature review focuses on another.

In the marketing field practitioners use the term identity to refer to brand imagery and often to visual identity, a product's get-up and logo. In fact many design companies market themselves as reputation consultants. While one can believe that visual identity has an important role in expressing desired reputation, visual identity and reputation cannot be usefully seen as synonymous, as the implications include the idea that changing reputation can be effected merely by changing a logo. A change in visual identity can refresh or update a tired perception in the market but only in something as fundamental as the refurbishment of a service outlet can the two be placed on the same platform. This chapter returns to this theme in a later discussion of corporate branding.

HOW ABOUT IMAGE?

At the time of preparing this chapter the writer has a paper under review in a journal and is considering a challenge from one reviewer along the lines of 'what is the difference between reputation and image?' Thus far in the work of Manchester Business School we have tended to use the term 'image' to refer to the view of an external stakeholder, normally the customer. However, the reviewer's challenge presumes that 'image' has a single meaning, which unfortunately it does not. Again you can read the work of highly respected researchers in the field who claim that 'image' is this and 'reputation' is that. In reality the two terms are often used interchangeably and 'image' is such a vague term that we doubt whether it is useful to see it as a clearly definable construct. Some do hold that reputation is more enduring than image which is more transient. At issue yet again is whether it is useful to distinguish between what can and cannot be easily changed in managing the way an organisation is perceived by its stakeholders and whether it is useful to have specific terms for each.

BRAND, IMAGE AND CORPORATE BRAND

Originally a brand was thought of as a device used to identify the origin of a product, so as to differentiate one similar product from another. The concepts of brand and reputation are similar. Strong brands, those with 'equity', tend to be thought of as those with a high level of awareness in their markets and with strong, positive associations. Thus a Mars bar is well known as a confectionary item, and in Britain was traditionally associated with a strap line of helping the eater to 'work, rest and play'. But what of the company, Mars itself? As an employer brand would this same strap line not signify a place to enjoy work through play, with of course plenty of opportunity to rest? The more recent slogan,

'Pleasure you can't measure' would be even more problematic as an employer brand. However, Mars the company and employer has its own associations, as a large, privately owned and global business with interests in a wide range of food products; one that offers high salaries, attracting good quality people. So the same name has quite different associations in different contexts even though the company and the name behind both are exactly the same. Here it is useful to distinguish between the product brand and the corporate brand.

Superficially in both cases we could be talking about the same idea, building associations around a name. But the writer believes and has argued elsewhere (Davies et al. 2003) that managing a product brand such as Mars and the corporate brand behind it are distinctly different tasks. Many successful product brands have an associated imagery which is above and beyond reality. Alcohol brands such as Martini work at a functional level because of taste and because they contain the recreational drug ethanol, which serves as a central nervous system depressant. (Interesting is it not that such a description cannot be found in the marketing of any alcohol brand?) Such products are marketed or rather branded by emphasising for example the social aspects of using the product, including fun and glamour. Particularly the latter is re-created by the user in his or her mind when using the product. Consequently it is seen as more sophisticated to serve and drink Martini than a supermarket own brand, which may be functionally identical to that same brand. Functionally at least they serve similar purposes, but emotionally they do not. Why then do we believe that using one brand is more sophisticated than using another? Quite simply because the advertising tells us it is more sophisticated to consume one product rather than another.

The same approach to branding does not necessarily work when marketing a service brand, where the intangibility of the product requires more solid associations. We trust a bank with our savings because it looks a solid, secure institution. The reality as we have found out to our cost is that banking has become or perhaps always was associated with risk taking of the type that most of would shun away from. So there *are* intangible associations that are (irrationally?) made with a service. But theorists argue that the design of a service outlet is key to creating the equivalent of product brand image and is the equivalent of a product brand's advertising. A stone façade makes a bank appear solid and strong. The example of banks and their promotion of an image that was not based upon reality (while equally fanciful advertising of product brands seems to work) suggests different mechanisms at work at least in our minds when we assess product and service brands.

So why do attempts to brand a service through advertising rarely seem to work as well as the equivalent with a tangible product? One reason is that when any imagery created by advertising or any other communication for a service proves false and the reality fails to match up to our expectations we can change our minds about the company (and remarkably quickly) leading to a change in our behaviour towards them. The reality of a service organisation has to live up to its external communication and advertising what you are not will at best be a waste of money. Instead what marketers call 'brand values' should reflect the real values of the organization (Davies et al., 2010). The customer enters temporarily and superficially into that culture when consuming a service, an experience that is often co-created with the employee. Most corporate brands that face the customer are service brands and the economies of developed nations are now predominantly dependent upon the service sector, making an understanding of corporate branding here absolutely vital. But to an employee the corporate name of any organisation is still a brand and one that is arguably similar in nature to a service brand. Some of our current work (as yet unpublished) shows that employees identify more strongly with and are more committed to strong corporate brands or corporate reputations. As will be argued later corporate brand imagery and corporate reputation can be measured using exactly the same measures, implying that they are similar if not identical constructs. Most service brands rely upon one name in their marketing, the company name. That same name has to appeal to many stakeholders and not just customers, which is akin to saying that at least in the service sector corporate reputation and corporate brand mean the same thing.

In summary the terms 'corporate brand' and 'corporate reputation' are very similar in the way they are used. In the former there is more emphasis on one stakeholder, the customer, but that is probably all that is worth noting.

A SHARED LEXICON?

There have been a number of attempts to find a shared way forward to address the confusion caused by the morass of terms in the reputation field. Brown et al. (2006) adopted the neat approach of stepping back from a dictionary-based approach to consider what are the key questions stakeholders might ask in this context. They identified four: Who are we as an organisation? What does the organisation want others to think about the organisation? What does the organisation believe others think of the organisation? and What do (external) stakeholders actually think of the organisation? They point out that the constructs represented by such questions have been variously labelled by different researchers and propose that researchers should agree on the following respective labels: identity, intended image, construed image and reputation. One problem with the lexicon is the use of reputation to refer to only external views while identity is used to refer to the internal but without differentiating between what is tractable and what is enduring. The wider problem is that their call for consistency has gone as yet unheeded.

Contemporaneously with Brown et al. (2006), Barnett et al. (2006) attempted to identify the various strands of meaning surrounding the term 'reputation'. They propose three different clusters of definition: Reputation as asset; Reputation as assessment; and Reputation as awareness. They consider that corporate reputation should be distinguished from corporate image as concepts and that reputation is more concerned with evaluative judgement, suggesting a cognitive construct, while 'image' should refer to the more impressionistic associations, essentially what comes to mind when one hears the corporate name, suggesting an affective construct. They define corporate reputation as: observers' collective judgements of the financial, social and environmental impacts attributed to the corporation over time.

Money and Hillenbrand (2006) offer another way to try to nail down a useful way of thinking about the meaning of reputation. They avoid the trap of definition and instead try to position reputation as a concept using in part the ideas of Fishbein and Ajzen on how attitudes are created and used. Our experiences of a corporation lead us to hold certain beliefs about them which in turn create attitudes towards them, leading to certain intentions and behaviours towards the company. Thus reputation should be seen as a set of beliefs and attitudes with certain antecedents and precedents. How one defines reputation more precisely becomes irrelevant. Neat, but reviewers of journal articles will still insist on a definition of terms.

One inevitable conclusion is that if it is possible for nine researchers in the same field to propose such radically different conceptualisations for the same thing then it is unlikely that a shared lexicon can or will emerge. The meaning of Reputation (and its allied constructs) will remain in terms of precision whatever the writer and reader deem it to be. It will then be the responsibility of the writer to ensure the reader understands what is meant by individual terms. Of interest to the reader for the second part of this chapter is the distinction between the rational/cognitive and affective perspectives that emerge from this review of definitions. But it is time for the writer to climb down from the fence and to offer to define reputation and to explain why.

A PERSONAL VIEW OF WHAT REPUTATION REPRESENTS

Reputation in the writer's opinion has been conceptualised (usefully) in two complementary ways: as our expectations of an organisation's future actions based upon our prior experience (e.g., Weigelt and Camerer, 1988) and as the accumulated impression that stakeholders form of the firm, resulting from their interactions with, and any communications they receive about, the firm (Fombrun and Shanley, 1990). This impression may be evaluative in the way that Barnett et al. (2006) suggest (e.g., I think that the Mars company is a profitable business and that is important to me) but such a cognitive stance ignores the issue of whether any stakeholder can make such judgement. The associations we make with a corporate name are created by a range of sources including actual experience, media comment and content, sponsored communication and word of mouth. But how many Mars customers or for that matter Mars employees have ever read their annual report and accounts? As a private company they are not of much interest to financial journalists so there is little media comment on the company. And what of a hospital within the British National Health Service or an organisation such as the police? Is the concept of financial impact even relevant here? If the answer is no then what is the value of defining reputation in such a way?

The media are a key source of information that we use to construct our perception of an organisation, but so is our experience of them. How much of this is concerned with a company's social or environmental actions? Do we care whether the police are environmentally responsible or more to the point is that a fundamentally relevant issue when considering their reputation? The various sources that we do use to evaluate a company and to form our picture of them will shape our expectations of an organisation and thus our own future behaviour towards it (Brown and Dacin, 1997) as customers or as employees. For example we will approach a firm that has gained our trust with a greater propensity to accept what they say. Consequently a reputation for being trustworthy can reduce transaction costs and create loyalty amongst customers. So having a reputation for being trustworthy appears to be good for business.

Here to the writer is the central issue for those who wish to impose a view as to what reputation means. Is it a useful definition? There is one other simple question to answer: what are the implications of your definition? Does a customer's or an employee's judgement of a company's financial, social and environmental impact influence their behaviour to a significant extent such that companies should attempt to both optimise these and ensure such stakeholders are aware of them? Or do such factors *potentially* contribute to our overall evaluation of an organisation so that one should not ignore them, but equally so not rely upon them as being the only or even the major issues for reputation managers? Where is even the evidence that stakeholders use their judgements of the financial, social and environmental impact of any or all organisations in determining their own behaviour? If the evidence is lacking or ambivalent, what is the value of the definition?

The conceptualisation of reputation the writer favours is to combine the four citations at the beginning if this section:

> *The reputation of an organisation is the impression stakeholders have of that organisation, accumulated from a range of sources including actual experience, media comment and content, sponsored communication and word of mouth. It shapes stakeholder expectations of that organisation's future actions and their own future behaviour towards that organisation.*

The statement makes it clear that reputation is largely subjective in nature and not necessarily based in whole or in part upon the objective evaluation of certain aspects of an organisation's behaviour. It recognises certain antecedents of this impression but do not specify what these are as they are many and various. The reason why reputation is potentially valuable is recognised as it is a determinant of customer and employee future behaviour as well as being an indicator of our expectations of that organisation. By implication it recognises that all stakeholders may hold an accumulated impression of the same organisation but may differ in that impression. At the highest level of abstraction the writer would argue that a reputation can be good, bad or neutral. What lies beneath that overall impression is the focus on the second part of this chapter and the issue of measurement.

How is Reputation Measured?

Reputation is a complex and intangible construct but it can be measured simply by asking respondents simply to rate the reputation of a firm from poor to good (Goldberg and Hartwick, 1990) but such global measures do not explain how reputation can be improved upon. And here is where the story of two routes to the same goal begins. Measures can be of two main types, cognitive or affective, or a mixture of both (Bolger, 1959). In the first respondents are asked to assess an organisation for example in its role as an employer, in providing products that are fit for purpose, and as a company to invest in. In the second respondents' feelings about a company are assessed; and there has been growing attention paid to more evaluative measures designed to capture the imagery that stakeholders associate with firms (Darden and Babin, 1994). The first type of measure is compatible with the type of reputation definition proposed by Barnett et al. (2006).

COGNITIVE MEASURES

The best known illustration of a cognitive measure is Fortune's annual America's Most Admired Companies (AMAC) survey, which has often been a key data source used to explore and argue positive linkages between reputation and financial performance. Fortune and its survey associate Hay Group have annually surveyed senior managers and analysts on their views about Fortune 500 companies (from 1984) and Fortune 1000 companies (from 1995) and a combination of American and global companies from 2009. The current survey covers 25 international industries and 39 primarily US-market industries. For the international industries up to 15 of the largest companies in an industry by revenue are chosen for inclusion and for the 39 US industries the 10 largest companies by revenue are chosen. Hay survey executives, directors and analysts, asking them to rate companies in their own industry on nine criteria, from investment value to social responsibility. In 2009 a total of 689 companies from 28 countries were surveyed by interviewing over 4,000 executives. Respondents are asked to rate a competitor's reputation in terms of nine key attributes: (1) Financial soundness, (2) Long-term investment value, (3) Use of corporate assets, (4) Innovativeness, (5) Quality of the company's management, (6) Quality of its products and services, (7) Ability to attract, develop, and keep talented people, (8) Acknowledgement of social responsibility and (9) Effectiveness in doing business globally. According to Hay these attributes were developed prior to the inception of the Most Admired Companies rankings in the mid 1980s through a series of interviews with executives and industry analysts to determine the qualities that make a company worthy of admiration (although the ninth criterion was added much more recently). Raters are asked to evaluate each eligible company on each attribute by assigning a score from zero ('Poor') to 10 ('Excellent'). For the purposes of the industry rankings, a company's overall score is determined through a simple average of the individual attribute scores. Companies who rank in the top half of their industry are defined as "most admired" within their industry. To create a top 50 overall list of Most Admired Companies, respondents to the industry surveys are asked to select the 10 companies they admire most in any sector. In other words the overall ranking survey is different from the industry survey and a strong position at the industry level is no guarantee of a strong position in the overall rankings.

Researchers have tended to use AMAC data to explore and argue links between reputation and financial performance. Three of the AMAC criteria are, however, financial in nature. A high Fortune score correlates with superior financial returns (Vergin and Qoronfleh, 1998) and can be used to imply that superior financial performance is sustainable (Roberts and Dowling, 2002). However, since financial performance is a major input to the Fortune ranking process the measure could be heavily influenced by a financial halo (Brown and Perry, 1994) leading to concern about the practical value to managers of AMAC data (Fryxell and Wang, 1994). The financial halo can be removed but the unadjusted Fortune rankings still suffer from poor face validity in explaining what is happening in the market, as it represents the evaluation of analysts and senior executives and not the customers and employees who create business performance. The reputations of companies in the eyes of business people certainly correlate with their financial performances, but it is more likely that financial performance causes such views rather than vice versa. For example, in both 1999 and 2000 Enron ranked first in the world for two of the Fortune criteria, 'Innovativeness' and 'Quality of Management'. It ranked first overall in its sector and would have been included in the list of the top 10 most admired companies on the basis of its raw score were it not for additional methodology used to devise the final ranking. High rankings are therefore no absolute guide to future financial performance and in this case would have misled. Nevertheless AMAC rankings are used by both academic researchers and business to identify companies with good or not so good reputations.

Concern over the validity of the Fortune approach led to alternatives being sought. One such attempt from Fombrun et al. (2000) was branded the RQ (Reputation Quotient) model. Through several stages of pilot studies and focus groups, the finalized total of 20 items was factor analysed into six dimensions from data gathered with members of the public. Items were generated mainly from existing media rankings with some additional items from the image and reputation literatures. Interestingly, the factors appeared to be almost identical to at least seven of eight factors in the Fortune study, which was originally criticised and led to the development of the RQ model (Chun, 2005).

Although RQ was developed in surveys with the public it was marketed as a scale suitable for use with multiple stakeholders in a joint venture between the Reputation Institute and research company Harris Interactive from 1999 and more recently by Harris themselves. In its current form, members of the public are asked to nominate companies they are familiar with and which have in their opinion either the best or worst overall reputation, the nomination phase. Over 6,000 interviews are used to develop a list of the 'Most Visible' companies in the USA. These companies are then used to obtain detailed evaluations from the public using the RQ scale and by surveying 20,000 respondents online. The overall RQ is calculated by averaging the scores across the RQ questions.

From 2006 the Reputation Institute have marketed their own measures, RepTrack and the Reputation Pulse. 70,000 on-line interviews are conducted in 32 countries. To seven criteria (products, innovation, workplace, governance, citizenship, leadership and performance) that are similar to those in the RQ and AMAC measures are added measures of affect: 'trust, admire, esteem, feeling'. The latter appear to be used to measure overall reputation as a single factor and the former to explain them; in other words reputation is seen as being more about affect but is achieved by what companies are actually seen to do.

In other sectors similar methodologies are used to assess reputation, similar in that a list of largely cognitive criteria are used to ask respondents for their opinions or about their experiences. However there are measures that many readers working in academia and particularly in business schools will be aware of that take an even stronger line as to what constitutes a positive reputation. The *Financial Times* Global MBA rankings aim to guide potential students as to their choice of school. To be included schools have to be accredited by an international accreditation body, have been running their MBA for at least four years and have graduated its first class at least three years before the year of ranking. Graduates from each participating school are surveyed and data is also gathered from each school directly. Twenty criteria are used to determine the rankings; eight are based on data from alumni questionnaires. The criteria used group into three main areas: salaries and career development, the diversity and international reach of the business school and its MBA programme, and the research of the school. Graduate salary and the percentage increase comparing earnings prior to study with salary after together contribute 40 per cent of the rank for each school. Other criteria include percentage of graduates employed at three months, percentage of women faculty, percentage of international members on the board, research and doctoral programme ranking. The FT research ranking is based on a database compiled by the FT which counts papers written by the faculty of each school in 40 specific academic and practitioner journals during the past three years. The measure contributes 10 per cent of the final score. The doctoral rank is calculated according to the number of doctoral graduates from each business school during the past three years. Additional points are given if these doctoral graduates took up faculty positions at one of the top 50 full-time MBA schools of 2008.

At the university level one similar and prominent ranking is that from China's Shangai Jiao Tong University, the Academic Ranking of World Universities. Twelve hundred higher education institutions worldwide are ranked according to a number of criteria. Thirty per cent of the weighting is given to the number of Nobel Prize or Field Medal winners among alumni or staff at each university. Employing highly cited researchers gets more points as does staff publishing in two specific journals (*Nature* and *Science*).

The problem with such measures and rankings is the choice of criteria. If it is difficult to understand where the theoretical justification came from for the choice of questions in the AMAC, RQ and RepTrack studies at least there was some attempt to involve the audience in creating the measure. As far as can be judged no student or potential student had much say in the criteria used to construct the FT or Shangai Jiao Tong measures let alone to decide what weightings to give to them. Reputation is being defined by its measure, which in turn is being determined by a third party.

There is no doubt that students use both the FT and Shangai Jiao Tong and other similar rankings to help them decide which university to study at. Companies use Fortune data in their advertising to customers. How much weight customers place on such measures is difficult to determine but choice theory would suggest that when faced with a plethora of choice deciders try first to reduce their choice set to more manageable proportions and do so using quite sweeping generalisations. Our own work on why students choose one business school over another suggested students start by considering which country to study in, then shortlist their options using rankings such as those we have described and the advice of agents or contacts in the education arena. They might also attend an event where different universities compete to promote their courses. So rankings form only one part of the decision-making process (although they might also influence others such as advisors). Nevertheless the criteria used to create the rankings are often things that university managers can do something about. The question is should they? The same question will be being asked in the boardrooms of companies who feel their ranking on AMAC or other similar measures does not reflect where they should be or want to be in relation to their peers.

Each year students studying at Manchester taking the reputation management options there are given the FT rankings for our school and the data that are used to compile them as an exercise. They are divided into groups, each group representing a different business school. The task set is to decide whether the school they represent should 'play the ranking game'? Soon it becomes obvious that the easiest way for our own school to improve its ranking would be by reducing the time taken for the programme from a year and a half to just one year and to reduce the fees proportionally. This reduces the cost to the student in two ways, less money expended and less income forgone while studying. The result is a better score for 'value for money', as long as starting salaries can be maintained. Interestingly, even when this is pointed out as an option, students even on the MBA programme rarely opt to play the reputation game. To do so they argue would be to change the character of their course and possibly that of the school. They feel they benefit from the extra six months and the major project that occupies much of this time. They and alumni argue that they can expect faster progression once they recommence work. There is some evidence that our graduates do move up faster after a year or so once employed but such a benefit is not measured in the calculation of the FT ranking. Should then our school and university ignore such rankings? At least in part we do follow them, seeking to employ Nobel Prize winners, publish in the journals that contribute to the rankings rather than equally prestigious ones that do not and so on. At the very least such ranking give you food for thought, to reflect on the kind of organisation you are and want to be. But should such rankings dominate strategy? Probably not.

The fundamental issue with most ranking approaches is the selection of the criteria used to compare one organisation with another. The accepted way to develop a measure for something in the academic world is first to define what that something is. Once that something, the construct, has been suitably scoped then and only then is it time to take on the next stage of identifying what sub-dimensions the construct *might* have. Finally the researcher should undertake secondary and qualitative research to identify potentially suitable measurement items. Both stages should consider the views of the audience(s) that the measure is intended to be used with. Secondly a scale developed in one context (in one language or with one stakeholder group for example) should not be assumed to be valid in another, different context. Taking the earlier example of Mars, the way a customer or an employee might think about the same name is likely to differ markedly. There is a risk in assuming that one scale fits all. Finally there are some quite basic mathematical techniques available to test the validity of a measurement scale and the independence of any sub-measures. For example are the three measures of financial performance in the AMAC survey independent or not? If they are the same or similar why should they each be included? To claim that right each should contribute something distinct.

The structure of many of the measures reviewed earlier is quite suspect. There is the assurance from Hay that the AMAC dimensions emerged from earlier research but apparently no published source to confirm that or to help us make up our own minds whether what was done was rigorous. The assurance also conflicts somewhat with the sudden introduction of a ninth criterion in 2009. RQ differs little from AMAC other than in the introduction of an emotional appeal dimension. The authors claim to have relied upon a survey of previous work to identify their dimensions. No qualitative work appears to have been done to check that measures such as those against the financial performance dimension have any meaning let alone relevance to the typical customer. Even in the revised measure that is RepTrack we would want to see evidence that customers buying a Mars bar feel comfortable giving their opinions about what it might be like to work in the Mars company. How can they tell?

There have been some attempts to justify the RQ and AMAC measures *post hoc*. One claim is that both reflect something called 'social expectation' theory, the idea that a company is expected by the public to fulfil a number of roles, employer, supplier of goods and services, a place to invest and so on (Berens and van Riel, 2004). Company reputation is equated to the perceived ability to fulfil such a role. A theoretical framework is indeed a promising place to start when developing a new measure but neither AMAC nor RQ appeared to have benefitted from such a starting point. Public sector organisations and charities are not expected to behave in the same way as those in the private sector so such a perspective, even if it existed, is not universally applicable. What probably happens when respondents are asked questions about an organisation they know little about is that they use what knowledge they have to attribute either positive or negative beliefs to any aspect of corporate reputation they are asked about. Thus if I have positive views about Mars I will rate them higher for being a good employer than Company X whom I think less of generally.

MEASURES OF AFFECT

'Trust' was mentioned earlier in discussing the potential for this to influence both employees and customers in a positive way. Yet one cannot really 'trust' an organisation. It is not a Gestalt and employees and managers will differ in terms of their trustworthiness. But we find it useful to think of organisations in this way. In doing so we are evoking a metaphor, that of a company as if it really were an individual person. Metaphor uses the equation of the unfamiliar with the familiar so as to communicate. For example the statement 'Roger is a Lion' is not meant to be taken literally but to provide us with a picture of Roger and his character (Black, 1962). Metaphor is more than a just something to enrich writing but a valid research tool. It is the sense-making role of a metaphor that is its most useful function in research. However, metaphors are quite literally false and critics of the metaphor stance argue that they only serve to distort and mislead, impeding the development of administrative science (Pinder and Bourgeois, 1982). Morgan (1983) in responding to the latter criticism advises that rather than seeing metaphor as posing a problem for science we need to see the problem as, potentially, science that is purged of metaphor. Who is right? For sure the use of metaphor works, but is that sufficient justification for its use?

Personification as an explanatory metaphor makes sense to most people, by allowing them to comprehend a wide variety of experiences with non-human entities in terms of human characteristics. Thus a company's reputation can then be usefully measured using human characteristics. What has become known as 'brand personality' is accepted as a way to identity the associations that are made with a brand so as to assess its worth or 'equity' (Keller, 1998). Our own work on Corporate Character (our term for the scale we developed to assess the personality of an organisation) drew upon the earlier work of Aaker (1997) and those before her who had tried to apply human personality measures to assess brand personality. Aaker's work demonstrated that brand personality does not share the same structure as its human equivalent. Our work in turn has shown that the dimensionality she identified and in particular its measurement items are to some extent context specific. But the fundamental idea holds, that people describe companies and the differences between them using a structure in language which is definable and which consists of traits such as 'trustworthy'.

We set out to develop a scale that would be valid for both employees and customers. We did this because we were interested in how the interaction of these two perspectives influenced the success or otherwise of business and in particular service organisations (Davies et al., 2004). Unlike Aaker we delved into the organisational behaviour literature and in particular into that of culture and culture measurement to help us identify potential dimensions of Corporate Character. Again unlike Aaker we did not identify a strong dimension similar to what she had labelled as 'Ruggedness' but with the help of the organisational literature we did identify a potentially negatively valenced dimension that we called Ruthlessness, which seemed to us to have face validity for employees and customers. Corporate Character is a measure of affect, compatible with our preferred definition of reputation. It represents an inventory of both the dimensionality and content of traits that are used by customers and employees to distinguish organisations. The scale was derived after appropriate qualitative work in a large scale study by collecting hundreds of items from various literatures (branding, corporate culture, as well as reputation) that were within the organization as person metaphor and then testing them in surveys to identify both groupings and the most useful terms. The five main dimensions or groupings of similar items identified and the items themselves are shown in Table 2.1.

Table 2.1   The Corporate Character Scale

Agreeableness	Enterprise	Competence	Chic	Ruthlessness
Cheerful	Cool	Reliable	Charming	Arrogant
Pleasant	Trendy	Secure	Stylish	Aggressive
Open	Young	Hardworking	Elegant	Selfish
Straightforward	Imaginative	Ambitious	Prestigious	Inward-looking
Concerned	Up to date	Achievement-oriented	Exclusive	Authoritarian
Reassuring	Exciting	Leading	Refined	Controlling
Supportive	Innovative	Technical	Snobby	
Agreeable	Extravert	Corporate	Elitist	
Honest	Daring			
Sincere				
Trustworthy				
Socially responsible				

Source: Davies *et al.*, 2004

Since our work one further study adopting a similar stance has been published (Slaughter et al., 2004) which aimed to identify a scale to assess the employee or rather the potential employee view of the firm. We believe that the measurement of brand/organisation personality has reached an interesting stage similar to that in the human personality literature prior to the acceptance of the Big Five structure. Three dimensions appear common to all three scale developments, the first three in Table 2.1. As with human personality measures there is no consensus on which set of items are most suitable to measure a particular dimension. That is not the point; the key breakthrough, if that is what it is, is that certain dimensions appear robust and replicable. There are two barriers to a universal measure; one is that different cultural contexts appear to influence the dimensionality of brand/organisational personality. Both Aaker's work and our own has found that different dimensions appear more relevant in certain cultures. In the human personality field workers appear more confident that a single structure might be applicable to the measurement of personality in all cultures. Views however differ as to whether there is any theoretical underpinning for the Big Five structure for human personality. One has to remember that the development of the human measures was empirically driven, with early work quite literally listing all the words from a dictionary that appeared to describe human traits and then using survey and factor analysis to identify dimensions. If personality measures are fundamentally lexicographic in nature, they will vary with language structure. The chances of a single structure emerging for brand/organisational personality are further remote due to their metaphorical nature.

The dimensions of Corporate Character were indentified using factor analysis with orthogonal rotation. The dimensions were seeded from prior literatures and are quite distinct. One question follows: are the dimensions separate measures as this implies or complex indicators of the underlying construct of reputation? Interestingly in our most recent work we used the entire scale as a single measure. It has an acceptable Cronbach alpha implying that reputation can be considered as a single construct at a suitably high level of abstraction. Put more simply, companies can have strong or weak reputations and this measure can identify where those strengths and weaknesses lie.

SOME ISSUES

There are benefits for the researcher in using a previously validated scale and there are drawbacks too. Some researchers prefer to develop their own context specific measures arguing that the increased colour and relevance is worth the additional investment. What this risks is the chance of missing a dimension or aspect of reputation that would have been at least covered by an existing scale. Others argue that no quantitative measure can do justice to a construct as complex as reputation. We agree to some extent in that in using our measure while more diagnostic than either AMAC or RQ some further work is often needed to identify what precisely needs to be done to improve reputation. We might for example identify that a company should improve on its ratings for 'supportiveness' one of the items within the dimension of Agreeableness. We then have to work with stakeholders to identify what specifically needs to be done in changing policies or behaviours to improve upon this trait.

In Summary

There are various definitions of reputation and various ways of measuring it. Two major options have been discussed, one based on a cognitive notion that stakeholders are able to judge the actual performance of companies on various criteria, the second based on the idea that reputation is an affective construct and such feelings can be accessed using the projective technique of the personification metaphor. From a theoretical perspective neither can claim the high ground as there is no accepted theory of reputation other than that we are all willing to judge whether we have positive or negative views of a company. Reputation can be thought of as an attitude.

What matters most is which approach, the cognitive or the affective, proves the more useful. The writer is best placed to report on the efficacy of his own measure. The Corporate Character scale works in many contexts in organisations as diverse as the giant Tesco and a small wealth management consultancy in Harrogate, and for different types of organisation including both the Catholic Church and the police. Cognitive measures by definition tend to be limited in their context. Having a measure that works in all contexts allows us to compare results and also to apply an existing measure without worrying about relevance. The Corporate Character scale has proven useful in measuring both country reputation and the reputation of individuals. It predicts satisfaction, affinity, perceived differentiation, voting behaviour, purchasing behaviour and commitment and identification among employees; but most importantly for business managers it can be used to demonstrate how financial performance (specifically sales growth) can be predicted and therefore understood and managed from measuring reputation in this way. Studies demonstrating such links have been published in the very best of peer-reviewed journals.

References

Aaker, J.L. (1997). Dimensions of brand personality. *Journal of Marketing Research*, 34: 347–56.

Albert, S. and Whetten, D. (1985). Organizational identity. *Research in Organizational Behavior*, 7: 263–95.

Barnett, M.L., Jermier J.M. and Lafferty B.A. (2006). Corporate reputation the definitional landscape. *Corporate Reputation Review*, 9(1): 26–38.

Berens, G. and van Riel, C. (2004). Corporate associations in the academic literature: three main streams of thought in the reputation measurement literature. *Corporate Reputation Review*, 7(2): 161–78.

Black, M. (1962). *Models and Metaphors*. New York: Cornell University Press.

Bolger, J.F. (1959). How to evaluate your company image. *Journal of Marketing*, October: 7–10.

Brickson, S.L. (2007). Organizational identity orientation: the genesis of the role of the firm and distinct forms of social value. *Academy of Management Review*, 32(3): 864–88.

Brown, B. and Perry, S. (1994). Removing the financial performance halo from Fortune's most admired companies. *Academy of Management Journal*, 37: 1347–59.

Brown, T.J. and Dacin, P.A. (1997). The company and the product: corporate associations and consumer product responses. *Journal of Marketing*, 61(1): 244–9.

Brown, T.J., Dacin, P.A., Pratt, M.G. and Whetten, D.A. (2006). Identity, intended image, construed image, and reputation: an interdisciplinary framework and suggested terminology. *Journal of the Academy of Marketing Science*, 34(2): 99–106.

Chun, R. (2005). Corporate reputation: meaning and measurement. *International Journal of Management Reviews*, 7(2): 91–109.

Darden, W.R. and Babin, B.J. (1994). Exploring the concept of affective quality: expanding the concept of retail personality. *Journal of Business Research*, 29: 101–109.

Davies, G., Chun, R., da Silva, R. and Roper, S. (2003). *Corporate Reputation and Competitiveness*. London: Routledge.

Davies, G., Chun, R. and Kamins, M. (2010). Reputation gaps and the performance of service organizations. *Strategic Management Journal*, 31(5): 530–46.

Dutton, J.E., Dukerich, J.M. and Harquail, C.V. (1994). Organizational images and member identification. *Administrative Science Quarterly*, 39: 239–63.

Fombrun, C.J., Gardberg, N.A. and Sever, J.M. (2000). The reputation quotient: a multiple stakeholder measure of corporate reputation. *The Journal of Brand Management*, 7(4): 241–55.

Fombrun, C.J. and Shanley, M. (1990). What's in a name? Reputation building and corporate strategy. *Academy of Management Journal*, 33(2): 233–58.

Fombrun, S. and van Riel, C. (1997). The reputational landscape. *Corporate Reputation Review*, 1 (1/2): 5–13.

Fryxell, G.F. and Wang, J. (1994). The Fortune corporate 'reputation' index: reputation for what? *Journal of Management*, 20(1): 1–14.

Gioia, D.A. and Thomas, J.B. (1996). Identity, image, and issue interpretation: sensemaking during strategic change in academia. *Administrative Science Quarterly*, 41(3): 370–403.

Goldberg, M.E. and Hartwick, J. (1990). The effect of advertiser reputation and extremity of advertising claim on advertising effectiveness. *Journal of Consumer Research*, 17 (September): 172–9.

Keller, K.L. (1998). *Strategic Brand Management: Building Measuring and Managing Brand Equity*. Englewood Cliffs, NJ: Prentice Hall.

Money, K. and Hillenbrand, C. (2006). Using reputation measurement to create value: an analysis and integration of existing measures. *Journal of General Management*, 32(1) 1-12

Morgan, G. (1983). More on metaphor: why we cannot control tropes in administrative science. *Administrative Science Quarterly*, 28: 601–607.

Pinder, C. and Bourgeois, V. W. (1982). Controlling tropes in administrative science. *Administrative Science Quarterly*, 27: 641–52.

Roberts, P. W. and Dowling, G. R. (2002). Corporate reputation and sustained superior financial performance. *Strategic Management Journal*, 23(12): 1077–93.

Slaughter, J. E., Zickar, M. J., Highhouse, S. and Mohr, D. C. (2004). Personality trait inferences about organizations: development of a measure and assessment of construct validity. *Journal of Applied Psychology*, 89: 85–102.

Vergin, R. C. and Qoronfleh, M. W. (1998). Corporate reputation and the stock market. *Business Horizon*, 41: 19–26.

Weigelt, K. and Camerer, C. (1988). Reputation and corporate strategy: a review of recent theory and applications. *Strategic Management Journal*, 9: 443–54.

3 Measuring the Impact of Corporate Reputation on Stakeholder Behavior

MANFRED SCHWAIGER, SASCHA RAITHEL,
RICHARD RINKENBURGER AND MATTHIAS SCHLODERER

Introduction

From academia to business community, corporate reputation radiates strong appeals. Corporate reputation is one of the most valuable intangible assets, and it is extremely hard to imitate by competitors. An effective reputation management concept therefore helps firms to achieve sustainable competitive advantages. Due to the topic's significance and attractiveness, a rapid increase in relevant studies has been witnessed in recent years. Conducting a survey of current literature, we can easily find ample research on corporate reputation ranging from its formation to measurement to management practice. However, there is still a lack of valid empirical studies proving the impact of reputation on stakeholder behavior. Following a description of our measurement approach we will therefore present empirical evidence of reputation impact on customers, investors and potential employees. Given these results, we then share some thoughts with the reader on how to effectively manage reputation in a company.

Proving Impact as Challenge

In order to cope with the fierce global competition, companies have to seek for drivers of sustainable, competitive advantages. In this regard, management academics traditionally investigated tangible resources (e.g., Barney, 1991; Wernerfelt, 1984, 1995). However, the last decade was characterized by a focus shift to studies of intangible assets. Analyzing the market-to-book ratio of stock quoted firms such a change is substantiated showing that, today, the major part of a company's value is based on intangible assets. Looking at the S&P 500, the share of intangible assets rose from 25 percent to 75 percent between 1980 and 2002 (Lev, 2001, 2003; Ballow et al., 2004). Similar findings can be drawn from the analysis of the HDAX in Germany. Here, more than two thirds of the companies' market value were based on intangible assets, excluding the financial crisis in 2008 (see Figure 3.1).

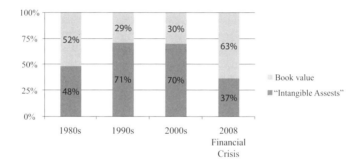

Figure 3.1   Ratio between market value and book value for HDAX companies (1980–2008)[1]

Hanssens et al. (2009), introducing a special issue of the *Journal of Marketing* ("Marketing Strategy and Wall Street: Nailing Down Marketing's Impact"), consider "exploring relationships along [the] chain from marketing actions to marketplace outcomes and the creation of market-based [i.e., intangible] assets and firm value" as a key research issue. In that respect, they regard (corporate) reputation as a key marketing metric next to customer satisfaction, customer retention and brand loyalty.

We can state that both the scientific community and the majority of practitioners consider corporate reputation as an intangible asset that is scarce, valuable, sustainable and difficult for a competitor to imitate. Therefore, reputation is an appropriate tool to achieve strategic competitive advantages, it helps the companies strengthen their competitive advantages and protect them from downturns. Indeed, authors such as Haywood (2002) and Sherman (1999) suggest that corporate reputation is "the ultimate determinant of competitiveness."

Due to the topic's significance and attractiveness, a rapid increase in relevant studies has been witnessed in recent years. Analyzing current literature, we can easily find numerous studies on corporate reputation ranging from its formation to measurement to management practice. However, there is still a lack of valid empirical research proving the effect of reputation on the behavior of various stakeholder groups. Before we present empirical evidence of reputation's impact on three selected stakeholder groups—namely customers, investors, and potential employees—we introduce definitions of reputation and describe our measurement approach. We finish this chapter by sharing some thoughts with the reader on how to effectively manage reputation and leverage its positive effects to create sustainable competitive advantage.

Operationalization of Corporate Reputation

Although there is a consensus on the importance of corporate reputation, the academic literature on the subject fails to provide a precise, commonly accepted definition. Common dictionaries define reputation as "beliefs or opinions that are generally

---

1   HDAX contains stocks of the 110 largest, publicly listed corporations in Germany (DAX, MDAX, TecDAX), 2008/2009 excluded in column 2000s.

held about someone or something" (Compact Oxford English Dictionary, 2009). In this line, some academic definitions see corporate reputation as a general attribute of organizations reflecting people's opinion as to whether a firm is substantially "good" or "bad" (Milgrom and Roberts, 1992; Weiss et al., 1999). However, such definitions do not provide information on how to measure reputation which is a prerequisite for the provision of empirical evidence for its impact on stakeholder behavior and, ultimately, financial performance.

Other definitions provide such hints for the measurement of corporate reputation. For Fombrun (1996), reputation is the stakeholder's overall estimation of a company expressed by affective reactions. The author excludes cognitive processes in his definition. On the other hand, other definitions focus only on a valuation of the firm's characteristics and do not include emotional components (e.g., Gray and Balmer, 1998). Hall (1992) considers both cognitive and affective dimensions by stating that reputation is composed by the knowledge and the emotions held by individuals. Schwaiger (2004) follows that definition, seeing reputation as an attitudinal construct consisting of a cognitive (competence) and an affective (likeability) dimension. He further broadens Hall's definition by allowing not only for (objective) knowledge about a company but also for more subjective perceptions and by following Dozier (1993) who highlights that reputation may be based also on processed communications and not only on factual experiences.

The increasing interest in corporate reputation by practitioners and academics alike has led to the emergence of numerous measurement tools for that concept (Schwaiger, 2004; Chun, 2005). Reviews of publicly available reputation metrics (Fombrun, 1996; Lewis, 2001; Wartick, 2002) accentuate Fortune's annual "America's" and "Global Most Admired Companies (AMAC, GMAC)" and the Harris-Fombrun-Reputation Quotient® (Fombrun et al., 2000) as the two most applied and discussed approaches in the field. However, both—like other concepts—show fundamental deficiencies:

- Many approaches are based solely on expert interviews, neglecting the variety of relevant stakeholders of a company, e.g., AMAC, GMAC and German *Manager* magazine's so-called "Imageprofile" (Eidson and Master, 2000; Hutton, 1986). Furthermore, corporate communication may have little or no impact on experts and so they only refer to their knowledge when they speak about the companies under evaluation. However, such knowledge does not have to be necessarily congruent with the actual attitudes and perceptions of relevant stakeholder groups.
- Some concepts exhibit serious drawbacks in operationalization. For example, the Fombrun-Harris-Reputation Quotient® calculates reputation using a weighted mean of 20 indicators. In doing so, the authors mix drivers and consequences of reputation: Whereas the item "good products and services" is a prerequisite of reputation, "admiration of a company" is obviously an outcome of a good reputation. Consequently, the interpretation of the measurement results is difficult and management recommendations are hard to derive.
- So far, the affective component of reputation is underestimated in most measurement models. Only Fombrun's approach considers emotions in three out of 20 items.
- Finally, stating only a single reputation score, nearly all rankings impede an explanation of a company's result. Firms are not able to analyze the key performance indicators of their corporate reputation. Accordingly, management implications cannot be drawn from such rankings respectively measurement models.

Schwaiger (2004) answered these shortfalls by developing a reputation measurement and explanation model in line with Rossiter's C-OAR-SE procedure (Rossiter, 2002) using a series of expert interviews as well as data from a large-scale representative survey carried out in Germany, the UK and the US. In each country, 300 randomly selected respondents were interviewed (CATI) and asked to evaluate the four companies Allianz, BMW, E.ON, and Lufthansa.

According to the previously presented definition of reputation, Schwaiger's model integrates an emotional component next to the cognitive dimension into the analysis of corporate reputation. The measurement model is composed of three reflective indicators— using a Likert scale with a range from 1 (strongly disagree) to 7 (totally agree)—for each of the two dimensions (see Table 3.1: Measurement Constructs). The first three items compose the affective dimension called "likeability" whereas the last three indicators are driven by the cognitive dimension called "competence". The two-dimensional structure was proven to be valid over time, industry sectors and cultural contexts (Schwaiger, 2004; Zhang and Schwaiger, 2009).

The explanation model was further developed to find out which aspects are responsible for a company's reputation. Twenty-one explanatory items were selected to disclose the drivers of reputation. In order to bundle the items to possible index constructs, a principal component analysis uncovered the following four factors: quality, performance, responsibility and attractiveness (see Table 3.1: Driver Constructs).

Table 3.1   Constructs and measurement items of reputation by Schwaiger (2004)

Construct		Item
Measurement Construct	Likeability	• [Company] is a company I would regret more if it didn't exist any more than I would with other companies. • [Company] is a company I can identify with better than with other companies. • I regard [Company] as a likeable company.
	Competence	• I believe that [Company] performs at a premium level. • As far as I know [Company] is recognized world-wide. • [Company] is a top competitor in its market.
Driver Construct	Quality	• The products/services offered by [Company] are of high quality. • I think that [Company]'s products/services offer good value for money. • The services [Company] offers are good. • [Company] seems to be a reliable partner for customers. • Customer concerns are held in high regards at [Company]. • In my opinion [Company] tends to be an innovator, rather than an imitator.

Table 3.1 *Concluded*

Construct		Item
	Performance	• [Company] is an economically stable company. • I assess the business risk for [Company] as modest compared to its competitors. • I think that [Company] has growth potential. • In my opinion [Company] has a clear vision about the future of the company. • I think [Company] is a well managed company.
	Responsibility	• I have the feeling that [Company] is not only concerned about profit. • I have the impression that [Company] is forthright in giving information to the public. • [Company] behaves in a socially conscious way. • [Company] is concerned about the preservation of the environment. • I have the impression that [Company] has a fair attitude towards competitors.
	Attractiveness	• I like the physical appearance of [Company] (Company buildings, branch offices). • In my opinion [Company] is successful in attracting high-quality employees.

The approach of Schwaiger (2004) has been validated in different countries (Eberl, 2009; Zhang and Schwaiger, 2009), frequently applied in research studies (Eberl and Schwaiger, 2005; Sarstedt et al., 2008) and adapted by several multinational companies as metric for reputation management (see European Centre for Reputation Studies)[2]. In addition, Wilczynski et al. (2009) have shown that in comparison to other approaches (AMAC, RQ, etc.) Schwaiger's (2004) approach exhibits the highest degree of criterion validity.

Linking Corporate Reputation to Stakeholder Behavior

Reviewing research, the strong link between a fine reputation and common management goals regarding the different stakeholder groups becomes evident. For instance, several studies state that a good reputation generally leads to overall advantages in conducting negotiations with stakeholders (Brown, 1997; Cordeiro and Sambharya, 1997; Deephouse, 1997; Fombrun, 1996; McMillan and Joshi, 1997; Roberts and Dowling, 1997; Srivastava et al., 1997).

Possessing a high reputation is also valuable for firms regarding specific stakeholder groups: customers of more reputable companies show not only an increased confidence in products and services as well as advertising claims, but also a lower cognitive dissonance (Eberl, 2006; Fombrun and van Riel, 1998; Goldberg and Hartwick, 1990; Lafferty and

---

2   http://www.reputation-centre.org.

Goldsmith, 1999). Through better customer retention (Caminiti, 1992; Preece et al., 1995; Rogerson, 1983) firms can achieve price premiums and higher purchase rates (Klein and Leffler, 1981; Milgrom and Roberts, 1986). Organizations with a stronger reputation are able to win the war for talent and to achieve higher employee retention rates (Caminiti, 1992; Dowling, 1986; Eidson and Master 2000; Preece et al., 1995; Nakra, 2000; Turban and Cable, 2003).

Companies showing a strong reputation have better access to capital markets, which decreases capital costs (Beatty and Ritter, 1986; Wiedmann and Buxel, 2005) and lowers procurement rates (Schwalbach, 2000). Moreover, for (private) investors, a high reputation increases a company's stock value, whereby this effect is intensified by unexpected negative price developments in the stock market (Schütz and Schwaiger, 2007). Given the impact of reputation on performance relevant outcomes, it is obvious that a company's market value *ceteris paribus* should grow with a better reputation. Eberl and Schwaiger (2005) as well as Roberts and Dowling (2002) show that corporate reputation supports the persistence of above-average profits and has a positive impact on net profit.

The following sections will provide a more detailed view on the results from selected empirical research regarding the reputation's impact on customers, investors and potential employees.

Reputation and Customer Behavior

Eberl (2006) has done extensive experimental research on two questions: Does corporate reputation (a) exert influence on the purchase intention and (b) on the willingness to pay of private bank customers? While the second question can be answered by means of conjoint analysis, the first question requires structural equation modeling (SEM).

THEORETICAL BACKGROUND

Based on relevant theory (Klein and Leffler, 1981; Milgrom and Roberts, 1986; Podolny, 1993; Zeithaml, 1988), Eberl uses the corporate reputation dimensions likeability and competence as exogenous constructs and purchase intention as an endogenous variable which is driven by attitude towards the product. Reputation is supposed to have direct effects on attitude towards the product, but also indirect impact mediated by identification (e.g., Bergami and Bagozzi, 2000; Sen and Bhattacharya, 2001), product–company fit (e.g., Keller and Aaker, 1992; Madrigal, 2000) and perception of product attributes (Feldman and Lynch, 1988; Fischhoff et al., 1980). Direct as well as indirect effects are moderated by the availability of information about product attributes (e.g., Kardes et al., 2004; Mantel and Kardes, 1999; Simmons and Lynch, 1991), by the degree of product and situational involvement (Haugtvedt and Wegener, 1994; Johnson and Eagly, 1989; Maheswaran et al., 1992; Petty et al., 1983), and by the extent of individual product knowledge (Jacoby et al., 1978; Bauer et al., 2003; Ratchford, 2001). The resulting SEM is depicted in Figure 3.2, so we may omit to explicitly formulate the hypotheses derived in this section (see Eberl, 2006 for details).

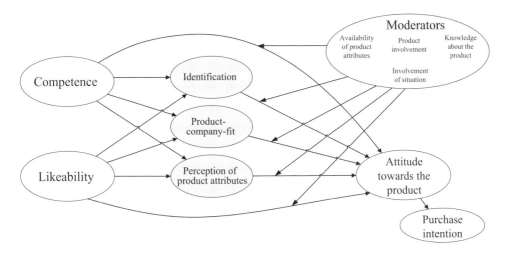

Figure 3.2   Hypothetical structural model

RESEARCH DESIGN

In order to get answers to the research questions formulated above an experimental design was developed (see Figure 3.3). The objects under investigation were financial institutes offering loans for students, which were considered most appropriate because the tuition system was not yet established in Germany during field time and therefore student loans were not in the market at the time the experiment was conducted. Hence, we could rule out detailed prior product knowledge on the one hand and make sure on the other hand that the degree of innovativeness of the product was small enough to prevent results from biasing influence. The companies under scrutiny were real banks (Deutsche Bank, Dresdner Bank, Postbank and Stadtsparkasse), whose reputation was manipulated by fictitious press releases. In line with international consumer research practice, we recruited undergraduate and graduate students of various fields of study, resulting in a total sample of 104 respondents.

Dresdner Bank and Postbank were selected for reputation manipulation. In a reversed treatment design according to Cook and Campbell (1979) one of the groups (group A) received a positive treatment for Dresdner Bank (assuming to build up Dresdner Bank's corporate reputation) and a negative treatment for Postbank (assuming to weaken Postbank's reputation), while group B received a negative treatment for Dresdner Bank and a positive treatment for Postbank. Reputation assessments for Deutsche Bank and Stadtsparkasse served as control factors. Both experimental groups were randomly split into two subgroups: the control group(s) received only limited information about the product attributes of the four products (student loans), while the experimental groups received detailed additional information (e.g., "lawmaker regulates interest rates..."). Model constructs were measured before and after treatment, so that Figure 3.3 describes a 2 (group A/B) × 2 (limited/detailed product information) before–after reversed treatment design. To assess the willingness to pay, all respondents had to go through a choice based conjoint analysis (including a non-option) subsequent to the measurement of the model constructs, i.e., before and after treatment, too.

Group	M1	CBC1	T1	T2	M2	CBC2
Group A						
Dresdner Bank AG	X	X	+		X	X
Deutsche Postbank AG	X	X	–	(none)	X	X
Deutsche Bank AG	X	X	neutral		X	X
Stadtsparkasse Munich	X	X	neutral		X	X
Control group A						
Dresdner Bank AG	X	X	+	X	X	X
Deutsche Postbank AG	X	X	–	X	X	X
Deutsche Bank AG	X	X	neutral	X	X	X
Stadtsparkasse Munich	X	X	neutral	X	X	X
Group B						
Dresdner Bank AG	X	X	–		X	X
Deutsche Postbank AG	X	X	+	(none)	X	X
Deutsche Bank AG	X	X	neutral		X	X
Stadtsparkasse	X	X	neutral		X	X
Control group B						
Dresdner Bank AG	X	X	–	X	X	X
Deutsche Postbank AG	X	X	+	X	X	X
Deutsche Bank AG	X	X	neutral	X	X	X
Stadtsparkasse Munich	X	X	neutral	X	X	X

(Control group A rows braced as "identic"; Control group B rows braced as "identic")

with:
M1/2   Measurement of the exogenous and endogenous model constructs (interview)
CBC1/2   Experimental conjoint-measurement of willingness to pay and partial utilities
T1   Treatment: Stimulus of reputation
T2   Treatment: Information about product attributes

Figure 3.3   The experimental design

Participation was incentivized by raffling off several cash prizes of between 50 and 100 euros. Before-measurement M1 and CBC1 were done by means of an online questionnaire. Then, students were randomly assigned to the four groups (experimental group A: 26, control group A: 25, experimental group B: 27, control group B: 26). Analyses of variance did not reveal significant differences for any of the items surveyed. Stimuli were handed out in form of a press kit containing 15 articles, among them six identical press releases. The remaining articles were customized according to group assignment. Respondents were not aware of this fact. Communication between respondents was not allowed during the experiment. Subsequent to the reading phase model constructs were surveyed again (M2), and CBC2 was conducted. Finally, respondents were informed about the research purpose and told that treatments were fictitious and the student loans evaluated not available in the market.

OPERATIONALIZATION AND DATA ANALYSIS

All constructs were operationalized in accordance with the C-OAR-SE procedure (Rossiter, 2002). Corporate reputation was operationalized in the way already outlined previously (see Table 3.1) and identification according to Bergami and Bagozzi (2000) via identity overlap scale. Product-company-fit has been measured as suggested by Keller and Aaker (1992) and Madrigal (2000). Perception of product attributes can be reduced to perceived interest rate, duration, and timing of payback (Epple, 1990; Wübker, 2004; Wübker and Baumgarten, 2004). Product involvement and situational involvement operationalization refer to Zaichkowsky (1985) and Laurent and Kapferer (1985a; 1985b), while product knowledge indicators were taken from Bauer et al. (2003).

Due to space restrictions we cannot go into details as far as methods of data analysis are concerned. Sawtooth CBC/HB 3.2 (Orme, 2004) has been used to conduct the choice-based conjoint analysis, PLS Graph 3.0 (Chin, 2001) was best suitable to parameterize the SEM and perform multi-group comparisons (Chin, 2000) to check for moderating effects. Details are reported in Eberl (2006).

RESULTS

Before we report results we would like to point out that manipulating corporate reputation by means of fictitious press releases (see Eberl, 2006 for stimulus material) had been successful. In other words: the treatment was significant at 5 percent level (Dresdner Bank's reputation score was raised from 53.15 percent to 54.75 percent, while Postbank's reputation declined from 44.45 percent to 42.84 percent).

The first research question was focusing on the impact of reputation on purchase intention. Figure 3.4 shows that competence and likeability have direct impact on attitude towards the product as well as indirect impact, mostly via perception of product attributes. While identification has impact on a 10 percent significance level only, product–company fit does not exert significant influence, which may be explained by the fact that student loans would fit with the product range of almost every bank.

Analyzing the impact of the moderators will give us more insights, under what conditions reputation seems particularly important. As we can see from Table 3.2 path coefficients from competence and likeability to attitude towards the product are considerably larger in the experimental group; that is, in that group where only limited information about the product was available. This supports the hypothesis that reputation can be seen as information surrogate in the decision process. It is notable that the affective reputation dimension (likeability) in these cases has more influence than the cognitive dimension (competence). Moreover, the higher the product involvement and hence the degree of cognitive information processing the lower the impact of reputation on the attitude towards the product will be.

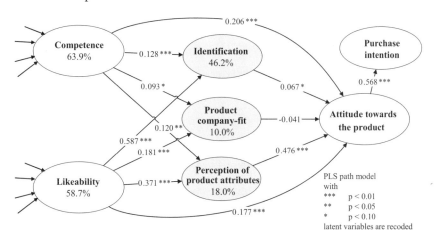

Figure 3.4   Results of the PLS main effect model

As far as the remaining moderator effects are concerned we would like to point out that the impact of the competence dimension on attitude towards the product decreases with an increase of recipients' (prior) product knowledge, whereas we could not detect a significant moderating effect of situational involvement.

Table 3.2   Model comparison if only limited product information is available (experimental group) vs. if detailed product information is provided (control group)

Relation	Coefficients in group			pooled s.e.	t	p	
	EG	CG	Diff.				
Competence → Identification	-.083	-.157	.074	.967	1.104	.270	
Competence → Product-company-fit	.090	.068	.022	1.294	.245	.806	
Competence → Perceived product attributes	-.076	-.080	.004	1.216	.047	.962	
Likeability → Identification	-.667	-.570	-.097	.773	1.810	.071	*
Likeability → Product-company-fit	.370	.209	.161	1.188	1.954	.051	*
Likeability → Perceived product attributes	-.368	-.392	.024	1.070	.323	.747	
Competence → Attitude towards product	.290	.162	.128	.840	2.196	.028	**
Likeability → Attitude towards product	.218	.046	.172	1.003	2.473	.014	**
Product involvement → Attitude towards product	-.151	.150	-.301	.935	4.644	.000	***
Situational involvement → Attitude towards product	.095	.027	.068	.970	1.011	.312	
Product knowledge → Attitude towards product	.015	.075	-.060	.797	1.086	.278	
Identification → Attitude towards product	-.011	-.162	.151	1.053	2.068	.039	**
Product-company-fit → Attitude towards product	.079	-.029	.108	.898	1.734	.083	*
Perceived prod. attributes → Attitude towards product	-.331	-.550	.219	.891	3.542	.000	***
Attitude towards product → purchase intention	.635	.462	.173	.809	3.083	.002	***
with: ***p<0,01 ** p<0,05 * p<0,1							

The second research question was focusing on the willingness to pay. Hierarchical-based choice-based conjoint analysis has shown fair goodness-of-fit measures (Certainty = .678, RLH = .595) and revealed part-worths of 52.7 percent for the interest rate, 17.3 percent for the bank name, 16.1 percent for the duration of the payback-period and 13.9 percent for the starting point of the payback period. The details reported by Eberl and Schwaiger (2008) prove that at a given interest of 3.10 percent reputation laggard Postbank would reach a market share of 13.81 percent, Dresdner Bank 14.09 percent, while reputation leaders Deutsche Bank and Stadtsparkasse would achieve market shares of 34.57 percent and 37.53 percent. In order to reach a market share of 10 percent Postbank and Dresdner Bank would have to fix the student loans' interest rate at 3.16 percent, while Deutsche Bank could demand an interest rate of 3.30 percent and Stadtsparkasse even 3.35 percent.

These results may be translated into a price premium of about 6 percent that can be traced back to corporate reputation only.

Reputation, Capital Markets, and Investor Behavior

CONCEPTUAL FRAMEWORK

The efficient market hypothesis, which is a central proposition of financial theory, argues that a stock price always fully reflects any available information (Fama, 1970). This stock price (i.e., market value or market capitalization) is a representation of the financial market's (i.e., investors') expectations of the sum of a firm's discounted future cash flows (e.g., Mizik and Jacobson, 2003; Srinivasan et al. 2009). These expectations, however, are not stable and change over time. Whenever investors become aware of new, unanticipated information, they interpret this information with respect to its value relevance, adapt their expectations of future cash flows accordingly, and sell or buy affected stocks until a new market equilibrium is reached. For that reason, market values (stock prices) increase or decrease. Now assuming a better corporate reputation induces incremental cash flows, investors should be willing to pay higher stock prices for firms with higher reputations. However, providing empirical evidence for the value relevance of this key marketing metric is challenging.

Scholars like Eberl and Schwaiger (2005), Roberts and Dowling (2002), Dunbar and Schwalbach (2002), Deephouse (1997), Fombrun and Shanley (1990), and McGuire et al. (1990) showed how persistent and superior financial performance of firms is created through a good reputation in terms of e.g., above average return on assets, return on invested capital, Tobin's q or net income. Thus, investors who are able to appreciate these long-term value implications of corporate reputation should adapt their expectations about future cash flows immediately after they become aware of information which is changing their perception of/knowledge about the level corporate reputation. Of course, investors buy and sell stocks not only because of new information about corporate reputation. Possibly, they are not even aware that reputation might be value-relevant. Undoubtedly, they will change their expectations about future cash flows when they process new information about fundamental data like changes in macroeconomic and industry specific conditions, the firm's property rights, strategies, and policies (Cutler et al., 1989). Investors, however, have only limited attention, cognitive capabilities, and memory and, thus, are not able to process immediately and accurately all available information about companies (Hirshleifer, 2001). Hence, they use heuristics and rules-of-thumb to simplify their (investment) decisions (e.g., Payne, 1976; Simon, 1955). Against this backdrop, a good reputation can serve as such a simplifying mechanism. Investors might (implicitly) use reputation as surrogate information to legitimate their investment decisions because they have learned that firms, for instance, offering high quality products and services (driver of reputation) and having an outstanding management record (driver of reputation), are recognized worldwide (outcome of reputation) (see Table 3.1) and are much more capable to increase the magnitude and reduce the volatility of their future cash flows and profits. Thus, a direct effect of reputation on investor behavior using reputation explicitly or implicitly as value-relevant information should be observable (see Figure 3.5).

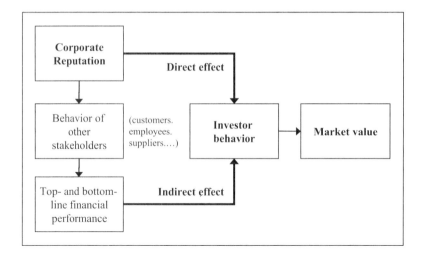

Figure 3.5   Effects of corporate reputation on investor behavior

On the other hand, investors might not be able to appreciate the long-term value implications of corporate reputation, and they are (possibly) not using information about reputation as simplifying heuristic. However, providing that positive effects of a good corporate reputation on other stakeholder groups' behavior (customers, employees, suppliers ...) in terms of, for instance, willingness to apply and willingness to pay price premiums hold true, firms with above average reputations show above average top-line (e.g., sales) and bottom-line (e.g., net income) financial performances. Since investors usually react to such information, they can be assumed to correct their initial misjudgment and will (unconsciously) overweight stocks of reputation leaders and underweight stocks of reputation laggards in the long run ("indirect effect" in Figure 3.5). This results in an observable mispricing effect (Jacobson and Mizik, 2009).

DIRECT IMPACT OF REPUTATION ON INVESTOR BEHAVIOR

In order to examine the direct effect of reputation on investor behavior and stock market performance methodologies like event studies (e.g., MacKinley, 1997; McWilliams and Siegel, 1997), econometric models (e.g., Greene, 2008), and experiments (e.g., Shadish et al., 2001) can be considered.

Focusing on private investors, Schütz and Schwaiger (2007) conducted a multi-period experiment: participants had to decide on the investment of 10,000 euros in three stocks—Lufthansa, Siemens, and Volkswagen—as well as a risk-free bond (max. 5,000 euros). Before conducting the experiment, the participants were informed that their investment decisions would have no effects on the stock price development and that short-selling was not possible. The objective was to maximize the final value of individual portfolios. As incentive participants could win three cash prices (100, 75, and 50 euros) which were assigned by a draw among the most successful 50 percent of participants in terms of final portfolio value. This kind of incentivizing made sure that participants' behavior was close to reality and did not change their individual risk aversion. Moreover, to avoid less successful participants showing an excessively risky trading behavior during the last period of the experiment, six periods were announced to the participants but the experiment was actually stopped after five periods. During the experiment participants were provided with information they could use for their investments decisions. Each individual got the same set of information about general macroeconomic and industry-specific conditions as well as information about Volkswagen and Siemens. However, the group of 63 participants was randomly split into two halves: the first half of participants additionally received positive information about Lufthansa facilitating an increase in positive perceptions of corporate reputation of Lufthansa while the second half of participants received additionally negative information about Lufthansa facilitating a decrease of its reputation. At the beginning as well as after periods 1, 3, and 5 participants had to evaluate reputations of all three companies—in order to limit the workload participants had not to evaluate reputations after each wave.

Figure 3.6 shows the results of this experiment. In period 0, before the start of the experiment, the differences between the two treatment groups in terms of perceptions of Lufthansa's reputation and the decision on the amount of capital invested in the Lufthansa stock did not vary significantly. However, manipulation of Lufthansa's reputation was successful and the reputation scores were significantly different between the two treatment groups. These changes in reputations did correlate significantly with the amount of capital invested in the Lufthansa stock. Results of an ANOVA confirmed these findings and showed that investment behavior varied at a 1 percent significance level between the two treatment groups in all five waves.

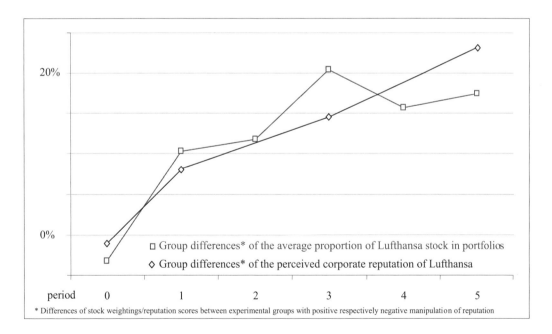

Figure 3.6   Dynamics in corporate reputation and stock trading behavior
Source: Schütz and Schwaiger, 2007

Another interesting finding is that during a simulated market crash in period 3, the treatment group (now) with a more positive perception of Lufthansa's reputation invested much more of their capital in the Lufthansa stock (please refer to the "peak" in Figure 3.6). This gives an indication that during critical developments of capital markets when stock prices decline rapidly and volatility of stock prices is excessively high—like, for instance, during the financial crisis in 2008 and the beginning of 2009—the influence of corporate reputation is increased. The flood of unforeseen and extraordinary events (possibly) prompts investors to rely on their heuristics when looking for an optimal investment decision (see also Jones et al., 2000). Raithel et al. (2009) provide corresponding results using the changes of competence and likeability scores of DAX companies between December 2007 and 2008 as an aggregate measure for events affecting corporate reputation during the financial crisis year 2008. Applying an econometric model controlling for value-relevant accounting variables like return on assets, sales, and total assets, a significant correlation between the changes in firm value—proxied by market-to-book ratios—and the different reputation scores was obtained.

INDIRECT IMPACT OF REPUTATION ON INVESTOR BEHAVIOR

Studying the long-term (indirect) mispricing effect of corporate reputation, Raithel and Schwaiger (2009) conducted a portfolio analysis which has become an accepted method for analyzing the value relevance of intangible assets (Srinivasan and Hanssens, 2009). Through the application of a momentum factor extended version of the Fama-French financial benchmark model (Fama and French, 1993; Carhart, 1997) to reputation-sorted portfolios of the German DAX companies, Raithel and Schwaiger (2009) were able to provide empirical evidence for a mispricing effect associated with corporate reputation. Stocks were divided into groups with high and low levels of reputation in order to be able to test the differences in the abnormal stock returns depending on the group's level of reputation. Performances of portfolios with equal-weighted and value-weighted investments in stocks of reputation champions/laggards were compared with performances of relevant stock market indices. For the period between December 2005 and June 2009, portfolios were updated at the end of June and December of every year using the latest reputation data stemming from surveys of representative samples of the German general public between 2005 and 2008. However, literature (e.g., Eberl and Schwaiger, 2005; Hildebrandt and Schwalbach, 2000) reports an investment effect—companies investing in reputation show better performance—as well as a performance effect—companies with a better financial performance obtain higher reputation values—associated with reputation. For that reason, the reputation scores were adjusted to control for the performance effect (halo effect) using a procedure developed by Brown and Perry (1994).

Results in Figure 3.7 show that the value of the Top 25 percent reputation portfolio—without removed halo effect which was quite small—has achieved an increase of 49 percent compared to 6 percent of the DAX index value (in USD). A notable fact is that the systematic risk—as expressed by the β factor—of the Top 25 percent Reputation portfolio is lower than the market risk—$\beta = .97$ using the DAX as benchmark on a daily basis. Hence, investors would not have to accept a higher risk in turn for the Top 25 percent reputation portfolio's outperformance. Referring to the (halo-removed) competence and likeability instead of the overarching reputation scores showed that likeability is more mispriced than the competence dimension.

Performing a similar portfolio analysis, Schwaiger et al. (2009) showed that the perceptions of the general public seem to be more indicative (i.e., value-relevant) than the reputation perceptions of different opinion leader groups (analysts, journalists, scientists, top executives, politicians, and representatives of non-governmental and non-profit organizations (NGOs and NPOs). This means, if one would rely on the recommendation to invest in reputation champions the best advice is to rely on the reputation perceptions of the general public. Focusing on the direct effect of reputation, Raithel et al. (2009) found an analogous result, i.e., reputation as perceived by the general public tends to be more value-relevant than the reputation as perceived by opinion leader groups.

Taking everything into consideration, we can state that corporate reputation is value-relevant, fosters higher shareholder value, and (directly and indirectly) affects investor behavior. However, from these findings new research challenges emerge (Hanssens et al., 2009): Can we observe similar effects when focusing the bond rather than the stock market? Is the right reputation metric, if any, communicated to investors? Are financial analysts influenced by corporate reputation? Do investors reward firms using their resources more efficiently than competitors when building up a fine reputation?

Figure 3.7   Performance of Top 25 percent reputation portfolio vs. DAX as benchmark index

Reputation and the War for Talent

FRAMEWORK AND TARGET VALUES IN THE RECRUITING MARKET

Winning the "war for talent" is considered as one of the central factors of a company's success and sustainability. Many studies about employer attractiveness show that monetary aspects on its own are not enough to recruit highly qualified potential employees, but there are important intangible drivers like corporate reputation that have a strong impact on one's willingness to apply for a job at a company (e.g., Lewandowski and Liebig, 2004; Ernst&Young, 2008). Surveys among highly skilled potential employees, for instance, have proven that reputation is one of these intangible factors of success (Grobe, 2003; Cable and Turban, 2003). For an employer with a good reputation it is easier to recruit skilled employees and to strengthen employee retention (e.g., Dowling, 1986; Caminiti, 1992; Preece et al., 1995; Eidson and Master, 2000; Nakra, 2000). Therefore, willingness to apply as one of the central target values in the recruiting market has to be linked to corporate reputation as it was done in one of our empirical studies (Schloderer, 2010) presented later.

Another important outcome of reputation is what we call a "salary premium." While it has already been shown several times that—referred to customers—companies with high reputation can earn price "mark-ups" called "price premiums" (Aaker, 1996; Crimmins, 1992; Park and Srinivasan, 1994; see also Eberl, 2006 as well as the section "Reputation and Customer Behavior" above), there still is—referred to the recruiting market—no empirical evidence in the scientific literature that good reputation results in a negative salary premium. The hypothesis is that potential employees would accept higher salary "mark-downs" if they were hired by a company with high reputation than they would accept working for a company with a mediocre or even low reputation. The existence of such premiums can be derived from the information lack about the potential employer (information asymmetry) and the caused uncertainness of the potential employees. As customers are willing to accept higher prices as a signal for high reputation and as this mark-up (price premium) can be interpreted as a company's compensation for its investment in reputation (Shapiro, 1983; Simon, 1992; Diller, 2000), in the recruiting market the compensation for a reputation investment leads to less salary (a negative salary premium) a company has to pay to its employees. Empirical evidence about the link between reputation and salary premiums will be obtained by the following empirical study (see in detail Schloderer, 2010).

EMPIRICAL RESULTS

In order to find out the strength of the link between a company's reputation on one hand and valuable outcomes as willingness to apply and salary demands on the other hand, an empirical study among students in business administration, economics and business education (n = 421) was conducted at LMU Munich in the summer term 2008. Every student had to evaluate 12 randomly selected companies from a list of 60 that was a selection of the members of the main German stock index (DAX30) and other companies that were considered as potential employers for the selected sample. Again, reputation measurement was done using the competence and likeability indicators shown previously in Table 3.1. The intention to apply was measured as an index of two indicators, namely "attractive employer" and "want to apply after studies".

In order to measure a salary premium, the preference-based approach of the price premium literature can be applied as well. Besides indirect approaches like regression analysis (Sattler, 1999; Nganje et al., 2008), choice experiment (Adamowicz et al., 1998), classical and choice-based conjoint analysis (Hauser and Rao, 2002; Sattler and Hartmann, 2002; Riediger et al., 2008), premiums can be measured by direct approaches like auctions (Hoffman et al., 1993; Lusk et al., 2004) and—applied here because of its simplicity— direct query (Aaker, 1996). Therefore, we asked the following question: "Please suppose that your preferred company would offer you a salary of 50,000 euros per annum for your choice of activities at your preferred location. How much salary per annum would ... have to offer you for the same activities at the same location for you to choose ... instead?"

As a result of the study, it has been shown that there is a strong significant correlation ($r = .77$) between perceived reputation and willingness to apply (see Figure 3.8). Obviously, successful reputation management can strongly drive the intention to be employed by a company and, hence, help to win the war for talent.

Assessing salary premiums, instead of comparing the absolute mean values (in this study for all companies ranging between mean values of 52,917 euros and 63,521 euros), it is more reasonable to look at the relative salary markups the companies have to pay in comparison to a salary of 50,000 euros of the preferred company. In doing so, we observe a higher salary demand of +4.49 percent for the Top Three reputation leaders (in this study: Audi, Porsche, BMW Group) compared to the desired company (see Table 3.3). It might be a surprising result that the Top Three's mark-up is above zero as practical experience has shown that at least in the first year(s) of their professional career young graduates might accept lower compensation when starting to work for a well-renowned company. However, we may assume that this potential bias is applied to any company under evaluation without substantial difference.

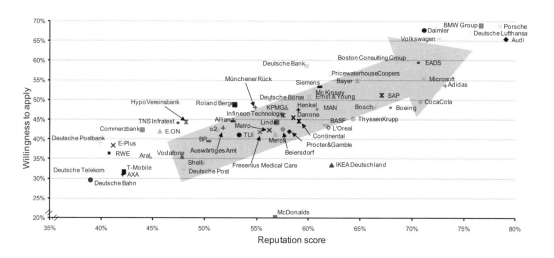

Figure 3.8   Reputation and willingness to apply among LMU students

Table 3.3   Reputation ranking and salary demands among LMU students

If a company's position at the reputation ranking is at place ...	... than there is a higher salary claim, compared to the preferred company, of about ...
Top Three	+ 4.49%
4–10	+ 10.12%
11–20	+ 13.99%
21–30	+ 14.61%
31–40	+ 15.63%
41–50	+ 17.56%
51–57	+ 18.17%
Bottom Three	+23.14%

When you compare the distance between the reputation Top Three (as an anchor) and e.g., the Bottom Three (in this study: Deutsche Telekom, Deutsche Postbank, Deutsche Bahn), on average a salary premium of 18.65 percent has to be paid by the laggards compared to the champions. Even if our sample is not representative for the whole recruiting market, we have obtained strong indication for the empirical evidence that the higher the reputation, the higher the salary deduction is. As this study may fulfill exploratory purposes only, further (experimental) research has to be done to discover to what extend the formation of a salary premium can causally be attributed to corporate reputation. For this purpose, multi-attributive job offers using the indirect approach of choice-based conjoint analysis might grant a more realistic and valid decision situation than direct approaches do.

Management Implications

Neither a good reputation nor its measurement is a goal for its own. Even though the evidence for the impact of reputation on stakeholder behavior is clear practitioners need guidance and tools when it comes to the management of reputation. Thus, we propose to consider professional reputation management as a closed loop system as shown in Figure 3.9.

First, reputation managers have to decide which outcomes should be focused on: customer retention, price/salary premiums, employees' commitment or investors' willingness to buy and hold stocks and so on. Then, we have to measure reputation and the outcomes within the relevant strategic group in order to locate the firm's position compared to its competitors. However, knowledge about the level of corporate reputation does not enable the firm to explore why it is a reputation leader or laggard. For that reason, driver analysis is required in order to find out which aspects are responsible for the respective level of reputation (see Table 3.1). Unlike the measurement concept, the driver analysis is dependent on time, markets, cultural context and industry. Hence, potential drivers (items, claims) are adapted according to the firm's sector and stakeholder group specifics. Estimating the relationships between constructs—driver constructs, measurement constructs, and outcome constructs—calls for structural modeling techniques like Partial Least Squares (PLS). Thus, all potential drivers are evaluated in cohesion with the defined outcomes. Exemplary results are illustrated in Table 3.4.

In that fictitious example the perceived degree of innovativeness accounts for more than 20 percent of the impact on the outcome customer loyalty via reputation. Regarding this indicator, the company is perceived as leader in its peer group (indicated by ++ in column 2 of Table 3.4). Focusing on the indicator "providing forthright information to the public," the firm is performing worse than the relevant benchmark. However, raising the perceived forthrightness of information by one scale point will have only one third of the impact than raising the perceived innovativeness by the same degree, as forthright information only explains 6.22 percent of the total impact on loyalty.

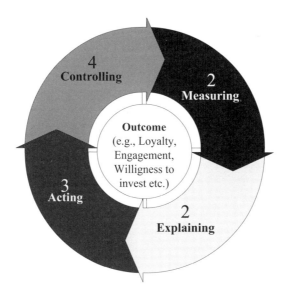

Figure 3.9   The Reputation Management Circle

Table 3.4   Exemplary results of a driver analysis

Rank (Impact on loyalty)	Position comp. to benchmark	Driver	Factor
1 (20.12%)	++	Rather innovator than imitator	Quality
2 (16.74%)	-	Well managed	Performance
3 (12.70%)	o	Customer centricity	Quality
4 (6.68%)	+	Physical appearance	Attractiveness
5 (6.22%)	--	Forthright information	CSR
6 ...		...	...

The results of the driver analysis enable the managers to put their focus on those drivers that show significant impacts on the outcome variable. Then, based on the positions within the benchmark group, the manager can plan actions like programs to improve product/service quality or rearrangement of the firm's corporate social responsibility (CSR) strategy. As these "new facts" about the company have to be perceived by the relevant stakeholder groups, information about these new/changed strategies and tactics has to be integrated into corporate communications. Once actions have been implemented and corporate communication activities are in place, controlling of measures' impact on the level of corporate reputation is required (effectiveness perspective). Relating improvements to the used resources enables judgments about the efficiency of activities. Thus, the loop is closed.

Beyond that, a thorough analysis of potential risk factors—product failure, social responsibility gap, executive and celebrity misbehavior, poor business results or loss of public support due to legal issues, environmental scandals, and communication disasters—is recommended as such crisis events may seriously put in danger over night the integrity as well as health of a company and, ultimately, its irreplaceable corporate reputation.

References

Aaker, D. A. (1996). *Building Strong Brands*. New York: Free Press.

Adamowicz, W., Louviere, J. and Swait, J. (1998). *Final Report: Introduction to Attribute-Based Stated Choice Methods*. URL: http://www.darrp.noaa.gov/library/pdf/pubscm.pdf [13.04.2009].

Ballow, J., Burgman, R., Roos, G., and Molnar M. (2004). *A New Paradigm for Managing Shareholder Value*. Wellesley, MA: Accenture Institute for High Performance Business.

Barney, J. (1991). Firm Resources and Sustained Competitive Advantage. *Journal of Management,* 17 (1), 99–120.

Bauer, H. H., Sauer, N. E. and Köhler, M. (2003). Der Einfluss des Produktwissens und der Produkterfahrung auf das Informationsverhalten und die Einstellung. *Jahrbuch der Absatz- und Verbrauchsforschung*, 49(3), 247–70.

Beatty, R. P. and Ritter, J. R. (1986). Investment Banking, Reputation, and Underpricing of Initial Public Offerings. *Journal of Financial Economics*, 15(1/2), 213–32.

Bergami, M. and Bagozzi, R. P. (2000). Self-Categorization, Affective Commitment and Group Self-Esteem as Distinct Aspects of Social Identity. *British Journal of Social Psychology*, 39(4), 555–77.

Brown, B. (1997). Stock Market Valuation of Reputation for Corporate Social Performance. *Corporate Reputation Review*, 1, 76–80.

Brown, B. and Perry, S. (1994). Removing the Financial Performance Halo from Fortune's Most Admired Companies. *Academy of Management Journal*, 37 (5), 1347–59.

Cable, D. M. and Turban, D. B. (2003). The Value of Organizational Reputation in the Recruitment Context: A Brand-equity Perspective. *Journal of Applied Social Psychology*, 33, 2244–66.

Caminiti, S. (1992). The Payoff from a Good Reputation. *Fortune*, 125(3), 49–53.

Carhart, M. M. (1997). On Persistence in Mutual Fund Performance. *Journal of Finance*, 52(1), 57–82.

Chin, W. W. (1998). The Partial Least Squares Approach to Structural Equation Modelling. G. A. Marcoulides (ed.), *Modern Methods for Business Research* (pp. 295–358). Mahwah, NJ: Lawrence Erlbaum Associates.

Chin, W. W. (2000). *Frequently Asked Questions—Partial Least Squares and PLS-Graph*. URL: http://disc-nt.cba.uh.edu/chin/plsfaq.htm [15.12.2005].

Chin, W. W. (2001). *PLS-Graph User's Guide*. Houston, TX: C.T. Bauer College of Business, University of Houston.

Chun, R. (2005). Corporate Reputation: Meaning and Measurement. *International Journal of Management Review*, 7, 91–109.

Compact Oxford English Dictionary (2009). Reputation. URL: http://www.askoxford.com/concise_oed/orexxputation?view=uk [02.03.2009].

Cook, T. D. and Campbell, D. T. (1979). *Quasi-Experimentation: Design and Analysis Issues for Field Settings*. Boston, MA: Houghton Mifflin.

Cordeiro, J. J. and Sambharya, R. B. (1997). Do Corporate Reputation Influence Security Analyst Earnings Forecasts. *Corporate Reputation Review*, 1(2), 94–8.

Crimmins, J. C. (1992). Better Measurement and Management of Brand Value. *Journal of Advertising Research*, 32(4), 11–19.

Cutler, D. M., Poterba, J. M. and Summers, L. H. (1989). What Moves Stock Prices? *Journal of Portfolio Management*, 15(3), 4–12.

Deephouse, D. L. (1997). The Effect of Financial and Media Reputations on Performance. *Corporate Reputation Review*, 1(1/2), 68–71.

Diller, H. (2000). *Preispolitik*. 3rd edn. Stuttgart/Berlin/Köln: Kohlhammer Verlag.

Dowling, G. R. (1986). Managing Your Corporate Images. *Industrial Marketing Management*, 15, 109–15.

Dozier, D. M. (1993). Image, Reputation and Mass Communication Effects. W. Armbrecht, H. Avenarius and U. Zabel (eds.), *Image und PR—Kann Image Gegen-stand einer Public Relations—Wissenschaft sein?* (pp. 227–50). Opladen: Verlag für Sozialwissenschaften.

Dunbar, R. and Schwalbach, J. (2002). Corporate Reputation and Performance in Germany. *Corporate Reputation Review*, 3(2), 115–23.

Eberl, M. (2006). *Reputation und Kundenverhalten*. München: Deutscher Universitätsverlag.

Eberl, M. (2009). An Application of PLS in Multi-Group Analysis: The Need for Differentiated Corporate-Level Marketing in the Mobile Communications Industry. In V. Esposito Vinzi, W. W. Chin, J. Henseler and H. Wang (eds.), *Handbook of Partial Least Squares: Concepts, Methods and Applications in Marketing and Related Fields*. Berlin: Springer.

Eberl, M., and Schwaiger, M. (2005). Corporate Reputation: Disentangling the Effects on Financial Performance. *European Journal of Marketing*, 39(7/8), 838–54.

Eberl, M. and Schwaiger, M. (2008). Die Bedeutung der Unternehmensreputation für die Zahlungsbereitschaft von Privatkunden. *Kredit and Kapital*, 41(3), 355–89.

Eidson, C. and Master, M. (2000), 'Top Ten ... Most Admired ... Most Respected: Who Makes the Call?' *Across the Board*, 37, 16–22.

Epple, M. H. (1990). Conjoint-Measurement—Neue Wege zur Ergründung von Kaufentscheidungen im Finanzmarkt. *Österreichisches Bankarchiv*, 38(3), 173–81.

Ernst&Young (2008). *Studenten 2008*. URL: http://www.ey.com/Global/assets.nsf/Germany/Studie_Studenten_2008/$file/Studie_Studenten_2008.pdf [15.03.2009].

Fama, E. F. (1970). Efficient Capital Markets: A Review of theory and Empirical Work. *Journal of Finance*, 25(2), 383–417.

Fama, E. F. and French, K. R. (1993). Common Risk Factors in the Returns on Stocks and Bonds. *Journal of Financial Economics*, 33(1), 3–56.

Feldman, J. M. and Lynch Jr., J. G. (1988). Self-Generated Validity and Other Effects of Measurement on Belief, Attitude, Intention and Behavior. *Journal of Applied Psychology*, 73(3), 421–35.

Fischhoff, B., Slovic, P. and Lichtenstein, S. (1980). Knowing What You Want: Measuring Labile Values. T. S. Wallsten (ed.), *Cognitive Processes in Choice and Decision Behavior* (pp. 117–42). Hillsdale, NJ: Lawrence Erlbaum Associates.

Fombrun, C. J. (1996). *Reputation. Realizing Value from the Corporate Image.* Boston, MA: Haver Business Scholl Press.

Fombrun, C. J., Gardberg, N. A. and Sever, J. M. (2000). The Reputation Quotient: A Multi-Stakeholder Measure of Corporate Reputation. *Journal of Brand Management*, 7(4), 241–55.

Fombrun, C. J. and van Riel, C. B. M. (1998). The Reputational Landscape. *Corporate Reputation Review*, 1(1), 5–14.

Fombrun, C. J. and Shanley, M. (1990). What's in a Name? Reputation Building and Corporate Strategy. *Academy of Management Journal*, 33(2), 233–58.

Goldberg, M. E. and Hartwick, J. (1990). The Effects of Advertiser Reputation and Extremity of Advertising Claim on Advertising Effectiveness. *Journal of Consumer Research*, 17, 172–9.

Gray, E. R. and Balmer, J. M. T. (1998). Managing Corporate Image and Corporate Reputation. *Long Range Planning*, 31, 695–702.

Greene, W. H. (2008). *Econometric Analysis.* Upper Saddle River, NJ: Pearson Prentice Hall.

Grobe, E. (2003). Corporate Attractiveness: Eine Analyse der Wahrnehmung von Unternehmensmarken aus der Sicht von High Potentials. *HHL-Arbeitspapier 50.* Leipzig: Leipzig Graduate School of Management.

Hall, R. (1992). The Strategic Analysis of Intangible Resources. *Strategic Management Journal*, 13, 135–44.

Hanssens, D. M., Rust, T. R. and Srivastava, R. K. (2009). Marketing Strategy and Wall Street: Nailing Down Marketing's Impact. *Journal of Marketing*, 73 (4), 115–18.

Haugtvedt, C. P. and Wegener, D. T. (1994). Message Order Effects in Persuasion: An Attitude Strength Perspective. *Journal of Consumer Research*, 21(1), 205–18.

Hauser, J. R. and Rao, V. R. (2002). *Conjoint Analysis, Related Modeling, and Applications.* URL: http://web.mit.edu/hauser/www/Papers/GreenTributeConjoint092302.pdf [13.04.2009].

Haywood, R. (2002). *Manage Your Reputation.* London: Kogan Page.

Henseler, J., Ringle, C. M. and Sinkovics, R. R. (2009). The Use of Partial Least Squares Path Modeling in International Marketing. *Advances in International Marketing*, 20, 277–320.

Hildebrandt, L. and Schwalbach, J. (2000). *Financial Performance Halo in German Reputation.* Data Forschungsbericht. Institut für Management der Humboldt-Universität zu Berlin.

Hirshleifer, D. (2001). Investor Psychology and Asset Pricing. *Journal of Finance*, 56(4), 1553–97.

Hoffman, E., Menkhaus, D. J., Chakravarti, D., Field, R. A. and Whipple, G. D. (1993). Using Laboratory Experimental Auctions in Marketing Research: A Case Study of New Packaging for Fresh Beef. *Marketing Science*, 12(3), 318–38.

Hutton, C. (1986). America's Most Admired Companies. *Fortune*, 6, 16–22.

Jacobson, R. and Mizik, N. (2009). The Financial Markets and Customer Satisfaction: Reexamining Possible Financial Market Mispricing of Customer Satisfaction. *Marketing Science*, 28(5), 810–19.

Jacoby, J., Chestnut, R. W. and Fisher, W. A. (1978). A Behavioral Process Approach to Information Acquisition in Nondurable Purchasing. *Journal of Marketing Research*, 15(4), 532–44.

Johnson, B. T. and Eagly, A. H. (1989). Effects of Involvement on Persuasion: A Meta-Analysis. *Psychological Bulletin*, 106(2), 290–314.

Jones, G. H., Beth, H., Little, J. and Little, P. (2000). Reputation as Reservoir: Buffering Against Loss in Times of Economic Crisis. *Corporate Reputation Review*, 3(1), 21–9.

Kardes, F. R., Posavac, S. S. and Cronley, M. L. (2004). Consumer Inference: A Review of Processes, Bases, and Judgment Contexts. *Journal of Consumer Psychology*, 14(3), 230–56.

Keller, K. L. and Aaker, D. A. (1992). The Effects of Sequential Introduction of Brand Extensions. *Journal of Marketing Research*, 29(1), 35–50.

Klein, B. and Leffler, K. B. (1981). The Role of Market Forces in Assuring Contractual Performance. *Journal of Political Economy*, 89(4), 615–41.

Lafferty, B. A. and Goldsmith, R. E. (1999). Corporate Credibility's Role in Consumers' Attitudes and Purchase Intentions. When a High versus a Low Credibility Endorser is Used in the Ad. *Journal of Business Research*, 44(2), 109–16.

Laurent, G. and Kapferer, J.-N. (1985a). Measuring Consumer Involvement Profiles. *Journal of Marketing Research*, 22(1), 41–53.

Laurent, G. and Kapferer, J.-N. (1985b). Consumer Involvement Profiles: A New Practical Approach to Consumer Involvement. *Journal of Advertising Research*, 25(6), 48–56.

Lev, B. (2001). *Intangibles: Management Measurement and Reporting*. Washington, DC: Brookings Institution Press.

Lev, B. (2003). Remarks on the Measurement, Valuation, and Reporting of Intangible Assets. *Economic Policy Review*, 9(3), 17–22.

Lewandowski, A. and Liebig, C. (2004). Determinanten der Arbeitgeberwahl und Relevanz des Personalimages für die Bewerbungsabsicht. *Mannheimer Beiträge zur Wirtschafts- und Organisationspsychologie*, 19(1), 15–28.

Lewis, S. (2001). Measuring Corporate Reputation, Corporate Communications. *An International Journal*, 6(1), 31–5.

Lohmöller, J. B. (1989). *Latent Variable Path Modeling with Partial Least Squares*. Heidelberg: Physica.

Lusk, J. L., Feldkamp, T. and Schroeder, T. C. (2004). Experimental Auction Procedure: Impact on Valuation of Quality Differentiated Goods. *American Journal of Agricultural Economics Association*, 86(2), 389–405.

MacKinlay, A. C. (1997). Event Studies in Economics and Finance. *Journal of Economic Literature*, 35(1), 13–39.

Madrigal, R. (2000). The Role of Corporate Associations in New Product Evaluation. *Advances in Consumer Research*, 27(1), 80–6.

Maheswaran, D., Mackie, D. M. and Chaiken, S. (1992). Brand Name as a Heuristic Cue: The Effects of Task Importance and Expectancy Confirmation on Consumer Judgments. *Journal of Consumer Psychology*, 1(4), 317–36.

Mantel, S. P. and Kardes, F. R. (1999). The Role of Direction of Comparison, Attribute-Based Processing, and Attitude-Based Processing in Consumer Preference. *Journal of Consumer Research*, 25(4), 335–52.

McGuire, J. B., Schneeweis, T. and Branch, B. (1990). Perceptions of Firm Quality: A Cause or Result of Firm Performance? *Journal of Management*, 16 (1), 167–80.

McMillan, G. S. and Joshi, M. P. (1997). Sustainable Competitive Advantage and Firm Performance. The Role of Intangible Resources. *Corporate Reputation Review*, 1(3), 81–5.

McWilliams, A. and Siegel, D. (1997). Event Studies in Management Research: Theoretical and Empirical Issues. *Academy of Management Journal*, 40(3), 626–57.

Milgrom, P. and Roberts, J. (1986). Price and Advertising Signals of Product Quality. *Journal of Political Economy*, 94(4), 796–821.

Milgrom, P. and Roberts, J. (1992). *Economics Organization and Management*. Englewood Cliffs, NJ: Prentice Hall.

Mizik, N. and Jacobson, R. (2003). Trading Off Between Value Creation and Value Appropriation: The Financial Implications of Shifts in Strategic Emphasis. *Journal of Marketing*, 67(1), 63–76.

Nakra, P. (2000). Corporate Reputation Management: "CRM" with a Strategic Twist. *Public Relations Quarterly*, 45(2), 35–42.

Nganje, W., Kaitibie, S., Wachenhiem, C., Acquah, E. T., Matson, J. and Johnson, G. (2008). Estimating Price Premiums for Breads Marketed as "Low-Carbohydrate Breads". *Journal of Food Distribution Research*, 39(2), 66–76.

Orme, B. (2004). *The CBC/HB System for Hierarchical Bayes Estimation*. Version 3.2. Sequim, WA: Sawtooth Software, Inc..

Park, C. S. and Srinivasan, V. (1994). A Survey-based Method for Measuring and Understanding Brand Equity and its Extendibility. *Journal of Marketing Research*, 31, 271–88.

Payne, J. W. (1976). Task Complexity and Contingent Processing in Decision Making: An Information Search and Protocol Analysis. *Organizational Behavior and Human Performance*, 16, 366–87.

Petty, R. E., Cacioppo, J. T. and Schumann, D. (1983). Central and Peripheral Routes to Advertising Effectiveness: The Moderating Role of Involvement. *Journal of Consumer Research*, 10(2), 135–46.

Podolny, J. M. (1993). A Status-based Model of Market Competition. *American Journal of Sociology*, 98(4), 829–72.

Preece, S., Fleisher, C. and Toccacelli, J. (1995). Building a Reputation Along the Value Chain at Levi Strauss. *Long Range Planning*, 28(6), 88–98.

Raithel, S. and Schwaiger, M. (2009). *The Value of Corporate Reputation for Shareholders*. Working Paper. München: Institute for Market-based Management.

Raithel, S., Wilczynski, P., Schloderer, M. and Schwaiger, M. (2009). *Corporate Reputation in Times of Economic Crisis*. Proceedings of the 5th International Conference of the Academy of Marketing's Brand, Identity and Corporate Reputation SIG. Cambridge, UK.

Ratchford, B. T. (2001). The Economics of Consumer Knowledge. *Journal of Consumer Research*, 27(4), 397–411.

Riediger, C., Sattler, H. and Völckner, F. (2008). *The Impact of Brand Extension Success Drivers on Brand Extension Price Premium*. Proceedings of the 37th Annual Conference of the European Marketing Academy. Brighton, UK.

Roberts, P. W. and Dowling, G. R. (1997). The Value of a Firm's Corporate Reputation: How Reputation Helps Attain and Sustain Superior Profitability. *Corporate Reputation Review*, 1(1/2), 72–6.

Roberts, P. W. and Dowling, G. R. (2002). Corporate Reputation and Sustained Superior Financial Performance. *Strategic Management Journal*, 23(12), 1077–94.

Rogerson, W. P. (1983). Reputation and Product Quality. *The Bell Journal of Economics*, 14(2), 508–16.

Rossiter, J. R. (2002). The C-OAR-SE Procedure for Scale Development in Marketing. *International Journal of Research in Marketing*, 19(4), 305–35.

Sarstedt, M., Ringle, C. M., Schloderer, M. P. and Schwaiger, M. (2008). *Accounting for Unobserved Heterogeneity in the Analysis of Antecedents and Consequences of Corporate Reputation: An Application of FIMIX-PLS*. Proceedings of the 37th Annual Conference of the European Marketing Academy (EMAC). Brighton, UK.

Sattler, H. (1999). Markenbewertung. S. Albers and A. Herrmann (eds.), *Handbuch Produktpolitik*. URL: http://www.econbiz.de/archiv/hh/uhh/marketing/markenbewertung2.pdf [02.12.2008].

Sattler, H. and Hartmann, A. (2002). Commercial Use of Conjoint Analysis in Germany, Austria, and Switzerland. Research Papers on Marketing and Retailing, University of Hamburg, 6.

Schloderer, M. P. (2010). *Reputation in the Recruiting Market*. Working Paper. München: Institute for Market-based Management.

Schütz, T. and Schwaiger, M. (2007). Der Einfluss der Unternehmensreputation auf Entscheidungen privater Anleger. *Kredit und Kapital*, 40(2), 189–223.

Schwaiger, M. (2004). Components and Parameters of Corporate Reputation—an Empirical Study, *Schmalenbach Business Review*, 56, 46–71.

Schwaiger, M., Raithel, S. and Schloderer, M. P. (2009). Recognition or Rejection—How a Company's Reputation Influences Stakeholder Behavior. In J. Klewes and R. Wreschniok (eds.), *Reputation Capital—Building and Maintaining Trust in the 21st Century* (pp. 39–56). Berlin: Springer.

Schwalbach, J. (2000). Image, Reputation und Unternehmenswert. B. Baerns and J. Raupp (eds.), *Information und Kommunikation in Europa. Forschung und Praxis. Transnational Communication in Europe. Research and Practice* (pp. 287–97). Berlin: Vistas.

Sen, S. and Bhattacharya, C. B. (2001). Does Doing Good Always Lead to Doing Better? Consumer Reactions to Corporate Social Responsibility. *Journal of Marketing Research*, 38(2), 225–43.

Shadish, W. R., Cook, T. D. and Campbell, D. T. (2001). *Experimental and Quasi-Experimental Designs for Generalized Causal Inference*. 2nd edn. Boston, MA: Houghton Mifflin Harcourt.

Shapiro, C. (1983). Premiums for High Quality Products as Returns to Reputation. *The Quarterly Journal of Economics*, 98(3), 659–79.

Sherman, M. L. (1999). Making the Most of Your Reputation. In Institute of Directors (ed.), *Reputation Management: Strategies for Protecting Companies, Their Brands and Their Directors*. London: AIG Europe.

Simmons, C. J. and Lynch Jr., J. G. (1991). Inference Effects without Inference Making? Effects of Missing Information on Discounting and Use of Presented Information. *Journal of Consumer Research*, 17(4), 477–91.

Simon, H. (1955). A Behavioral Model of Rational Choice. *Quarterly Journal of Economics*, 69(1), 99–118.

Simon, H. (1992). *Preismanagement: Analyse, Strategie, Umsetzung*. 2nd edn. Wiesbaden: Gabler.

Srinivasan, S. and Hanssens, D. M. (2009). Marketing and Firm Value: Metrics, Methods, Findings, and Future Directions. *Journal of Marketing Research*, 46(3), 293–312.

Srinivasan, S., Pauwels, K., Silva-Risso, J. M. and Hanssens, D. M. (2009). Product Innovations, Advertising, and Stock Returns. *Journal of Marketing*, 73(1), 24–43.

Srivastava, R. K., McInish, T. H., Wood, R. A. and Capraro, A. J. (1997). The Value of Corporate Reputations: Evidence from the Equity Markets. *Corporate Reputation Review*, 1(1), 62–7.

Turban, D. B. and Cable, D. M. (2003). Firm Reputation and Applicant Pool Characteristics. *Journal of Organizational Behavior*, 24, 733–52.

Wartick, S. L. (2002). Measuring Corporate Reputation: Definition and Data. *Business and Society*, 41(4), 371–92.

Weiss, A. M., Anderson, E. and MacInnis, D. J. (1999). Reputation Management as a Motivation for Sale Structure Decisions. *Journal of Marketing*, 63, 74–89.

Wernerfelt, B. (1984). A Resource-Based View of the Firm. *Strategic Management Journal*, 5(2), 171–80.

Wernerfelt, B. (1995). A Resource-Based View of the Firm: Ten years after. *Strategic Management Journal*, 16(3), 171–4.

Wiedmann, K.-P. and Buxel, H. (2005). Corporate Reputation Management in Germany: Results of an Empirical Study. *Corporate Reputation Review*, 8 (2), 145–63.

Wilczynski, P., Sarstedt, M., Melewar, T. C. (2009). *A Comparison of Selected Reputation Measures' Convergent and Criterion Validity*. Proceedings of the 2009 Annual Conference of the Academy of Marketing Science. Baltimore, MD.

Wübker, G. (2004). Pricing-Prozesse: Gewinnpotenziale erschließen. *Die Bank*, 44(1), 7–11.

Wübker, G. and Baumgarten, J. (2004). Der Markenwert von Banken—Messung komplexer Sachverhalte mit modernen Verfahren. *Zeitschrift für betriebswirtschaftliche Forschung*, 56(9), 577–92.

Zaichkowsky, J. L. (1985). Measuring the Involvement Construct. *Journal of Consumer Research*, 12(3), 341–52.

Zeithaml, V. A. (1988). Consumer Perceptions of Price, Quality, and Value: A Means-End Model and Synthesis of Evidence. *Journal of Marketing*, 53(3), 2–21.

Zhang, Y. and Schwaiger, M. (2009). An Empirical Research of Corporate Reputation in China. *Communicative Business*, 2(1), 80–104.

Developing a Corporate Reputation

4 Reputation and Corporate Social Responsibility: A Global View

PHILIP H. MIRVIS

A survey of US companies finds that two of every three business leaders today believe that corporate social responsibility (CSR) makes a tangible contribution to the bottom line (BCCCC, 2009).[1] Another poll finds that 80 percent of CEOs believe that CSR contributes to their company's reputation (Hill and Knowlton and Crown Ferry International, 2006). That poll also reports that the CEOs believe that reputational benefits can significantly increase their company's ability to recruit and retain employees, appeal to and attract consumers, differentiate their firm and its offerings in the market place, generate additional sales, and achieve many of the other business benefits.

For the past several years, practitioners have built a business case for action based on this linkage between CSR and reputation. Books, seminars, and corporate programs on "competing on reputation" and the "CSR advantage" abound. But today, even as the global financial crisis ebbs, trust in business remains low, few (27 percent) trust the credibility of CEOs, and large majorities of the public are suspicious of advertisements and messages that portray a corporation as "green" or "socially responsible" (Edelman, 2010). In this context, practitioners need a more sophisticated understanding of how the public sees CSR and which of its multiple dimensions are the most significant drivers of corporate reputation. And, in a global economy, where reputational risks abound and CSR investments are expected to create reputational value, a more nuanced view on how national culture and traditions factor into this CSR → Reputation equation is essential.

Consider these fundamental questions: We know that the public says that CSR is important to trust and reputation, but do people make this link when they think about a *specific* company? Is it a stronger or weaker link when compared to, say, their views of the financial performance or leadership of a firm? Is the link between CSR and a company's reputation pretty much the same in countries around the world or are their key variations?

For the past several years, Reputation Institute has measured and studied the components of corporate reputation through in depth studies of individual firms and an annual global study of the reputations of over 600 companies through 30,000 online

---

1   The terms "corporate citizenship," "corporate responsibility," and "corporate responsibility" are used interchangeably.

interviews with consumers in some 27 countries (see appendix to this chapter for details on the survey). For the 2008 data collection, the author worked with Reputation Institute to analyze how CSR, in its several dimensions, factors into companies' reputations. This chapter overviews the findings and highlights some of the implications for managing reputation and responsibility on a global scale.

Managing Reputation and Responsibility on a Global Scale

Business leaders today face an increasingly complex operating environment. Markets are global. Customers, suppliers, and staff are located around the world in vastly different cultural, linguistic, and economic operating environments. As a result, intentions and practices that may be valued or prudent in a home market can instead backfire, be misunderstood, or at best seem irrelevant in another country. This has significant implications for managing corporate reputation and CSR.

One major factor reshaping the corporate environment today has been the rapid rise in the public's expectations of business. This, combined with the absence of global regulation and gradual withdrawal of the state from public services provision, has increased both the expectation of and need for a more responsible, stakeholder-driven approach to business wherever a firm operates—what is called global corporate citizenship.

As many corporations expand their business reach and operations across the world, they are also globalizing their CSR programs. Just as misreading the business culture in a new environment can prove disastrous, so can adopting the wrong approach to CSR—whether that be in terms of corporate governance, workplace practices, environmental investments, or community relations. As practitioners begin (or continue) to expand their programs abroad, it is important that they are aware of the unique citizenship landscape in each country in which they do business.

INFLUENCES ON CSR

There are global as well as local (national, cultural) forces that shape public expectations and set the context for CSR around the world (GERN, 2008). Let's start with some *global* trends. Consider, first, how the past decades saw a dramatic surge in the relative power of the private sector as the globalization of the world's economy opened up new opportunities for businesses. The number of multinational corporations has doubled in just the past 15 years. And the number of their foreign operations and affiliates nearly tripled in the same period. Today 200 corporations account for 23 percent of the world's GDP, and 51 of the top 100 economies in the world are corporations.

The integration of a global marketplace, the internationalization of capital and labor markets, and the retraction of the public sector in the United States and abroad have together spurred this unprecedented growth in business activity. Productivity gains and innovation have improved competitiveness and efficiency; greater market opportunities worldwide have raised revenues and expanded the scope of business opportunity; and access to cheaper sources of labor and raw materials continually lowers costs. These advantages have raised the power position of business, often beyond national governments. They have also produced undeniable economic, social, and environmental costs. Not surprisingly, this rise in business power has led to calls among the world's populace for business to assume broader social and environmental responsibilities in the twenty-first century.

One consequence is that CSR is itself in a state of transformation. Most countries are experiencing a shift from a traditional view of the responsible corporate citizen as providing jobs, earning profits, and paying taxes while "giving back" through philanthropy, to a new view that is more encompassing of the impact of business on society. Furthermore, the global media, most especially the internet, has put corporate conduct into the spotlight. As a result, leading companies themselves are going beyond traditional definitions of a "good company" and are taking steps to increase transparency about their doings and to move CSR from the margins to the mainstream of their business management (Googins et al., 2007).

DIMENSIONS OF CSR

What is involved in CSR? To begin, the field, whether termed "citizenship," "corporate responsibility" or "sustainability," has its roots in *ethics*. This stresses the importance of moral corporate conduct, very much in the spotlight this decade given Enron and its ilk, corporate human rights violations in supply chains, and the latest financial misdoings by banks and brokerage firms. At a minimum, this translates into *compliance*: behaving in line with current law, accepted business principles, and codes of conduct. But companies can choose to comply not only with the *letter* but also with the *spirit* of regulations; and to *exceed the law* in product safety, environmental protection, or employee relations. Taking this to a global scale, companies also have to decide whether to apply the high standards for ethics and transparency found in the US and Europe to their operations in nations where there is no legal requirement or strong public expectation that they do so.

Beyond compliance, *philanthropy* is an important part of the business–society equation. Firms, in the US and increasingly globally, are more or less expected to give back a portion of their profits to help the disadvantaged, support community life, and, when necessary, provide disaster relief. This translates into a voluntary contribution to society in exchange for business benefits like market infrastructure and a general license to operate. Of course, corporate giving and employee volunteerism can also yield firm-specific benefits such as an improved reputation and stronger community relationships (Porter and Kramer, 2002).

Business has its biggest impact on society through (1) its own operations and (2) its interactions with suppliers, distributors, and other stakeholders through the entire value chain to end users (including business-to-business or B2B customers and/or consumers). In this context, the social and economic impact of philanthropy is comparatively modest. Most would agree then that corporate citizenship encompass the *harms* and *benefits* of a company's *commercial activities on society*.

Front and center today are worries over climate change and *environmental sustainability*. McKinsey & Co. (Bonini et al., 2008) finds that over 50 percent of consumers and business leaders in over 10 countries sampled rate "environmental issues, including climate change" as the most important issues facing business. Finally, it is well documented that *how employees are treated* is the "litmus test" for how the public evaluates its corporations. In GolinHarris (2004–2009) surveys in the US, for instance, the public's perception of whether or not a company "values and treats employees fairly and well" has been the number one criteria in ratings of corporate citizenship, more so than charity, community involvement, environmental performance, and other citizenship factors. This raises a central question of this study: what are public expectations of a corporate citizen around the globe?

THE RESPONSIBILITIES OF BUSINESS—A GLOBAL VIEW

The short answer is that the public today expects a lot from business and holds firms responsible for their conduct. GlobeScan (2001–2010) has asked the public around the world whether or not companies are "not at all" or "somewhat" or "completely" responsible for various aspects of business operations and their impact on society. For the past several years, the pollster found that large majorities in 25 countries hold companies *completely* responsible for the safety of their products, fair treatment of employees, responsible management of their supply chain, and for not harming the environment. These are, of course, *operational* aspects of firms and well within their control. But, in addition, a significant number held them completely responsible for improving education and skills in communities, responding to public concerns, increasing global economic stability, reducing human rights abuses, and reducing the rich–poor gap. Add in the category of *partially* responsible, and business is responsible, in the public's eye, not only for minding its own store but also for addressing myriad of the world's ills.

How is business doing overall on its responsibility scorecard? A multiyear look at public opinion worldwide by GlobeScan shows that while public expectations of companies have been rising, ratings of their social responsibility have been dropping. Surveys from Reputation Institute, in turn, document that in 25 countries studied, an average of just one in five people agree that "most companies are socially responsible." Roughly 16 percent of Americans see it this way—fewer than in Mexico (35 percent) and Canada (26 percent) but more than in the UK (11 percent) and Japan (9 percent).

No database or set of surveys is sufficient to parse out the relative importance of global versus the many sociocultural factors in shaping the public's expectations of business in different parts of the world. Nor can a survey study document how these influence corporate practices and the public's perception of corporate conduct. Still, a closer look at how the public views the CSR of companies in their nation yields some hunches and insights into both its global and local dimensions.

Measuring Corporate Reputation and Responsibility

Through its annual Global Pulse Study, Reputation Institute measures the reputations of the world's largest companies around the world selected on the basis of their total revenues. Rated companies had to have significant consumer presence and be minimally familiar to the general public. All companies are measured in their home country only, and the results standardized to remove unique country-level variation and enable cross-country comparisons. This put some 150 US companies on the list, as well as 40 companies from Japan, 35 each from China and the UK, 30 each from France and Germany and 20 from Russia, and smaller numbers from the other countries studied.

What is important to note is that most polls on corporate citizenship address the public's expectations of *business overall* and/or their ratings of *business conduct in general.* The Global Pulse, by comparison, measures public perceptions of *specific* companies.

Through the survey, consumers are asked to opine on the reputation and conduct of individual companies based in their home countries. The data here represents how countries see their companies. This allows us to test the relationship between social responsibility and reputation with actual companies as a referent point.

DIMENSIONS OF REPUTATION: THE GLOBAL PULSE STUDY

Reputation Institute has identified several different dimensions of firm activity and its overall reputation. The *pulse* measure—what is termed the "heartbeat"—reflects the public's good feeling about, respect for, and trust in a company. This is a summative indicator of reputation *overall*. The global survey also asks the public to rate a selected company in terms of its *performance* (financial results), *innovation* (in products and ways it does business), *products and services* (quality and reliability), *leadership* (visibility and effectiveness), *citizenship* (support for causes and protecting the environment), *workplace* (treatment of employees), and *governance* (ethics, openness and transparency).

A first analysis looks at the relationship of these seven factors with the overall reputation ratings for a company (see Figure 4.1). In the 2008 Global Pulse Survey, the top predictor of reputation—as in prior years—is ratings of products and services. Products and services are of course the most visible representation and presence of a company in the marketplace and the most familiar indication of corporate conduct to consumers that purchase them, see them in stores, the media, and advertisements, and learn about them from other consumers. In statistical language, ratings of a company's products and services are the strongest *driver* (predicting 17.6 percent) of reputation.

What is notable is that the next higher predictors of reputation are perceptions of a company's citizenship (16.3 percent), governance (14.5 percent), and workplace (14.6 percent) practices. In some instances, these aspects of a company may be experienced directly by consumers but for most are learned about through corporate communications, media coverage, and word of mouth. As you see in the exhibit, perceptions of innovation, leadership, and financial performance all factor into corporate reputation, but somewhat less so among a nation's general public.

Attention in this study turns to the three of the dimensions of reputation most germane to social responsibility. In the 2008 survey, the combined ratings of a company's citizenship, governance, and workplace practices—what we term the *CSR Index*—accounted for 45.4 percent of the variation in ratings of its reputation. To understand how the world sees the CSR of companies, we next look at how specific companies are rated on these counts (mean ratings).

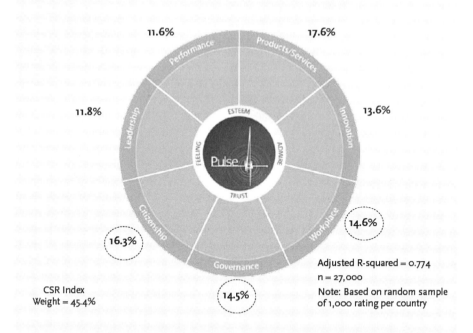

RepTrak™ Pulse scores are based on questions measuring Trust, Admiration & Respect, Good Feeling and Overall Esteem (captured in the Pulse score on a 0-100 scale)

Dimension scores are based on the evaluations of the following statements:

Product/Services: 'Company' offers high quality products and services -- it offers excellent products and reliable services

Innovation: 'Company' is an innovative company -- it makes or sells innovative products or innovates in the way it does business

Workplace: 'Company' is an appealing place to work -- it treats its employees well

Citizenship: 'Company' is a good corporate citizen -- it supports good causes & does not harm the environment

Governance: 'Company' is a responsibly-run company -- it behaves ethically and is open & transparent in its business dealings

Leadership: 'Company' is a company with strong leadership -- it has visible leaders & is managed effectively

Performance: 'Company' is a high-performance company -- it delivers good financial results

Figure 4.1   The RepTrak™ Model—dimensions and global drivers of reputation

Source: Global Reputation Pulse, Reputation Institute. Copyright © Reputation Institute. All rights reserved. Adapted from Mirvis, P. H. et al., *Building Reputation Here, There, and Everywhere*. Reputation Institute and Boston College Center for Corporate Citizenship, 2009.

GLOBAL RATINGS OF CITIZENSHIP, GOVERNANCE, AND WORKPLACE

Figure 4.2 presents the public's ratings of 600 or so corporation's citizenship, governance, and workplace practices around the world. A quick look shows that there is a larger range across countries in ratings of corporate governance compared to the other two. The global mean for governance (62.0) is also somewhat higher than for the workplace (60.4) and citizenship (59.0). Who are the leaders versus laggards on each dimension?

2008 Ratings (*Means*) of Citizenship, Governance, and Workplace Dimensions by Country

Citizenship		Governance		Workplace		CSR Index	
Netherlands	65.8	South Africa	71.8	Norway	66.0	Netherlands	65.5
Norway	64.0	India	67.3	Netherlands	65.8	Sweden	64.8
Denmark	63.2	Portugal	67.1	Sweden	65.6	Norway	64.7
India	63.1	Sweden	66.1	USA	64.4	India	64.7
Sweden	62.6	Poland	65.2	India	63.6	South Africa	64.6
Russia	61.9	Netherlands	65.0	Canada	63.0	USA	63.5
Japan	61.6	USA	64.8	United Kingdom	62.0	Portugal	62.6
Italy	61.3	Norway	64.2	South Africa	61.7	Canada	62.2
USA	61.2	Canada	64.2	South Korea	61.7	Japan	62.2
Poland	60.9	Japan	64.0	Denmark	61.3	Italy	61.7
South Africa	60.4	Brazil	64.0	Japan	61.0	Russia	61.7
Portugal	60.2	Russia	63.8	Portugal	60.6	Denmark	61.5
France	60.2	Italy	63.6	AVERAGE	60.4	Poland	61.5
Canada	59.5	Finland	62.9	Italy	60.3	Brazil	61.0
South Korea	59.3	France	62.6	Switzerland	59.8	France	60.8
Germany	59.3	AVERAGE	62.0	Brazil	59.7	AVERAGE	60.5
Brazil	59.1	Germany	61.9	France	59.7	Finland	59.9
AVERAGE	59.0	Denmark	60.1	Greece	59.6	South Korea	59.5
Switzerland	58.5	China	59.9	Russia	59.5	Germany	59.4
Finland	57.6	Switzerland	59.7	Finland	59.2	Switzerland	59.4
United Kingdom	56.5	Greece	58.9	Poland	58.3	United Kingdom	58.9
Spain	55.6	Spain	58.6	Argentina	58.3	Greece	57.8
China	55.1	United Kingdom	58.3	Mexico	58.0	Spain	57.3
Greece	54.9	Mexico	57.8	Spain	57.6	China	57.1
Mexico	54.2	South Korea	57.6	Germany	57.1	Mexico	56.7
Australia	54.0	Argentina	56.0	China	56.3	Argentina	56.0
Argentina	53.6	Chile	55.5	Chile	55.9	Australia	54.6
Chile	50.0	Australia	54.4	Australia	55.5	Chile	53.8

Note: Ratings are a mean of company scores collected in each country. All scores are globally adjusted. The CSR Index is a mean of the citizenship, governance and workplace dimension scores per country.

Figure 4.2   2008 ratings (means) of citizenship, governance, and workplace dimensions by country

Source: Global Reputation Pulse, Reputation Institute. Copyright © Reputation Institute. All rights reserved. Adapted from Mirvis, P. H. et al., *Building Reputation Here, There, and Everywhere*. Reputation Institute and Boston College Center for Corporate Citizenship, 2009.

When it comes to ratings of corporate citizenship, specifically the extent to which a firm *supports good causes* and *does not harm the environment*, firms in the Netherlands, Norway, Denmark, and Sweden are ranked highest on this dimension by their nation's public. This should not surprise because companies in Scandinavia have a long heritage of environmental stewardship and many of the larger ones are connected to national, EU-wide, and global initiatives aimed at remedying social ills.

Interestingly, India scores highly on the citizenship dimension as well. Several of the nation's leading companies have gained a reputation on the world's stage for their outreach to society and green agenda. A closer look shows that Indians give their companies comparatively high marks on all three dimensions of CSR.

Also highly rated on citizenship, but in the next tier, are companies in Russia, Japan, Italy, and the US. There may be an objective basis to these public perceptions: an EIRIS (2007) study finds that European companies are generally ahead of US firms in adopting responsible business practices. When it comes to managing environmental impacts, for example, European and Japanese companies (also rated highly on citizenship) are clear leaders. Where US firms stand out is in their community engagement through philanthropy, volunteerism, and cause marketing.

Comparatively lower ratings of corporate citizenship come from the public in Chile, Argentina, and Mexico, as well as Australia and China. (The "average" rating in each nation is near to the midpoint on a five-point rating scale.) Obviously, corporate conduct is a factor in these ratings. Remember, too, that the largest companies in these smaller commercial markets are being rated. As such, they are highly visible targets for the public's disappointment with its material and social circumstances.

A different pattern across nations emerges in ratings of corporate governance—the extent to which a company is *open and transparent* and *behaves ethically*. Here the highest scores come from two emerging markets: South Africa and India. One hypothesis is that strong and highly publicized guidelines on corporate conduct from the King Commission have shaped corporate conduct and influenced public perceptions of the same in South Africa. In the case of India, Infosys Technologies and the Tata Group, highly visible companies and early signatories to the United Nation's Global Compact Principles, score among the world's leaders in ratings of governance. Governmental crackdowns on business misbehavior in India may also feature here.

The US scores in the top third of countries in the governance measure. This may seem a bit surprising in light of corporate scandals during the past decade. Remember, though, that the legal system and codes of corporate conduct in the US are far more developed than in other nations where corruption is commonplace. Firms in Portugal, Sweden, Poland and the Netherlands also score high with their publics on ethics and transparency. Interestingly, Denmark and the UK typically score highly in experts' rankings of corporate transparency and governance. In this study, however, the public rates them comparatively lower. This may have something to do with corporate scandals in each nation in 2008.

On the other end of the rating scale, companies in Latin American countries (not Brazil) and in Australia score lower on governance in the public eye. South Koreans also give their firms low marks on governance too—not surprising given that several of the big South Korean chaebols have been involved in highly visible financial and influence-peddling scandals. Under ratings of workplace conditions or *how companies treat their people*, the Netherlands, Norway, and Sweden reappear at the top of the list. The US and Canada give their companies high ratings in this regard, too.

Look now at how the UK rates the CSR of its companies. Brits give their firms high marks on the workplace (ranked 7th), but comparatively low scores on citizenship (20th) and governance (22nd). One wonders about the impact of extensive media coverage of citizenship and governance issues in the UK in this regard. Contrast, for example, the achievements of Tesco and Marks & Spencer versus the failings of BP in these areas.

Russia public opinion about corporate conduct, by contrast, moves in the opposite direction. Russians give their companies relatively lower marks on the workplace (ranked 18th) versus citizenship (6th) and governance (12th). The same pattern is found in Poland. Here a factor could be the absence of media coverage of corporate citizenship and governance in these nations. By comparison, people can form opinions about workplace practices from their own experiences and that of friends and neighbors.

Again, the Latin American and Australian companies rate lower on the how they treat their workers. German firms also scores lower on ratings of the workplace (24th). A strong pro-labor tradition in Germany running up against downsizing and layoffs may help to explain lower workplace ratings found here.

COMBINED RATINGS: CORPORATE SOCIAL RESPONSIBILITY INDEX

Summing these three ratings of citizenship, governance, and the workplace yields what we term the CSR Index. Companies in the Netherlands score highest on this summative index followed by Sweden and Norway. India and South Africa rank highly too—largely on the strength of their strong governance scores. US companies, ranked in the top third in all three dimensions, score sixth overall. Firms based in Portugal, on the strength of governance ratings, and in Canada and Japan round out the top tier on the overall CSR Index.

In the middle tier of the CSR Index are firms based in Italy (upgraded on citizenship ratings), Denmark (downgraded on governance), and Germany (downgraded on the workplace). In the lower tier are firms based in Latin America, China, and Spain.

Reputation and Corporate Social Responsibility: What Matters Most

To assess to what extent the public's ratings of the CSR of companies factor into ratings of reputation overall, Reputation Institute researchers undertake regression analyses that parse out the relative contribution of each of these "drivers" to a firm's reputation pulse score. Figure 4.3 presents the distinctive contribution of the CSR ratings to a company's reputation in the countries sampled.

A close look at this chart shows that there is considerable variation in the power of CSR Index to predict a company's reputations—ranging from very high predictive power in Finland (55.3 percent) to the global average (45.4 percent) to relatively low power in Spain (41.4 percent). This means that CSR is a more robust "driver" of the reputation of companies in Finland and in other nations near the upper end of the scale and far less significant a driver for companies in Spain and in other nations on the lower end. The picture gets more granular in the case of the predictive power of the individual CSR Index components.

Consider the relative importance assigned to corporate citizenship—supporting good causes and not harming the environment. The Scandinavian countries and the Netherlands give citizenship a high weight in their judgments about a company overall. By comparison, the Latin Americans, Spanish and Italian publics assign citizenship much less importance when assessing the reputations of companies in their nations. Interestingly, the public in the US, the UK, and Canada don't give citizenship near as strong a weighting in overall reputation ratings in their nations. This story changes in the case of governance.

Importance (Driver Weights) of Citizenship, Governance, and Workplace Dimensions by Country

Citizenship		Governance		Workplace		CSR Index	
Finland	21.8%	Chile	18.1%	Finland	18.9%	Finland	55.3%
Norway	20.8%	South Korea	17.4%	Portugal	17.0%	France	49.6%
Netherlands	20.1%	Australia	17.1%	Denmark	16.6%	Denmark	49.4%
Denmark	20.0%	Canada	16.5%	Canada	15.7%	Netherlands	47.5%
Sweden	19.1%	India	16.5%	France	15.6%	Portugal	47.4%
Portugal	18.7%	United States	16.4%	Brazil	15.3%	South Korea	47.4%
France	18.6%	Italy	16.3%	Switzerland	14.9%	Canada	47.1%
Russia	18.5%	Mexico	16.1%	Netherlands	14.7%	Sweden	46.5%
Poland	18.3%	Un Kingdom	15.8%	AVERAGE	14.6%	Switzerland	46.3%
Switzerland	17.5%	Argentina	15.7%	Poland	14.5%	Norway	46.2%
Japan	16.7%	France	15.4%	Argentina	14.4%	Poland	46.2%
AVERAGE	16.3%	Spain	15.1%	China	14.4%	AVERAGE	45.4%
Brazil	16.1%	Germany	14.8%	Japan	14.4%	Brazil	45.3%
Greece	15.9%	Finland	14.6%	South Korea	14.3%	Australia	45.0%
South Korea	15.7%	AVERAGE	14.5%	Greece	13.9%	Chile	44.7%
China	15.5%	South Africa	14.5%	Sweden	13.9%	Argentina	44.4%
South Africa	15.5%	Greece	14.3%	Chile	13.7%	United States	44.3%
India	15.3%	Brazil	13.9%	Germany	13.7%	India	44.2%
Germany	15.1%	China	13.9%	United Kingdom	13.7%	United Kingdom	44.2%
Australia	15.0%	Switzerland	13.9%	Mexico	13.3%	Japan	44.1%
Canada	14.9%	Russia	13.7%	United States	13.3%	Greece	44.1%
United Kingdom	14.7%	Sweden	13.5%	Italy	13.0%	China	43.8%
United States	14.6%	Poland	13.4%	South Africa	13.0%	Germany	43.6%
Argentina	14.3%	Japan	13.0%	Australia	12.9%	Mexico	43.0%
Mexico	13.6%	Denmark	12.8%	Spain	12.8%	Russia	43.0%
Italy	13.5%	Norway	12.8%	Norway	12.6%	South Africa	43.0%
Spain	13.5%	Netherlands	12.7%	India	12.4%	Italy	42.8%
Chile	12.9%	Portugal	11.7%	Russia	10.8%	Spain	41.4%

Note: Weights are derived from the Driver Analysis (see Exhibits 1 and 2). Each weight represents unique contribution of given dimension to explaining companies' reputation. The CSR Index weight is a sum of weights for citizenship, governance and workplace dimension weights.

Figure 4.3   Importance (driver weights) of citizenship, governance, and workplace dimensions by country

Source: Global Reputation Pulse, Reputation Institute. Copyright © Reputation Institute. All rights reserved. Adapted from Mirvis, P. H. et al., *Building Reputation Here, There, and Everywhere*. Reputation Institute and Boston College Center for Corporate Citizenship, 2009.

The highest weights given to governance—*behaving ethically and being open and transparent*—are found in emerging global business markets (Chile, Mexico, India) and in the most advanced countries with Anglo-Saxon capitalism (Australia, Canada, US, UK). What accounts for this? Consumers in these emerging markets may be especially sensitive to ethics as their corporations gain more power and have the potential to do more harm with misbehavior. Scandals by companies in emerging markets naturally reinforce the importance of governance in the public's mind. The same is true in the Anglo-Saxon countries where corporate scandals are given a high profile in the media. Note how South Koreans—who have witnessed repeated misdoings by their biggest companies—also see corporate governance as a significant driver of reputation.

The relative weight assigned to citizenship versus governance may also have something to do with the freedom of business versus its regulation in particular countries.

For example, the "cowboy capitalism" practiced in the US and other English-speaking countries emphasizes self-regulation by business. This may make the public especially attentive to corporate ethics. By contrast, stronger social norms ("soft governance") and the regulatory environment in Northern Europe put more constraints on business conduct. Not surprisingly, the public in Denmark, Norway, and the Netherlands, who put a high value on citizenship in judging their companies, don't put near as much stress on ethics, openness, and transparency—where this is more or less expected from firms.

Finally, when it comes to the workplace—*how companies treat their people*—the Fins and Danes stand out along with the Portuguese in putting a heavy emphasis on it when judging companies. It's much less of a driver in the UK and US where decent working conditions are more or less expected from employers. Interestingly, the Russians, who give some primacy to corporate citizenship in reputational ratings compared to other nations, put less stress on the workplace. The same pattern is found in Norway.

CORPORATE REPUTATION VERSUS CSR SCORES

Overall, there is a strong, positive alignment between Global Pulse reputation ratings of corporations and their CSR Index scores in almost every country in this study (Figure 4.4 displays this relationship graphically in terms of ranks of the countries 1–27 on the two scores). The power of CSR as a reputational driver is plain: the public in nations that give their companies high marks on CSR tend to trust, admire, and respect them. And the public in nations that think less of their companies overall tend to give them lower CSR scores. There is, however, by no means a one-to-one correspondence between these ratings. Remember, this relationship is influenced a) the statistical error involved in any measurement, b) the weights attached to other reputational drivers, and c) distinctions people make between their feelings about a company overall and perceptions of its ethics, citizenship, and how it treats its employees.

A cursory look at this chart shows there are some significant gaps between reputation and CSR ratings in select countries. South Africans, for example, rank their firms comparatively high on CSR but have much lower regard for them. The same pattern, albeit with lower ratings on both scales, is found for Greece. On the other side, the public in Spain and Latin America—Chile, Argentina, and Brazil—have more positive feelings about their companies overall than they do about their CSR performance.

What are the implications of these comparative ratings? Obviously where there are significant gaps between ratings of reputation and CSR, companies can reduce them by 1) *strengthening their CSR performance* and/or 2) *strengthening, in stakeholder's mind, the relationship between CSR and company reputational overall*. This twin prescription is especially relevant to firms operating in nations where firms are scored relatively low on overall reputation and on CSR. This includes developing global business markets, like Mexico and China, and mature ones like Australia and to some degree the UK, Germany, and Switzerland. The broader point is that is that strengthening CSR has the potential to yield reputational rewards to firms wherever they operate around the world.

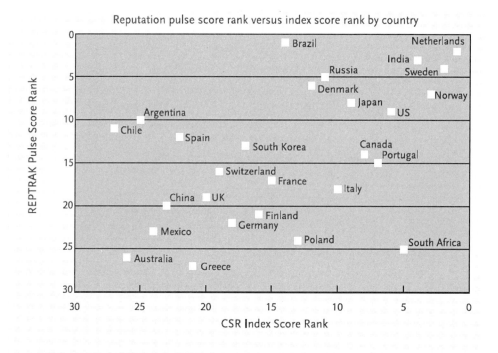

Figure 4.4 **Reputation pulse score rank versus index score rank by country**

Source: Global Reputation Pulse, Reputation Institute. Copyright © Reputation Institute. All rights reserved. Adapted from Mirvis, P. H. et al., *Building Reputation Here, There, and Everywhere*. Reputation Institute and Boston College Center for Corporate Citizenship, 2009.

On Managing Reputation and Social Responsibility Globally

Partly because of rising stakeholder expectations and partly because of the evident payoff in reputation and returns, many firms are striving to improve their social and environmental performance, governance, and workplace practices. On the social front, for instance, there has been growth in strategic corporate philanthropy, in business-relevant volunteering, and in cause-related marketing. More firms are "greening" their plants and products and reducing their carbon footprints. Corporate governance reform continues to evolve. And innovations in work–life programs, flextime, and such complement other CSR-type initiatives aimed at working people.

Doing CSR on a global stage adds complexity to all of this. Strategic and value choices have to be made at the enterprise level. Should, for example, CSR policies and practices developed in the context of laws and expectations in the US and Europe be extended to operations throughout Asia, Africa, and Latin America? Does this mean applying world class standards to governance and environmental management everywhere a firm does business or just where it's required by rule or custom? How much should companies invest in social programs on a global versus regional or local scale? Such decisions are surely informed by internal corporate values and codes of conduct. But careful consideration of how much they will pay off in terms of reputational gains and other business benefits is an important strategic consideration.

At the operating level, there's the challenge of engaging stakeholders and factoring their inputs into design and delivery decisions (see Freeman et al., 2008). What's most relevant to consumers, employees, and civil society organizations? Should these inputs be gathered globally or in-country? To what extent should programs be pushed out globally versus tailored to social and environmental priorities in distinct locales and markets around the world? Here, too, corporate values have to be clarified and strategic directions and priorities set. In turn, tradeoffs may have to be made in light of what matters most to different stakeholders; and with the respect to the commercial question: where's the biggest bang for the buck?

Scholars are only beginning to study the linkages between reputation management and CSR and there are not a lot of well-tested corporate practices on how to integrate these two thrusts. There are nevertheless some guidelines on how to build a CSR strategy that improves business performance and corporate reputation (see Porter and Kramer, 2006; Schultz and Hatch, 2006; Mirvis and Googins, 2008). To begin, this is not simply a matter of a firm taking sensible actions and then publicizing how improved performance serves to benefit both the business and society. Rather it is taking a holistic approach to reputing and CSR that takes account of and often engages directly a firm's multiple stakeholders in clarifying expectations, setting directions, and shaping actions in each relevant reputational domain (see Figure 4.5).

Figure 4.5   Using CSR to drive improvements in reputation

Source: Global Reputation Pulse, Reputation Institute. Copyright © Reputation Institute. All rights reserved. Adapted from Mirvis, P. H. et al., *Building Reputation Here, There, and Everywhere*. Reputation Institute and Boston College Center for Corporate Citizenship, 2009.

1. IDENTIFY AND ENGAGE STAKEHOLDERS

The world's most progressive companies in CSR, such as Royal Dutch Shell, Novo Nordisk, IBM, General Electric, BBVA and others have developed a core competence in stakeholder engagement and regularly work with panels of stakeholders on key issues pertaining to community needs, environmental challenges, transparency, human rights, and economic and social development. On a global scale, this means engaging stakeholders in key regions or nations in which a firm does business and factoring these inputs into global *and* local strategies.

Studies show that investors, not surprisingly, are most concerned with financial performance, and certainly how products and services and innovations might affect corporate growth and return on capital (Bonini et al., 2009). These reputational dimensions would naturally be part of a firm's engagement with them. At the same time, investors are also quite interested in corporate ethics and transparency (governance is a significant risk factor) and more are honing in on social and environmental performance for the same reasons (citizenship is also a risk factor and a proxy for how well a firm is managed).

The media and regulators, by comparison, might focus on products and services and also on citizenship, governance, and workplace factors as these mirror the public's prime interests and their regulatory scope respectively. Select non-governmental organizations, in turn, might be more or less interested in one or another of the seven reputation dimensions.

Stakeholder consultation is core to determining what's most relevant to corporate constituents and to deciding what to invest in, how much, and where. As a start, however, global scans and multi-country data sets can be especially useful in seeding consultations and helping practitioners estimate to what extent CSR investments might improve their reputations. On this count, there are some global data on employee and customer expectations.

In one of its annual surveys, Reputation Institute asked what extent people would "prefer to work for a company that is known for its social responsibility." On average, two thirds of those polled in some 25 countries would "prefer to work for a company that is known for its social responsibility." The highest interest (based on globally adjusted scores) was shown in Norway, South Korea, Germany, Finland, Denmark, and Poland—all highly industrialized countries. The least interest was found in the UK, US Mexico, France, India, South Africa, and Australia. All of this ranking is relative—interest levels in working for a socially responsible company across the countries ranged from a low of 50 percent of the populace to a high of 80 percent.

How about consumer's views of CSR? How does it factor into their buying behavior (see Bhattacharya and Sen, 2004)? On this point, Reputation Institute data shows that, on average, roughly 40 percent of consumers have personally "refused to buy the products of a company that was not socially responsible." Consumers most apt to make this claim are again found in Finland and Scandinavia, and South Korea. The Italians and Chinese, who don't especially prefer to work for a socially responsible company, say in comparatively large numbers that they have chosen not to buy products from an irresponsible firm. Consumers in Japan, the UK, and the US are in the middle of the pack on this dimension. Relatively fewer consumers in South Africa, India, Mexico, and Chile say that they have boycotted a product because of CSR issues.

2. UNDERSTAND EXPECTATIONS OF BUSINESS

More general but relevant data is available about expectations of business in various countries around the world. This data can inform a company's understanding of the business climate in markets of interest. In one of its Global Pulse studies, Reputation Institute asked the world about its expectations of corporate conduct. Specifically, the public was asked to what extent companies should: 1) *Provide assistance to local communities where they operate?* 2) *Be concerned about the personal well-being of their employee?* and 3) *Not support initiatives that are unethical, even if they are legal?* The research team combined these expectations to compute a TCE (Total Corporate Expectations) Index. The global average for each question registered strong support from between 80 to 90 percent of the public. This reinforces the main point that the world expects CSR from companies. Still, there are local differences in degree of expectations across the countries sampled.

Firms that want to find what matters most to their stakeholders can gather and mine data like these to get a sharper picture of CSR expectations around the world. Obviously, more detailed surveys among targeted stakeholder groups can yield a clearer picture of how, for example, a firm's employees, consumers, and other relevant groups think about social responsibility and the other dimensions of corporate reputation. This global data is a starting point, but not a substitute for more hands-on engagement with stakeholders in these regards.

3. CONSIDER COMPANY VISION AND VALUES

Even as companies gather an "outside in" perspective on what society expects of them, equal attention has to be given to understanding the firm's vision and values and how these play together with what stakeholders want. Here's when an "inside out" perspective fits into the strategic calculus.

Scholars emphasize that reputational strategy, like CSR strategy, emerges from a "conversation" between a company and its stakeholders that takes place in the context of a firm's strategic vision and aims. Branding experts refer to this new orientation as *enterprise branding* (see Hatch and Schultz, 2009). This orientation calls for the redesign of organizations to emphasize the brand in the full portfolio of corporate interactions, not only in marketing and communication campaigns, but also in product and service innovations, and in the firm's engagement with relevant social and environmental issues. New models of employee, community, and stakeholder engagement dovetail neatly with the idea of enterprise branding. When CSR is added to enterprise branding, for instance, this conversation extends to the development and delivery of healthier, socially useful, and sustainable products and services at every stage of the value chain from sourcing to disposal (see Hatch and Mirvis, 2010). The challenges both branding and CSR face are to deliver corporate social innovations that their stakeholders desire *and* that fit the values and style of the brand.

4. IDENTIFY PERFORMANCE GAPS

One key to improving CSR performance and reputation is to locate and redress gaps between expectations and performance. Polling data on national expectations of business and ratings of its performance have a place in corporate management of reputation and

CSR. It can serve as a "wake up" call about, say, a loss of trust or confidence in business in select regions. Or it can signal, more specifically, CSR challenges in entering into new markets or not keeping pace with changing expectations in established ones.

The Reputation Institute global data provides a global picture of potential performance gaps. We compared the public's ratings of their *general expectations of business* in the various countries with *ratings of the performance of specific companies* on citizenship, governance, and the workplace. In ranking across the nations, several high expectation versus low performance gaps stand out:

- German's expectations about the workplace (7th) versus low corporate ratings (24th).
- Argentina's expectations about citizenship (7th) versus low corporate ratings (26th).
- South Korean's expectations about governance (8th) versus low corporate ratings (24th).
- Australian's expectations about all aspects of CSR (2nd) versus low corporate ratings (26th).

Obviously, these would be target areas for CSR activity for companies in these nations. In other countries, there is more alignment between expectations and performance— for better and worse. For instance, we find lower expectations and performance ratings for CSR in China, Mexico, and Chile (in the lower third on both measures), mid-range expectations and performance scores in France, Poland, and Brazil, and slightly higher scores on both counts in Japan and Canada. The public and companies in Norway and Sweden match on high expectations and high performance ratings.

5. TAKING STRATEGIC ACTION TO REDUCE GAPS

Any manager knows that implementing any program to use CSR to drive improvements in business performance and reputation is no mean feat. Effective reputation and CSR management involves new levels of cooperation between multiple departments within a firm, and with external consultants and contractors as well. This means breaking down silos within a firm between, say, investor and community relations, public affairs, environmental, health, and safety, human resources, and communication functions. And many matters require close coordination with marketing, product development and stewardship, and other business functions.

There are also important corporate and national culture elements to consider when attempting to improve reputation through CSR. On the supply side, for instance, companies whose actions and messaging are seen as distinct, authentic, and "true to the brand" tend to score best on brand trackers and reputation ranking systems. On the demand side, in turn, the public and savvy NGOs and media monitors are wary of and vocal about empty PR exercises and "greenwashing." One implication, then, is that companies need to think through how they want to configure CSR in their home market and around the world. Another is that they need to gain a more sophisticated understanding of how CSR initiatives "work" on a global and local level.

On this first point, Gardberg and Fombrun (2006) argue that citizenship programs are strategic investments comparable to advertising and R&D. As such there are global and local dimensions to consider when devising a CSR and reputing strategy. On one side, for instance, a case can be made that a company's CSR platform should originate from its *"home"* market and thus reflect core competencies, brand traditions, and home cultural inputs. This adds to its authenticity and to its global differentiation versus other firms. On the other side, a case can be made that a firm's CSR strategy be adapted to *"host"* markets where, after all, there are different requirements, expectations, and needs in play ...

Take a company based in a market with lower expectations for CSR. It might choose to fit in its local market by simply meeting these expectations. But what happens when it moves into a higher expectation host market? Here it would be expected to increase its CSR investments. Thus many Japanese, Korean, and Indian firms moving into the US and Europe have had to expand their CSR agendas accordingly.

How about a company operating in a relatively high expectation home market? US firms tend to rank highly in a home market that expects a lot from companies. Moving into a lower expectation market, such firms might lower their CSR attention and investments. This may sound sensible buts it's risky. Look, for example, at how Nike, Home Depot, and others were pilloried for exploiting people and natural resources in their global supply chains. In these instances, a host country may not have expected or been in a position to demand higher CSR from a company but the world expected better and corporate reputations suffered. This is why many of the world's leaders in CSR have chosen to operate as global corporate citizens.

6. COMMUNICATE CREDIBLY

Even with country differences in rankings and weightings of CSR, there is a worldwide appetite for it. GlobeScan, for instance, finds that the majority of people in every country it surveys are very interested in "learning more about the ways companies are trying to be more socially responsible." This runs from a high of 90 percent in Mexico to 78 percent in the US to 68 percent in South Korea to 56 percent in Russia. The challenge for companies is to communicate credibly about CSR in countries where there is interest in but endemic skepticism about what companies are up to.

In this Reputation Institute data set, we found some interesting relationships between the public's ratings of a company's CSR and its credibility as a communicator. The global survey asked the public to rate a company's communication in terms of visibility, distinctiveness, consistency, transparency, sincerity, and responsiveness. Looking across the 27 countries, we found a correlation of .57 between ratings of CSR and the six communication factors summed together

In media-savvy markets, the public is increasingly interested in the CSR performance of companies. A Fleishman-Hillard/National Consumer's League (2007) survey found that some 54 percent of US consumers seek out information "sometimes" about the social responsibility of particular companies. Increasingly, they are turning to the internet to search for information. Interestingly, over half of the consumers surveyed turned to the websites of independent groups, such as consumer-watch groups or accrediting agencies, to garner data, a substantial increase from prior years. When it comes to judging the credibility of data, consumers favor independent (cited by 43 percent as credible) versus company websites (cited by 29 percent). The most credible sources are personal experience (cited by 60 percent) and word of mouth (56 percent).

7. MEASURE, ASSESS, CORRECT

It was noted earlier that companies can reduce the gaps between stakeholder expectations, ratings of CSR and its connection to reputation by 1) *strengthening their CSR performance* and/or 2) *strengthening, in stakeholder's mind, the relationship between CSR and company reputational overall*. Here's how these prescriptions' might pay off for a global company that has used CSR to improve its reputation in different parts of the world.

Figure 4.6 shows the overall positive relationship between citizenship and reputation pulse ratings across the globe. Assume, for the sake of illustration, that these represent public ratings of one company doing business globally. Assume, too, that it adopted an activist strategy and improved its CSR performance. How would you document the result? The dotted lines in this graph show the current intersection between 1) ratings of its citizenship (environmental and social performance) and 2) its overall reputation at the mean of each scale (X1). Now suppose in a subsequent measurement, the company improved perceptions of its citizenship globally (from 58.5 to 60.5 or one standard deviation). This would improve its mean reputation rating (X2) accordingly (from 63.0 to 65.0).

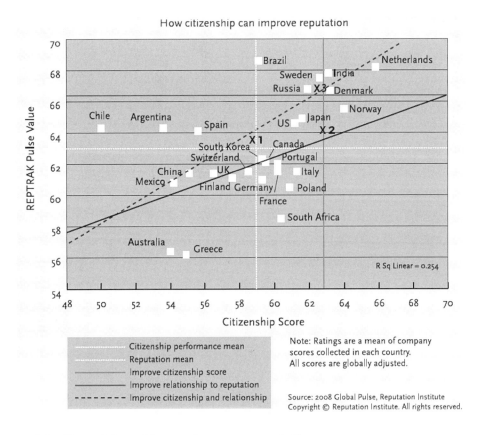

Figure 4.6   How citizenship can improve reputation

Source: Global Reputation Pulse, Reputation Institute. Copyright © Reputation Institute. All rights reserved. Adapted from Mirvis, P. H. et al., *Building Reputation Here, There, and Everywhere*. Reputation Institute and Boston College Center for Corporate Citizenship, 2009.

Now assume that a company not only improves in its ratings of citizenship, but that the driver weight of citizenship as a predictor of reputation also increases (represented as a dotted line with a higher slope). Given a higher rating of citizenship, and an increase in the relationship between citizenship and reputation, a firm's global reputation rating (X3) would increase even more (from 63.0 to nearly 66.5).

While this is only a hypothetical example (using real data), it shows how a company can use survey tools to track its CSR performance globally and in different markets. It's possible, too, to even put an economic value on reputation improvements (or declines) by, for instance, assigning a value to reputation (estimates are that reputation accounts for between 4 and 8 percent of a firm's market value). These are the tools by which companies track their product and innovation performance. Why not CSR?

Obviously good CSR performance, when communicated effectively, can yield increases in public perceptions of a firm. But is it possible to increase the linkage between ratings of CSR and Reputation in the public's minds? There is organic movement afoot as a global appetite for CSR by companies has made the CSR → Reputation linkage more salient (and strong CSR "driver weight" in predicting reputation shows). Research is needed to show whether the linkage is even stronger among select stakeholders like, for instance, members of the Millennial Generation born 1978–98 who are entering and moving up in companies today. *The Cone Millennial Cause Study* (Cone Inc./AMP Insights, 2006) found that over three of four young people who are part of or entering the US workforce want to work for a company that "cares about how it impacts and contributes to society." The relationship may well be stronger also among growing numbers of ethical consumers worldwide who make a strong connection between CSR and the brands they purchase.

A case could be made, of course, that perhaps a company need not improve its CSR to enhance its reputation, but rather choose to improve and emphasize more so its products and services, innovativeness, leadership and financial performance—the other reputational drivers. In our estimation, this argument falls short on two dimensions. First, there is considerable evidence that the public expects and even demands social responsibility from companies in every nation in this sample. Failing to improve on this front risks losing public support and dampening a company's reputation. Second, public perceptions of the various facets of a company are inter-related and mix both cognition and emotions. Thus, failing to meet to meet the public's expectations for social responsibility could, in turn, affect not only depress the "likeability" of a company overall, but even judgments about its products, leadership, and so on.

In short, when it comes to reputation, CSR matters now and offers firms a chance to use their CSR performance to differentiate themselves among stakeholders and drive reputational improvements around the world.

References

BCCCC (2009). *The State of Corporate Citizenship in the U.S.* Boston, MA: BCCCC.

Bhattacharya C. B. and S. Sen. (2004). "Doing Better at Doing Good: When, Why, and How Consumers Respond to Corporate Social Initiatives." *California Management Review*, 47/1: 9–24.

Bonini, S., G. Hintz, and L. T. Mendonca. (2008). Addressing Consumer Concerns About Climate Change. *The McKinsey Quarterly*, March, accessed November 28, 2010 at ttps://www.mckinseyquarterly.com/Addressing_consumer_concerns_about_climate_change_2115.

Bonini, S., T. M. Koller, and P. H. Mirvis. (2009). Valuing Social Responsibility. *McKinsey on Finance*, 32 (Summer): 11–18.

Cone Inc./AMP Insights. (2006). *The 2006 Cone Millennial Cause Study*, October 24, accessed November 28, 2010 at http://www.coneinc.com/stuff/contentmgr/files/0/b45715685e62ca5c6c eb3e5a09f25bba/files/2006_cone_millennial_cause_study_white_paper.pdf .

Edelman Trust Barometer. (2010). Accessed November 28, 2010 at http://www.edelman.com/ trust/2010/docs/2010_Trust_Barometer_Executive_Summary.pdf .

EIRIS. (2007). *The State Of Responsible Business: Global Corporate Response to Environmental, Social and Governance (ESG) Challenges*, accessed November 28, 2010 at http://www.eiris.org/files/ research%20publications/stateofespbusinessexecsumsep07.pdf.

Fleishman Hillard/National Consumers League (2007), *Rethinking Corporate Social Responsibility*, May, accessed November 28, 2010 at http://fleishmanhillard.com/wp-content/uploads/2007/05/ csr_white_paper.pdf.

Freeman, R. W., J. S. Harrison, and A. C. Wicks. (2007). *Managing for Stakeholders*. New Haven, CT: Yale University Press.

Gardberg, N. A. and C. J. Fombrun. (2006). Corporate Citizenship: Creating Intangible Assets across Institutional Environments. *Academy of Management Review*, 31(2): 329–46.

GERN (2008). *Corporate Citizenship around the World*. Boston: Global Education Research Network and Center for Corporate Citizenship.

GlobeScan (2001–2010). *Corporate Social Responsibility Monitor*, accessed November 28, 2010 at http://www.globescan.com/csrm_overview.htm.

GolinHarris (2004–2009). *"Doing Well by Doing Good: The Trajectory of Corporate Citizenship in American Business,"* accessed November 28, 2010 at http://www.golinharris.com/resources/gh/ flash/The%20Buck%20Stops%20Here.pptx.pdf.

Googins, B, P. H. Mirvis, and S. Rochlin. (2007). *Beyond "Good Company": Next Generation Corporate Citizenship*. New York: Palgrave.

Hatch, M. J. and P. H. Mirvis. (2010). Corporate Branding and CSR: Design Considerations, In T. Thatchenkery, D. Cooperrider, and M. Avital (eds.). *Positive Design and Appreciative Construction: From Sustainable Development to Sustainable Value*. Advances in Appreciative Inquiry, v. 4. New York: Emerald, 35–56.

Hatch, M. J. and M. Schultz, (2008). *Taking Brand Initiative: How Companies Can Align Strategy, Culture, and Identity through Corporate Branding*. San Francisco, CA: Jossey-Bass.

Hill and Knowlton and Crown Ferry International. (2006). *Return on Reputation: Corporate Reputation Watch*, accessed November 28, 2010 at www2.hillandknowlton.com/crw/downloads.asp.

Mirvis, P. H. and B. Googins. (2008). *Moving to Next Generation Corporate Citizenship*. Berlin: Centrum for Corporate Citizenship Deutschland.

Porter M. E. and M. Kramer. (2006). Strategy and Society: The Link between Competitive Advantage and Corporate Social Responsibility. *Harvard Business Review*, December, 2–15.

Porter, M. E. and M. R. Kramer. (2002). The Competitive Advantage of Corporate Philanthropy. *Harvard Business Review*, December, 5–16.

Schultz, M. and M. J. Hatch. (2006). The Cycles of Corporate Branding. *California Management Review*, 46 (1): 6–26.

Appendix: Global Pulse Measurement

The Global Pulse 2008 is the third annual study of the reputations of the world's largest companies. The study was developed by the Reputation Institute to provide executives with a high-level overview of their company's reputation with consumers. More than 60,000 online interviews with consumers in 27 countries on six continents were conducted in February and early March 2008. More than 150,000 ratings were used to create reliable measures of the corporate reputation of more than 1,000 companies. Rated companies had to have significant consumer presence and be minimally familiar to the general public. All companies are measured in their home country only.

Companies selected for inclusion in the Global Pulse 2008 met the following criteria: 1. They were among the largest companies in their country of origin based on the most recent record of their total revenues; 2. They engaged in commercial activities and so were not purely investment trusts or holding companies; 3. They were not wholly owned subsidiaries of another foreign company; 4. If they were large B-to-B companies, they were only included if they had reasonably high familiarity to the public.

Survey methodology. The Global Pulse 2008 was conducted online in all countries, except South Africa. The Global Pulse is a measure of corporate reputation calculated by averaging perceptions of four indicators of trust, esteem, admiration and good feeling obtained from a representative sample of at least 100 local respondents who were familiar with the company. All Global Pulse scores are standardized on both the country and global level. Scores range from a low of 0 to a high of 100.

Measure standardization. Market research shows that people are inclined to rate companies more or less favorably in different countries, or when they are asked questions directly or online. When asked in a personal interview, for example, it's known that people tend to give a company higher ratings than when they are asked by phone, or when they are asked to answer questions about the company online. This is a well-established source of "systematic bias." Another source of systematic bias comes from national culture—in some countries, people are universally more positive in their responses than in other countries. In statistical terms, it means that the entire distribution of scores in a "positive" country is artificially "shifted" because of this propensity for people in that country to give higher ratings to all companies, good or bad. The distribution of scores in that country may also be more spread out than in another because people have more information and are able to make more subtle differences between companies. To overcome these sources of systematic bias, Reputation Institute's policy is to adjust reputation scores by standardizing them against the aggregate distribution of all scores obtained from the RI's annual Global Pulse study. Standardization has the effect of lowering scores in countries where consumers tend to overrate companies, and has the effect of raising scores for companies in countries in which consumers tend to rate companies more negatively. The Reputation Institute uses its cumulative database of reputation scores measured internationally to carry out two adjustments:

1. *Country adjustment*: All scores derived from surveys are standardized by subtracting the country mean and dividing by the standard deviation of all known scores previously obtained in that country. In statistical terms, this adjustment "normalizes" the distribution of scores in the country to a mean of 0 and a standard deviation of 1, producing a "z-score" for the company.
2. *Global adjustment*: A global mean and standard deviation are calculated from all of the country-adjusted ratings. A Global Pulse score is scaled back by multiplying each company's z-score by the global standard deviation and adding back the global mean. The resulting number is the Global Pulse or Dimension score that is reported.

5

Organizational Identity, Corporate Social Performance and Corporate Reputation: Their Roles in Creating Organizational Attractiveness

KRISTIN B. BACKHAUS

At 3:00 p.m. on a Monday afternoon, managers of three Hyatt Hotels in Boston and Cambridge, Massachusetts, called a meeting of their housekeeping staff and fired all of them, outsourcing their jobs to a staffing firm in another state. The housekeepers, mostly female and mostly immigrants, had long tenure with the firm and were shocked. In a matter of minutes they found themselves left with small severance packages and no job. Within days, hotel workers around the United States were protesting Hyatt's actions, the governor of Massachusetts called for a boycott of Hyatt, and a labor union stepped in to represent the discharged workers. Within a week, Wikipedia entries and blogs around the world had information about Hyatt's actions (Whitford, 2009). With an active media, easy access to information online, and a scandal-oriented public, Hyatt's seemingly small local action presented a significant threat to their corporate reputation, their record of social responsibility and their attractiveness as an employer.

Corporate Reputation, Corporate Social Performance and Organizational Attractiveness

Corporate reputation is a coveted and carefully guarded intangible asset. It affects virtually every aspect of firm performance including customer satisfaction and loyalty, investor awareness, firm equity, and employee attraction and retention (Highhouse et al., 2009). Defined as a perceptual assessment of a company by external audiences (Fombrun, 1996), corporate reputation is built through activities that differentiate the organization from others in a positive way, and present a consistent image to the public (Fombrun, 1996). Research on reputation reveals a number of factors that drive reputation, with corporate social performance (CSP) consistently emerging as a compelling factor in the public's evaluation of reputation (Schnietz and Epstein, 2005). Corporate social performance is comprised of the activities of a firm that relate to treatment of employees, natural environment, workplace diversity, customers, product and other issues (Berman et al., 1999). As the opening vignette illustrates, even corporate decisions regarding staffing and outsourcing can be interpreted as a social performance issue, particularly when one stakeholder group has been adversely affected. Hence, corporate social performance is an area of particular concern with regard to reputation management (Fombrun, 2005).

Just as there are many factors that go into the formation of corporate reputation, reputation also affects organizational outcomes. A review of corporate financial records indicates that corporate reputation is significantly related to financial performance (Duhe, 2009). In a broader sense, reputation also affects the perceptions of attractiveness of a firm to multiple stakeholders including customers, investors and potential employees (Carmeli et al., 2006; Fombrun, 2001; Turban et al., 1998). Corporate social performance plays a role in these organizational outcomes as well. Research suggests that just as corporate social performance affects reputation; it also directly affects the attractiveness of an organization to customers, investors and potential employees (Backhaus et al., 2002; Marin and Ruiz, 2007; Wright et al., 1995).

Moreover, it is clear that corporate reputation plays a significant role in achieving competitive advantage (Fombrun, 1996), and that CSP is an important aspect of that reputation management process. Further, the organizational attractiveness that is developed as an outcome of a strong reputation enables the firm to access resources that provide the basis for the firm's strategy and profitability (Barney, 2001). This chapter presents a model of the relationships among these constructs and discusses their interrelationships.

Relationships among Constructs: A Design-Evaluation-Outcomes Model

This chapter is based on a design-evaluation-outcomes model like that presented by Martin (2009). The focal issues in the model are organizational identity, corporate social performance, corporate reputation and organizational attractiveness (See Figure 5.1). Within the design phase of the model are organizational identity and corresponding corporate social performance. The evaluation phase of the model includes the external evaluation of firm actions, which are the basis for development of legitimacy beliefs and corporate reputation. Organizational attractiveness is conceptualized as the outcome of the evaluation, and also as a feedback loop to the ongoing redefinition of organizational identity. We now turn to the issue of organizational identity.

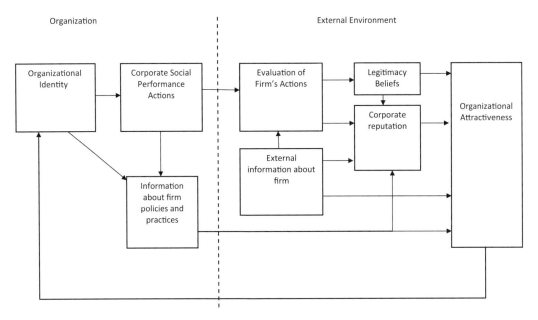

Figure 5.1   **Model of organizational identity, corporate social performance, corporate reputation and organizational attractiveness**

Organizational Identity

The founder of Zappos.com, Tony Hsieh, built his online shoe and apparel company around the belief that a happy workforce could create happy customers. Through an innovative process of employee selection and careful attention to the workplace environment, Hsieh was able to create an organizational identity focused on meeting customer needs. The employees were united around the belief in "personal emotional connection" with customers that came to define the company and each employee's job (Chafkin, 2009).

Organizational identity is defined as the central, enduring and distinctive character of an organization (Albert and Whetten, 2004) and the foundation of corporate reputation (Gioia et al., 2000; Scott and Lane, 2000). Albert and Whetten (2004) describe three important aspects of organizational identity:

- the essential character of the organization—its essence
- the differentiating aspects of the organization—how is it different from other firms?
- its longevity—identity is an aspect of an organization that remains fairly static over time.

Stated another way, organizational identity describes the way the members of the organization view it. It is the self-defined description of the firm as conceptualized by key members of the organization (Bromley, 2000). As illustrated in the Zappos example, both the founder, Hsieh, and his employees saw the firm as a customer service organization that happened to sell shoes. Hatch and Schultz (1997) describe organizational identity formation as a reciprocal process of sense making that occurs between organizational leaders and members in which top management guides the development of identity and members interpret and mold it. Hatch and Schultz (1997, p. 361) also address the role of external forces on organizational identity formation: "Who we are is reflected in what we are doing, and how others interpret who we are and what we are doing."

As part of the organizational identity formation process, firms make choices regarding how to self-categorize and how to position themselves relative to rival firms (King and Whetten, 2008). In the positioning process, firms seek to be distinctive enough to differentiate themselves from competitors, but similar enough to conform to industry norms (King and Whetten, 2008). Ultimately, the organizational identity process frames firm strategy development and tactical decision-making (Ravasi and Schultz, 2006). Organizational identity, therefore, is an action force (Dutton et al., 1994). As figure one indicates, corporate social performance is the focal set of actions examined here, so we now move on to that topic.

Corporate Social Performance

The Disney Corporation was ranked number one in 2009 for corporate social responsibility by the Boston College Center for Corporate Citizenship and Reputation Institute for its efforts to build strong governance practices, create positive working conditions, and support the needs of the community and environment. According to a spokesperson for the Reputation Institute, the public has increased its expectations for firms to be socially responsible, and corporate leaders perceive their firms' corporate social performance to be tied directly to their firm's reputation (CSRwire, 2009).

Corporate social performance (CSP) is the "configuration of principles of social responsibility, processes of responsiveness and policies, programs and observable outcomes as they relate to the firm's social relationships" (Wood, 1991, p. 693). CSP is voluntary action that has social or third-party effects (Schuler and Cording, 2006). CSP is an outcome-oriented construct, in keeping with the model presented in this chapter. Specifically, as discussed above, organizational identity decisions drive corporate actions and certain of these actions fall into the category of CSP.

The appropriateness of CSP is not embraced by all. Friedman, in his classic comment on CSP, said that for managers to focus on social concerns rather than strictly financial concerns is an abrogation of investors' trust (Friedman, 1970). On the other hand, some argue that CSP is a pre-requisite for establishing legitimacy with external audiences (Freeman, 1984).

Before discussing the relationship between corporate reputation and CSP, it is important to briefly review the evolution of the CSP construct. Most models of CSP used in academic and practitioner research today trace back to Carroll's (1979) theory. Carroll suggested that the firm assess its overall responsibility to society, identify social issues that needed to be addressed and prepare ways to respond. Using these three factors, he proposed a three-dimensional model of CSP. One dimension included philosophies of CSP that ranged from reactive to proactive. Second, he enumerated a set of social responsibilities: discretionary, ethical, legal and economic. Third, he identified a number of potential social issues that firms should consider when formulating social performance strategies (Carroll, 1979).

Building on Carroll's concepts, Wood (1991) developed the CSP model that is considered by most to be the seminal model in the literature. Wood presents a principles-processes-outcomes model. The underlying principles of CSP are legitimacy, public responsibility and managerial discretion. Processes of corporate social responsiveness are assessment of the environment, management of stakeholders and issue management. Outcomes of corporate behavior are social impacts, programs and policies (Wood, 1991). Wood's CSP model is significant to researchers for a number of reasons. First, it included the stakeholder view, which was absent from Carroll's model, and is particularly important when understanding the outcomes of corporate behavior. Second, it includes two important drivers of social actions, duty to the public and economic responsibility. Duty to the public is reflected in the principle of public responsibility. Economic constraints are implied through the institutional principle of legitimacy—firms behave in a socially responsible manner because the market restrains them from doing otherwise (Swanson, 1995).

Stakeholders are an important element of Wood's model, and central to the discussion here. Although Wood's model gave tacit recognition to stakeholders, hers is not a stakeholder model. Clarkson (1995) instead presents a framework for understanding corporate social performance using a stakeholder-based model. He gave voice to the notion that even though the corporation is designed to create and distribute value and wealth, there are stakeholders other than shareholders that need to be considered when developing corporate policies. By definition, a stakeholder is "any group or individual who can affect or is affected by the achievement of the organization's objectives" (Freeman, 1984, p. 46). As such, CSP should be perceived by the firm to be important to an audience that extends beyond financial stakeholders, and that this wider audience is evaluating firms' legitimacy on the basis of its actions. Should these stakeholders find that the firm does not have an acceptable level of CSP, they can withdraw from the firm just as shareholders might (Clarkson, 1995).

CSP IN ACTION

Corporate social performance is an objective characterization of the impact of corporate decisions on society (Clarkson, 1995). CSP ratings take into consideration both the intentional actions that firms take with regard to society (e.g., philanthropy, supporting social issues, etc.) and all other strategic actions taken as a part of their regular business operation (Clarkson, 1995). There are a variety of measures of CSP, most of them conducted by external rating agencies. For example, Kinder, Lydenberg, Domini (KLD) ratings measure social performance in seven qualitative areas: environment, community, corporate governance, diversity, employee relations, human rights and product quality/safety (KLD, 2009). The Boston College Center for Corporate Citizenship and Reputation Institute has a Corporate Social Responsibility Index that measures public perceptions of citizenship, governance, and workplace practices.

It is important to note that although CSP is measured objectively on the basis of particular agency criteria (which vary widely), CSP is constantly evolving. A firm's record of corporate social responsibility may change dramatically from one year to the next as a result of firm actions. Further, standards for CSP behavior also evolve over time; CSP is a normative construct and changes with stakeholder demands (de Quevedo-Puente et al., 2007).

Finally, while CSP is an objective measure of firm actions, it becomes important to our discussion when we examine both outcomes of those actions and stakeholder perceptions of those actions. Those perceptions are the forces that drive legitimacy beliefs, corporate reputation and ultimately, organizational attractiveness.

IMPLICATIONS OF CSP

Much research has been conducted to explicate the connections between corporate social performance and outcomes. The primary interest has been the exploration of a connection between firm CSP and financial performance. Researchers continue to seek support for the "doing well by doing good" hypothesis—in other words, better CSP records relate to better financial results. Although these studies have had mixed results, a few have found a positive link between financial performance and CSP (Callan and Thomas, 2009; Cochran and Wood, 1984; Coffey and Fryxell, 1991; Makni et al., 2009; Waddock and Graves, 1997).

Some clearer results have come from investigations of CSP and customer preferences. Creyer and Ross (1997) found that customers would bear higher prices from firms with higher CSP ratings. Brown and Dacin (1997) found a relationship between CSP and company and product evaluations, and Marin and Ruiz (2007) found a relationship between CSP and ratings of company attractiveness by consumers.

With regard to employees, there has not been a great deal of academic research to explore the implications of CSP on employees, although the practitioner literature contains a number of anecdotal observations (Van Buren, 2005). Among the few academic studies that have been conducted, researchers found a positive relationship between CSP and organizational commitment (Brammer et al., 2007) and job satisfaction (Peterson, 2004). There has been more work done with regard to potential employees, but that will be discussed later in the chapter.

Evaluation by Stakeholders

In 2008, Gap, Motorola and Apple began a joint philanthropic campaign to raise funds to benefit the Global Fund to Fight AIDS, Tuberculosis and Malaria. After a year and upwards of $100 million invested, the "RED" campaign has raised about $18 million and many questions. Because the campaign allowed the partners to profit from their charitable efforts, critics expect its poor performance to spur a backlash against the companies involved. Parodies of the campaign advised people to buy less and give more—directly to the charity (Frazier, 2007).

As the previous section suggests, stakeholders evaluate the corporate social performance records of firms. The experience of Gap, Motorola and Apple suggests that even a seemingly well-intentioned charitable campaign can be interpreted in an unfavorable light. It also illustrates that stakeholders receive their information about firm CSP from a number of sources. Customers shopping at Gap or Apple might have seen merchandise that was part of the Red campaign. They might have seen promotional advertisements for Red products in the media, or during television programming like the Grammy Awards

(Frazier, 2007). Or, they might have read more critical reviews of the Red campaign online or in newspapers.

Clearly, stakeholders have a wide variety of information sources from which to evaluate CSP efforts. Objective ratings of CSP are provided by agencies like KLD, Center for Corporate Citizenship or *Fortune* magazine. Stakeholders are also presented with information provided directly by the firm through carefully crafted messages designed by marketers, public relations officers, or human resource officers (Fombrun, 1996), or through the firm's corporate social performance officer. The messages conveyed through corporate communications are targeted to create intended images of the organization for specific stakeholders. By so doing, firms create multiple images that might include a general image, a market image or an employer image (Lievens et al., 2007).

Alternatively, stakeholders may receive information about firms' corporate social performance through their own direct experience with the firm as a consumer, job applicant, investor, supplier, etc. Or, they may receive information through general representations of the firm in the media. Studies show that information from external entities like the media contain stronger and more compelling messages than information provided by the firm (Gilly and Wolfinbarger, 1998; Yoon et al., 2006).

In summary, stakeholders use information garnered through multiple sources to evaluate corporate social performance as a means of drawing conclusions about the firms' legitimacy and corporate reputation. The next section touches briefly on the meaning of the term "legitimacy," and the way it relates to corporate reputation.

Legitimacy

Legitimacy is defined as congruence between an organization's goals, operating procedures and outcomes and the expectations of significant stakeholders (Lindblom, 1994). Institutional theory posits that in order to survive, firms must maintain legitimacy in the eyes of their stakeholders (Daft, 2008). Failure to maintain legitimacy can mean failure of the firm entirely (Shocker and Sethi, 1974). The struggle to maintain legitimacy in a rapidly changing environment requires the firm to continually perform environmental scanning and update its practices and procedures. Firm's corporate social performance plays a strong role in the development of legitimacy beliefs among stakeholders (de Quevedo-Puente et al., 2007). We need only look at the results of poor CSP records to see how quickly firms lose legitimacy in the eyes of stakeholders. After mishandling a contamination of its products in Belgium, Coca-Cola faced full loss of legitimacy in France, Belgium ,and Luxemburg. All three countries demanded that Coke withdraw its products (Regester, 2002).

The struggle to maintain legitimacy is tied directly to corporate reputation, in that a positive reputation cannot be developed without a firm first having met the minimum standards of organizational legitimacy (King and Whetten, 2008). We next discuss the formation, antecedents, and consequences of corporate reputation.

Corporate Reputation

"Corporate reputation" is defined as a "resilient and enduring evaluation anchored in core characteristics of the company" (Fombrun, 1996). It is a general and global (Highhouse et al., 2009) assessment of a firm, and is perceptual in nature (de Quevedo-Puente et al., 2007). Corporate reputation is an affective evaluation and is judged in relation to other firms (Fombrun and Shanley, 1990). A firm's reputation serves as a guarantor of future actions to external audiences (Fombrun, 2001).

The value of a positive reputation is explained by the resource based view (Fombrun, 1996). According to the resource-based view, firms acquire resources and develop unique capabilities as a result. Firms that acquire rare and valuable resources that are difficult to imitate or substitute are more readily able to achieve competitive advantage (Barney, 2001). Good reputations have strategic value for firms because they are rare, valuable and difficult to imitate (Roberts and Dowling, 1997). Further, firms have a greater chance of sustaining their superior performance if they have a good reputation (Roberts and Dowling, 1997). A positive corporate reputation improves an organization's ability to recruit a talented workforce (Turban and Greening, 1997). Positive corporate reputations are seen by some as a reservoir of good will, in that good will remains available to them as long as they keep their reputation clean (Fombrun, 2001; Schnietz and Epstein, 2005).

ANTECEDENTS OF CORPORATE REPUTATION

As the model suggests, corporate reputation is a perception formed on the basis of evaluation of a firm's actions. Legitimacy beliefs also inform the development of corporate reputation (King and Whetten, 2008). Research has identified the relationship between specific firm actions and attributes and corporate reputation. For example, Fombrun (1996, p. 186) illustrates the relationship between corporate reputation and six factors, showing positive relationships between reputation and profitability, charitable contributions, advertising and company size, and negative relationships between reputation and volatility and visibility in the media.

Financial performance is one of the most frequently noted and powerful antecedents of corporate reputation. Studies have shown that reputation is predicted by general financial performance measures (Preston and O'Bannon, 1997; Sobol and Farrelly, 1988), stock market returns and accounting based measures of financial performance (McGuire et al., 1988) and firm profitability (Cable and Graham, 2000; Turban and Greening, 1997).

Familiarity with a firm has also been shown to be related to positive reputation perceptions in a number of studies (Brooks et al., 2003; Cable and Graham, 2000; Cable and Turban, 2003). In a related vein, Cable and Graham (2000) and Fombrun and Shanley (1990) found that firm size was related to reputation, with larger firms having more positive reputations.

CSP AND CORPORATE REPUTATION

A Google search of corporate social performance yields thousands of web pages, many of which actually refer to corporate reputation. The reverse is also true. Both the general and academic literatures on corporate reputation often conflate the terms, or discuss them as virtually interchangeable constructs. To be clear, corporate social performance is an objective measure of activity, while corporate reputation is a perceptual evaluation of a firm (de Quevedo-Puente et al., 2007). However, their ties go beyond a simple conflation of terms. Firms that are strong social performers, able to adapt to different stakeholders, are able to strengthen and consolidate their corporate reputation (de Quevedo-Puente et al., 2007). Periods of homogeneous evaluations of a firm's social performance are linked closely to strong corporate reputation (Logdson and Wood, 2002).

More specifically, firms that embrace CSR standards have been shown to have more positive reputations (Fombrun 2005). Reputation is also related to involvement in social causes (Hess et al., 2002), philanthropic giving (Brammer and Millington, 2005) and community involvement (Brammer and Pavelin, 2006). In general, reputation is enhanced when firms conform to the social norms of their stakeholders (Fombrun and Shanley, 1990). Stakeholders expect a certain level of social responsibility, and firms that meet that expectation accrue more positive reputations.

Firms are awarded for outstanding records of corporate social performance by a variety of organizations. For example, as mentioned earlier, the Boston College Center for Corporate Citizenship—Reputation Institute recognizes outstanding performers in their CSR Index. *Fortune* magazine ranks global socially responsible organizations in their Global 500. Firms are also recognized for performance in specific dimensions of CSP. The Environmental Protection Agency, United Nations Environment Program, and Global Green USA are examples of agencies that confer awards on firms with outstanding performance in environmental management practices. According to Fombrun (1996), these awards are highly coveted and contribute significantly to corporate reputation. Fombrun (1996) suggests that rankings and awards provide important information to stakeholders about firm CSP that allow them to more closely examine and judge reputation.

CONSEQUENCES OF REPUTATION

As the resource-based view asserts, firms that acquire and cultivate resources that are rare, valuable and difficult to imitate are able to achieve competitive advantage (Barney, 2001). A strong corporate reputation is seen as a rare and valuable resource, providing firms with a form of intangible wealth (Keller, 1993). Reputation is a differentiator—allowing firms to highlight their differences from other firms, while attesting to their legitimacy within the industry (Deephouse and Carter, 2005; King and Whetten, 2008) While most research examines antecedents and correlates of reputation, there is empirical research that confirms reputation has a positive influence on financial performance and profitability (Flatt and Kowalczyk, 2008; Roberts and Dowling, 2002).

In the human resources domain, a number of studies have examined outcomes of corporate reputation. There is a positive relationship between reputation and size of applicant pool, the number of applicants bidding on jobs, and job pursuit intentions and behaviors among job seekers (Turban and Cable, 2003). Corporate reputation has also been found to positively impact applicant perceptions of recruiter behaviors and organizational attributes (Turban et al., 1998). Overall, reputation enhances organizational performance because it allows the firm to attract a wider applicant pool from which it can select higher quality employees (Belt and Paolillo, 1982; Gatewood et al., 1993) Better quality employees lead to better quality work output, and increased competitive advantage (Barney, 2001).

Organizational Attractiveness

The last piece of our model is an outcome variable, organizational attractiveness. As the previous discussion has shown, organizational identity drives decision and actions with regard to corporate social performance. These actions are evaluated by stakeholders to determine their beliefs regarding the legitimacy of an organization and ultimately its reputation.

Beliefs about reputation influence stakeholders' attraction to organizations, whether it be related to investing in the firm, purchasing product or services from the firm, or seeking employment with the firm. This section focuses on issues of organizational attractiveness from the job seeker's point of view.

There are two theories most frequently used to explain organizational attractiveness. The first is Fishbein and Ajzen's (1975) theory of planned behavior. This theory states that behavior is a function of intentions, which are driven by attitudes toward the behavior. Attitudes here relate to potential applicants feelings about the organization's attributes, and behavior is related to seeking employment with a firm (Highhouse et al., 2003). The second theory that supports an examination of organizational attractiveness is signaling theory. Signaling theory suggests that individuals use clues or bits of information provided by the firm to draw conclusions about the firm's future actions (Srivastava and Lurie, 2001). Job seekers use any available information to improve their efforts to make a wise decision (Wanous, 1992).

Recruitment researchers have done considerable exploration to determine the key factors that attract potential employees to their organization. Employment processes (Barber and Roehling, 1993), work values (Chatman, 1991), and recruiter characteristics (Rynes, 1990; (Rynes and Miller, 1983), influence attraction. Also, job and organizational attributes like compensation, work environment and type of work have a positive effect on attraction (Harris and Fink, 1987; Powell, 1984; Rynes and Miller, 1983; Taylor and Bergmann, 1987). Familiarity with the firm is related to attractiveness (Luce et al., 2001), as is the perception that mentorship will be provided (Spitzmueller et al., 2008).

While some researchers have pursued universal attractors, others have investigated a contingent variable in attraction, person-organization fit (PO fit). PO fit is a subjective judgment by job applicants of the extent to which their values mesh with the values of the firm (Kristof-Brown et al., 2005). These evaluations relate to their assessment of the extent to which the firm is going to be able to meet their personality and psychological needs (Harold and Ployhart, 2008). Perceived fit has been shown to affect both organizational attraction and job choice decisions (Bretz and Judge, 1994; Kristof-Browne, Jansen and Colbert, 2002). PO fit is consistent with a stakeholder evaluation model because it highlights the extent to which stakeholders use their own perceptual lens to judge the organization.

CORPORATE SOCIAL PERFORMANCE AS A PREDICTOR OF ATTRACTION

Because of the importance of CSP to stakeholders, researchers have investigated the role of firm CSP records in increasing organizational attractiveness. In general, CSP has a positive effect on attraction (Backhaus et al., 2002; Bauer and Aiman-Smith, 1996; Greening and Turban, 2000; Turban and Greening, 1997). Specifically, positive ecological ratings (Aiman-Smith et al., 2001) and pro-environmental stance (Bauer and Aiman-

Smith, 1996) increase attraction. Proactive diversity practices (Williamson et al., 2008), affirmative action policies (Smith et al., 2004; Wright et al., 1995) and gender and diversity management programs (Martins and Parsons, 2007) also affect attractiveness.

CORPORATE REPUTATION AS A PREDICTOR OF ATTRACTION

The role of corporate reputation in creating organizational attractiveness functions mainly through the process of social identification. Social identification derives from group identification (Ashforth and Mael, 1989). Individuals tend to identify themselves and others on the basis of the groups to which they belong (Ashforth and Mael, 1989). Belonging to the group confers the characteristics of the group to the individual (Ashforth and Mael, 1989). Belonging to a highly reputed organization confers positive characteristics to the individual, whether or not he or she actually possesses those characteristics. Naturally, people want to be identified with, and identified by, the positive attributes of their organization, so more highly reputed organizations become more attractive. Empirical research supports the connection between reputation and attraction (Highhouse et al., 2003; Zhang, 2008).

The Feedback Loop

The causal chain from organizational identity to organizational attractiveness doesn't end with attractiveness. Organizational attractiveness relates back to organizational identity, launching a virtuous cycle of potential organizational improvement. Organizational attractiveness creates a larger applicant pool for employers, and hence a better opportunity to select excellent employees. Highly skilled employees who are closely aligned with the values of the firm are more likely to identify with the firm and engage in behavior that supports the firm's mission and goals (Edwards, 2005). These employees help to drive forward actions that support the development of positive reputation, like corporate social performance, strong financial performance and profitability. Studies linking employee behavior to customer behavior (Rucci et al., 1998; Ulrich and Smallwood, 2005) illustrate these positive outcomes. These employees also serve as ambassadors of the firm carrying a positive message about the firm to external audiences (Edwards, 2005). The cycle repeats as firms maintain a positive reputation and strong attractiveness.

The presentation of the model in the chapter has described the ways in which organizational attributes relate to one another, and provide a framework for understanding reputation. There are practical considerations, however, that have not been addressed. The final section of the chapter presents and discusses these issues.

Corporate Reputation Issues

CORPORATE REPUTATIONS IN JEOPARDY

Between 2006 and 2008, seven out of 11 industries experienced declines in their reputations (Harris Interactive, 2008). More than 50 percent of America's most admired companies lost their top rankings over the past five years (Gaines-Ross, 2008). It seems that the overall reputation of corporations in America reached an all-time low in 2008 (Harris Interactive, 2008). The revelations of abuses in the banking industry and the resulting global economic downturn that occurred in 2008 and 2009 shook the faith of stakeholders around the world.

At that same time that corporate reputations declined, the recession claimed millions of jobs in the United States (Cook, 2009). So while organizations became less attractive as employers, there are also fewer jobs to choose from. Research on job choice suggests that job seekers place more weight on attributes related to person-organization fit when they have a greater number of job offers to choose among (Harold and Ployhart, 2008). Concern for organizational reputation also decreases when there are fewer job choices (Harold and Ployhart, 2008). This presents a contingency issue for the relationship between corporate reputation and organizational attraction. Research conducted during periods of high unemployment and weak job markets may find weaker connections between organizational attractiveness and CSP records, legitimacy, and corporate reputation.

However, at a time when corporate reputation has dipped precipitously, organizations cannot afford to overlook the importance of regaining their reputation, first to increase sales and investment, and second to rebuild a strong workforce. Gaines-Ross (2008) suggests that firms maintain attention to corporate values and high levels of communication during reputational crises. A firm that undermines its policies supporting a positive workplace environment, for example, will only further reduce its credibility with stakeholders.

Further research is required to understand the contingency factors that affect the link between reputation and attractiveness. What are the boundary conditions? At what point in an economic crisis do job seekers stop considering reputation when considering job offers? Are there particular reputational issues that have specific impact on job seekers? For example, do product issues, corporate philanthropy or environmentally proactive policies have the same effect on job seekers in a lean job market as they do under other circumstances? Can employers craft communications in such a way as to maintain their level of attractiveness despite a damaged reputation? Can organizations separate their employer images from their product or financial images, or is reputation only a unidimensional attribute?

THE RIGHT MESSAGE FOR THE RIGHT AUDIENCE

The stakeholder perspective is critical to understanding the links between organizational actions, corporate reputation and attractiveness. Stakeholders need information relevant to their own needs in order to make determinations about firms (Schuler and Cording, 2006). Job seekers are looking for information that will signal their potential future with a firm. Cues like a record of sustainable development including sensitivity to environmental concerns may suggest that an employer has integrity and strong standing in society. In fact, studies have found that positive environmental records are related to higher levels of employee commitment among current employees (Brammer et al., 2007). However, job seekers may be more concerned with "internal" social performance records like excellent working conditions, diversity programs, and support for families, and may be looking for cues from the organization that those conditions are present.

While it may be clear, and perhaps even self-evident, that messages need to be tailored to the appropriate stakeholder, the execution is not so simple. First, firms complain that it is difficult to get stakeholders to read their CSP reporting, even when they provide detailed information on their websites ("New Monthly Index", 2009). Second, messages about CSP, particularly with terms like sustainability, green, and environment confuse people because they do not know precisely what the firm means (*Greenbiz.com*, 2009). Further, people tend to give less credence to messages that emanate directly from the firm, and find external sources of information more believable (Yoon and Garban-Canli, 2003). This becomes a greater issue when there is a lack of congruence between external messages and those sent by the firm (Schuler and Cording, 2006).

So, what is a firm to do? The first step is to understand the stakeholder. What are the particular concerns of that stakeholder group? What are the minimum requirements for them to consider a firm legitimate? Second, going beyond legitimacy, what attributes does that stakeholder group consider highly respectable? Does the firm possess those attributes? If so, how can they be communicated? Ratings and rankings by external organizations provides one means of conveying accurate messages to targeted groups. There are lists of all kinds that cater to job applicants with varying needs: Fortune, Inc., Working Mother, Fast Company, and the Society for Human Resource Management are just a few of the organizations that provide employer ratings. In addition, there are much more specific ratings that address particular stakeholder needs, like the Human Rights Campaign, Diversity Edge, Asian Enterprise, and Hispanic Business. Each of these rating services provides employers with a list of criteria, which can be used developmentally as a means of developing strategies and actions consistent with stakeholder needs. Second, once they qualify for ranking, they can use these external sources of information to supplement and corroborate their own information, thereby strengthening the credibility of their message.

THE ROLE OF HUMAN RESOURCES

This chapter focuses on the implications of reputation for potential employees, so it is appropriate that the final issue raised in the chapter relate to the human resource function. Human resource research underpins the framework presented here, ranging from the resource based view, a strategic human resource model, to person-organization fit and recruitment issues. Friedman (2009) presents a model illustrating the ways in which the human resource (HR) management function can support corporate reputation development. For example, HR can provide employee development and training programs to enhance strategically important skills (Friedman, 2009). Second, HR can work as a member of the top management group to clarify its employee communications to make them consistent with, and supportive of, corporate mission and vision (Friedman, 2009). Put together, consistency of message and specific employee training programs help to create a workplace that supports the identity of the organization. Potential employees looking at these programs will have a realistic view of the organization's values, helping to improve person-organization fit at the organizational entry point. Friedman's (2009) model provides specific support to the model presented here, and also supports the cyclical properties of the model—the virtual cycle of corporate reputation and attractiveness.

Conclusion

Our information intensive culture makes the process of reputation management increasingly difficult. A carefully managed corporate reputation can be undermined in minutes, as the opening vignette illustrates. Firms can depend on the services of corporate reputation managers and public relations officers, but it is increasingly important to involve employees in the process of reputation building and management. This chapter has provided an overview of the relationships among the organizational attributes that affect reputation and ultimately, organizational attractiveness. Using this framework, firms can consider the decisions they make, they way in which they impact their reputation and their present and future workforce. The virtuous cycle that flows from identity to attractiveness can be leveraged to maintain a legitimate and robust corporate reputation.

References

Aiman-Smith, L., Bauer, T. N., and Cable, D. M. (2001). Are you attracted? Do you intend to pursue? A recruiting policy-capturing study. *Journal of Business and Psychology*, *16*(2), 219–37.

Albert, S., and Whetten, D. A. (2004). Organizational identity. In M. J. Hatch and M. Schultz (eds.), *Organizational Identity: A Reader* (pp. 89–118). Oxford, England: Oxford University Press.

Ashforth, B. E., and Mael, F. (1989). Social identity theory and the organization. *Academy of Management Review*, *14*, 20–39.

Backhaus, K. B., Stone, B. A., and Heiner, K. (2002). Exploring the relationship between corporate social performance and employer attractiveness. *Business and Society*, *41*(3), 292.

Barber, A. E., and Roehling, M. V. (1993). Job postings and the decision to interview: A verbal protocol analysis. *Journal of Applied Psychology*, *78*, 845–56.

Barney, J. B. (2001). Resource-based theories of competitive advantage: A ten-year retrospective on the resource-based view. *Journal of Management*, *27*(6), 643–50.

Bauer, T. N., and Aiman-Smith, L. (1996). Green career choices: The influences of ecological stance on recruiting. *Journal of Business and Psychology*, *10*, 445–58.

Belt, J. A., and Paolillo, J. G. P. (1982). The influence of corporate image and specificity of candidate qualifications on response to recruitment advertisement. *Journal of Management*, *8*(1), 105–12.

Berman, S., Wicks, A. C., Kotha, S., and Jones, T. (1999). Does stakeholder orientation matter? The relationship between stakeholder management models and firm financial performance. *Academy of Management Journal*, *42*(5), 488–505.

Brammer, S., and Millington, A. (2005). The effect of stakeholder preferences, organizational structure and industry type on corporate community involvement. *Journal of Business Ethics*, *45*, 213–26.

Brammer, S., Millington, A., and Rayton, B. (2007). The contribution of corporate social responsibility to organizational commitment. *International Journal of Human Resource Management*, *18*(10), 1701–19.

Brammer, S. J., and Pavelin, S. (2006). Corporate reputation and social performance: The importance of fit. *Journal of Management Studies*, *43*(3), 435–55.

Bromley, D. B. (2000). Psychological aspects of corporate identity, image and reputation. *Corporate Reputation Review*, *3*, 240–52.

Brooks, M. E., Highhouse, S., Russell, S. S., and Mohr, D. C. (2003). Familiarity, ambivalence, and firm reputation: Is corporate fame a double-edged sword? *Journal of Applied Psychology*, 88(5), 904.

Brown, T. J., and Dacin, P. A. (1997). The company and the product: Corporate associations and consumer product responses. *Journal of Marketing*, 61, 68–84.

Cable, D. M., and Graham, M. E. (2000). The determinants of job seekers' reputation perceptions. *Journal of Organizational Behavior*, 21(8), 929–47.

Cable, D. M., and Turban, D. B. (2003). The value of organizational reputation in the recruitment context: A brand-equity perspective. *Journal of Applied Social Psychology*, 33(11), 2244–66.

Callan, S. J., and Thomas, J. M. (2009). Corporate financial performance and corporate social performance: An update and reinvestigation. *Corporate Social Responsibility and Environmental Management*, 16(2), 61–78.

Carmeli, A., Gilat, G., and Weisberg, J. (2006). Perceived external prestige, organizational identification and affective commitment: A stakeholder approach. *Corporate Reputation Review*, 9(2), 92–104.

Carroll, A. B. (1979). A three-dimensional conceptual model of corporate performance. *Academy of Management Review*, 4(4), 497–505.

Chafkin, M. (2009). The Zappos way of managing. *Inc. Magazine*. Retrieved October 27, 2009 from http://www.inc.com/magazine/20090501/the-zappos-way-of-managing.html.

Chatman, J. A. (1991). Matching people and organizations: Selection and socialization in public accounting firms. *Administrative Science Quarterly*, 36, 459–84.

Clarkson, M. E. (1995). A stakeholder framework for analyzing and evaluating corporate social performance. *Academy of Management Review*, 20(1), 92–117.

Cochran, P. L., and Wood, R. A. (1984). Corporate social responsibility and financial performance. *Academy of Management Journal*, 27, 42–56.

Coffey, B. S., and Fryxell, G. (1991). Institutional ownership of stock and dimensions of corporate social performance. *Journal of Business Ethics*, 10, 437–44.

Cook, J. (2009). Small business gets its bailout. *Reuters Blog*, October 30. Retrieved October 31, 2009 from http://blogs.reuters.com/small-business/2009/10/30/small-business-gets-its-bailout/.

Creyer, E. H., and Ross, W. T., Jr. (1997). The influence of firm behavior on purchase intention: Do consumers really care about business ethics? *Journal of Consumer Marketing*, 14, 421–32.

CSRwire (2009). Disney and Microsoft Top List of 50 U.S. Companies Recognized as Leaders in Corporate Social Responsibility. *CSRwire* press release, October 28. Retrieved October 30, 2009 from http://www.csrwire.com/press/press_release/27944-Disney-and-Microsoft-Top-List-of-50-U-S-Companies-Recognized-as-Leaders-in-Corporate-Social-Responsibility.

Daft, R. L. (2008). *Organization Theory and Design, 8th edition*. Mason, OH: Southwestern Cengage.

de Quevedo-Puente, E., de la Fuente-Sabato, J. M., and Delgado-Garcia, J. B. (2007). Corporate social performance and corporate reputation: Two interwoven perspectives. *Corporate Reputation Review*, 10(1), 60–72.

Deephouse, D. L., and Carter, S. M. (2005). An examination of differences between organizational legitimacy and reputation. *Journal of Management Studies*, 42, 329–60.

Duhe, S. C. (2009). Good management, sound finances, and social responsibility: Two decades of U.S. corporate insider perspectives on reputation and the bottom line. *Public Relations Review*, 35(1), 77–8.

Dutton, J. E., Dukerich, J. M., and Harquail, C. V. (1994). Organizational images and member identification. *Administrative Science Quarterly*, 39(2), 239–64.

Edwards, M. R. (2005). Organizational identification: A conceptual and operational review. *International Journal of Management Reviews*, 7(4), 207–30.

Fishbein, M., and Ajzen, I. (1975). *Belief, Attitude, Intention and Behavior: An introduction to theory and research*. Reading, MA: Addison-Wesley.

Flatt, S. J., and Kowalczyk, S. J. (2008). Creating competitive advantage through intangible assets: The direct and indirect effects of corporate culture and reputation. *Advances in Competitiveness Research, 16*(1), 13–30.

Fombrun, C. (1996). *Reputation: Realizing Value from the Corporate Image*. Boston, MA: Harvard Business School Press.

Fombrun, C. (2001). Corporate reputations as economic assets. In M. Hitt, R. Freeman and J. Harrison (eds.), *Handbook of Strategic Management*. Oxford, England: Blackwell.

Fombrun, C. (2005). Building corporate reputation through CSR initiatives: Evolving standards. *Corporate Reputation Review, 8*(1), 7–11.

Fombrun, C., and Shanley, M. (1990). What's in a name? Reputation building and corporate strategy. *Academy of Management Journal, 33*, 233–58.

Frazier, M. (2007). Costly red campaign reaps meager $18 million. *Advertising Age*. Retrieved October 28, 2009 from http://adage.com/article?article_id=115287.

Freeman, E. (1984). *Strategic Management: A Stakeholder Approach*. Boston, MA: Pitman.

Friedman, B. (2009). Human resource management role: Implications for corporate reputation. *Corporate Reputation Review, 12*(3), 229–44.

Friedman, M. (1970). The social responsibility is to increase its profits. *New York Times Magazine*, September 30.

Gaines-Ross, L. (2008). How to avoid reputation stumbles. *PR Week*, February 25. Retrieved on October 30, 2009 from http://www.prweekus.com/How-to-avoid-reputation-stumbles/article/107172/.

Gatewood, R., Gowan, M., and Lautenschlager, G. (1993). Corporate image, recruitment image, and initial job choice decisions. *Academy of Management Journal, 36*, 414–27.

Gilly, M. C., and Wolfinbarger, M. (1998). Advertising's internal audience. *Journal of Marketing, 62*(1), 69–88.

Gioia, D. A., Schultz, M., and Corley, K. G. (2000). Organizational identity, image, and adaptive instability. *Academy of Management Review, 25*(1), 63–81.

Greenbiz.com. (2009). New monthly index reveals pent-up demand for green purchases. *Greenbiz.com*, press release. October 28. Retrieved October 31, 2009 from http://www.csrwire.com/press/press_release/28056-New-Monthly-Index-Reveals-Pent-Up-Demand-For-Green-Purchases.

Greening, D., and Turban, D. (2000). Corporate social performance as a competitive advantage in attracting a quality workforce. *Business and Society, 39*(3), 254–80.

Harold, C. M., and Ployhart, R. E. (2008). What do applicants want? Examining changes in attribute judgments over time. *Journal of Occupational and Organizational Psychology, 81*(2), 191–218.

Harris, M. M., and Fink, L. S. (1987). A field study of applicant reactions to employment opportunities: does the recruiter make a difference? *Personnel Psychology, 40*(4), 765–84.

Harris Interactive. (2008). Seventy-one percent of consumers say the reputation of corporate America is "poor", but consumers will buy, recommend and invest in companies that concentrate on building their corporate reputation. June 23. Retrieved from October 30, 2009 from http://www.harrisinteractive.com/news/allnewsbydate.asp?NewsID=1318.

Hatch, M. J., and Schultz, M. (1997). Relations between organizational culture, identity and image. *European Journal of Marketing, 31*(5/6), 356.

Hess, D., Rogovsky, N., and Dunfee, T. W. (2002). The next wave of corporate community involvement: Corporate social initiatives. *California Management Review, 44*, 110–25.

Highhouse, S., Broadfoot, A., Yugo, J. E., and Devendorf, S. A. (2009). Examining corporate reputation judgments with generalizability theory. *Journal of Applied Psychology, 94*(3), 782–9.

Highhouse, S., Lievens, F., and Sinar, E. F. (2003). Measuring attraction to organizations. *Educational and Psychological Measurement, 63*(6), 986–1001.

Keller, K. L. (1993). Conceptualizing, measuring, and managing customer-based brand equity. *Journal of Marketing, 57*(1), 1–22.

King, B. G., and Whetten, D. A. (2008). Rethinking the relationship between reputation and legitimacy: A social actor conceptualization. *Corporate Reputation Review, 11*(3), 192–207.

KLD (2009). KLD research methodology. Retrieved October 28, 2009, from http://www.kld.com/research/methodology.html.

Kristof-Brown, A.L., Jansen, K.J. and Colbert, A.E. (2002). A policy-capturing study of the simultaneous effects of fit with jobs, groups, and organizations. *Journal of Applied Psychology, 87*(5), October: 985–93.

Kristof-Brown, A. L., Zimmerman, R. D., and Johnson, E. C. (2005). Consequences of individuals' fit at work: a meta-analysis of person–job, person–organization, person–group, and person–supervisor fit. *Personnel Psychology, 58*(2), 281–342.

Lievens, F., Van Hoye, G., and Anseel, F. (2007). Organizational identity and employer image: Towards a unifying framework. *British Journal of Management, 18*, 45–59.

Lindblom, C. K. (1994). The implications of organizational legitimacy for corporate social performance and disclosure. Paper presented at the Critical Perspectives on Accounting Conference, New York, NY.

Logdson, J., and Wood, D. J. (2002). Reputation as an emerging construct in the business and society field: An introduction. *Business and Society, 41*(4), 365–70.

Luce, R. A., Barber, A. E., and Hillman, A. J. (2001). Good deeds and misdeeds: A mediated model of the effect of corporate social performance on organizational attractiveness. *Business and Society, 40*(4), 397.

Makni, R., Francoeur, C., and Bellavance, F.O. (2009). Causality Between Corporate Social Performance and Financial Performance: Evidence from Canadian Firms. *Journal of Business Ethics, 89*(3), 409–22.

Marin, L., and Ruiz, S. (2007). "I need you too!" Corporate identity attractiveness for consumers and the role of social responsibility. *Journal of Business Ethics, 71*(3), 245–60.

Martin, G. (2009). Driving corporate reputations from the inside: A strategic role and strategic dilemmas for HR? *Asia Pacific Journal of Human Resources, 47*(2), 219–35.

Martins, L. L., and Parsons, C. K. (2007). Effects of gender diversity management on perceptions of organizational attractiveness: the role of individual differences in attitudes and beliefs. *Journal of Applied Psychology, 92*(3), 865–75.

McGuire, J. B., Sundgren, A., and T., S. (1988). Corporate social responsibility and firm financial performance. *Academy of Management Journal, 31*, 854–72.

Peterson, D. K. (2004). The relationship between perceptions of corporate citizenship and organizational commitment. *Business and Society, 43*(3), 296–319.

Powell, G. N. (1984). Effects of job attributes and recruiting practices on applicant decisions: A comparison. *Personnel Psychology, 37*(4), 721–32.

Preston, L. E., and O'Bannon, D. P. (1997). The corporate social-financial performance relationship: a typology and analysis. *Business and Society, 36*(4), 419–30.

Ravasi, D., and Schultz, M. (2006). Responding to organizational identity threats: Exploring the role of organizational culture. *Academy of Management Journal, 49*(3), 433–58.

Regester, M. (2002). The role of corporate social responsibility in managing reputation. *Ethical Corporation*, February 25. Retrieved October 28, 2009 from http://www.ethicalcorp.com/content.asp?ContentID=48.

Roberts, P. W., and Dowling, G. R. (1997). The value of a firm's corporate reputation: How reputation helps attain and sustain superior profitability. *Corporate Reputation Review*, *1*, 72–5.

Roberts, P. W., and Dowling, G. R. (2002). Corporate reputation and sustained superior financial performance. *Strategic Management Journal*, *23*, 1077–93.

Rucci, A., Kirn, S., and Quinn, R. (1998). The employee customer profit chain at Sears. *Harvard Business Review* (January–February), 82–9.

Rynes, S. L., and Miller, H. E. (1983). Recruiter and job influences on candidates for employment. *Journal of Applied Psychology*, *68*(1), 147–54.

Schnietz, K. E., and Epstein, M. J. (2005). Exploring the financial value of a reputation for corporate social responsibility during a crisis. *Corporate Reputation Review*, *7*(4), 327–45.

Schuler, D. A., and Cording, M. (2006). A corporate social performance–corporate financial performance behavioral model for consumers. *Academy of Management Review*, *31*(3), 540–58.

Scott, S. G., and Lane, V. R. (2000). A stakeholder approach to organizational identity. *Academy of Management Review*, *25* (1), 43–62.

Shocker, A. D., and Sethi, S. P. (1974). An approach to incorporating social preferences in developing corporate action strategies. In S. P. Sethi (ed.), *The Unstable Ground: Corporate social policy in a dynamic society* (pp. 67–80). Los Angeles, CA: Melville Publishing Company.

Smith, W. J., Wokutch, R. B., Harrington, K. V., and Dennis, B. S. (2004). Organizational attractiveness and corporate social orientation: Do our values influence our preference for affirmative action and managing diversity? *Business and Society*, *43*(1), 69–96.

Sobol, M. G., and Farrelly, G. (1988). Corporate reputation: A function of relative size or financial performance? *Review of Business and Economic Research 24*, 45–59.

Spitzmueller, C., Neumann, E., Spitzmueller, M., Rubino, C., Keeton, K. E., Sutton, M. T., et al. (2008). Assessing the influence of psychosocial and career mentoring on organizational attractiveness. *International Journal of Selection and Assessment*, *16*(4), 403–15.

Srivastava, J. N., and Lurie, L. (2001). A consumer perspective on price-matching refund policies: Effect on price perceptions and search behavior. *Journal of Consumer Research*, *28*, 296–307.

Swanson, D. L. (1995). Addressing a theoretical problem by reorienting the corporate social performance model. *Academy of Management Review*, *20*(1), 43–64.

Taylor, M. S., and Bergmann, T. J. (1987). Organizational recruitment activities and applicants' reactions at different stages of the recruitment process. *Personnel Psychology*, *40*(2), 261–85.000

Turban, D. B., and Cable, D. M. (2003). Firm reputation and applicant pool characteristics. *Journal of Organizational Behavior*, *24*(6), 733–751.

Turban, D. B., Forret, M. L., and Hendrickson, C. L. (1998). Applicant attraction to firms: Influences of organization reputation, job and organizational attributes, and recruiter behaviors. *Journal of Vocational Behavior*, *52*(1), 24–44.

Turban, D. B., and Greening, D. W. (1997). Corporate social performance and organizational attractiveness to prospective employees. *Academy of Management Journal*, *40*(3), 658–672.

Ulrich, D., and Smallwood, N. (2005). HR's new ROI: Return on intangibles. *Human Resource Management*, *44*(2), 137–142.

Van Buren, H. J. (2005). An employee-centered model of corporate social performance. *Business Ethics Quarterly*, *15*(4), 687–709.

Waddock, S. A., and Graves, S. B. (1997). The corporate social performance-financial performance link. *Strategic Management Journal*, *18*(4), 303–320.

Wanous, J. P. (1992). *Organizational Entry: Managing Human Resources*. Reading, MA: Addison-Wesley.

Whitford, D. (2009). A mess: Hyatt's housekeeping scandal. *Fortune*. Retrieved October 27, 2009 from http://money.cnn.com/2009/09/30/news/companies/hyatt_hotels_boston.fortune/index. htm.

Williamson, I. O., Slay, H. S., Shapiro, D. L., and Shivers-Blackwell, S. L. (2008). The effect of explanations on prospective applicants reactions to firm diversity practices. *Human Resource Management, 47*(2), 311–330.

Wood, D. J. (1991). Corporate social performance revisited. *Academy of Management Review, 16*(4), 691–718.

Wright, P., Ferris, S. P., Hiller, J. S., and Kroll, M. (1995). Competitiveness through management of diversity: Effects on stock price valuation. *Academy of Management Journal, 38*(1), 272–284.

Yoon, Y., and Garban-Canli, Z. (2003). The effects of partnering with good cause on corporate and organization image. *Advances in Consumer Research, 30*(1), 322–324.

Yoon, Y., Garban-Canli, Z., and Schwarz, N. (2006). The effect of corporate social responsibility activities on companies with bad reputations. *Journal of Consumer Psychology, 16*(4), 377–390.

Zhang, L. (2008). Corporate social responsibility, applicants' ethical predispositions, and organizational attraction: A person-organization fit perspective. Doctoral dissertation, George Washington University Dissertation Abstracts International, 68/12.

PART III

Managing a Corporate Reputation

6 *Employer Branding, the Psychological Contract and the Delicate Act of Expectation Management and Keeping Promises*

KERRY GRIGG

Introduction

While a tight labour market foreshadowed the emergence of employer branding at the turn of the century, employer branding has remained an important strategic human resource management (HRM) consideration for organisations around the world despite the global slowdown and particularly among multinational enterprises (Martin, 2008b). Employer branding activities establish the identity of the organisation in the minds of the potential and existing labour market as a 'great place to work' above and beyond other organisations (Ewing et al., 2002) by promoting a clear view of what makes the organisation different and desirable as an employer (Backhaus and Tikoo, 2004).

Despite the emergence of employer branding activities, researchers have lagged behind in their understanding of how these communication activities shape the expectations of individual employees and the potential consequences for organisations that flow from their ability, or lack thereof, to live up to employees' expectations. The psychological contract concept provides a useful framework to examine the making and keeping of employer brand promises by the organisation in its employer branding and organisational communication activities. The term 'psychological contract' refers to a commonly used exchange concept that provides a framework for understanding the expectations employees and employers have about the employment relationship (Maguire, 2003). According to Sims it is 'the set of expectations held by the individual employee that specify what the individual and the organisation expect to give and receive from each other in the course of their working relationship' (Sims, 1994, p. 375).

It is widely accepted that employees expect a certain range of inducements from the organisation (e.g. training, salary, satisfying and fulfilling work assignments) and in exchange employees reciprocate by demonstrating their commitment to the organisation by performing work duties and exhibiting good organizational citizenship behaviours

(Deery et al., 2006). The important role of organisational communication (e.g. mission statements, HR handbooks, line management briefings) to communicate psychological contracts to employees was demonstrated in a study by Guest and Conway (2002), but both HR and marketing academics and practitioners recognise that more work needs to be done to understand the impact employer branding and organisational communication activities have on psychological contract development and consequences of perceived psychological contract fulfilment or breach (Martin and Hetrick, 2006).

In an attempt to stimulate further discussion and research on this gap in the employer branding literature this chapter sets out to explore how the psychological contract can be used to better understand the function of employer branding at the individual level. First a discussion of the psychological contract – employer branding link is presented. Second, the potential consequences of keeping or breaking employer branding promises (referred to as psychological contract breach or fulfilment) are presented and factors that may act to moderate the outcomes are briefly discussed. The chapter concludes with a short discussion on the practical implications of the psychological contract perspective for employer branding practitioners. Throughout the chapter examples from organisations around the world are used to illustrate the relevant concepts.

Employer Branding and Organisational Communication

Employer branding is a strategic HRM concept derived from the marketing discipline that relies on external and internal organisational communication activities to attract, retain and engage high-quality employees (Barrow and Mosley, 2005). The employer brand is what the organisation's management wants to communicate to existing and potential employees about what makes the organisation different and desirable as an employer (Backhaus and Tikoo, 2004). Employer branding practitioners embrace the tools of marketing and brand management, including recruitment advertising events and publicity (Ewing et al., 2002) to promote the organisation's employer brand.

The employer brand concept has been subject to academic criticism and practitioner scepticism (Martin, 2008a), perhaps due to the scarcity of empirical research (Edwards, 2005), the reticence of academics to borrow concepts from other disciplines (Gunasekara, 2002) and the unwillingness of academics to look to practitioners for inspiration in setting their research questions (Rynes et al., 2001). However, it is now a widely used HR, communications and marketing tool in the USA, the UK, continental Europe, Asia and Australasia (Martin, 2008a; Zhang et al., 2008)

However, despite academic cynicism an emerging body of research reports on the positive organisational outcomes associated with employer branding. According to the available research a strong employer brand can positively affect the pride that individuals expected from organisational membership (Cable and Turban, 2003), positively affect applicant pool and quality (Collins and Han, 2004), and provide firm performance advantages over the general market (Fulmer et al., 2003). A more recent empirical study demonstrated the role of the employer brand in influencing employees' perceived organisational differentiation, affinity, satisfaction and loyalty (Davies, 2008). While the cited empirical studies demonstrate the potential value of a strong and identifiable employer brand at an organisational level they do not consider the impact employer branding activities have on the development of the employee's psychological contract at an individual level.

Organisational communication is utilised by organisations to promote the instrumental and symbolic attributes of an organisation and/or job to existing and potential employees. Applying instrumental attributes to the employment context involves describing the job or organisation in terms of the objective, concrete, and factual attributes (e.g. pay, benefits, training and development) inherent in a job or organisation (Lievens, 2007, p. 53). Extending the concept of symbolic attributes involves understanding employee's need to maintain their self-identity, enhance their self-image or express themselves (Highhouse et al. , 2007). Organisations that promote their symbolic attributes (e.g. innovative, caring and prestigious) may describe the job/organisation in terms of subjective and intangible attributes. In turn, applicants and existing employees may ascribe specific traits to organisations and therefore be attracted to the organisation, or motivated to stay, because those traits align with how they see themselves personally (Lievens, 2007). In China, Motorola's career website uses emotive and aspirational language and visual images to communicate the Motorola employment experience and a range of instrumental and symbolic attributes are explicitly and/or implicitly communicated via the site's multimedia video clip entitled 'Inspiration – who we are, what we stand for and what it's like to work at Motorola' (Motorola Careers, 2010). While on the Lenovo careers website the promised employment experience is explicitly communicated:

> *Lenovo believes in the power of ideas and helps you create, nurture, preserve, share and realize them. At Lenovo, the culture we've built is defined by diversity of work styles, willingness to take risks and the ability to think globally. It's a place where smart dedicated people can achieve their highest potential. This culture fosters an organization that the world has never seen before, and the excitement within is breathtaking (Lenovo Careers Website, 2010).*

Beyond the symbolism of the previous quote, the website also highlights the instrumental attributes associated with a job at Lenovo including an outstanding compensation/benefits package of base pay, pay for performance, short and long – term incentive plans, work–life balance programmes, health plans and retirement and savings plans (Lenovo Careers Website, 2010). The symbolic and instrumental attributes of the Lenovo employment offering represent the company's unique employer proposition, that is, 'what the organisation stands for, offers and requires as an employer' (CIPD, 2008, p. 5).

While the above examples only highlight one form of the employer branding arsenal (i.e. the recruitment website) given the sophisticated employer branding programmes in place at multinational enterprises like Motorola and Lenovo one would expect similar messages would be found across all forms of organizational communication including other recruitment advertising material, induction programmes, employee handbooks/ intranet sites etc. Given the explicitness of the communication this may lead to psychological contract formation around those various content items, or symbolic and instrumental attributes of the employer brand, including high pay, access to work–life balance, health and savings programmes, and a risk taking and innovative organisational culture. The discussion now turns to the application of the psychological contract concept to employee perceptions of employer branding activities.

The Psychological Contract

While definitional inconsistencies have plagued the development of the psychological contract concept (Guest, 1998) there is widespread agreement it is a useful concept to examine the explicit and implicit, or hidden, aspects of the relationship between employer and employee (Maguire, 2003). Social exchange theory and the norms of reciprocity underpin psychological contract (Deery et al., 2006) and these themes feature in the various definitions used in the literature. According to Rousseau (1995), the psychological contract outlines the unwritten beliefs held by the employee and organisation about the exchange relationship that operates between both parties. The psychological contract is a reflection of the individual employee's perceptions that promises have been made and considerations offered in exchange, which bind the employee and employer to a set of reciprocal obligations (Rousseau and Tijoriwali, 1998). Because this chapter is examining the impact employer branding and organisational communication activities have on the individual employee's formation of the psychological contract, for the purposes of this discussion the psychological contract refers to the individual employee's beliefs about the terms and conditions of a reciprocal exchange agreement between that person and the organisation (Rousseau, 1990). The employees expectations about what the organisation will provide are based around a range of promises and commitments, often referred to as psychological contract content items including job security, training and recognition (Herriot et al., 1997).

THE EMPLOYER BRANDING–PSYCHOLOGICAL CONTRACT LINK

The ensuing discussion outlines the process through which employer branding activities potentially impact on the individual employee's psychological contract. Drawing on signalling theory I argue that when an employee (or potential applicant) becomes aware of the employer brand attributes via the organisation's internal and external communications this will heighten the employee's psychological contract in relation to the specific content items. For example if an organisation promotes global career development opportunities through its employer branding activities this will heighten employees' expectations in terms of the career development and global relocation opportunities the organisation will provide. However if the employee believes the organisation has failed to keep it's 'promise' to provide these opportunities, according to psychological contract research, he/she may react by experiencing lower levels of trust in the organisation, job satisfaction and commitment; intentions to leave and lower levels of job performance. However if the promises contained in the psychological contract are kept, referred to as psychological contract fulfilment, the employee may react by experiencing higher levels of the aforementioned outcomes. Of course other factors, including perceptions of organisational justice and attributions for perceived breach, may work to influence (i.e. moderate) the negative or positive consequences of psychological contract breach/fulfilment and they are briefly discussed later in the chapter.

PSYCHOLOGICAL CONTRACT FORMATION

Following the conceptual work of Suazo et al. (2009) and Aggarwal and Bhargava (2009) this discussion relies on signalling theory to examine the means by which effective communication of psychological contract content items and awareness of the complementary HRM policies may create psychological contracts in the minds of individual employees.

Signalling theory has been used to examine perceptions of organisational attractiveness from the job applicant's perspective (Rynes, 1991). It's an important concept because it helps to understand how HRM policies (Aggarwal and Bhargava, 2009; Guzzo and Noonan, 1994) and the communication of those policies (e.g. via employer branding activities) work to form the individual employee's psychological contract (Suazo et al., 2009).

According to signalling theory, job applicants and/or existing employees use cues or signals, including HRM policies, from the organisation to form views about the organisation including the organisation's intentions, actions and characteristics (Casper and Buffardi, 2004; Casper and Harris, 2008; Rynes, 1991).

While signalling theory has been used to explain the role of HRM policies in shaping the employee's psychological contract, the role of effective communication of those policies from the employee's perspective is less well understood. Research by Guest and Conway (2002) demonstrated the importance of effective organisational communication (e.g. recruitment, induction, staff handbook) by the employer in communicating the psychological contract to the organisation's employees. Given that many organisations are now using a range of organisational communication methods to communicate their HR policies and practices to position themselves as 'employers of choice' and strengthen their employer brand (Joo and McLean, 2006), signalling theory and the empirical work of Guest and Conway (2002) would suggest effective use of employer branding communication and awareness of various HR policies and practices will develop psychological contracts for individual employees.

OUTCOMES OF PSYCHOLOGICAL CONTRACT FULFILMENT AND BREACH

The employee-related outcomes of the employee's assessment of psychological contract breach or fulfilment is one of the most widely researched aspects of the psychological contract literature (Xu, 2008). When the promises and commitments inherent in the psychological contract are fulfilled by the organisation the employee is more likely to exhibit positive work-related attitudes and behaviours (Rousseau, 1995). Alternatively Robinson and Morrison (1995) argue that if the employee perceives the organisation has failed to keep its promises, this constitutes a breach of the psychological contract and a fall in engagement, trust and productivity can result while staff turnover intentions will increase. Referring back to the Lenovo example, psychological contract research suggests that if the individual employee believes the organisation has failed to keep the promises made around an innovative risk-taking culture or organisational support for work–life balance he or she may experience a sense of psychological contract breach.

Social exchange theory and the norms of reciprocity have been frequently used as a means of explaining how employees might respond to psychological contract breach (Deery et al., 2006). Applying the principles of social exchange theory, employees are motivated by a desire to maintain a reciprocal or balanced relationship with their employer in terms of inducements offered by the employer, and the work-related contributions made by employees (Deery et al., 2006). Should the employee feel the organisation has not fulfilled its psychological contract obligations, this perceived breach will tend to undermine expectations of reciprocity and fair dealing that underpin long-term employment relationships (Rousseau and McLean Parks, 1993) and in turn erode trust in the organisation (Deery et al., 2006).

While research has yet to test the direct consequences of failing to keep employer branding promises to employees, there is a significant body of research outlining the negative impact psychological contract breach has on the individual employee's trust in the organisation, job satisfaction, affective commitment, intention to leave and job performance.

Trust is the cornerstone of the social exchange relationship between employee and employer and as the relationship evolves over time into trusting, loyal and mutual commitments as long as both parties fulfil their promises (Aggarwal and Bhargava, 2007). In summary it is important for employees to trust the organisation they work for. Research has demonstrated the negative impact perceptions of psychological breach have on employee trust in the organisation (Dulac et al., 2008; Robinson, 1996) and the flow on effect mistrust can have on other important employee outcomes including job satisfaction, commitment, intentions to stay and performance (Zhao et al., 2007).

Perceptions of psychological contract breach have also been linked directly to the important employee attitude of job satisfaction. Given that the working day can absorb a very large part of a person's waking hours it is not surprising that dissatisfied employees may attempt to avoid or change their place of employment or recalibrate their work performance (Nielsen and Smyth, 2008). Job satisfaction has been widely examined in the context of psychological contract outcomes and while the keeping of psychological contract promises (i.e. fulfilment) has been linked to enhanced levels of employee job satisfaction (Robinson et al., 1994; Pate et al., 2003) psychological contract breach has undermined employees' job satisfaction (Tekleab and Taylor, 2003) and this should be a particular concern for management.

Affective organisational commitment and intentions to leave the organisation are two additional and important employee attitudes linked to psychological contract breach. A range of studies have demonstrated that employees' perceptions of contract breach tend to yield diminished levels of organisational commitment and heighten employee intentions to leave the organisation (Coyle-Shapiro and Kessler, 2000; Dulac et al., 2008). Given the important role committed employees play in pursuing departmental and organisational goals and the well-reported financial and intellectual property and capital 'costs' associated with voluntary turnover, these consequences of psychological contract breach provide further cause for concern.

Finally, employee perceptions of psychological contract breach can have a negative impact on employee in-role and extra-role performance (Coyle-Shapiro and Kessler, 2000; Robinson, 1996). So when employees believe the organisation has failed to keep its promise on psychological contract items such as career development or job security they are likely to respond by reducing their 'on-the-job' work performance and demonstrate diminished discretionary effort around the workplace (e.g. assisting and encouraging colleagues), often referred to as 'organisational citizenship behaviour' (OCB) or 'extra-role performance'. Both enhanced individual in-role and extra-role (i.e. OCB) performance make important contributions to the variance in organisational effectiveness and performance at an organisational level (Podsakoff and MacKenzie, 1997) and underline the importance of better managing the employer–employee relationship.

However, it is important to acknowledge that not all perceived breaches of psychological contracts will result in the negative consequences outlined in the previous discussion. How an employee chooses to respond to a perceived psychological contract breach is likely to be determined by a range of factors. First the extent of the breach may play an important role in that a minor breach as perceived by the employee may not impact on the employee's sense of trust, job satisfaction or commitment (Morrison and Robinson, 1997).

The second factor that may explain how an employee responds to psychological contract breach is the degree of importance the employee places on the particular psychological content item (De Vos and Meganck, 2009). For example, it is reasonable to expect that an employee who places a high level of importance on their career trajectory will respond more negatively (e.g. reduced sense of commitment to the organisation and intentions to leave) to a breach of promise around career development opportunities to a breach of promise around work–life balance support if they do not particularly value organisational support for work–life balance at this point in their career or life stage.

Thirdly, the individual employees' attribution regarding why the discrepancy or breach actually occurred in the first place will influence the employee's response to the perceived breach (Turnley and Feldman, 1999). A range of important studies provide support for the notion that employees are most likely to reduce their work effort or exhibit other negative work emotions, attitudes or behaviours when they perceive the organisation has intentionally failed to live up to its promises and commitments (e.g. Deery et al., 2006; Turnley et al., 2003).

Finally, perceptions of how fairly he or she was treated, operationalised in the organisational behaviour literature as organisational justice (Morrison and Robinson, 1997), will also play an important role in determining how an employee responds to psychological contract breach. Psychological contracts involve managers making decisions about the employment relationship, that is the discretionary decisions, and how they are made and communicated, about access to career development opportunities and work–life balance support will have an important influence on how employees respond when decisions aren't made in their favour. According to the organisational justice literature employees evaluate the fairness of decision outcomes (distributive justice), the decision-making process (procedural justice), the sincerity and respect shown towards the employee (interpersonal justice) and the extent of adequate and honest explanations provided to the employee (informational justice) (Judge and Colquitt, 2004).

While the relevance and role of employee perceptions of organisational justice and attributions for breach, within the employer branding context, require robust empirical testing the concepts are intuitively appealing and present important considerations for HR practitioners, line managers and researchers. Organisations, and their agents, won't always be able to keep the promises they make as part of their employer branding strategies but the preceding discussion highlights the importance of setting realistic expectations about the employment experience to ensure employees don't attribute the psychological contract breach to a deliberate deception about what the organisation (or job) could offer. In consumer marketing parlance the term used would be 'deceptive or misleading advertising'. Furthermore, to minimise the negative consequences of psychological contract breach, line managers or representatives from the HR function should clearly explain and justify their decisions to ensure the employee feels they have been treated fairly if they do not receive what they thought they were entitled to as part of the employment relationship 'deal'.

Practical Implications for HR Practitioners

The job-related emotions, attitudes and behaviours discussed in the previous section are considered critical to the performance of the organisation when applying a strategic HRM approach to organisational performance (Wright et al., 2001) and should provide the impetus for all organisations to better manage the making and keeping of psychological contract promises via employer branding activities.

However, in a rush to keep up with its competitors in the recent 'talent wars', organisations, via their employer branding activities, make claims about their employment experience that are often challenging to deliver upon. One area of employer branding that proved an important plank for organisations pursuing 'employer of choice' status was in the promise of organisational support and policies for work–life balance including the provision of part-time, telecommuting and job-sharing opportunities. In the Australian banking sector, the strategy of St George Bank to leverage their well-publicised success in a string of high-profile work–life balance HRM awards to complement and reinforce their 'Good with People, Good with Money' corporate branding strategy over recent years is instructive. The organisation has successfully built its employer brand around the promise of a supportive work–life balance organisational culture while at the same time cleverly linking it to the organisation's broader corporate strategy. In the St George example the implicit message to their market was clear – 'trust us to provide outstanding customer care and service (and do the right thing with your money) because we are the most caring and trusting employer in the industry, we even have the awards to prove it.' These consistent messages and images were conveyed to a diverse audience including customers, employees, shareholders and the broader community with the help of advertising and public relations and an obliging media interested in the work–life balance issue (e.g. Raine, 2007; Robertson, 2007; St George Bank, 2010).

In China the global professional services firm PriceWaterhouseCoopers symbolises a job at PWC on its careers website as a recipe for life requiring '1 part work – 1 part leisure – 1 part learning, Mix Well!' (PriceWaterhouseCoopers, 2009) and work–life balance (among other inducements) feature heavily. Despite the economic global downturn organisational support for work–life balance is still an important component of the employer brand offering for many organisations across the world because of the importance of work–life balance in many societies (Choi, 2008; Spector et al., 2007). However, delivering on the promise of work–life balance organisational support is difficult. There is widespread agreement that an organisation's commitment to enhancing the employee's sense of work–life balance must go beyond HRM policy considerations. Creating a set of high-commitment HR policies is only the first step in providing genuine support for the work–life balance needs of employees. Fostering an organisational culture that encourages and supports the use of available policies through the role of the supportive supervisor is critical (Bardoel, 2003; De Cieri et al., 2005) if organisations are to deliver on the employer branding claims they are making around the promise of work–life balance.

The critical role of high-commitment HR policies and organisational culture to underpin employer branding strategies stretches far beyond the use of work–life balance as an employer branding attribute. Other attributes that feature prominently in employer branding strategies include employee advancement (e.g. career management, professional development, mentoring), corporate social responsibility and competitive compensation packages (Backhaus, 2004). In the case of the former, to deliver on the promise of employee advancement organisations require a suite of high-performance HRM policies (effective training, internal labour mobility) and a supportive organisational culture including decentralised decisional-making to ensure HR and/or line managers have the autonomy and leadership expertise to implement the relevant HR practices (Purcell and Hutchinson, 2007).

Herein lies the challenge for employer branding practitioners. While employer branding activities work to differentiate the organisation and make promises about the employment experience it is the organisations use of high-performance HR policies and the requisite organisational culture that will determine how well the organisation can deliver on those promises. Given that perceived psychological contract breach can lead to the negative consequences of diminished trust, commitment, job satisfaction, performance and intentions to stay with the organisation it is important for employer branding practitioners to ensure organisations have the necessary HR policies and organisational culture in place to deliver on the employer branding promises made by the organisation. Returning to the Lenovo example, if the organisation's recruitment advertising makes claims of an innovative and risk-taking culture with opportunities for career development then HR policies that support innovation and career development should be in place and line managers must be equipped to implement and support these HR policy prescriptions. As Purcell and Hutchinson (2007, p. 4) observe, 'Poorly designed or inadequate policies can be "rescued" by good management behaviour in much the same way as "good" HR practices can be negated by poor front-line management behaviour or weak leadership'. The latter requires devolvement of HR practices to line managers and this is still an emerging and challenging practice for many organisations (Harris et al., 2002; Purcell and Hutchinson, 2007; Zhu et al., 2008). This is concerning for HR practitioners because successful employer branding strategies require close co-operation between the communications and HR functions of the organisation to develop the external and internal communications strategy *and* the co-operation of middle and line managers to 'live the brand' and deliver on the employer branding promises (Moroko and Uncles, 2008).

Another challenge for employer branding practitioners is to ensure employer branding strategies do not undermine efforts to develop the requisite harmonious organisational culture that facilitates social capital development. Social capital is conceptualised as 'the bonds, bridges and trust among people and partners that provide the glue that binds the organization together' (Martin et al., 2009 p. 11) and is a critical determinant of knowledge transfer, often described as a key source of competitive advantage (Makela and Brewster, 2009). Social capital development is built on, among other things, interpersonal trust and exchange between individual employees (Kang and Snell, 2009) and it has been suggested that employer branding strategies focusing on attracting and retaining 'the best talent' may be counterproductive to nurturing the organisation's social capital (Martin et al., 2009). There is a considerable body of literature highlighting the strategic value of employees with unique skills and experience, variously referred to as 'A-players' (Becker et al., 2009), 'pivotal talent' (Boudreau and Ramstad, 2007) or 'knowledge workers' as part of the HR architectures concept developed by Lepak and Snell (2002). According to

Davies (2008), employer branding activities are tailored to attract and retain valuable and strategically important employees, a view shared by other employer branding researchers (Ewing et al., 2002). Rousseau and colleagues also refer to the ability of high-status employees to negotiate preferable idiosyncratic deals with their line manager around a range of employment conditions (e.g. work–life balance) (Hornung et al., 2008). In the same vein, Coyle-Shapiro and Kessler (2000) suggest that organisations load psychological contract contents with attractive inducements to valued employees and those employees are typically more likely to have their promises fulfilled by the organisation. Questions are already being raised about the suitability of these forms of exclusive talent management strategies in the West (e.g. Groysberg et al., 2004; Martin et al., 2009) and in emerging economies where the practice of employer branding is gaining momentum the risks of exclusive talent management strategies are even more pronounced. For example, in China's collectivist society in which the greater good of the society or organisation is given precedence over 'individual' goals (Warner, 2008), exclusive employer branding activities and high-commitment/performance HR practices directed solely at employees earmarked as strategically valuable could be even more problematic.

Finally, employer branding practitioners working in multinational enterprises must have the autonomy to reconfigure the employer brand at a local level to best meet the nuances of the organisation's workforce, organisational HR capabilities, broader labour market conditions and cultural sensitivities. Simply exporting and imposing an employer branding strategy on the subsidiary or joint venture partner that was originally developed in and designed for the parent organisation is problematic. Successful employer brands are authentic, genuine and resonate with those they are targeted at (Martin, 2008b). In addition, the successful development and promotion of employer brands is dependent on a good relationship between the organisation's headquarters and foreign subsidiaries, the nature and quality of personal relations among managers in headquarters and sensitivity of the local cultural and business system context (Martin 2008b). So while the employer branding activities at a corporate level may shape the employee's psychological contract it is the HR policies, organisational culture and line manager support at the subsidiary local level that will determine if the employee's psychological contract is breached or fulfilled and the resulting work based emotions, attitudes and behaviours.

Successful employer branding strategies at the organisational level require employer branding to work at the individual employee level. Promises made about the employment experience on offer, whether symbolic or instrumental, must be reinforced and underpinned by HR practices and policies, a complementary organisational culture and consistent line manager support. The potential pay-offs for effective deliverance of employer branding promises, in the form of fulfilled psychological contracts and enhanced employee trust, job satisfaction , commitment, performance and intentions to stay, should form an important part of an organisation's approach to strategic HRM. While the concept is appealing, HR practitioners should endeavour to understand and respond to the challenges involved with designing and implementing effective employer branding strategies to ensure employees develop realistic expectations about the employment experience on offer. Furthermore, to reap the positive work outcomes associated with psychological contract fulfilment the organisation must develop the capacity to deliver on the expectations they have conspired to create through their employer branding strategies.

References

Aggarwal, U., Datta, S., and Bhargava, S. (2007). The relationship between human resource practices, psychological contract and employee engagement – implications for managing talent. *IIMB Management Review, 19*(3), 313–25.

Aggarwal, U., and Bhargava, S. (2009). Reviewing the relationship between human resource practices and psychological contract and their impact on employee attitude and behaviours: A conceptual model. *Journal of European Industrial Training, 33*(1), 4–31.

Backhaus, K. B. (2004). An exploration of corporate recruitment descriptions on Monster.com. *Journal of Business Communication, 41*(2), 115–36.

Backhaus, K., and Tikoo, S. (2004). Conceptualizing and researching employer branding. *Career Development International, 9*(5), 501–17.

Bardoel, E. A. (2003). The provision of formal and informal work-family practices: The relative importance of institutional and resource dependent explanations versus managerial explanations. *Women in Management Review, 18*(1/2), 7–19.

Barrow, S., and Mosley, R. (2005). *The Employer Brand: Bringing the best of brand management to people at work*. London: Wiley.

Becker, B. E., Huselid, M. A., and Beatty, R. W. (2009). *The differentiated workforce: Transforming talent into strategic impact*. Boston, MA: Harvard Business Review Press.

Boudreau, J. W., and Ramstad, P. M. (2007). *Beyond HR: The new science of human capital*. Boston, MA: Harvard Business School Publishing Corporation.

Cable, D. M., and Turban, D. B. (2003). The value of organizational reputation in the recruitment context: A brand-equity perspective. *Journal of Applied Social Psychology, 33*(11), 2244–66.

Casper, W. J., and Buffardi, L. C. (2004). Work-life benefits and job pursuit intentions: The role of anticipated organizational support. *Journal of Vocational Behavior, 65*(3), 391–410.

Casper, W. J., and Harris, C. M. (2008). Work–life benefits and organizational attachment: Self-interest utility and signaling theory models. *Journal of Vocational Behavior, 72*(1), 95–109.

Choi, J. (2008). Work and family demands and life stress among Chinese employees: The mediating effect of work–family conflict. *The International Journal of Human Resource Management, 19*(5), 878–95.

CIPD. (2008). *Employer Branding: A no-nonsense approach*. London: Chartered Institute of Personnel and Development.

Collins, C. J., and Han, J. (2004). Exploring applicant pool quantity and quality: The effects of early recruitment practice strategies, corporate advertising, and firm reputation. *Personnel Psychology, 57*(3), 685–717.

Coyle-Shapiro, J., and Kessler, I. (2000). Consequences of the psychological contract for the employment relationship: A large scale survey. *Journal of Management Studies, 37*(7), 903–30.

Davies, G. (2008). Employer branding and its influence on managers. *European Journal of Marketing, 42*(5/6), 667–81.

De Cieri, H., Holmes, B., Abbott, J., and Pettit, T. (2005). Achievements and challenges for work/life balance strategies in Australian organizations. *International Journal of Human Resource Management, 16*(1), 90–103.

Deery, S. J., Iverson, R. D., and Walsh, J. T. (2006). Toward a better understanding of psychological contract breach: A study of customer service employees. *Journal of Applied Psychology, 91*(1), 166–75.

De Vos, A., and Meganck, A. (2009). What HR managers do versus what employees value: Exploring both parties' views on retention management from a psychological contract perspective. *Personnel Review*, 38(1), 45–60.

Dulac, T., Coyle-Shapiro, J. A. M., Henderson, D. J., and Wayne, S. J. (2008). Not all responses to breach are the same: The interconnection of social exchange and psychological contract processes in organizations. *Academy of Management Journal*, 51(6), 1079–98.

Edwards, M. R. (2005). Employer and employee branding: HR or PR? In S. Bach (ed.), *Managing Human Resources: Personnel Management in Transition*. Oxford: Blackwell Publishing.

Ewing, M. T., Pitt, L. F., de Bussy, N. M., and Berthon, P. (2002). Employment branding in the knowledge economy. *International Journal of Advertising*, 21(1), 3–22.

Fulmer, I. S., Gerhant, B., and Scott, K. S. (2003). Are the 100 best better? An empirical investigation of relationship between being a 'great place to work' and firm performance. *Personnel Psychology*, 56(4), 965–93.

Groysberg, B., Nanda, A., and Nohria, N. (2004). The risky business of hiring stars. *Harvard Business Review*, 82(5), 92–100.

Guest, D. E. (1998). Is the psychological contract worth taking seriously? *Journal of Organizational Behavior*, 19, 649–64.

Guest, D. E., and Conway, N. (2002). Communicating the psychological contract: An employer perspective. *Human Resource Management Journal*, 12(2), 22–38.

Gunasekara, C. (2002). *Employer Branding: The perils of transdisciplinary extension*. Charles Sturt University Faculty of Commerce Working Paper. Bathurst: NSW.

Guzzo, R. A., and Noonan, K. A. (1994). Human resource practices as communications and the psychological contract. *Human Resource Management*, 33(3), 447–62.

Harris, L., Doughty, D., and Kirk, S. (2002). The devolution of HR responsibilities – perspectives from the UK's public sector. *Journal of European Industrial Training*, 26(5), 218–29.

Herriot, P., Manning, W. E. G., and Kidd, J. M. (1997). The content of the psychological contract. *British Journal of Management*, 8(2), 151–62.

Highhouse, S., Thornbury, E. E., and Little, I. S. (2007). Social-identity functions of attraction to organizations. *Organizational Behavior and Human Decision Processes*, 103(1), 134–46.

Hornung, S., Rousseau, D. M., and Glaser, J. (2008). Creating flexible work arrangements through idiosyncratic deals. *Journal of Applied Psychology*, 93(3), 655–64.

Joo, B.-K., and McLean, G. N. (2006). Best employer studies: A conceptual model from a literature review and a case study. *Human Resource Development Review*, 5(2), 228–57.

Judge, T. A., and Colquitt, J. A. (2004). Organizational justice and stress: The mediating role of work–family conflict. *Journal of Applied Psychology*, 89(3), 395–404.

Kang, S.-C., and Snell, S. A. (2009). Intellectual capital architectures and ambidextrous learning: A framework for human resource management. *Journal of Management Studies*, 46(1), 65–92.

Lenovo Careers Website (2010) *Opportunities at Lenovo*. 20 February. Available online at http://www.lenovocareers.com/, accessed 20 Februrary 2010.

Lepak, D. P., and Snell, S. A. (2002). Examining the human resource architecture: the relationships among human capital, employment, and human resource configurations. *Journal of Management*, 28(4), 517–43.

Lievens, F. F. (2007). Employer branding in the Belgian Army: The importance of instrumental and symbolic beliefs for potential applicants, actual applicants, and military employees. *Human Resource Management*, 46(1), 51.

Makela, K., and Brewster, C. (2009). Interunit interaction contexts, interpersonal social capital, and the differing levels of knowledge sharing. *Human Resource Management*, 48(4), 591-613.

Maguire, H. (2003). The changing psychological contract: Challenges and implications for HRM, organisations and employees. In R. Weisner and B. Millett (eds.), Human resource management: Challenges and future direction (pp. 87–103): John Wiley and Sons.

Martin, G., and Hetrick, S. (2006). Managing corporate brands and reputations, *Corporate Reputations, Branding and People Management B2 – Corporate Reputations, Branding and People Management*. Oxford: Butterworth-Heinemann.

Martin, G. (2008a). Employer branding and corporate reputation management: A model and some evidence. In C. L. Cooper and R. Burke (eds), *The Peak Performing Organization*. London: Routledge.

Martin, G. (2008b). *Employer Branding and Corporate Reputation Management in an International Context*. Paper presented at the 2008 Academy of Management Meeting. Anaheim: CA.

Martin, G., Gollan, P., and Grigg, K. (2009). A future for employer branding: Dealing with negative capabilities in strategic HRM. Paper presented at the International Industrial Relations Association World Congress (HRM Study Group).

Moroko, L., and Uncles, M. D. (2008). Characteristics of successful employer brands. *Journal of Brand Management, 16*(3), 160–75.

Morrison, E. W., and Robinson, S. L. (1997). When employees feel betrayed: A model of how psychological contract violation develops. *Academy of Management Review, 22*(1), 226–56.

Motorola Careers (2010) *Motorola Careers*. Available online at http://www.motorolacareers.com/moto.cfm?flashover=1, accessed 20 February 2010.

Nielsen, I., and Smyth, R. (2008). Job satisfaction and response to incentives among China's urban workforce. *Journal of Socio-Economics, 37*(5), 1921–36.

Pate, J., Martin, G., and McGoldrick, J. (2003). The impact of psychological contract violation on employee attitudes and behaviour. *Employee Relations, 25*(6), 557–73.

Podsakoff, P. M., and MacKenzie, S. B. (1997). Impact of organizational citizenship behavior on organizational performance: A review and suggestion for future research. *Human Performance, 10*(2), 133.

PriceWaterhouseCoopers (2009). *Careers with us*. 27 August. Available online at http://www.pwccn.com/home/eng/joinusmain.html, accessed on 20 February 2010.

Purcell, J., and Hutchinson, S. (2007). Front-line managers as agents in the HRM-performance causal chain: Theory, analysis and evidence. *Human Resource Management Journal, 17*(1), 3–20.

Raine, L. (2007). *Life Matters: Grandparent' Leave*. Radio broadcast, Australian Broadcasting Commission, 19 September. Available at http://www.abc.net.au/rn/lifematters/stories/2007/2036739.htm, accessed on 20 February, 2010.

Robertson, A. (2007). *Lateline Business: St George CEO juggles work, family life*. Television broadcast, Australian Broadcasting Commission, 21 May. Available at http://www.abc.net.au/lateline/business/items/200705/s1929272.htm, accessed on 20 February, 2010.

Robinson, S. L. (1996). Trust and breach of the psychological contract. *Administrative Science Quarterly, 41*(4), 574–99.

Robinson, S. L., Kraatz, M. S., and Rousseau, D. (1994). Changing obligations and the psychological contract: A longitudinal study. *Academy of Management Journal, 37*(1): 137–52.

Robinson, S. L., and Morrison, E. W. (1995). Psychological contracts and OCB: The effect of unfulfilled obligations on civic virtue behavior. *Journal of Organizational Behavior, 16*(3), 289–98.

Rousseau, D. M. (1990). New hire perceptions of their own and their employer's obligations: A study of psychological contracts. *Journal of Organizational Behavior, 11*(5), 389–400.

Rousseau, D. M. (1995). *Psychological Contracts in Organizations*. Thousand Oaks, CA: Sage.

Rousseau, D. M., and McLean Parks, J. (1993). The contracts of individuals and organizations. *Research in Organizational Behavior, 15,* 1–43.

Rousseau, D. M., and Tijoriwala, S. A. (1998). Assessing psychological contracts: Issues, alternatives and measures. *Journal of Organizational Behavior, 19,* 679–95.

Rynes, S. L. (1991). Recruitment, job-choice, and post-hire consequences: A call for new research directions. In M. D. Dunnette and L. M. Hough (eds), *Handbook of Industrial and Organizational Psychology.* Palo Alto: CA: Consulting Psychologists Press.

Rynes, S. L., Bartunek, J. M., and Daft, R. L. (2001). Across the great divide: Knowledge creation and transfer between practitioners and academics. *Academy of Management Journal, 44*(2), 340–55.

Sims, R. R. (1994). human resource management's role in clarifying the new psychological contract. *Human Resource Management, 33*(3), 373–82.

Spector, P. E., Allen, T. D., Poelmans, S. A. Y., Lapierre, L. M., Cooper, C. L., O'Driscoll, M., et al. (2007). Cross-national differences in relationships of work demands, job satisfaction, and turnover intentions with work-family conflict. *Personnel Psychology, 60*(4), 805–35.

St George Bank (2010). St George Awards. Accessed at http://www.stgeorge.com.au/about-us/awards.asp on February 20, 2010.

Suazo, M. M., MartÃnez, P. G., and Sandoval, R. (2009). Creating psychological and legal contracts through human resource practices: A signaling theory perspective. *Human Resource Management Review, 19*(2), 154–66.

Tekleab, A. G., and Taylor, M. S. (2003). Aren't there two parties in an employment relationship? Antecedents and consequences of organization–employee agreement on contract obligations and violations. *Journal of Organizational Behavior, 24*(5), 585.

Turnley, W. H., Bolino, M. C., Lester, S. W., and Bloodgood, J. M. (2003). The impact of psychological contract fulfillment on the performance of in-role and organizational citizenship behaviors. *Journal of Management, 29*(2), 187–206.

Warner, M. (2008). Reassessing human resource management 'with Chinese characteristics': An overview and introduction. *The International Journal of Human Resource Management, 19*(5), 771–801.

Wright, P. M., Dunford, B. B., and Snell, S. A. (2001). Human resources and the resource based view of the firm. *Journal of Management, 27*(6), 701.

Xu, X. (2008). *Explaining the Impact of Work Interference with Family: The role of work–family psychological contract and cultural values.* Unpublished PhD dissertation. Gainesville, FL: University of South Florida.

Zhang, H., Liu, G., and Zhao, P. (2008). *China Employer Brand Management.* Beijing: Post and Telecom Press.

Zhao, H., Wayne, S. J., Glibkowski, B. C., and Bravo, J. (2007). The impact of psychological contract breach on work-related outcomes: A meta-analysis. *Personnel Psychology, 60*(3), 647–80.

Zhu, C., Cooper, B., De Cieri, H., Bruce Thomson, S., and Zhao, S. (2008). Devolvement of HR practices in transitional economies: Evidence from China. *The International Journal of Human Resource Management, 19*(5), 840–55.

7 *Managing Corporate Reputations, Strategic Human Resource Management and Negative Capabilities*

GRAEME MARTIN, PAUL GOLLAN AND KERRY GRIGG

Introduction

As recent events have shown, particularly the global financial services crisis, how organizations manage their staff can have a significant impact on corporate reputations. One need look no further than the worldwide debate over executive pay and the use of incentive bonuses to attract, motivate and retain talent in certain sectors of the financial services industry, a problem one of us forecast might occur in an earlier case on the financial service industry in the UK when we described it as potentially 'unfit for the future' (Martin and Hetrick, 2006). This is not meant to demonstrate our particular brand of wisdom, since we were merely expressing what others had claimed, including the much maligned British regulatory body – the Financial Services Authority – regarding the use of incentives and the lack of a strategic approach to HR in the sector. What we were also trying to highlight was a collective blindness among senior leaders and HR staff in the industry concerning a single-minded faith in incentives, which would do long-term damage to the reputation of firms and, indeed, the industry. Financial services may be the most high profile example of a lack of strategic thinking in Human Resource Management (HRM) but most large organizations in other industries face similar problems created, we argue, by an inability to manage tensions between the simultaneous need for firms to be *different* and *the same*. In this chapter we discuss these tensions and propose a way of resolving them, which may help organizations become fit for the future in reputational terms.

Though there is an extensive literature in strategic HRM (SHRM) (Becker and Huselid, 2005; Boxall and Purcell, 2008; Lengnick-Hall, et al., 2009), we do not propose to review it here. Instead we wish to analyse some of the most recent contributions in the SHRM normative literature to logics in strategic management and set these against the lessons from the corporate reputation literature. By doing so, we draw attention to a set of 'negative capabilities' that HR practitioners, managers, line managers and employees face, especially in large, complex organizations. We believe the term 'negative capabilities' is a useful one to explain what the poet John Keats referred to when he pointed out that people need to remain open-minded and accepting of a world of irreconcilable ideas which cannot (easily) be resolved. Such potentially irreconcilable ideas are found in the many paradoxes and tensions in business and management, including the distinction between management and leadership (Grint, 2005), in the needs for organizations to exhibit simultaneous differentiation and integration (Lawrence and Lorsch, 1969; Roberts, 2004) and the now clichéd 'thinking global and acting local' mantra of many global companies and large complex organizations, perhaps more accurately expressed in the *integration-responsiveness* duality (Rosenzweig, 2006).

As noted above, we focus on two such dominant logics: the logic of distinctiveness (from others) and the logic of similarity (among others). We then raise the possibility of a third logic, strategy-in-action (with others), which might help SHRM academics and practitioners work with the negative capabilities generated by the simultaneous search for difference and similarity. We begin by summarizing our views in Table 7.1 and explain them in some detail. By doing so, we hope to address a gap in the HRM and corporate reputation management literature, which has yet to deal with these negative capabilities, a paradox which characterizes (some might say terrorizes) the corporate reputation literature (Deephouse and Carter, 2005; Martin and Hetrick, 2006).

Table 7.1 Three strategic logics and strategic HRM

Strategic logics	The need to be distinctive (from others)	The need to be similar (to others)	The need for action (with others)
Focus	Competitive positioning and differentiation. Transformative business model change	Legitimacy with stakeholders	Dealing with 'negative capabilities', politics and emergent strategy in action
Locus	Mid-level business unit. Strategic capabilities and value-adding workforce segments, jobs and people. Business unit architectures	Corporate-level reputation for being different but legitimate	'Acting your way in to thinking' and 'strategizing' through negotiations between corporate and local
Strategic aim	Local responsiveness, differentiation and identity	Corporate respectability and approval from peers. Global integration. Economies of scale and scope. Leveraging and aligning benefits of corporate identity among stakeholders	Resolving the 'integration-responsiveness tension. Organizational dexterity by being integrated and differentiated. Knowledge transfer
SHRM implications	Focus on talent management of key workforce segments or 'A' jobs and people. Specific employee value propositions for segments. 'Employee of choice' approach. 'Enterprise branding'	Corporate/global approach to talent management. 'Best practice' HR architectures. Following industry recipes. Corporate employer branding. 'Employer of choice' approach	Resolving corporate-local tensions through 'equivocal' values and bottom-up authenticity. Focus on the 'journey' more than outcomes. 'Regaining control by sharing control'

Distinctiveness (from Others)

Much of the classical strategic management literature has focused on how organizations position themselves in their environment and have recommended various positioning or product-market strategies for superior organizational performance e.g. differentiation through customer captivity, customer relations and innovation, cost leadership and economies of scale. Michael Porter's work and variations thereof have been at the heart of this approach, which can be summed up in his heavily quoted aphorism that strategy is and should be about differentiation: creating value for customers by doing different things and/or by doing things differently.

This logic of differentiation has been at the heart of recent work by a number of well-known American strategic HR scholars. Writing from an essentially normative perspective, they have sought to identify *actionable* and *mid-level strategic capabilities* in firms which are a unique source of competitive advantage for the organizations (Becker and Huselid, 2005; Becker et al., 2009; Boudreau and Ramstad, 2007; Cascio and Boudreau, 2008; Lepak and Snell, 2002). These scholars draws on each other's work to focus on their own brand of high value adding and uniquely skilled segments of the workforce (Lepak and Snell, 2002) – variously described as 'A jobs' and 'A-players' (Becker et al., 2009) or 'pivotal talent' (Boudreau and Ramstad, 2007) – on which these strategic capabilities rest and so help form a resource-base (Boxall and Purcell, 2008) that makes organizations truly different and difficult to imitate, unlike abstract generic strategies, missions or values.

In the UK, there has been a parallel stream of research linking HR strategy to *business models* rather than strategic positioning models. The key message of this research conducted with senior HR practitioners is that the future credibility of HR needs to be tied into business model change (Sparrow et al., 2008). Business models are distinct from the traditional product-market strategies identified by Porter (2008) and others in that they try to capture how organizations seek to create distinctiveness by specifying new organizational arrangements among firms and *external* partners and customers, now popularized in the social networking and network analysis literature. Though there are a variety of business models, typically they focus on *novel* ways of conducting their transactions, e.g. by connecting previously unconnected partners or by linking participants through technology, or on more *efficient* ways of doing business, e.g. through reducing transaction costs (Zott and Amit, 2008).

The contribution of Sparrow et al. (2008) is to extend this external focus of business models to the specification of new organizational arrangements or architectures among the focal firm and business partners by applying it to the problem of how new and distinctive organizational architectures can be developed in the relations between the focal firm and *internal* partners, most notably different groups or segments of employees, contractors, consultants and the like. So although their work is arguably broader in its concerns from some of the American HR strategy writers, the core of their argument is similar because they propose that overarching strategic success relies on transformational business model change, this time linking the business to internal as well as external partners in distinctive ways. Sparrow et al. (2008) argue that for HR to gain credibility it must ensure that all of its activities are tied to supporting changes in the business model by helping design the organizational architecture and to make it work through, among other activities, appropriate 'future-proofing' of talent management and employer branding, keys concern of theirs (Balain and Sparrow, 2009).

Arguably common elements in these new approaches to SHRM lead organizations to focus on the business unit or line of business rather than the corporation for its true source of differentiation or novelty because:

1. Strategic capabilities and business model change tend to be located at the business unit/ line of business level rather than at corporate level, or else located in key processes and even functions at the business unit level, e.g. supply chain management, relationship management, partnership working, etc.
2. Identity, as the social philosopher Baumann (2007) has argued, is essentially a local phenomenon rather than a global one. Thus local workforce identification and engagement with the business unit rather than corporate identification and engagement with global values are a major potential source of strategic value creation and support for business model transformation.
3. HR strategies, especially talent management, need to be aligned directly with specific business unit strategies and business model change, ideally by helping shape it or at least following it. Often, however, this is not how HRM has seen its contribution because of concerns and desires to implement universal professional standards developed by professional HR bodies, and a sometimes overly simplistic notion of transferable 'best practice' and corporate control. These factors have led some corporate HR functions to try to impose one-size-fits-all HR practices in unreceptive contexts for change and unconnected with the concerns of line managers and employees, with the attendant consequences of being seen as irrelevant and lacking credibility with these people who have the task of implementing global values and polices locally (Sparrow et al., 2008).

Thus whether product market or business model driven, this logic of distinctiveness provides a strong argument for segmentation of the workforce and of HR architectures, in much the same way that marketing approaches customer segmentation with specific value propositions rather than one-size-fits-all global messages. This is especially true of the American writers. For example, Becker et al. (2009) argue for an 'employee of choice' approach, so rejecting 'best practice' work systems and employer of choice approaches for all employees, which they see as a recipe for mediocrity. The intellectual bedrock of this logic is the resource-based view (RBV) of strategy, which sees internal resources as the true source of differentiation when they are valuable, rare, inimitable and non-substitutable (Barney, 1991). This is the justification for the 'exclusive' talent management focus described above, based as it is on a version of the 'power law' or Pareto principle of human capital investment in which 80 per cent of value is thought to be created by 20 per cent of people. So, the intended audience for the messages of this logic is largely internal stakeholders (including business partners) because differentiation and novelty in business model change lies in identifying and working with internal bundles of resources, including key talent pools (Sparrow and Balain, 2009). However, this distinctiveness/differentiation logic, which rests on exclusivity and the classical liberal notion of equity rather than equality, is potentially and, perhaps, intentionally divisive as a motivational strategy: *in focusing on the few it creates the problems of integrating the many* necessary but currently less value-adding segments of the workforce, especially those that have the potential in the longer term to contribute (Sparrow et al., 2008).

Similarity (among Others)

The above, largely internally facing logic of distinctiveness, can be contrasted with an external strategic decision-making logic that seeks to make organizations legitimate in the eyes of industry peers and society at large (Highhouse et al., 2009; King and Whetten, 2008). This alternative logic sees strategic decisions as influenced by a need to be the same as others by seeking approval and respectability from relevant stakeholders. Sometimes decisions are driven by the need for legitimacy in society at large, and thus are influenced by institutional pressures and isomorphism; sometimes, however, they are driven by an historically shaped industry recipe that seems to define success, which managers use as an heuristic device to make decisions in uncertain conditions (Spender, 1989). Although there are inconsistencies arising from these two sources of legitimacy – society at large and industrial peers, both sets of drivers cause organizations to look and feel the same because of the following demands on them:

1. meeting ever-changing standards expected of large companies to develop a strong sense of 'corporateness' (Balmer and Greyser, 2003; Martin and Hetrick, 2006, 2009), respectability and impressiveness (Highhouse et al., 2009),
2. creating integration through corporate brand and values (Hatch and Schultz, 2008), high standards of corporate governance (Martin and McGoldrick, 2009), and
3. achieving a corporate reputation for being socially responsible, contested though such a concept is (Devinney, 2009).

Such standards are increasingly demanded by stakeholders, especially investors, the financial press, discerning customers and, increasingly, prospective and existing employees in companies in developed economies, probably explaining why large, complex organizations, especially multinational enterprises (MNEs), are so concerned with corporate branding and employer branding. In doing so, they constitute the necessary but not sufficient conditions to exist. A good example of this search for legitimacy is the adoption of sustainability and social responsible policies by many organizations during the last few years (Devinney, 2009).

A corporate identity allows organizations to achieve economies of scale and global cost leadership through integration of businesses and by reducing transaction costs in functions such as marketing, IT, HR, supply chain management, to secure new business through 'doing well by doing good' and to establish reputations internationally and locally for being good corporate citizens among governments and the investor community (Love and Kraatz, 2009; Martin and Hetrick, 2006). Thus the mimetic institutional pressures to copy others' strategies and values, and the impact of social networking and recruitment among a small cadre of business leaders leads to bandwagon effects, coercive comparisons in the form of benchmarking best practice and national legal standards or codes of conduct in accounting, governance and CSR drive companies to achieve legitimacy by becoming the same corporately. This logic ensures that firms develop a strong corporate value system, often for investors' consumption, and to ensure that rogue subsidiaries or divisions do not damage hard won corporate reputations and brand equity.

The SHRM implications of this drive towards corporateness are that firms becoming similar in their branding, thus seeking to become employers of choice with a global employer brand and set of HR 'best practices'. The audience for such signals are largely external – to send a message to investors, governments, customers and potential employees that they are engaging with a prestigious, well-run, high-performing and respectable company that is as least as good as others, to help internal stakeholders identify and engage even more with the organization because identity and engagement are formed by what employees think significant outsiders feel about their organization – their so-called construed image (Highhouse et al, 2009; Martin, 2009; Price et al., 2008).

Negative Capabilities?

These different strategic logics lead organizations and their corporate and business unit managers to work with ideas that are not easily resolved because they require of them the simultaneous need to be, on the one hand, locally responsive and to adopt exclusive talent management policies, focusing on talented individuals and human capital, while on the other hand, they strive to be similar in employing corporate-wide standards of legitimacy, inclusive talent management policies and to focus on the all important social capital – the bonds, bridges and trust among people and partners that provide the glue which binds the organization together. The two sets of needs can be linked theoretically in terms of meeting accountability standards (King and Whetten, 2008). The similarity/legitimacy logic drives strategists towards strategic decision-making that meets the minimum standards or expectations for membership of an industry or global company, while the differentiation logic sets a higher standard for competitive performance and esteem. Practically, however, we have found in our research in large organizations, especially MNEs (e.g. Martin and Beaumont, 2001; Martin and Dyke, forthcoming), that they lead to three linked but conceptually distinctive problems which HR practitioners and line managers find great difficulty in resolving when dealing with the integration-responsiveness problem.

TENSIONS BETWEEN GLOBAL AND LOCAL VALUES

The exhortation to think global and act local mantra is recognition that organizations, especially ones that grow through acquisition or internationally, are characterized by multiple identities. Global companies seek to exercise control over these identities because of the need to have business units and their workforce 'on message' with the corporate logic, global cost leadership and corporate stakeholder management. However, as we noted earlier philosophers and management scholars of identity have argued that identity is essentially a local phenomenon and has to resonate or be authentic with employees and other local stakeholders because both are a product of local cultures (Baumann, 2007; Hatch and Schultz, 2004). This localization of identity requires organizations to be in tune with local employees and other stakeholders and to encourage constant expressions of employee voice and speaking truth to power (Gollan and Wilkinson, 2007), an argument recently receiving official government backing in countries such as the UK from the MacLeod Report on engagement (2009).

THE TENSIONS BETWEEN EXCLUSIVE AND INCLUSIVE HR STRATEGIES

The exclusive approach to talent management that focuses on the few at the expense of the many has its critics (Pfeffer and Sutton, 2006; Sparrow et al., 2008) for ethical, economic and rational reasons. Especially in coordinated market economies, which have a heritage of integration among firms and employees (Whitley, 1999), the liberal market philosophy on which this exclusive talent management approach is based is a difficult idea to swallow for many organizations, managers and employees. This debate is reflected among many organizations in their approach to talent management. Again turning to the UK, a recent Chartered Institute of Personnel and Development survey showed that 63 per cent of firms surveyed pursued an inclusive talent management strategy while 37 per cent had more focused policies (CIPD, 2007). The debate over elitism following the collapse of the world financial system is also central to the discussions over what kinds of organizations will be fit for the future and the calls for a new management 2.0 paradigm based less on market and hierarchical principles and more on those that are evident in firms in coordinated market business systems (Hamel, 2009).

Even within the liberal market economies of the USA, however, there is emerging evidence that the exclusive version of talent management hasn't worked well and, given the unpredictability of economic environments, can't work well. As noted earlier, Groysberg and his colleagues have produced a series of articles showing the negative side of the 'star' system, which the exclusive version of talent management has helped fuel (Groysberg et al., 2004; Groysberg, 2008; Groysberg et al., 2008). Their research into the recruitment and performance of investment analysts demonstrated how much recruiting 'star' analysts could backfire on the hiring companies and on the subsequent poorer performance of the supposed star, in part because of the resentment of lesser lights in the hiring companies and the difficulty of stars' abilities to embed themselves in new supportive 'soil'. More recent work on US football stars and women managers has begun to refined their arguments and begin to hint at the importance of social capital rather than the human capital of investment in stars (Groysberg et al., 2008). For example, they found a significant difference in the subsequent performance of star players transferred from one team to another who played in positions that relied on supportive team work from those who played in positions that relied less on a supporting cast. Similarly women managers were found to have and use greater skill in creating and leveraging networks when changing jobs to new organizations than their male counterparts (Groysberg, 2008).

On the unpredictability of the future argument, part of the premise of talent management and the ubiquitous talent pipeline metaphor used by many organizations is that it is possible to forecast with some degree of accuracy into the future what skills and types of people will be needed and that once recruited and developed that such talent will remain in the pipeline. However, as Sparrow et al. (2008) have argued, in an increasingly unknowable world, premises based on typical workforce talent planning assumptions are not only fraught with problems but can lock organizations into long-term talent strategies that are inappropriate in a volatile environment. Hesketh and Hird (2009) also make an excellent point in the partial truth of metaphors when describing the typical talent pipeline of organizations in the UK as more of a sieve, with leaks appearing at many junctures because of the failure of organizations to manage careers through the pipeline and because of declining levels of loyalty among talented employees who have got the message delivered by acquisitive organizations that job change is the fastest route to increased salary.

TENSIONS BETWEEN HUMAN AND SOCIAL CAPITAL AND INNOVATION

Related to the above, HR initiatives and other management techniques and functions are increasingly being judged against how they impact the innovation agenda in these organizations. One useful way of conceptualising this potential relationship is to see innovation as the product of three, interrelated forms of capital – human, social and organizational capital – that combine and complement each other to create intellectual capital in an organization, which is its collective stocks and flows of knowledge and learning (see Figure 7.1). This is sometimes referred to as the collective 'IQ' of an organization on which different types of innovation rest (Munsi et al., 2005). Human capital is usually defined in terms of the investment and capacities of individuals and is a product of individualist cultures and business systems. It refers to the capabilities, knowledge, skills, attitudes and experiences of individual employees and managers which have been at the heart of the talent management agenda in organizations and in the growing interest in leadership. Though not without its critics, few practitioners and management academics disagree that the case for human capital and talent management is a compelling one. Yet, as we have argued, recent research has shown it is only one element in creating intellectual capital (Bontis and Serenko, 2009). Moreover, it has been shown to have a 'dark side' to it (Pfeffer and Sutton, 2006; Sennett, 2009). The key message in much of the talent management literature is of a direct link between investment in human capital (talented individuals) and innovative organizations, though this relationship in more sophisticated work is thought to be mediated by an organization's stock and flow of intellectual capital or, in more common parlance, capacity for organizational learning. Yet, practitioners and some researchers often commit the fundamental 'attributional error' of over-emphasizing individuals and their talents (or lack of them) as the cause of organizational performance and under-emphasizing the social and organizational context in which performance occurred. For example, a longitudinal study of 208 US firms found that increased emphasis on human capital had a *negative* impact on an organization's capacity to produce radical innovation and only had a positive effect when combined with social capital investment (Subramaniam and Youndt, 2005).

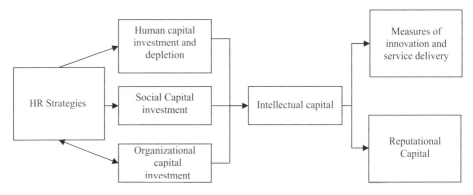

Figure 7.1   Modelling HR's potential contribution to innovation and reputational capital

The series of studies by Groysberg mentioned in the previous section of this paper helps explain why such counter-intuitive findings may have occurred. Their longitudinal study of financial services analysts posed major risks associated with hiring 'stars' on the basis of past performance and then expecting them to repeat similar levels of performance in new contexts; the evidence points to the likelihood that both the performance of the star and the recipient organization will decline for some considerable time following hiring. This was because stars relied on a supportive context for them to perform effectively in their original employment, which could not be transferred to their new employment; moreover, disruption and low morale often resulted from parachuting stars into unreceptive contexts for change. Thus, by talking up the value of individual human capital, there is a danger that we neglect to invest in these other key elements of context, most notably, *social capital* and *organizational capital*. Both of these forms of capital, according to some evidence at least, can have a greater impact on intellectual capital in certain circumstances; moreover, they can have an earlier impact, another key factor in appraising investment decisions (Bontis and Serenko, 2009). So our core argument is that HR has an important potential influence on intellectual capital formation, and so on innovation and the corporate reputations that ensue, because HR can not only influence human capital formation but also social capital by strengthening organizational engagement or identification (Edwards and Peccei, 2007), work engagement (Salanova and Schaufeli, 2008) and engagement with each other, otherwise known as relational collaboration (Gittell et al., 2009). This reasoning is also evident in the work by Sparrow et al. (2008) on HR and engagement. They stress the need for HR to focus not just on human capital but also on the organizational architecture that binds individuals and teams together, through a greater emphasis on organizational design and organizational development.

HR Strategy as Practice

We have found in our research and clinical work with senior HR managers that they have significant if not insurmountable difficulties in reconciling these logics of difference and similarity (Martin and Hetrick, 2006, 2009). So, is there a model that might help them to do so, and what might it imply for corporate reputation management in industries such as financial services? We believe the strategy as practice perspective offers some guidance in this respect. This perspective has become an important theme in the academic literature on strategic management in recent years, though it draws on a classic literature in the field of strategic change and HRM which emphasized the role of context and process in strategy and strategic HRM (Pettigrew and Whipp, 1991; Tyson, 1987). The key messages of this new and, indeed, earlier literature are that strategy needs to be understood not necessarily as a position nor as the outcome of legitimate actions but in terms of the problems experienced by strategists at all levels in organizations in how they strategize and what do they do when they strategize to resolve often difficult or irreconcilable issues.

This perspective emphasizes the verb, 'strategizing', rather than the outcomes of strategy, so focusing on three factors, *strategists*, the *practice* of strategy and strategic *practices* (Jarzablowski et al., 2007). The first of these refers to the *people* doing the strategizing, that is, the different types and levels of practitioners involved in creating strategic decisions

– who they are, how they act and what resources they draw on when strategizing. In the conventional normative strategic literature, usually these key actors are assumed to be senior managers involved in strategic planning teams, drawing on rational and political resources to achieve their ends, but this is not always or even mainly the case; HR managers, line managers, union representatives, employees at all levels and external consultants are often heavily involved in the process not only of implementing strategies but also in helping develop them through their actions and conversations. The second factor refers to the *practice* of strategy, which refers to the relationships between the actions of these different levels and groups of strategists and how they are socially, politically and economically embedded in the institutions of the particular organizations and societies in which they act. In strategic HR terms this can be illustrated by the problems local HR managers and line managers have in implementing corporate values especially in business units and contexts that are institutionally and culturally distant, which is the case in many global companies (Martin and Beaumont, 2001). The third refers to strategic practices, which are the routines of behaviour consisting of mental and interpersonal activities, background knowledge, knowhow, motivations and material and discursive resources that strategists draw on for constructing strategic activity. Again, translating this notion into strategic HR terms, this could refer to how specific HR practices such as talent management and employer branding are used to influence strategic practice and, indeed, strategists.

Thus the focus of this perspective is on how HR strategists through their actions, interactions and negotiations skilfully accomplish situated strategic HR practice that has important implications for the firm, and how they combine cognitive, behavioural, procedural, motivational, symbolic and physical resources to construct strategic HR practice that has meaning in specific contexts and time periods (Jarzabkowski et al., 2007; Johnson et al., 2007; Whittington et al., 2003). As such it is concerned with 'thinking your way into acting' and 'acting your way into thinking' (Weick, 2001), seeing strategy as a planned and emergent or learning process, so allowing organizations to manage the inevitable tensions that face them when strategizing. Such tensions include those we have already identified – 'the think global, act local paradox'. It is also evident in the need to simultaneously innovate and exploit (O'Reilly and Tushman, 2004), the need to create wealth and protect wealth (Martin and McGoldrick, 2009) and the problems of transferring learning across business units and between the centre and business units in multinational environments (Bjorkman et al., 2009; Martin and Beaumont, 2001).

The SHRM implications of this perspective are most obvious in helping explain how organizations can and perhaps should resolve the differentiation/segmentation/exclusive approach with the integration/corporate/inclusive approach of the two dominant logics. By foregrounding various HR strategists and employees at all levels and their practices, that is putting people back into strategic management, this approach not only helps us understand how the dilemmas and paradoxes are worked through but also suggests that it is only by focusing on the *journey* – the skilful accomplishments of HR strategists and employees at *all* levels in creating workable HR strategies – that distinctiveness and similarity can be reconciled. It is maybe only through this route, rather than the legislative one currently pursued by governments, that sectors such as financial services can become 'fit for the future' again.

References

Balain, S. and Sparrow, P. (2009) *Engaged to Perform: a new perspective on employee engagement.* White Paper 2009-04. Lancaster: Centre for Performance-Led HR, University of Lancaster. Available online at http://www.lums.lancs.ac.uk/research/centres/hr/WhitePapers/.

Barney, J. (1991). Firm resources and sustained competitive advantage. *Journal of Management,* 17(1), 99–120.

Baumann, Z. (2007). *Liquid Times: living in an age of uncertainty,* Cambridge: Polity Press.

Becker, B. E. and Huselid, M. A. (2005). Strategic human resource management. Where do we go from here? *Journal of Management,* 32(6), 898–925.

Becker, B. E., Huselid, M.A. and Beatty, R.W. (2009). *The Differentiated Workforce: transforming talent into strategic impact.* Boston, MA: Harvard Business Review Press.

Bjorkman, I., Barner, Rasmussen, W., Ehrnrooth, M. and Makela, K. (2009) Performance management across borders. In P. Sparrow (ed.), *Handbook of International Human Resource Management:* integrating people, process and context (pp. 229–50). Chichester: John Wiley.

Bontis, N. and Serenko, A. (2009). A causal model of human capital antecedents and consequents in the financial services industry. *Journal of Intellectual Capital,* 10, 53–69.

Boudreau, J.W. and Ramstad, P.M. (2007). *Beyond HR: the new science of human capital.* Boston, MA: Harvard Business School Publishing Corporation.

Boxall, P. and Purcell, J. (2008). *Strategy and Human Resource Management* (2nd ed.). New York: Palgrave Macmillan.

Cascio, W. and Boudreau, J. (2008). *Investing in People: financial impact of human resource initiatives.* Upper Saddle, NJ: FT Press/Pearson Education.

CIPD (2007). *Talent Management.* London: Chartered Institute of Personnel and Development.

Deephouse, D. L. and Carter, S. M. (2005). An examination of differences between organizational legitimacy and organizational reputation. *Journal of Management Studies,* 42(2), 329–60.

Devinney, T. M. (2009). Is the socially responsible corporation a myth? The good, the bad, and the ugly of corporate social responsibility. *Academy of Management Perspectives,* 23, 44–56.

Edwards, M.R. and Peccei, R. (2007) Organizational identification: development and testing of a conceptually grounded measure. *European Journal of Work and Organizational Psychology,* 16, 25–57.

Gittell, J.H., Seidner, R. and Wimbush, J. (2010). A relational model of how high-performance work systems work. *Organization Science,* 21(2): 490–506.

Gollan, P. and Wilkinson, A. (2007) Contemporary developments in information and consultation. *International Journal of Human Resource Management,* 18, 1133–44.

Grint, K. (2005). Problems, problems, problems: the social construction of 'leadership'. *Human Relations,* 58(11), 1467–94.

Groysberg, B. (2008). How star women build portable skills. *Harvard Business Review,* 86(2), 74–81.

Groysberg, B., Nanda, A. and Nohria, N. (2004). The risky business of hiring stars. *Harvard Business Review,* 82(5), 92–100.

Groysberg, B, Sant, L. and Abrahams, R. (2008). When 'stars' migrate, do they still perform like stars? *MIT Sloan Management Review,* 50, 41–6

Hamel, G. (2009) Moonshots for management. *Harvard Business Review,* 1 February.

Hatch, M. J. and Schultz, M. (2008). *Taking Brand Initiative: how companies can align strategy, culture and identity through corporate branding.* San Francisco: Jossey Bass.

Hesketh, A. and Hird, M. (2009). The golden triangle: how relationships between leaders can leverage more value from people. *Human Resource Business Review,* 2, 24–38.

Highhouse, S., Brooks, M. E. and Gregarus, M. (2009) An organizational impression management perspective on the formation of corporate reputations. *Journal of Management*, 35, 1481–93.

Jarzabkowski, P., Balogun, J. and Seidl, D. (2007). Strategizing: The challenges of a practice perspective. *Human Relations*, 60(1), 5.

Johnson, G., Langley, A., Melin L. and Whittington, R. (2007). *Strategy as Practice: research directions and resources*. Cambridge, UK: Cambridge University Press.

King, B. G. and Whetten, D. A. (2008). Rethinking the relationship between reputation and legitimacy: a social actor conceptualization. *Corporate Reputation Review*, 11(3), 192–207.

Lawrence, P. R. and Lorsch, J. W. (1969). *Developing Organizations: diagnosis and action*. Reading, MA: Addison-Wesley Publishing Company.

Lengnick-Hall, M. L, Lengnick-Hall, C.A., Andrade, L. and Drake, B. (2009) Strategic human resource management; the evolution of a field. *Human Resource Management Review*, 19, 64–85.

Lepak, D. P. and Snell, S. A. (2002). Examining the human resource architecture: the relationships among human capital, employment, and human resource configurations. *Journal of Management*, 28(4), 517–43.

Love, E. and Kraatz, M. (2009). Character, conformity, or the bottom line? How and why downsizing affected corporate reputation. *The Academy of Management Journal*, 52(2), 314–35.

MacLeod, D. and Clarke, N. (2009). *Engaging for Success: enhancing performance through employee engagement*. London: Department for Business Innovation and Skills.

Martin, G. (2009). Employer branding and corporate reputation management. In R. J. Burke and C. L. Cooper (eds), *The Peak Performing Organization* (pp. 252–74). London: Routledge.

Martin, G. and Beaumont, P.B. (2001) Transforming multinational enterprises: towards a process model of strategic human resource management change. *International Journal of Human Resource Management*, 12, 1234–50.

Martin, G. and Groen-In't-Woud, S. (forthcoming) Employer branding in multinational firms. In H. Scullion and D. Collings (eds), *Global Talent Management*. London: Routledge.

Martin, G. and Hetrick, S. (2006*) Corporate Reputations, Branding and Managing people: a strategic approach to HR*. Oxford: Butterworth Heinemann.

Martin, G. and Hetrick, S. (2009) Employer branding and corporate reputation management in an international context. In P.R. Sparrow (ed.), *Handbook of International Human Resource Management* (pp. 293–320). Chichester, Sussex: John Wiley.

Martin, G. and McGoldrick, J. (2009) Corporate governance and HR: some reflections and a case study from the UK National Health Service. In S. Young (ed.), *Contemporary Issues in International Governance*. Melbourne: Tilde University Press.

Munsi, N., Oke, A., Stafylarkis, M., Puranam, P., Towells, S., Moslein, K. and Neely, A. (2005) *Leading for Innovation: the impact of leadership on innovation*. Advanced Institute of Management Report, AIM/ESRC. Available at: http://www.aimresearch.org/index.php?page=81, accessed 8 December 2008.

O'Reilly, C. A., III, and Tushman, M .L. The ambidextrous organization. *Harvard Business Review*, 82, 74–81.

Pettigrew, A. M. and Whipp, R. (1991) *Managing Change for Competitive Success*. Oxford: Blackwell.

Pfeffer, J. and Sutton, R. I. (2006). *Hard Facts, Dangerous Half-truths, and Total Nonsense: profiting from evidence-based management*. Cambridge, MA: Harvard Business School Press.

Porter, Michael F.. (2008) The five competitive forces that shape strategy. *Harvard Business Review* 86 (special issue on HBS centennial), 1.

Price, K. N., Gioia, D. A. and Corley, K. G. (2008). Reconciling scattered images: managing disparate organizational expressions and impressions. *Journal of Management Inquiry*, 17(3), 173–85.

Roberts, J. (2004). *The Modern Firm: organizational design for performance and growth.* Oxford: Oxford University Press.

Rosenzweig, P. (2006) The dual logics behind international human resource management: pressures for global integration and local responsiveness. In Günter K. Stahl and Ingmar Björkman (eds) Handbook of Research in International Human Resource Management (pp. 36–48), Cheltenham, UK: Edward Elgar.

Salanova, M. and Schaufeli, W. B. (2008). A cross-national study of work engagement as a mediator between job resources and proactive behavior: a cross-national study. *International Journal of Human Resources Management*, 19, 226–31

Sennett, R. (2009) *The Craftsman.* London: Penguin.

Sparrow, P. (ed.) (2009) *Handbook of International Human Resource Management: integrating people, process and context.* Chichester, UK: John Wiley.

Sparrow, P. and Balain, S. (2009) Talent-proofing the organization. In C. Cooper and R. Burke (eds), *The Peak Performing Organization.* London and New York: Routledge.

Sparrow, P., Hesketh, A., Hird, M., Marsh, C. and Balain, S. (2008) *Reversing the Arrow: using business model change to tie HR into strategy.* Academic report. Centre for Performance-Led HR, University of Lancaster. Available online at http://www.lums.lancs.ac.uk/research/centres/hr/WhitePapers/, accessed 14 February 2010.

Spender, J. C. (1989) *Industrial Recipes: an enquiry into the nature and sources of managerial judgement.* Oxford: Basil Blackwell.

Subramaniam, M. and Youndt, M. A. (2005) The influence of intellectual capital on the types of innovative capabilities. *Academy of Management Journal*, 48, 450–63.

Tyson, S. (1987) The management of the personnel function. *Journal of Management Studies*, 24, 523–32.

Weick, K. E. (2001) *Making Sense of the Organization.* Oxford: Blackwell.

Whitley, R. (1999). *Divergent Capitalisms: the social structuring and change of business systems.* Oxford: Oxford University Press.

Whittington, R. (2001). *What is Strategy – and Does it Matter?* London: Thomson.

Whittington, R., Jarzabkowski, P., Mayer, M., Mounoud, E., Nahapiet, J. and Rouleau, L. (2003). Taking strategy seriously: responsibility and reform for an important social practice. *Journal of Management Inquiry*, 12(4), 396–409.

Zott, C. and Amit, R. (2008). The fit between product market strategy and business model: implications for firm performance. *Strategic Management Journal*, 29, 1–26.

8 *From Applause to Notoriety: Organizational Reputation and Corporate Governance*

CHARLES MCMILLAN

Defend your reputation, or bid farewell to your good life forever.
William Shakespeare

Introduction

For business organizations, survival of the firm is an operating premise of MBA programs, with an assumption that longevity depends on corporate reputation, i.e. public acceptance in the marketplace. In truth, most firms have limited survival rates. Many firms fail, even big ones, despite the Wall Street dictum, Too Big to Fail! Often firms are absorbed by bigger firms, or get merged, and many firms simply and quietly disappear. Why is survival a real challenge? The Catholic Church has remained strong for some 2,000 years. Its management has few MBAs. The ancient universities of Europe, like Krakow, Bologna, and Oxford, have almost a thousand years of history. Some monarchical families—the Windsors in Britain, the Japanese imperial family—are dated in millennia. Certain corporate groups like Mitsui and Hudson's Bay date back hundreds of years. Japan has more firms in the top 1,000 global companies that survive more than 200 years than any other nation. Most corporations survive less than a century, and the failure of mergers and acquisitions is about 60 per cent. General Electric is the only surviving American entity in the top 100 firms at the turn of the twenty-first century (for background, see Stinchcome, 1965; McMillan, 2007).

Common sense (which may not be so common) and everyday experience indicate that individual, companies, and organizations from universities to charities can gain a reputation varying from good to terrible. "Everyone has 15 seconds of fame," an aphorism from a famous Andy Warhol quote, illustrates the modern cult of celebrity, reinforced by Western popular culture, reality TV shows, and gossip magazines, and fostered by the internet and new tools of social networks. Today, a hit record, a catastrophe, a lottery winner, and a heroic action vie for 24/7 media space, a measure of idolatry, and celebrity status. Even for business corporations, executives vie for cover stories, and compete to be listed as the most admired companies in magazines like *Fortune*.

In a world of global forces, where trade, technology, and communications greatly enhance competitive forces, organizational reputation now stands as a central strategic concern. Corporate scandals illustrate how firms like Enron, Arthur Anderson, Nortel, Hollinger, and the investment banks on Wall Street can fail, but the issues both of managerial and corporate reputation are more complicated than illegal activities. Around the world, the external risk environment is well documented (World Economic Forum, 2010). Risks affecting organizations and societies are enormous: economic (energy, fiscal, underinvestment in infrastructure, asset price bubbles), geopolitical (from terrorism and nuclear proliferation to failed state collapse and international crime), environmental (biodiversity loss to climate change), medical (infectious diseases, HIC-AIDS, and pandemics) to technological (cyber crime, data fraud, nano-particle toxicity). Decision-risk and reputation are related phenomena.

Three dominant paradigms surround studies of corporate reputation. Economic theory builds on the market exchange ideas of Milton Friedman (1962), where sellers and buyers trade products and services, firms suffer reputation damage from substandard performance, thus impacting future exchange. In this sense, firm reputation is a constant in an economic equilibrium model, unless through faulty products or bad services, the consuming public provides a market signal through abandonment, product switching, and severe punishment (e.g. financial penalties). In this sense, as set out by Klein and Leffler (1981), reputation is a corporate asset, where value is enhanced or destroyed by performance incentives and constant new investments that create perceived uniqueness. The conceptual challenge of these models is complicated by the boundaries of the firm, the purchasing decision varies with information: immediate to the customer buying fresh produce, subsequent to purchase (buying a car, getting an MBA), or post-sale comparison (e.g. medical treatment). Markets are often imperfect, hence the real problems of asymmetric information (Spence, 1975; Akerlof, 1970).

Legal scholars also consider economic exchange, usually in the framework of contracts, e.g. between buyers and sellers on a repeated basis, thus forming a relational contract, or a more formal, legal contract, such as a purchase of a house or an employment contract (MacNeil, 1974). A vast literature has developed (MacLeod, 2007) combining legal contractual studies and issues like reputation uncertainty (sellers allowing price discounts to maintain buyer–seller reciprocity), asymmetric information and cheating, rules enforcement, and firm reputation as tradable assets, including contract purchasing and imperfect monitoring.

Business school academics and managerial consultants address similar issues, but often with fewer abstractions, formal mathematical models, and prescriptive theorizing. Two themes emerge. The first is that organizations engage in reputation building and enhancement as a process of external communications with the public and key stakeholders, but often as an asymmetric exercise where the organization and top management control the messaging with time lags between sender and receiver (March and Simon, 1958). Organizational reputation is constructed around brand imaging, ranging from logos and trade marks to formal brands like the *iPhone* and *Lexus* where branding strengthens and accentuates organizational competencies. A second theme is institutionalism, where organizations construct identities using language, symbols, rhetoric, and actions that lead to an autonomous domain and repetitive routines, built around a unique portfolio of events, successes, and people (Thompson, 1967; Eccles and Nohria, 1990; Martin and

Hetrick, 2006). Universities are a classic example, exemplified by the question answered by a president of Harvard: "What makes a great university? 350 years."

This chapter addresses corporate reputation, providing a model of organizational reputation, what sustains it, and what damages it. What are the models of corporate governance that will guide future organizational behavior and does the model entertain appropriate risk assessments and models of action? How reputation risk assessments impact corporate governance as a result of corporate scandals? The paper concludes with recommendations to build and maintain corporate reputation.

Values and Organizational Reputation

In general terms, corporate reputation comes from multiple sources of self-esteem, e.g. from key stakeholders like employees, shareholders, suppliers and customers, or social claimants, including society at large, the media, or reputation enhancers like governments, bankers, professional critics, or competitors (Bonini et. al, 2009; Worcestor, 2009; Weigelt and Cameron, 1988). Corporate surveys around the world show a correlation between expressed values and corporate reputation. Globalization enhances but elevates the risk elements of corporate reputation, because new competitors can now encroach on entrenched positioning. In theory, there are five general elements, or social values, that impact corporate reputation, discussed below.

MORALITY

Both immediate stakeholders and the public at large have a general sense of morality, even if there are differences by country or region. Slavery is a case in point, impacting the textile trade, shipping and cargo, and the output of plantation landholdings in the nineteenth and twentieth centuries in the United States (or the gulags of China and the Soviet Union), but today, similar moral issues effect industries and firms in terms of child labor, illegal immigration, or other forms of maltreatment of people because of skin color, religious beliefs, country of origin, or gender inequities.

LEGALITY

Legal issues transcend moral issues, because many issues that seem morally repugnant once were not illegal (the slave trade) and many issues that are illegal may not be widely seen as moral issues (smoking marijuana or tobacco). In general, once a society makes certain activities illegal, and corporations adhere to old practices and habits, corporate reputation will decline. Pollution, asbestos, tobacco and, more recently, a high carbon footprint, are cases in point.

CONSISTENCY

In general, most corporations serve multiple industries with multiple products/services, so there is an enormous challenge to develop consistency across the product portfolio, especially when some products can readily damage the corporate brand. The attempt to exit or diversify from the tobacco or asbestos industry is an example.

COHERENCE

Corporate reputation comes from actions and behaviors at the strategic level, in products and markets served. But reputation also comes in operational tactics and functions, which steadily enhance or undermine corporate reputation. The Japanese case studies of quality management illustrate both the reputation of Japanese corporations, but also the country reputation of "Made in Japan," similar to "Made in Switzerland," as a source of high-quality, high-value products and services.

INCLUSIVENESS

Organizations have indeed multiple stakeholders and corporate reputation must have wide appeal, or perhaps more accurately, a sense of inclusion that different stakeholders are being treated in the same way. For corporations, this immediately means workers, shareholders, and customers. The corporate scandals of Wall Street follies of recent years have at their core the perception, more real than imagined, that some groups like managers and select shareholders are ripping off the system for their own ends. The rising spread between the ratios of total compensation for CEOs to workers, once 20:1, now closer to 470:1, illustrates the real risk to corporate reputation and managerial legitimacy.

Corporate Reputation: Theory and Practice

Standard dictionaries define reputation as the quality or skills of a person or organization, as judged by the public at large, or recognition of character or ability. In a practical sense, this meaning implies that an individual or organization (the sender) communicates to the public or relevant stakeholders (the receiver) skills and strengths. Reputation is related to communications, in conventional sense via public relations, or novel, like the internet and social media. Clearly, the role of the media, today so ubiquitous, from cell phones and BlackBerry to the internet and social media tools like Twitter and Facebook, creates and enhances instant identities where managers may prefer to create a narrative of illusions and make-believe, divorced from authentic performance (Fombrun, 1996; Jue et al., 2009; Shih, 2009).

Executive decisions can advance actions and behaviors that depart from experience, past learning, organizational memory, and familiar routines by extending resource commitments to less predictable (high-variability) routines, leading to increasing risk and misalignment of skills and competences to shareholder perceptions of acceptable performance. The result is reputation failure. Management behavior is the intermediary aligning the organization's reputation to the critical stakeholders (see Figure 8.1).

The media has an inherent interest in celebrity CEOs, and CEOs in turn cultivate a celebrity status, much as governments and the military foster heroic models of leadership, as attested in the writings of the celebrated Scottish scribe, Thomas Carlyle (1841) and his classic work on heroes. Top management, controlling the critical resources for communications—the message and the messenger—can instigate a bias in both performance and reputation. (For overview, see March 2000; Weigelt and Cameron, 1988; Hayward et al., 2004; Pavelin and Brammer, 2006; and Villette and Viellermat, 2009.) Too often, both CEO biographies and organizational case studies rationalize management

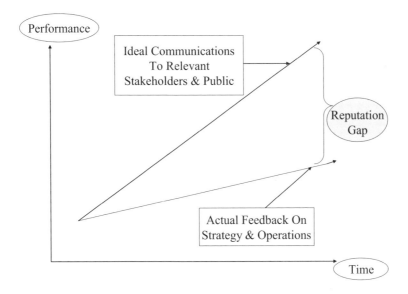

Figure 8.1   Corporate alignment, performance and reputation

actions and rarely question or evaluate leadership behavior and its negative consequences (Higgs, 2009; Pfeffer and Sutton, 2006). In the extreme, organizational misconduct comes from many facets of misaligned incentives, such as financial misrepresentation, violation of legal codes, and organizational hypocrisy about actual performance (Baucus and Baucus, 1997; Chatterjee and Hambrick, 2007; Farber, 2005; Staubus, 2005).

Organizations occupy a space in a network, sometimes called industries, sometimes labeled environments, but they cultivate a measure of autonomy or self-sufficiency to leverage power, applause, and personal esteem. An organization's culture fuses skills, competencies, and decision choices that create a sense of virtue, illusions, and incentives. The construction of such traits and beliefs lead to reputation, communicated and embedded within members and external constituents. Within the organization, the executive coalition justifies its power and position by communicating a measure of uniqueness called a distinct competence, usually justified to provide solutions to problems that pose moral hazards—conserving animals and natural landscapes, assuring safety of food and health, providing educational services, preserving the people's savings, protecting children from pornography and evil ways. Organizations seek a measure of autonomy as a license to carry out these functions, and thereby leverage information and power to cultivate a scarce good, corporate reputation (Carpenter, 2006).

Reputation is a process of learning, of cultivating organizational memory, and of communicating and interpreting positive beliefs and emotions about organizational performance and thus sources of leverage in the environment. Rising reputation, allied to rising aspirations and performance, improve conditions of organizational slack—emotional, judgmental, financial—and decisions are settled by analytic and bargaining processes. By contrast, reputation damage, or even reputation destruction, comes from decision styles that are political, personal, and conflict-driven (March and Simon, 1958).

These perspectives are consistent with a view of organizations as a coalition of actors (individuals, groups, subunits, teams) where senior executives communicate actions and values to external groups about critical strategic contingencies, where organizations combine problems, routines, and solutions (Cyert and March, 1963; Thompson, 1967; Hickson et al., 1971). Scarcity of resources, or organizational slack, preserves power relations within the organization, providing a general desire to maintain a measure of perceived uniqueness to secure and protect both individual and organizational reputation. Coalition behavior allows senior executives to mold recognition, identity, cognition, and decision premises by controlling communication tools, office layout, luxury goods (board rooms, cars, corporate jets, expenses), and executive placements positions that preserve power and status (March and Olsen, 1976; Kay et al., 2004).

Carpenter (2006: 26) outlines the history of bureaucratic agencies in the US government and how they built reputations through autonomous activities:

> The reputations that autonomous agencies established were diverse. Some agencies became known for their ability to conserve the nation's natural resources. Others were celebrated for protecting American consumers from the hazards of adulterated food and medicines. The Post Office earned esteem for moral guardianship (a powerful role in the culturally conservative Progressive Era), that is, for shielding American families from the evils of pornography and gambling. Whatever their specific content, organizational reputations had two common traits. First, they were grounded in actual organizational capacity. Agencies with strong reputations possessed greater talent, cohesion, and efficiency than agencies with reputations for weakness, corruption, or malfeasance. Second, organizational reputations were not ethereal but socially rooted. They were grounded in diverse political affiliations maintained by career bureaucratic officials. Reputations that were embedded in multiple networks gave agency officials an independence from politicians, allowing them to build manifold coalitions around their favored programs and innovations.

> Two features of bureaucratic legitimacy—reputational uniqueness and political multiplicity— are crucial … Autonomous agencies must demonstrate uniqueness and show that they can create solutions and provide services found nowhere else in the polity. If politicians can easily find compelling policy alternatives to an agency's plans, then agency autonomy will not be stable. Autonomous agencies also have a legitimacy that is grounded—not among the voters of one party or one section, not in a single class or interest group, but in multiple and diverse political affiliations. Agencies are able to innovate freely only when they can marshal the varied forces of American politics into coalitions, coalitions that are unique and irreducible to lines of party, class, or parochial interest. Network-based reputations as such are the very essence of state legitimacy in modern representative regimes.

Corporate or individual reputation comes from public recognition of unique, special qualities and attributes. In theory, the "good" or competencies should be virtuous, valuable, and noteworthy, i.e. generally accepted according to social norms. But they may not be, because they are offensive, illegal, or even notorious (e.g. a personality like Bernie Madoff or Al Capone, or perhaps the most wanted man in the world, Osama Bin Laden). However, they still have a reputation.

Implicitly, relevant publics have a belief or trust in the message, i.e. that competencies lead to high performance (retailers selling quality goods, universities providing a quality education). Sustained performance judged by the public leads to corporate reputation as a social asset. In theory, the higher the reputation, the higher the organization can price its product/service, relative to other market participants. Whether the example is Tiger Woods in the golf industry, or Toyota's resale value for its used cars, or a book signed and written by a personality like Winston Churchill, reputation assets carry a premium over time. But there are two other variables in organizational reputation. As shown in the simplified model of corporate reputation in Figure 8.2, organizations communicate their strengths/competencies to the public by evoking these links to actual performance. Reputation comes from the social process of identification, what Alvesson (1990, p. 373) terms "experienced distinctiveness, consistency, and stability".

The first is organizational branding, a formal strategy of identifying the organization with expected performance. In theory, brand value is a portfolio of attributes perceived by customers and other stakeholders that enhance stock prices and provide repetitive purchasing and enhanced customer services (Merrilees and Miller, 2008). Organizational branding and managerial tools like brand equity, brand loyalty schemes, and brand association tactics may create sustained competitive advantage (Aaker, 2008). Organizations stake enormous financial and reputation commitment to a brand, because the public at large and specific consumer groups identify with four attitudes towards brands—trust, regard, awareness, and esteem. A huge marketing literature has developed, showing positive correlation between brand value and financial metrics of organizational performance, annual revenues, and stock performance (Pavelin and Brammer, 2006; Gerzema and Lebar, 2008).

Generally accepted best marketing practices suggest that organizations communicate organizational competences and mission values through brands, linking the organizational name to a brand image, associating with such virtues as trust, awareness, regard and esteem. High brand awareness, leading to brand equity, suggests sustained consumer purchasing and nigh loyalty that reinforces reputation (universities like Harvard and Oxford cultivate these issues through alumni around the world). Because brands and brand management create and maintain stakeholder loyalty, intangible assets are created, a reputation premium that leads to rising share prices. However, because of globalization, where information is more readily available, and minimizes the time spread between sender and receiver, stakeholders face information overload, cynicism increases with

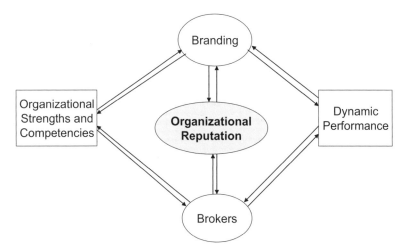

Figure 8.2   A simplified model of corporate reputation and communications

transparency, and organizations may face reputation loss because of a brand bubble (Gezema and Lebar, 2008; Bonini et al., 2009).

Branding represents a communications game between the organization and the public, real or contrived, two-way symmetry or asymmetrical, on-line and authentic, or gimmick PR imagery (Gilmore and Pine, 2007; Jue et al., 2009; Showkeir and Showkeir, 2008). However, other issues are at play. A central one includes what March and Simon (1958) call the "brokerage function." From movies to hotels, airlines to business schools, corporate bonds to country and corporate finance, rating agencies, the classic reputation brokers, attempt to decrease asymmetric information. Organizational brokers alleviate imperfect information flows by providing external quality certification, even though there may be enormous discrepancies in data flows, data analysis, and data intelligence. Indeed, most industries operate with imperfect information between the product and subsequent service, monitoring, and the timing of feedback mechanisms. Because there may be a desire to hide potential conflicts, the double agency problem arises. Double agency exists where firms pay the raters for their work, but need the rating outcomes to sell products (for one study, see Becker and Milbourn, 2009).

Increasing, corporate reputation is not based on direct consumer experience, but on the broker communications function of middlemen, serving as communications filters, who can make a reputation instantly, as illustrated by a film critic or movie review after the first performance. When Winston Churchill received two free tickets from George Bernard Shaw for the opening night of *Pygmalion*—which later was was the basis of the musical *My Fair Lady*—with an offer for the politician to bring a friend, if he had one, Churchill responded, "I can't make the opening night, but can go the next night, if you have one." Or, as Marie Antoinette found at the court of Versailles, underscored in a widely read novel, *Les Liaisons Dangereuses*, "Old women must not be angered, for they make young women's reputations."

Brokers filter actions, communications, and perceptions, as evidenced between innovation proposals and funding groups like investors. March and Simon (1958, p. 188) describe this function as follows:

> when decisions are satisficing rather than optimizing decisions, resource allocation to new programs will depend substantially on the communications structure through which proposals are processed from entrepreneurs to investors and on the order of presentation of alternatives ... Organizational decisions depend at least as heavily on attention cues as on utility functions.

Who Owns An Enterprise? Whose Reputation?

The owner-manager, the stereotype of small business, is an easy model to understand. So are family firms (Caspar et al., 2010), sports personalities, movie stars, or political figures, whose reputation and performance become aligned. It is no accident that an entrepreneur like Richard Branson built his brand around Virgin, not around himself. A basic question remains: Who owns most firms? Whose reputation is at risk: the organization, or the managers who run them? Are their interests aligned? This is the classic agency problem, and it often leads to the double agency dilemma—when things go well, management and the organization are rewarded via share price premiums, compensation, and the like.

When things go badly, it is the organization which is jeopardized by reputation risk, even though, too often, management does very well indeed. Moral hazard is real.

Most organizations have a separation of ownership and managerial control. The assessments and implications of governance structure and agency challenges stem from financial engineering devices: corporate diversification, re-investment of earnings or dividend payouts to shareholders, dual class shares, holding companies, make or buy purchasing, to name a few. Even for public institutions owned and funded by government, such as universities, hospitals, and public agencies, there is confusion about the rights and responsibilities of managers, the forms of reporting, and protection of ownership rights. Public policy towards corporations, as enshrined by law, often leaves ambiguous disclosure policies, the rights of stakeholder groups, and the priority given to different stakeholders when an institution is in trouble, as in bankruptcy or court protection (for an overview, see Hillman and Keim, 2001). Where, for instance, are employee pensions when managers, who are not the owners, place a firm in bankruptcy? Hired managers and their salaries may be preserved, but retired employees may lose their pension stakes.

Figure 8.3 illustrates the complexity of corporate governance, where decision choices, processes, and outcomes vary widely. In the most straightforward model, where two dimensions are examined, the level of ownership and operating management, the role of proprietors is the simplest to define. In essence, the owner-manager is the traditional *homo economicus*, where the firm and the owner share identical goals, compensation, and performance criteria.

At the other extreme, where operating management is low (casting a vote at a shareholder's meeting, or selling a few shares), many shareholders are investing for share appreciation; they are in effect absentee shareholders. If shareholding is widely dispersed, with no one shareholder group dominating, senior management may act as proprietors, but not necessarily in the interest of shareholders. Perversely, many public organizations operate on similar premises.

The two other models illustrate coalition behavior in organizations. With hired guns, i.e. professional managers recruited to operate the enterprise, executives have unequivocal control over the central resources, i.e. all aspects of strategy and treasury management.

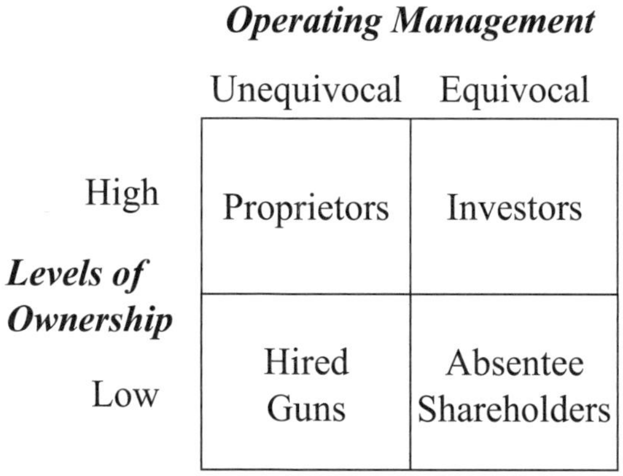

Operating Management

		Unequivocal	Equivocal
Levels of Ownership	High	Proprietors	Investors
	Low	Hired Guns	Absentee Shareholders

Figure 8.3　Understanding stakeholder models of the firm

Family-owned companies often elevate managers to these roles to maintain corporate survival, e.g. Hewlett-Packard, Bombardier, Seagram, and Disney have used this approach, with mixed success. Shareholder activism in the US has put many hired gun managers on a short leash, and turnover has been high (but often with enormous compensation for retiring executives). Another model first developed in the USA but now widely copied is the case of shareholder groups (e.g. equity funds, sovereign wealth funds, and private equity players, like the Carlyle Group). They take significant equity position in companies, work with existing managers or recruit hired guns to enhance corporate reputation by develop strategies to improve shareholder value, with the view of selling their interests to outside shareholders (Bishop, 2004; Briody 2003).

Corporate governance has two dominate paradigms. The first is the traditional maximizing model of the firm, with agency theory accounting for managers who align stock-based compensation to maximize shareholder wealth (for a review, see Cyert and March, 1963; Ghoshal, 2005). A second model, rooted in potential conflicts between managerial malevolence and self-promotion, as well as in a wider view of the corporation in the community, is the stakeholder view of the corporation, sometimes supported in corporate law through "constituency statues" (Hillman and Keim, 2001). The stakeholder perspective can be narrowly cast, such as employees, suppliers and customers, or it can be more extensive, from the community at large to specific groups, like NGOs, charities, or even educational institutions. The theory is that wider non-shareholder constituencies legitimize organizational action, even by creating illusions of actual performance through cheating, misrepresentation, and other forms of malfeasance (Harris and Bromiley, 2007; Pavelin and Brammer, 2006).

Shareholder activists argue that free markets are the closest thing that human nature can devise for openness, transparency, competitive markets for ideas and opinions. In this perspective, market adjustments of corporate behavior are self-regulating. Self-adjustment and feedback from strong corporate performance, i.e. profitability and innovation, lead to incentive rewards to the entrepreneurial winners and high shareholder value. Poor performance leads to a downward spiral and destruction of shareholder value, although other factors may influence attention, such as the impact of executive narcissism and, too often, managerial incompetence (Argyris, 1986; McMillan, 2007).

Critiques of shareholder interests, aside for moral and ethical issues related to corporate malfeasance, frame a new model: corporate social responsibility (CSR). It is a managerial creed, widely taught in business schools, and endorsed by many multinationals like Shell Oil and corporate industry groups. CSR is a mantra for many capitalist managers, an alignment of shareholders with the interests of society at large. Just how CSR actually works, and why a multitude of stakeholders add to ethical behavior, remains a mystery. Advocates wanting to transform companies offer a balance between corporate philanthropy and corporate culture, a so-called 1 percent solution—1 percent to shareholders, 1 percent to employees, and 1 percent of profits to philanthropy (Benioff and Southwick, 2004; Porter and Kramer, 2006). Concrete and less doctrinaire approaches suggest that, whatever the merits of CSR, organizations can benefit from a clean eco-system (*neighborhood effects*), appreciate the direct social costs of a carbon footprint (*reputation effects*), and attract public identity through information brokers and mavens, and indirectly from stakeholders (*legitimacy effects*).

Corporate scandals engulfing North America—Enron, Tyco, Citibank, Global Crossing, BreX Mining, Hollinger, Nortel and the like—unmask corruption at the height of the organizational pyramid: bribery, collusion, embezzlement, fraud, kickbacks, money-laundering, and tax evasion. Such scandals expose a hornet's nest of information misrepresentation and weak transparency. Corporate treasury functions are at the heart of these scandals. The lies of senior executives, the deliberate manipulation of accounting statements, and the willful distortion of managerial performance reveal how quickly good reputations can vanish. Small firms are influenced by the crowd moods of investors and bankers who fund them, and where herding, euphoria, and other irrational behaviors guide so-called sophisticated treasury decision rules. Fueling this trend has been the mix of managerial hubris—big is better, being huge is better still—and a cadre of young MBAs knowing, not thinking, that spreadsheet models are unquestioned. Traditional, risk-averse conventional accountants are in decline, replaced by MBAs whose goals are short term, individualistic, and monetary. Organizational reputation is a side bar when you can change jobs without changing parking lots. Capitalism may be a surprisingly productive and robust system, but it has its own troubles (Bishop, 2004; Ghoshal, 2005).

Accounting and regulatory reform is spreading on Wall Street and other global financial centers, suggesting separating positions like CEO and board chairman, appointing more independent board members, removing crass conflict of interest (mixing auditing and consulting fees), immediate public disclosure of executive insider trading—these are minimum reforms demanded by the public. European and American companies are attempting to coordinate international accounting standards, through the Financial Accounting Standards Board of the US and the European Roundtable. Social network internet sites are activating shareholders towards greater disclosure of information and risk practices. Globally, shareholder activism, aided by social networking, extends transparency, led by institutional investors, vulture funds, consumer groups, and individuals like Warren Buffett. Unfortunately, reputation destruction may be self-inflicted, as shown in surveys of global brands, showing a marked downward spiral (Gerzema and Lebar, 2009; Bonini et al., 2009). What has changed profoundly is the corporate treasury function.

Treasury Functions and Reputation Risk

The treasury function is the financial life-blood of organizations in a market economy. In essence, to know what is going on, follow the money. Reputation comes in part for organizational slack, a measure of excess resources that calibrate virtuous incentives. Corporations have business models determining the revenue streams from product sales, less costs, that create operating margins, but time lags require regular financing. Hospitals and schools require similar treasury models, even when they are supported by governments and public financing. For corporate treasurers, there are two basic environments: one where finance is cheap and plentiful and one where finance is expensive and hard to find. Most treasury functions operate in the middle, allowing incentives—financial, social, status—to vary enormously in an organization (McMillan, 2010).

Corporate strategies are more than product-market placements: they realign incentives and power relations, the critical leverage points for diverse stakeholders, and communications to the external world (Carpenter, 2006; March and Simon, 1958).

Treasury managers need to understand risk profiles and how funding options impact corporate reputation. Corporate treasurers are in the position of a manager of a great golfer: which tournaments to play in, what are the stakes, who is the competition, what is the risk of reputation failure? Companies, governments, universities, and hospitals around the world have witnessed a wide range of scandals. Corporate white collar crime exists, and regulatory systems are inadequate (Rosen, 2008). Many stakeholders have a vested interest in non-compliance. As a result, a universal corporate governance problem is that, in too many cases, crime pays! It is relatively easy to manipulate critical items, overstate others, and generally misrepresent the true financial health of enterprises, thus undermining corporate reputation with key stakeholders (Harris and Bromiley, 2007; Staubus, 2005).

The role of the chief financial officer (CFO) is now a central function in executive suites, controlling and influencing organizational contingencies, including organizational reputation. In small business, the owner is the dominant shareholder and the main financial officer. In most organizations, these roles are separate. The CFO's job determines the firm's prospects for growth, survival and reputation—among workers and fellow managers, but also suppliers, customers, and lenders. Firms today are slowly including risk profiles and risk assessments in a range of operational and strategic activities (see Figure 8.4).

Historically, the CFO position was primarily an accounting task to monitor money flows, i.e. detailed reviews of financial operations, on an annualized basis, based on a quarterly (or monthly) budget projections agreed by top management. Operational performance was primarily governed by engineering process requirements (workflows and detailed cost analysis, including time) and the need to assess informational needs for management decision-making, the relationships among different plants or divisions, and the outlays of financial expenditures within capital budgets (for a detailed case study, see Cyert and March, 1963, Ch. 7).

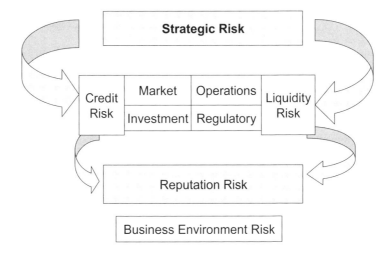

Figure 8.4 Organizational risk profiles

Source: Adapted from TD Bank Financial Group

Budgets include simple and conservative assumptions on the state of the economy, interest rates, energy prices, or other factors that have direct influence on the company. Information needs for management centered on such operational issues as "management by objectives," "management by exception," and "management of budget deviations" (Drucker, 1977). Certain organizations are combining treasury functions with risk assessment, including linkages to functions like human resources and production, where strike action, product safety, and quality design can insidiously undermine organizational reputation. Some organizations are actually designating senior managers as "risk officers" (Economist Intelligence Unit, 2008).

As a result of scandals and accounting shenanigans, the CFO function has been elevated by regulators, shareholders, and corporate law. Corporate treasury functions are more publicized because of media attention, thus subject to scrutiny and review. Increasingly, stakeholders understand strategic risk and organizational consequences when management refuse to play by agreed rules. Big firms can go bankrupt. Executives can go to jail. For publicly listed companies, fiduciary responsibilities now require detailed disclosure with quality information transparency. For companies listed on the New York Stock Exchange, firms must now produce detailed financial statements, reviewed by independent auditors. Falsified financial reports, or failure to disclose key information on material issues, can lead to criminal prosecutions, prison sentences, and financial fines and potential reputation destruction.

New organizational tools of risk management, stress tests combined with models of scenario planning, have changed the treasury function by turning reporting and performance data into new tasks for information officers. Strategic risk and reputation risk means that education, training, and special exams are becoming mandatory. Treasury management has moved from reporting past behavior and financial results to projecting future performance. Corporations are in a global race to build brands and adopt first mover positions for market share. The goal is to maximize the corporate value of the firm, largely by increasing the price/earnings ratio against industry benchmarks and the historical indices of the stock market. In the US, the New York Exchange was for traditional companies and industries and NASDAQ is for knowledge firms in the new economy (Gordon, 2000).

Organizational Reputation and Institutional Governance

The dynamics of organizational reputation and malfeasance are a money matter. The sheer amounts of money circulating around the world, some from the gray economy of tax evasion, some from illegal activities like drugs, prostitution, and armament sales, combine with unprecedented technological capacity to move money instantly across borders. So too is the willingness of some corporate executives, fostered with hubris and personal greed, to commit financial fraud and plunder shareholder wealth (Hayward et al., 2004). Although boards of public companies have fiduciary obligations to shareholders, scandals are widespread (e.g. Figure 8.5). Around the world, shareholder destruction is unprecedented, including conventional strategies like mergers and acquisitions to enhance executive bonuses and managerial wealth. Morgenson (2005) summarizes the challenge:

deals represent an opportunity for management to throw everyday expenses into the merger bucket and make operating results look better than they actually are. It's probably no coincidence that some of the biggest frauds in recent years have involved serial deal makers like Tyco International, Waste management, and WorldCom... there are people for whom they make perfect sense: the executives and the Wall Street bankers behind them.

Many of the conventions on institutional governance are derived from legal principles of limited liability of the public corporation, one of the historic innovations of modern capitalism (Mason, 1959). Globally, challenges to accepted practices have forced governments, financial regulators and boards to review all aspects of corporate governance: board membership, senior management responsibilities and practices, the impact of multiple and global shareholders, the tools to assess performance criteria, and the information requirements of corporate effectiveness, including the responsibilities of independent auditors.

In theory, in publicly listed firms, there is a clear hierarchy of corporate governance: a board representing shareholders, a senior management team, and an operating management team, with regular financial reporting (monthly or quarterly), public disclosure of financial data and other relevant issues, and an annual audit process by independent accounting firms. In reality, corporate governance was opaque, murky, and often a shady money green. Moral hazard and reputation risk are often ignored,

A spreading scandal
Selected companies

Company	Source of investigation	Charge/ investigation	Result
Alliance Capital	New York state/ SEC	Market timing	2 employees fired; booked $190m charge
Bank of America	New York state/ SEC	Market timing/ late trading	3 employees fired; booked $100m charge
Bank One	New York state	Market timing	2 managers resigned
Bear Stearns	Client lawsuit	Market timing	6 employees fired
Charles Schwab	Internal	Questionable trades	2 employees fired
Citigroup	Internal	Market timing/late trading	5 employees fired
Federated Investors	New York state/SEC	Market timing	Ongoing investigation
Fred Alger & Company	New York state/ SEC	Market timing/ late trading	Vice-chairman convicted of felony and fined $400,000
Janus Capital	New York state/ SEC	Market timing	Janus International CEO and others resigned
Merrill Lynch	Notified by SEC	Market timing	3 employees fired
Morgan Stanley	New York state/ MA/SEC	Directed brokerage	$50m settlement to compensate investors
Pilgrim, Baxter & Associates	Internal	Market timing	2 founders resigned
Prudential Securities	MA/SEC	Market timing	12 employees fired; 7 employees facing charges
Putnam Investments	MA/SEC	Market timing	CEO resigned; undisclosed SEC settlement
Strong Capital Management	New York state	Market timing	Chairman of mutual-funds unit resigned (remains chairman of group)

Sources: Morningstar; Reuters; SEC; state prosecutors; TheStreet.com; *Wall Street Journal*; *Washington Post*   MA=Massachusetts

Figure 8.5   A spreading scandal

Source: the Economist

suspended, or downplayed. Conflicts of interest abounded. Minority shareholders were squeezed by majority shareholder groups. Auditors sided with managers, not shareholders. Audit firms played double agents, collecting audit fees and consulting fees. Globalization in all its forms has jolted this traditional concept of corporate governance. More recently, American, European and Japanese practices, while different in their precise legal forms, force a gradual convergence around such basic issues like limiting the role of banks and insurance firms to hold equity in public corporations, and strengthening through legal and other incentives the fiduciary roles of management towards individual shareholders. Complacent managers from Toronto to Tokyo comfortably point to the stupidity of politicians and the sins of speculators as the prime culprits of corporate misfortunes. Academics and consultants wantonly write about corporate capitalism, and the usefulness of corporate boards to rebuild corporate reputations and protect shareholder rights (Byron, 2004; Bonini et al., 2009).

In too many cases, senior management can use the legal form of the public corporation, and its access through public markets, to acquire immense amounts of money, often because public policy dictates that pension funds must invest mostly in domestic companies. Given enormous flows of capital—now a trillion dollars per day—corporate governance has become the rage of the media, with immense coverage in *Business Week*, *Fortune*, the *Economist*, and management publications. The public at large and the individual shareholder, or shareholder blocs like pension funds, and equity firms demand quality information and public transparency. Firms that rank high in the performance rating, providing superior returns, openness to investors, and excellent management, can also be the firms that fall fastest when reputations are on the line (Byron, 2004).

New Rules for Corporate Governance

Slowly, managers can no longer shift organizational risk to the public. Corporate governance has five basic criteria: financial disclosure; shareholder review of management performance; composition of board members in terms of quantity, national origins of the members and their international experience; and external auditing and corporate disaggregation of related firms in the group.

The sheer magnitude and the consequence impact of corporate governance fraud— "You Bought, They Sold" as *Fortune* magazine put it in a cover story—brought out the inevitable reactions from public authorities, including the US Congress. Fraud revelations had direct impacts—share price declines, reputation destruction—leading to CEO firings, corporate bankruptcy, financial fines, and jail sentences for many perpetrators. Aggressive countervailing investigations in New York, with muted responses from Washington, as well as similarly muted reactions from regulatory officials in Canada and Europe, led to passage of Sarbanes-Oxley Act (SOA). The SOA legislation was mirrored by new listing obligations of the New York Stock Exchange, which fundamentally changed the corporate risk profile obligations of member companies and also applied to foreign firms listing in the USA, thereby beginning to have a global reach (McMillan, 2007).

The Sarbanes-Oxley Act, enacted on July 30, 2002, directly impacts corporate governance and management of treasury functions. Corporate management is compelled to follow governance rules affecting the choice and membership of boards of directors, detailed reporting obligations of the board and senior management, the role of independent auditors, and obligations over a range of corporate behavior—disclosure reporting, insider trading, fraud accountability, conflicts of interest that, if statements are false, lead to crimes punishable by severe fines and jail sentences.

Governments want to protect the benefits of capital markets and publicly listed companies. Academics, trade groups, accounting bodies, and industry associations have recommended additional changes in governance. These include new disclosure rules for security commissions, regulatory bodies, accounting and audit firms, board mandates, and corporate reporting of all payment terms of senior executives. These global pressures help disclosure, but they won't detract from corporate inefficiencies and the capacity of managers to control incentives, organizational communications, and the desire to stifle organizational dissent and internal decision conflict (McMillan, 2010).

In theory, boards are the ultimate arbiter of organizational reputation because they have legal and fiduciary responsibilities beyond short term performance or immediate payback (Drucker, 1977; Weston et al., 2004). As recent experience on Wall Street demonstrates, boards may fail to perform even minimum fiduciary duties, despite the quality and reputation of individual directors. Boards over time operate with groupthink, herd instinct, myopic visions, operational malfeasance, and perverse double agency incentives (high compensation for immediate rewards, including tolerance of managerial hubris and narcissism). Reputation as a learning process requires decision mechanisms that separate information from understanding, short-term incentives from long-term legitimacy, and performance efficiency from organizational effectiveness.

As depicted in Figure 8.6, boards have fiduciary responsibilities, and must be reflective, socially responsive, and seek out understanding of executive decision premises. Executive leaders often summon heroic personal attributes, but disguise the fact that the control the main communication cues (rhetoric, data, intelligence, ambiguous signals, even mere propaganda) for the organization. Organizational reputation comes from organizational strengths and competencies, cultivated around redundant systems and routines, not heroic attributes of leaders (March 2000). To be effective, boards can preserve organizational reputation only by addressing stakeholder risk and avoiding the yes-man mentality desired by too many executives.

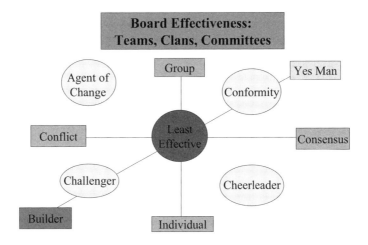

Figure 8.6 Board effectiveness: Teams, clans, committees

Conclusions

Corporate reputation is an asset, a process, and a form of legitimacy. As a reputation asset, organizations communicate internal capabilities and competences, embedded around knowledge and know-how. As a process, reputation is an organizational style of decision-making around wide decision search processes, sharing of information, and open transparencies about likely outcomes. Organizational reputation comes from environmental legitimacy, because external stakeholders perceive recurring performance results that are widely accepted and embedded in values, consistency, and reasonable preferences.

Current turmoil in the financial markets may be an academic issue for corporate boardrooms and managers, but in reality, this view may a colossal misjudgment. Conventional practice stress short-term issues, based mainly on internal consensus and immediate impact, not on long-term results, expert opinion, or serious planning tools, from scenario analysis to public opinion research. The real impact for organizational reputation will be on the strategic issues of corporate governance: shareholder review of managerial performance and accountability. Corporate risk assessments, and risk management are strategic functions. Corporations around the world will be faced with annual reports on the Worst and Best Boards, as *Business Week* publishes annually.

CFO responsibilities must integrate all aspects of treasury management, from the operational risk performance, to all aspects of investments, including allocating capital to future obligations (like pension funds). The management of treasury decisions now includes some of the following:

- all budgets, expressed usually by product lines, geography, types of business, expressed in quarterly or monthly accounting, with detailed explanations for special provisions;
- regular reviews of stakeholder assessments, critical reputation reviews based on internal analysis and external assessments, premised on the assumption that reputation threats comes from executive impulses ranging from benign (misconceptions or repudiation) to self-aggrandizement (denial or even delusional);
- managerial operating performance standards against operational budgets, reviewed by internal managers but also outside groups, including auditors and board members of the board through periodic reviews and external benchmarking;
- treasury risk management tools guiding strategic management, including risks associated with loans, liquidity risk, unexpected losses, and receivables outstanding, regulatory risks (e.g. health, environmental, quality and safety) and future financial obligations (pension), via cash shortages, and risk adjustments so that apples are compared to apples, not oranges (a problem for diversified organizations, from hospitals and universities to corporations and state enterprises).

In a world of cynicism and media-based skepticism, reputation management requires transparency, board accountability, and clear rules of management performance. Stakeholders don't want empty apologies: they want problems to be acknowledged, and action protocols to solve them. Activist shareholders, slowing helped by social networks and the internet, are forcing management to face scrutiny for under performance and reputation destruction. Executives who choose to ignore this fundamental dictum of scrutiny will pay a heavy price indeed. Firms with the best reputation will get ahead of the growth curve by instituting internal reforms. Senior executives, boards, and treasury managers face new scrutiny and transparency from stakeholders, but increasingly from risk management consultants, brokers in social media, and regulatory personnel assessing corporate risk and performance.

New organizational scenarios will institute corporate strategies for risk management— just what are the parameters for risk exposure for such issues as diversification, currency risk, commodity risk, political risk, unfounded liabilities risk, to name a few. Best practice firms will design board-level, CEO and senior executive-level treasury procedures to monitor and assess corporate risk on a regular basis—earnings at risk, cash flow at risk, even catastrophic risk, as a basic strategic tool of reputation management. Firms which play their cards well are going to experience financial gains from a reputation premium. By contrast, organizations which fail to understand the impact of Enron *Enronitis*, a Wall Street disease, in the public mind should take a walk in New York's Central Park, and advertise their presence beforehand. They may get mugged, but no one will come to their rescue.

References

Aaker, D.A. (2008), *Strategic Marketing Management*. New York: Wiley.

Akerlof, G. (1970), "The Market for 'Lemons': Quality Uncertainty and the Market Mechanism," *Quarterly Journal of Economics*, 51: 488–500.

Alvesson, M. (1990), "Organizations: From Substance to Image?" *Organizational Studies*, 11: 373–94.

Argyris, C. (1986), "Skilled Incompetence," *Harvard Business Review*, 64: 74–80.

Baucus, M.S. and D.A. Baucus (1997), "Paying the Piper: An Empirical Examination of Longer-Term Financial Consequences of illegal Corporate Behaviour," *Academy Management Journal*, 40: 129–51.

Becker, B. and T. Milbourn (2009), "Reputation and Competition: Evidence from the Credit Rating Industry" Boston, MA: Harvard Business School, Working Paper #09-051.

Benioff, M. and K. Southwick (2004), *Compassionate Capitalism*. London: Career Press. (For a critical view, see *Behind the Mask: The Real Face of Corporate Social Responsibility* (www.christianaid.org. uk).)

Bishop, M. (2004), "Private Equity: The New Kings of Capitalism," *Economist* (November 25), pp. 1–26.

Bonini, S., D. Court and A. Marchi (2009), "Rebuilding Corporate Reputations," *McKinsey Quarterly*, June.

Boyd, D. and N. Ellison (2007), "Social Network Sites: Definition, History and Scholarship," *Journal of Computer-Mediated Communication*, 10: 210–30.

Briody, D. (2003), *The Iron Triangle: Inside the Secret World of the Carlyle Group*. New York: John Wiley.

Byron C. (2004), *Testosterone Inc.: Tales of CEOs Gone Wild*. New York: John Wiley.

Carlyle, T. (1841). *On Heroes, Hero Worship, and the Heroic in History*. London.

Carpenter, D.P. (2006), *The Forging of Bureaucratic Autonomy: Reputations, Networks, and Policy Innovations in Executive Agencies, 1862–1928*. Princeton, NJ: Princeton University Press.

Caspar, C., et al. (2010), "The Five Attributes of Enduring Family Businesses," *McKinsey Quarterly*, January.

Chatterjee, A. and Hambrick, D.C. (2007), "It's All About Me: Narcissistic CEOs and their Effects on Company Strategy and Performance," *Administrative Science Quarterly*, 52: 351–86.

Cyert, R. and J. G. March (1963), *A Behavioural Theory of the Firm*. Englewood Cliffs, NJ: Prentice-Hall.

Drucker, P.F. (1977), *Management*. Heinemann: Pan Books.

Economist Intelligence Unit (2007), *Best Practice in Risk Management*. London: EIU.

Eccles, R.G. and N. Nohria (1992), *Beyond The Hype: Rediscovering the Essence of Management*. Boston, MA: Harvard Business School Press.

Farber, D.B. (2005), "Restoring Trust After Fraud: Does Corporate Governance Matter?" *Accounting Review*, 80, 2: 539–61.

Friedman, M. (1962), *Capitalism and Freedom*. Chicago, IL: University of Chicago Press.

Fombrun, C. (1996), *Reputation: Realizing Value from Corporate Image*. Boston, MA: Harvard Business School Press.

Gerzema, J. and E. Lebar (2009), "The Trouble with Brands," *Strategy + Business*, 55: 1–12.

Ghoshal, S. (2005), "Bad Management Theories Are Destroying Good Management Practices," *Academy of Management Learning and Education*, Vol. 4/1: 75–91.

Gilmore, J. and J. Pine (2007), *Authenticity: What Consumers Really Want*. Boston, MA: Harvard Business School Press.

Gordon, R. (2000), "Does the New Economy Measure Up to the Great Inventions of the Past?" *Journal of Economic Perspectives*, 4 (Fall): 49–74.

Harris, J. and P. Bromiley (2007), "Incentives to Cheat: The Influence of Executive Compensation and Firm Performance on Financial Misrepresentation," *Organizational Science*, 18: 350–67.

Hayward, M. et al. (2004), "Believing One's Press: The Causes and Consequences of CEO Celebrity," *Strategic Management Journal*, 25: 637–53.

Hickson, D. et al. (1971), "Strategic Contingencies Model of Interdepartmental Co-ordination," *Administrative Science Quarterly*, 16: 216–29.

Higgs, M. (2009), "The Good, the Bad, and the Ugly: Leadership and Narcissism," *Journal of Change Management*, 9: 165–77.

Hillman, A.J. and G.D. Keim (2001), "Shareholder Value, Stakeholder Management, and Social Issues: What's The Bottom Line?" *Strategic Management Journal*, 22: 125–39.

Jue, A., J.A. Marr and M. Kassotakis (2009), *Social Media At Work*. New York: Jossey-Bass.

Kay, A.C., S.C. Wheeler, J.A. Bargh and L. Ross (2004), "Material Priming: The Influence of Mundane Physical Objects on Situational Construal and Competitive Behavioral Choice," *Organizational Behavior and Human Decision Processes*, 95(1): 83–96.

Klein, B. and K.B. Leffler, "The Role of Market Forces in Assuring Contractual Performance," *Journal of Political Economy*, 89 (4): 615–41.

MacLeod, W.B. (2007), "Reputations, Relationships, and Contractual Enforcement," *Journal of Economic Literature*, XLV (September): 595–628.

Mailath, G.J. and L. Samuelson (2001), "Who Wants a Good Reputation?" *The Review of Economic Studies*, 89, 4 (August): 615–41.

March, J.G. (2000), "Organisations Prosaïque et Leaders Héroïques," *Gérer et Comprendre* (June): 44–50.

March, J.G. and J.P. Olsen (1976), *Ambiguity and Choice in Organizations*. Bergen: Universitetsforlaget.

March, J.G. and H.A. Simon (1958), *Organizations*. New York: Wiley.

Martin, G. and S. Hetrick (2006), *Corporate Reputation, Branding, and People Management*. London: Butterworth-Hamilton.

Mason, E.S. (1959) (ed.), *The Corporation in Modern Society*. New York: Atheneum.

McMillan, C.J. (2007), *The Strategic Challenge*. Toronto: Captus Press.

McMillan, C.J. (2010), "Five Competitive Forces of Leadership and Innovation," *Journal of Business Strategy*, 31 (1): 11–22(12).

McNeil, L.R. (1974), "The Many Futures of Contracts," *Southern California Law Review*, 47 (68): 691–816.

Merrilees, B. and D. Miller (2008), "Principles of Corporate Rebranding," *European Journal of Marketing*, 42: 537–52.

Morgenson, G. (2005), "What Are Mergers Good For?" *New York Times Magazine* (June 5)

Pavelin, S. and S. Brammer (2006), "Corporate Reputation and Social Performance," *Journal of Management Studies*, 43: 3.

Pfeffer, J. and R. Sutton (2006), *Hard Facts, Dangerous Half-Truths, and Total Nonsense*. Boston, MA: Harvard Business School Press.

Porter, M. and M. Kramer (2006), "Strategy and Society: the Link Between Competitive Advantage and Corporate Social Responsibility," *Harvard Business Review*, 78–92.

Rosen, L.D. (2010), *Rewired: Understanding the iGeneration and the Way They Learn*. New York: Palgrave MacMillan.

Rosen, L.S. (2008), "Canadian Corporate Corruption," in R.J. Burke and C.L. Cooper (eds), *Research Companion to Corruption in Organizations*. Cheltenham: Edward Elgar.

Shih, C. (2009), *The Facebook Era*. Upper Saddle River, NJ: Prentice Hall.

Showkeir, J. and M. Showkeir (2008), *Authentic Conversations: Moving from Manipulation to Truth and Commitment*. San Francisco, CA: Berrett-Koehler.

Spence, M. (1975), *Market Signaling*. Cambridge, MA: Harvard University Press.

Staubus, G. (2005), "Ethics Failure in Corporate Financial Reporting," *Journal of Business Ethics*, 57: 5–15.

Stinchcome, A.L. (1965), "Social Structure and Organizations," in J.G. March (ed.), *Handbook of Organizations*. Chicago, IL: Rand McNally.

Sundaram, A. and A. Inkpen (2004), "The Corporate Objective Revisited," *Organizational Science*, 15: 350–63.

Thompson, J. (1967), *Organizations in Action (New York: McGraw-Hill)*.

Van Lee, R., L. Fabish and N. McGaw, (2005), "The Value of Corporate Values," *Strategy+ Business*, 39: 1–16.

Villette, M. and C. Vuillermot (2009), *From Predators to Icons: Exposing the Myth of the Business Hero*. Ithaca, NY: Cornell University Press.

Weigelt, K. and C. Cameron (1988), "Reputation and Corporate Strategy," *Strategic Management Journal*, 9: 443–54.

Weston, J. F., K.S. Chung, and J.A. Siu, (2004), *Takeovers, Restructuring, and Corporate Governance*. Upper Saddle River, NJ: Pearson-Prentice Hall.

World Economic Forum (2010), *Global Risks 2010: A Global Risk Network Report*. Geneva: WEF.

9

The Role of the CEO and Leadership Branding – Credibility not Celebrity

JULIE HODGES

In this chapter, we examine the role of the CEO and leadership branding. We will seek to shed some light on this issue by examining how leadership branding works in theory and in practice. We do so, firstly, by reviewing the leadership literature and discussing the concept of leadership and then leadership branding. Secondly, we set out some of the available evidence on leadership branding to address the questions: what role does the CEO play in leadership branding? Finally, we will examine some of the critical success factors and the potential problems that organisations might face in establishing effective leadership brands.

The Role of the CEO

The role of the CEO in determining the reputation of an organisation has long been advocated (Kitchen and Laurence, 2003; Van Riel, 1999). This was particularly evident after the economic crises in the early twenty-first century when the financial world was littered with CEOs who had destroyed not only their own reputation but also that of their company. There was a perception that some companies in certain sectors, particularly financial services, had violated their social contract with consumers, shareholders, regulators and taxpayers (Cable, 2009) and their CEOs were considered as being much to blame.

Fred Goodwin, for instance, was desperate to restore his reputation after leading RBS, Britain's second largest bank in 2008, to a £24bn loss – the largest in UK corporate history. Goodwin had led an ad hoc strategy of rapid acquisition in an attempt to create a global company and brand. Having presided over a culture of fear and bullying, he left an organisation with no public or shareholder credibility or trust, along with a legacy of greed, individual rewards and unmitigated risk taking. Goodwin abused his power to serve personal gains and to reinforce his self-image and enhance perceptions of his personal performance: behaviours which the literature describe as the roots of 'bad' leadership (Aasland et al., 2008; Benson and Hogan, 2008; Kets de Vries, 1993).

The breadth and depth of a reputational challenge is a consequence not just of the speed, severity, and unexpectedness of economic events but also of underlying shifts in the reputation environment that have been under way for some time. Those changes include the growing importance of Web-based participatory media (Martin, 2009), the increasing significance of non-governmental organisations (NGOs) and other third parties (Hatch and Schultz, 2009; Worcester, 2009), including shareholder activist groups such as the Pensions Investment Research Consultants Ltd (PIRC) and a declining trust in advertising (Larsson, 2007). Together, these forces are promoting a wider, faster scrutiny of companies and rendering traditional public-relations tools less effective in addressing reputational challenges.

The reputation of Adam Applegarth, the CEO of the beleaguered Northern Rock Building Society, was left in tatters as he was slated for failing to protect the bank from volatility in the global financial markets and for using a business model that took on too much risk. It resulted in the ultimate collapse of Northern Rock's corporate reputation, with a run on the bank and the reputation of the banking system destroyed. Other financial sector CEOs who destroyed their own and their firm's reputations include Richard Fuld (Lehman Brothers); Dan Tully (Merrill Lynch); Hal Paulson (Goldman Sachs) and Any Hornby (HBOS). To name but a few.

In the aftermath of the financial storm the reputation of corporations and their CEOs was at an all-time low. A McKinsey survey (March 2009) of senior executives around the world revealed that most senior executives believed that trust in business (85 per cent) and commitment to free markets (72 per cent) had deteriorated, while a Harris poll (2009) found that the companies with the worst reputations were troubled insurer American International Group Inc., oilfield services company Halliburton Co., automakers General Motors Co and Chrysler LLC, and failed savings and loans company Washington Mutual. The five with the best reputations were Johnson & Johnson, Google Inc., Sony Corporation, Coca-Cola Company and Kraft Foods Inc. The poll showed that consumers were less likely to invest in or do business with companies with poor reputations (Harris, 2009).

One financial organisation which has weathered the economic storm is Berkshire Hathaway whose corporate reputation remains intact as does that of its CEO – Warren Buffet. In 2009 in his annual letter to investors in his company Berkshire Hathaway, he said the errors included buying stakes in two Irish banks. He also regretted investing in oil company Conoco Philips when the crude price was at its peak. Berkshire's profits fell 62 per cent in 2008 – the worst performance in its 44 years. The company's net earnings totalled US$4.99bn (£3.5bn) in 2008 compared with US$13.2bn in 2007. In the letter to shareholders, Mr Buffett was candid about his failings, saying 'the tennis crowd would call my mistakes "unforced errors".' 'During 2008, I did some dumb things in investments,' he said. 'I in no way anticipated the dramatic fall in energy prices that occurred in the last half of the year,' he added (BBC News Online, 2 March 2009; http://news.bbc.co.uk/1/hi/business/7918448.stm). As one financial advisor told Reuters: '[Buffett] admits when he is wrong. You don't get candor from other CEOs. That's why his credibility is so high.'

Although the role of the CEO in making or breaking the reputation of their company is evident, one of the characteristics of strong brands would appear to be their resilience to abuse by their CEOs. One such example is truculent Irishman Michael O'Leary, CEO of Europe's largest airline, Ryanair. O'Leary has taunted customers with the possibility of standing-room-only aircraft and coin-slot toilets – the ultimate customer experience at 35,000 feet. What's interesting is the self-assurance with which O'Leary parodies the meanness of the Ryanair brand offering and his cult of cheapness.

However, not all brands are immune from the abuse hurled at them by their owners. The case of Gerald Ratner is a salutary reminder. Ratner built up a highly successful chain of jewellers based around the idea of cheap bling. His mistake was to tell his customers exactly what he thought of them. Here is an extract from the speech delivered at the Institute of Directors on 23 April 1991 that virtually destroyed his business overnight: 'We also do cut-glass sherry decanters complete with six glasses on a silver-plated tray that your butler can serve you drinks on, all for £4.95. People say "How can you sell this for such a low price?" I say "Because it's total ****".'

The flamboyant, arrogant CEOs who are initially perceived as 'heroic' or 'visionary' may end up damaging their company's reputations. The widespread perception of their unbounded greed, such as that of Goodwin and Applegarth, and the excess with which they had been celebrated over previous decades has precipitated a severe crisis of leadership, adding weight to Burns' (2003) comment that, 'if it is unethical or immoral it is not leadership ...' (p. 48).

Now more than ever, it will be action, not spin which builds strong reputations. CEOs need to enhance their listening skills so that they are sufficiently aware of emerging issues and to reinvigorate their understanding of and relationships with, critical stakeholders. Doing so effectively means stepping up both the sophistication and the coordination of reputation efforts. One key to cutting through the organisational barriers that might impede such efforts is the model of leadership demonstrated by CEOs, who have an opportunity to differentiate their companies by bolstering the reputations of their companies.

Literature

The study of leadership is characterised by a focus on the individual leader (Groon, 2002; Bryman, 1992); the dyadic relationship between the individual CEO and his/her followers (Kellerman, 2008; Pearce, 2004) and the impact of an individual leader on the effective performance of an organisation or the members of that organisation (Khurana, 2002; Wade et al., 2006).

With the exception of a few (Conger, 1998; Hogan and Hogan, 2001; Hogan and Kaiser, 2005), most leadership studies have explored only the positive relationships and the actions of leaders (Aasland et al., 2008; Benson and Hogan, 2008), ignoring those that may be harmful to corporate reputations. Instead there has been a focus on the heroic/celebrity conceptualisation of leadership (Hayward et al., 2004; Rindova et al., 2006; Wade et al., 2006) which has lead to organisational personality cults and follower dependence (Higgs, 2009).

In the context of corporate reputations leadership styles are important in translating organisational identity into an image. Fred Goodwin's image as 'Fred the Shred' led to the image of the RBS Group as being mean and lean. In contrast, Starbuck's firm identity is about enthusiasm, excellence and contributing positively to communities and the environment and that is exactly what Howard Schultz did when he set up the company. He personified the leadership style of the Starbuck's brand.

Celebrity explanations of leadership focus on the apex of the organisation, privileging the significance of one individual – the CEO – to the exclusion of all others. In the 1990s Intel was portrayed in the media as simply Andy Grove (or later Craig Barrett) while GE was in turn Jack Welsh. Lee Iacocca was Chrysler, Victor Kiam was Remington, and Alan Sugar was Amstrad. In the twenty-first century Donald Trump is the Trump Organization and Richard Branson is the Virgin Group.

There is good reason to believe that employing a 'celebrity' CEO could be valuable to a firm's reputation. As Fombrun (1996) stated, having a highly recognised CEO at the helm may reassure stakeholders that the firm's future prospects are bright and, that in turn, will enhance the firm's ability to attract higher quality employees, increase its leverage over suppliers and gain better access to needed capital. On the other hand, some arguments in the management literature suggest that the CEO celebrity status has other consequences for a company's reputation, such as over-confidence and hubris, than may have detrimental effects on future performance (Wade et al., 2006).

The obsession with celebrity has reached epidemic proportions in recent years, with 'the attribution of glamorous or notorious status to an individual ...' (Rojek, 2001, p.12). The media is often cited as over attributing the reputation of individual's with that of the company they led and playing a crucial role in creating the CEO celebrity (Hayward et al., 2004). Flattering media accounts of medal-winning CEOs may encourage boards to believe in the distinct ability of winners (Wade et al., 2006).

This 'celebrification' of leadership contributes to the production of a particular set of discourses and practices of leadership (Rojek, 2001). It is distinguished by a relationship between the leader and the led in which belief in the leader is based on personage rather than experience or past performance (Burns, 1978).

Despite academic scepticism over the pejoratively labelled 'leadership industry' in countries seemingly obsessed with individualism and celebrity (Barker, 2001; Chhokar et al., 2007), the leadership phenomenon has gripped practitioners to such an extent that its importance goes largely unquestioned and so rarely evaluated (Pfeffer and Sutton, 2006; Rosenzweig, 2007). Though there is substantial evidence of leadership's impact on their organisations and followers (Fiol et al., 1999; Munshi et al., 2005), there are also increasingly concerns over these claims and of leadership's 'dark side' (Higgs, 2009).

For every person that reveres Bill Gates as a great business leader, there seems to be another who despises him as a power-hungry monopolist. As with the construction of the celebrity CEO, their deconstruction and that of the firm's reputation have been described as being built up by the media (Jackson and Guthey, 2006). Some even say that the backlash is a rhetorical device or cliché that gets mobilized by various management fashions, as well as a minor management fashion in its own right (Guthey et al., 2008).

No one seems immune from the celebrity backlash, even Jack Welsh, as vehemently illustrated by the following quote, 'Rogues at companies like WorldCom and Enron were bad enough, but even superstar executives like Jack Welsh contributed to the staining of corporate America' (O'Neal, 2002). Former GE employees reported that 'Welsh conducts meetings so aggressively that people tremble. He attacks almost physically with his intellect – criticizing, demeaning, ridiculing, humiliating' (O'Toole and Warren, 2009, p. 57). While Carly Fiorina, CEO of Hewlett Packard in 2005, was castigated for her celebrity profile and failure to fit into HP's egalitarian corporate culture.

The extraordinary trust in the power of the celebrity CEO has been said to resemble less a mature faith than it does a belief in magic (Khurana, 2002). Such critics have gone on to say that there is no conclusive evidence that a company's top leadership actually has much impact on its performance. Khurana (2002) spoke of the 'fervent though erroneous belief that the quality of the CEO is the primary determinant of firm performance – and therefore that it is realistic to hope that a high-powered CEO can be a corporate saviour' (2002, p. XIII). Pfeffer and Sutton (2006, p. 192) summarised this critical perspective on the contribution of leaders to organisational performance as:

> *modest under most conditions, strong under a few conditions, and absent in others ... Studies from leaders from large samples of CEOs ... university presidents to managers of colleges and professional sports teams show that organizational performance is determined largely by factors that no individual – including a leader – can control.*

The backlash reaction against business celebrities exemplifies the manner in which such figures can function as flashpoints for debates and conflicts over what business leadership should be like. The complex cultural and ideological dynamics of business celebrity bashing exert considerable influence over discussions about what leadership is (Guthey et al., 2008).

Some leadership scholars have advocated the replacement of the dominant and entrenched celebrity model of leadership with more inclusive and collective distributed models (Carroll and Levy, 2008) which are anti-celebrity. Some believe that we have become overly preoccupied with individual leaders when, in fact, we should have been focusing more on the long taken-for-granted and largely unnoticed role of the follower (Grint, 2005; Kellerman, 2008). While others believe that the essential ingredient is having what has been termed 'level 5 leadership', which involves a paradoxical blend of humility and intense professional will (Collins, 2001).

There is no doubt that there are individuals behind some brand successes, such as Inguare Kamprad at IKEA and Erling Persson at H&M. However, focusing on the leader as hero, the leader as the firm, twists how we think about leadership, according it too much credit while paradoxically demeaning its achievements. Indeed, the notion of the celebrity CEO as heroic stands in sharp contrast to the traditional notion of a hero, a person who is willing to make personal sacrifices necessary so that others may benefit' (Morris et al., 2005, p. 1331).

The celebrity school of leadership has based many of its assertions on the basis of case study and anecdotal evidence drawn from either biographies or media material (Clark et al., 2008). This combined with interest in understanding the failures of CEOs to deliver sustainable performance or even corporate failure has led to the emergence of interest in and criticism of narcissistic leadership (Higgs, 2009; Vogel, 2006).

As well as possessing charisma and a strong sense of vision, narcissistic CEOs are grandiose, intolerant of criticism, unwilling to compromise, arrogant, self-absorbed and have a sense of entitlement and a need to be admired (Higgs, 2009).

Narcissism occurs when leaders become self-referential, attributing success to their actions and failing to be 'inclusive' by not listening to criticisms from key stakeholders, including employees and customers (Brown, 1997; Brown and Starkey, 2000; Kets de Vries, 2001; Price et al., 2008). Narcissistic leadership behaviour results from a need to reinforce their self-image and aggrandisement that reduces an organisation's desires and capabilities to listen, search for and use information that upsets its dominant ways of working. As Maccoby (2004) comments, 'even at their best, narcissistic leaders are bound to leave damaged systems and relationships in their wake' (p. 12). Narcissistic CEOs have been found to engage in more grandiose and dramatic actions, such as acquisitions and strategic dynamism and to take bold actions that attract attention, with their organisations experiencing dramatic performance fluctuations (Chatterjee and Hambrick, 2007). At its most virulent, narcissism can result in leaders attempting to manipulate stakeholder images of the organisation in unethical ways. This has been a feature of the financial history of the modern world, with cases such the Lehman Brothers, Enron and the 'Madoff' affair (Ferguson, 2008).

Some leadership scholars are becoming more and more adamant in their criticism of the usefulness of celebrity leadership, and in their rejection of the kinds of models of leadership implied by the very phenomenon of celebrity leadership. First on the grounds that leadership is or should be a much more distributed process, involving input and interaction from a variety of different concerned parties. Secondly, on the basis that leadership is not merely an empirical object to be studied, nor a set of desirable attributes to be developed, or a collection of best practices to be disseminated.

The focus on leaders and the so called 'New Leadership theory' (Bass, 1985; Bryman, 1992; Tichy and Devanna, 1990) that emerged as transformational leadership in the 1980s is to some largely misplaced and seen as little more than a rebranding of earlier charismatic leadership; moreover, it is even dangerous to organisational health (Kellerman, 2004; Kets de Vries, 2001; Khurana, 2002; Mintzberg, 2004).

In a critical vein, Rosenzweig (2007) included much leadership theory in his list of eight delusions that deceive managers, so puncturing deep holes in some of the popular theorising and evidence of leaders' contributions to lasting organisational success.

According to leadership sceptics, mainstream thinking in New Leadership theory is overly focused on the 'vision thing' and in aligning followers behind these visionary goals, usually by tapping into or shaping the motivations and identities of individuals so that they coincide with corporate identities and aims. This line of reasoning is based on two questionable premises. The first is that the study of leadership is, and should be, about leaders and their role in organisations; the second is that organisational performance can be attributed to leadership characteristics rather than anomalies in the organisation's environment. This has led to the emergence of pillars of interest in the field of leadership such as authentic leadership (Avolio and Luthans, 2006; Luthans and Avolio, 2003). Yet work on defining and measuring authentic leadership is in the early stages of development and there is a need to examine how it is viewed across situations and cultures (Avolio et al., 2009).

Current theorising on leadership seems to have moved away from the singular focus on leaders and, indeed, in 'romanticising' the need for leaders per se (Meindl et al., 1985) to reflect leader–member exchanges (Flynn, 2006) and the role of followership in shaping leader behaviour (Kellerman, 2004, 2008). Such approaches treat leadership as emerging from context. Rather than using the formula and direction of cause and effect implied in the 'great men' theory that good leaders cause people to perform in ways that they might not have otherwise done, it is argued that people perform in less self-interested ways because they value important outcomes that the leader holds out a real promise of achieving for them. Here the focus is less on the qualities of leaders and more on the motivations, attributions, inferences and social identities of followers. A feature of this approach is to see leadership as a process, which it might be better conceived of as part of an unfolding dynamic collaboration between the motivations and values of individuals, on the one hand, and the demands of the organisational context on the other (Grint, 2005). Thus leadership results from this collaboration but also helps produce it. In this way, leadership is different from management in that it is produced by and helps produce change in organisations rather than stability, and is a function of situations rather than of the characteristics of individuals. Seen from this perspective, leaders come to symbolise change rather than cause it to happen, which is one of the key messages of implicit leadership theory (Lord and Brown, 2004). This theory postulates that leadership is an attribution based on the degree of fit between leaders' characteristics and the implicit ideas held by followers of what 'leaders' are or should be. Such implicit ideas are seen to be a product of upbringing, education and national cultural values (Bass and Avolio, 1994; Hofstede, 1998).

Although leaders may at times be characterised by singular events, leadership is rarely the result of a sole action or behaviour. Rather, leadership is an inherently multi-level phenomenon with relationships occurring between leaders and subordinates, leaders and teams, leaders and other organisational leaders, as well as leaders and leaders of other organisations (Hunter et al., 2007).

Yet despite the continuous epidemic of leadership studies it would appear that there is still a need for a new model of leadership, generally dubbed 'post-heroic' leadership (Fletcher, 2004), that acknowledges and responds to the qualitatively different context within which contemporary organisations have to work. Post-heroic models of leadership recognize that effectiveness in knowledge-based environments depends less on the actions of a few individuals at the top of the organisation and more on collaborative leadership practices distributed throughout it (Manz and Sims, 1991). What has begun to emerge is a less individualistic, more relational concept of leadership, one that focuses on dynamic, interactive processes of influence and learning intended to transform corporate reputations.

Leadership as a Brand

One of the most recent and potentially interesting leadership concepts which is also an extension of employer branding is leadership branding. This was an idea developed by Ulrich and Smallwood (2007) as a way of helping organisations develop a greater sense of corporate agreement on what leadership means internally and as a means of conveying to customers, employees and other key stakeholders what an organisation wants its leadership to be known for externally.

A leadership brand is consistent with a firm's brand, or identity in the marketplace. For example, Amazon.com is known as a company with exceptional service, so its leaders are expected to be competent in identifying and delivering great service. Leaders at all levels reflect the brand when they think and act in ways consistent with the desired product or firm brand and demonstrate an ongoing reputation for both quality and results. Leadership brand is a true extension of an organisation brand or identity because it shows up in behaviours and results. Companies with strong leadership brands are generally not as strongly affected by changes in management as companies with weaker leadership brands. In some cases firms are so confident about their bench strength that they turn what most organisations view as a negative, the loss of a leader, into a positive. The consulting firm PWC (PricewaterhouseCooopers) for example, continues to build its leadership brand reputation by tracking and publishing the feats of its successful alumni.

According to Ulrich and Smallwood (2007), leadership needs to be branded because leadership practices are often piecemeal and seldom integrated with the corporate brand, let alone with the daily operations of an organization. Drawing loosely on organisational identity theory (Ashforth et al., 2008; Dutton et al., 1994; Walsh and Gordon, 2008), Ulrich and Smallwood (2007) define a leadership brand as the desired identity of leaders in an organization, bridging customer expectations and employee and organisational behaviour. It is what leaders should be known for and how they act to support that identity.

The key antecedent of leadership branding appears to be *corporate identity*, which is defined as 'how we are perceived right now' and 'how we want to be perceived' (Balmer and Geyser, 2003). This can be articulated in a company's image, branding, reputation and communications, as well as in logos, missions, strategies and values. A leadership brand needs to be consistent with a company's corporate identity in the marketplace. Leaders at all levels reflect the brand when they think and act in ways consistent with the corporate identity and demonstrate an ongoing reputation for quality and results.

Leadership branding focuses on leadership more than leaders, from the outside to the inside of the organization. According to Ulrich and Smallwood (2007), leadership branding not only bridges the connection between the inside culture and the outside firm brand, but also assists in building and developing future leaders and strengthening of the organisation. 'The collective leadership capacity in an organization – institutional leadership – is the sum total of leadership behavior at all hierarchical levels. When this is strong, we may say that the organization has a strong leadership brand' (Gill, 2006, p. 33). Referring to examples from well-known organisations, Ulrich and Smallwood (2007) further suggest that companies with a strong leadership brand enjoy reputations for developing exceptional leaders with a distinct set of talents that meet customer, employee and investor expectations. Thus organisations with leadership brands take an 'outside-in' approach to their business: they begin with a clear statement of what they want to be known for by their customers and then link it with a required set of leadership skills. For example, the Lexus division of Toyota translates its strap line 'The pursuit of perfection' into an expectation that its leaders excel at managing quality processes (Liker and Hoseus, 2008). While at UPS, leadership branding is aligned with the promise of outstanding customer service. Companies such as Johnson & Johnson; PepsiCo, Boeing, Disney, Nordstrom, and McKinsey have also built leadership brands (Ulrich and Smallwood, 2007).

The key features of a leadership brand are a focus on building distributed leadership in an organisation rather than a focus on the CEO alone. It is about being known externally for high quality leadership among key stakeholders as well as having a good internal reputation among employees for excellent leadership. Organisations with branded leadership win with customers because the customers have the confidence that their needs will be addressed in a consistent and appropriate way. An effective leadership brand also appeals to employees because it helps shape a positive organisational culture (Ulrich and Smallwood, 2007).

Reflecting the tensions acknowledged in the corporate reputations literature between being simultaneously *legitimate* and *different* (Deephouse and Carter, 2005; Hatch and Schultz, 2008), a leadership brand consists of two major elements: the 'leadership code' and the 'leadership differentiators' (Ulrich and Smallwood, 2007). The leadership code refers to the core elements of leadership that the CEO and all leaders must demonstrate to be effective (Ulrich et al., 2009). These can be thought of as 'derailers' that cause leaders to fail if not avoided. They are 'competencies' that leaders possess and deploy if they are to succeed, as well as 'commitments' to employees and customers. Ulrich and Smallwood (2007) postulate that leaders clearly need to acquire and master the fundamentals of leadership so that they meet the requirements for success and can communicate a sense of belonging to employees. Following some of the lessons of organisational identity theory, a leadership brand also has to communicate a sense of being different from other organisations. Ulrich and Smallwood (2007), however, define 'differentiators' in external terms as the elements of leadership that are uniquely aligned to an organisation's customers and investors. Leaders must think and act in ways, congruent with the desired corporate brand. Moreover, as company strategies and corporate brands change, so too must the leadership brand change to reflect these.

Changing external images in the eyes of customers and investors need to be made real to employees through the organisation's policies and actions. This is evident, for instance, with Walmart, whose corporate reputation has undergone a stunning metamorphosis. In the summer of 2004, towns all over the USA were fighting expansion of Walmart's giant stores that were seen as the epitome of urban sprawl. At the behest of Walmart's board, headed by Rob Walton, the son of the company founder Sam Walton, the corporate communications department commissioned a reputation survey and found that Walmart in just a short time had gone from corporate darling to demon. The board gave then-CEO Lee Scott distinct orders: Fix it. Scott stopped defending the company's practices and started changing them. He built the brand successfully around low prices and leaders who are known for managing cost and logistics efficiently and getting things done on time (Fishman, 2006).

So, what is the role of the CEO in developing and sustaining a leadership brand? On the one hand, there is a good case for, and some anecdotal evidence of, iconic global leadership brands that contain strong identity myths, emotional links and symbolism from the CEO. Novell serves as an example. CEO Ron Housespian symbolises Novell's leadership brand and acts as the brand manager. The leadership is known for developing the company's supreme network architecture, and their high technical competence. The attributes which Novell foster are industry knowledge, interpersonal skills, ability to integrate product concepts, and trustworthiness. The integration of these desired results with these attributes provides a picture of a leadership brand at Novell as being: collaborative, knowledge-seeking, integrative and looking for new opportunities.

In 2009 IBM's president, chairman and CEO, Samuel Pamisano, spoke of the deeper innovation, new workforce models, forward-thinking policies and strong business ethics and values managed consistently across global operations. Taken together, this amounts to a leadership brand of global citizenship among individuals, organisations and society at large.

Technology companies such as the ones above are good examples, and though many of these leadership brands are American in origin and speak to American myths, their appeal is often worldwide. On the other hand, there is a strong argument and some evidence that leadership brands are less dependent on the CEO, but need to be locally authored or co-created to be contextually authentic, if they are to achieve the cultural authenticity that some organisations seek from investment in employer branding. This may apply particularly to firms in certain kinds of industries, such as retailing and in those operating in experience goods markets, such as tourism, personal services, financial services and even healthcare and education, arguably all of which are characterised by a greater degree of culture-boundedness than technology.

Leadership Branding in Practice

Even the most sceptical academic would acknowledge that leadership has an important impact on corporate reputations among employees, customers, investors and other stakeholders. Barry Gibbons, former CEO of Burger King, said that, 'Leadership and ... branding are seamlessly merged into one' (cited in Gill, 2006, p. 33). Yet considering the criticisms of the leadership industry the notion of leadership branding might be seen as a step too far.

There are indeed some potential problems with Ulrich and Smallwood's (2007) use of leadership as a branding concept for managing corporate reputations, especially in trying to reconcile multiple identities in complex organisations, in general, and in multinational organizations, in particular (Hodges and Martin, forthcoming).

Global brands, as the name suggests, are global in their reach. They operate in a number of markets, have huge resources to support their market entry and communication efforts, have the requisite expertise and have deep enough pockets to absorb initial losses. Though this answer seems quite logical, it overlooks one very key component – the role of visionary leadership. Most of the hugely successful brands have had the benefit of being led by leaders who had a vision. These leaders have led their brand from the front, been the brand's chief ambassador, understood the strategic importance of branding and nurtured the brand as a favoured child. Not many local brands have had this critical success factor to boost their equity.

Ulrich and Smallwood's (2007) use of leadership as a vehicle for reputational management has to resolve a key issue facing organisations, especially multinational ones. The 'global-local' paradox (Deephouse and Carter, 2005; Larsson et al., 2003) of managing the tensions and paradoxes connected with *integration* and *differentiation* (Roberts, 2004) within global companies. It has become an axiom that multinational organisations need to integrate to achieve economies of scale and global branding advantages, yet they also need to respond to local situations to achieve strategic differentiation and local authenticity. To establish a strong corporate brand, it is argued that organisations should strike a dynamic balance between a corporate identity with the needs to reflect these local differences (Martin, 2009; Martin and Hetrick, 2009; Roberts, 2004).

One of the few companies that has been able to cross from the global to the local is Coca-Cola, which remains one of the most successful and innovative brands in the world today. Its success is as a result of thinking globally and acting locally (McDonald and Keegan, 2002). The company is adept at adopting sales promotion, distribution and customer service efforts to local needs. Coca-Cola has enjoyed its brand equity for many decades and become a billion-dollar-plus global brand (Keegan and Green, 2005). At the firm's annual meeting in 2009, CEO Muhtar Kent said Coca-Cola should be able to increase market share despite the global recession by pushing its top brands in emerging markets such as China and in strong markets such as the US and Mexico.

A company which has recently implemented a leadership brand strategy is Sage – a large UK-based business software company, which has grown rapidly through acquisitions overseas. Sage grew rapidly during the 1990s and the first years of the millennium to resemble what its senior managers describe as a 'federation of businesses' embracing a global perspective with local expertise. The decentralised model of how Sage relates to key stakeholders (Patzelt et al., 2008) is seen as a critical contributor to the company's success as it allows for constructive local adaptation of the global company principles.

The CEO Paul Walker joined the firm as financial controller in 1984 when it only had seven employees on its payroll. Sage's firm brand is about acquisitive and organic growth and innovation. Its reputation is built on product innovation and customer support with the small and medium enterprise (SME) marketplace. Walker personifies Sage's firm identity with his strong conviction about the merits of free enterprise and the ineffectiveness of large, ponderous organisations. Despite the rapid growth of the company, these convictions have prevailed within a decentralised business model.

In the early 2000s the increasingly competitive landscape lead to a generalised perception among the CEO and senior managers that the company needed a much stronger leadership base so that it could continue to compete successfully. The company's '2010 and beyond' strategy focused on moving the company from a product- to a customer-driven approach and aimed to position the brand to meet customer requirements more closely. Despite the differences within the federal business model and the stated desire of the managers in Sage's operating companies to be able to continue to run their own 'business within a business' there was widespread and strong agreement for a more consistent approach to leadership. To address these issues and to align the leadership of the company more closely to the company brand and the strategic goals the CEO and executive board set up a leadership branding exercise. In accordance with the recommendations of Hatch and Schultz (2008) for organisations to adopt an 'enterprise' approach to leadership branding, Walker had engaged a wide range of stakeholders in identity conversations over the symbolic meaning of leadership in the company. A leadership brand statement was adopted, in line with Ulrich and Smallwood's (2007) approach, to signal to all stakeholders what the company meant by leadership.

Overall the leadership branding process in Sage was not owned by a single person or function, but was multidisciplinary in nature, with senior leaders from a wide range of functions contributing to the design and implementation process. Managers were given the autonomy to create a leadership brand statement, and to define the 'leadership code' and the 'differentiators'. This approach mirrors that of companies that have a strong leadership brand, such as IBM, Pepsico and Apple: all have CEOs who have strong leadership brands and who see developing leadership capability as key.

As CEO Walker role-models the reputation he expects from his company. He makes a point of managers being evaluated not only on their ability to 'make their numbers' (the 'what') but also on their ability to do it in a way that will work in the long-term best interests of the organisation (the 'how'). He has continued the tradition of investing in leadership development at Sage as economic instability rocks the formerly stable business software industry. Not surprisingly, as they have recast their business strategy and organisational structure to compete more effectively in an increasingly competitive marketplace Sage have revised their brand to better support the accomplishment of the results for which they are now striving.

When companies can develop leaders at every level who have their own style that fits within the context of the differing firm identities, the company has a leadership brand that is appreciated by customers and employees and rewarded by financial markets as an envied capability (Ulrich et al., 2008).

Sage's leadership brand is sustainable as it is not tied to any one person, no matter how charismatic or talented. The company is attempting to embed it throughout the organisation. However, the process of implementing the leadership brand has been long and drawn out. The model proposed by Ulrich and Smallwood (2007) gives the impression that it is linear process and that if a company goes through each step it will come out at the end with a workable leadership brand.

There are lessons to be learnt from Sage's approach to implementing a leadership brand in a multinational context. The CEO's response was not to impose a central brand but to allow local leaders to take it and make it their own. This is in line with ideas already proposed by researchers in the field of international management in attempting to manage the paradoxes and tensions of local branding (Roberts, 2004). For Sage this has involved developing a corporate leadership brand credo in a language that reflects the different cultures (Martin and Hetrick, 2006). Such an approach has avoided the trap of compromise that suits no-one and the trap of resolution when faced in choosing between two horns of a dilemma (Hatch and Schultz, 2008).

It represents 'both-and' thinking in which the CEO has communicated a sustainable corporate story about the need for general principles for leadership but also allowed subsidiary organisations in different countries to write what they want into these principles which follows the suggestions of Price, Gioia and Corley (2008) for reconciling scattered images in corporate reputational management. A leadership brand represents the identity and reputation of leaders throughout the company. It exists when leaders at all levels of an organisation demonstrate a consistent reputation for both attributes and results. The reputation is thus with the company. In the case of Sage, when Paul Walker leaves the reputation will stay with the company.

Although leadership branding can be seen as an integral part of corporate reputation management, because employees expect strong leadership and thus thrust upon them their expectations and hopes, for it to work it has to tread a delicate and dynamic balance between integration and differentiation.

Conclusion

In this chapter we have discussed the impact and significance of the role of the CEO and leadership branding upon our understanding of the practice of leadership. Thinking about leadership as a brand instead of simply something a leader does, offers a number of insights into leadership effectiveness and into creating a sustained and consistent corporate reputation that enhances firm value. So what can we learn from this the theory and practice? There are some lessons that might be of value to practitioners.

Firstly, leadership branding is about the process, not just the characteristics of the leader. The potential of leadership branding lies in bridging the firm brand to employee actions. In many companies leadership is not tied to the company brand or to the business. It is often tied to a person or to competences. When that person (often the founder) leaves, the quality of leadership dissipates. In contrast, the focus of leadership branding is on the organisation, and not just the CEO. It is the leadership brand that helps ensure that corporate reputation is delivered and sustained and meets customers' expectations. The critical success factor to a leadership brand is working from the 'outside in' rather than the traditional 'inside out'. By starting at the outside the leadership is beginning with the reason for the firm's existence, its customers. This practice involves specific, targeted leadership rather than traditional, generic qualities that are similar in each business. By analysing what customers think and expect of the brand, leaders can shape the organisation and its employees to create a culture that is conducive to meeting its expectations. In essence, leadership branding involves aligning customers' expectations with employees' behaviours. It is not dependent on an individual leader.

Secondly, the role of the CEO and senior management in the development and implementation of the brand is crucial. Enunciating a leadership brand statement is the easy part and, on its own not very effective. Most statements are too vague and too abstract to have much impact. Leaders must give specific meaning to the values, which then sets the basis for their generating norms of expected behaviour (Roberts, 2007, p. 285). The CEO and top management have to be deeply involved, reach tough-minded conclusions, then ensure that those decisions are enforced and executed across the company. 'It takes guts, it takes time, and it takes superb execution' (Gerstner, 2003, p. 246). Sage's CEO had to get leaders to listen to him, to understand where they needed to go, to follow him there; he needed to stop them being autonomous independent beings. The CEO had to learn to do more than merely define and understand the brand which would maintain and continue to grow the business; he and the rest of his executive team had to live it and teach it to others. They also had to celebrate and reward those who acted in appropriate ways and correct those who did not. A leadership brand must have efficacy. This occurs when employees, customers and investors believe and see that promises made at the top are promises that will be kept. Leaders, who declare a leadership brand, must live and breathe it or they will create cynicism and lose credibility.

Thirdly, the CEO has to ensure that a leadership brand is applied across the entire organization. It should avoid 'situational leadership which results in confusion and alienates people' (Lawler, Worley and Porras, 2006, p 221). Employees don't want to be uncertain about how they will be treated or unable to count on being involved in decisions or informed by their manager (Lawler et al., 2006). Branding viewed in its totality transcends the functional barriers within an organization and thus requires brand guardians to have an overall view of the business. The CEO in consultation with his senior management team can provide consistent strength to the reputation of the company. Strong initiatives from CEOs and corporate boards will help anchor and sustain brands in the highly competitive global market.

Finally, organisations need to maintain their leadership brand regardless of the economic conditions which they face. What they need to change when the business environment changes is their tactics, business practices and business models (Lawler et al., 2006).

We conclude that leadership branding can be seen as an integral part of corporate reputation management, because employees expect strong leadership and thus load leaders with expectations and their hopes. Second, for leadership branding to work it requires the back-up of a strong leadership team. By being a strong brand evangelist, a CEO can define and defend the actions of a brand.

In summary, the process of leadership branding is more complicated than most practitioners would acknowledge and although evidence so far is piecemeal it does hold potential opportunities for the fields of leadership and corporate reputational management.

When we think of companies with great corporate reputations, we often think of strong leaders that are behind them and the characteristics that those leaders possess. While the characteristics are important, leadership branding goes beyond the characteristics of a dynamic, celebrity leader; it encompasses every aspect of the organisation, the internal employees and the external customers, as well as suppliers and partners and is enduring.

References

Aasland, M., Skogstad, A., and Einarsen, S. (2008). The dark side: defining destructive leadership behavior. *Organisations and People*, 15(3), 19–26.

Ashforth, B. E., Harrison, S. H., and Corley, K. G. (2008). Identification in organizations: an examination of four fundamental questions. *Journal of Management*, 34: 325–74.

Avolio, B., and Luthans, F. (2006). *The High Impact Leader: moments matter in accelerating authentic leadership*. New York: McGraw-Hill.

Avolio, B., Walumbwa, F., and Weber, T. (2009). Leadership: current theories, research, and future directions. *Annual Review of Psychology*, 60: 421–49.

Balmer, J. T., and Greyser, S. A. (2003). *Revealing the Corporation: perspectives on identity, image, reputation, corporate branding and corporate-level marketing*. London: Routledge.

Barker, R. (2001). The nature of leadership. *Human Relations*, 54(4), 469–94.

Bass, B. M. (1985). *Leadership and Performance beyond Expectations*. New York: Free Press.

Bass, B., and Avolio, B. (1994). Transformational leadership and organizational culture. *International Journal of Public Administration*, 17 (3/4): 541–54

Benson, M. J., and Hogan, R. S. (2008). How dark side leadership personality destroys trust and degrades organizational effectiveness. *Organisations and People* 15(3), 10–18.

Bok, D. (1993). *The Cost of Talent: how executives and professional are paid and how it affects America*. New York: Free Press.

Brown, A. (1997). Narcissism, identity, and legitimacy. *Academy of Management Review*, 22, 3 (July), 643–86.

Brown, A., and Starkey, K., (2000). Organizational identity and learning: a psychomatic perspective. *Academy of Management Review*, 25(1), 102–20.

Bryman, A. (1992). *Charisma and Leadership in Organizations*. London: Sage.

Burns, J. (2003). *Transformational Leadership*. New York: Atlantic Monthly Press.

Cable, V. (2009). *The Storm: the world economic crisis and what it means*. London: Atlantic Books.

Carroll, B., and Levy, L. (2008). Defaulting to management: leadership defined by what it is not. *Organization*, 15(1), 75–96.

Chatterjee, A., and Hambrick, D.C. (2007). It's all about me: narcissistic chief executive officers and their effects on company strategy and performance. *Administrative Science Quarterly*, 52, 351–86.

Chhokar, J. S., Brodbeck, F. C., and House, R. E. (2007). *Culture and Leadership across the World: the GLOBE book of in-depth studies of 25 societies*. London: Routledge.

Clark, T., Guthey, E., Greatbach, D., and Jackson, B. (2008). *Demystifying Business Celebrity: leaders and guru*. London: Taylor and Francis.

Collins. J. (2001). *Good to Great*. New York: HarperCollins.

Collins, J. (2001). Level 5 leadership. *Harvard Business Review*, January, 79 (1), 66–76.

Conger, J. A. (1998). The dark side of leadership. In G.R. Hickman (ed.), *Leading Organisations: perspectives for a new era* (pp. 250–60). Thousand Oaks, CA: Sage.

Deephouse, D.L., and Carter, S.M. (2005). An examination of differences between organizational legitimacy and reputation. *Journal of Management Studies*, 42, 329–60.

Dutton, J. E., Dukerich, J. M., and Harquail, C.V. (1994). Organizational images and member identification. *Administrative Science Quarterly*, 39, 239–63.

Ferguson, N. (2008). *The Ascent of Money: a financial history of the world*. London: Allen Lane.

Fiol, C. M., Harris, D., and House, R.E. (1999). Charismatic leadership: strategies for effecting social change. *Leadership Quarterly*. 10, 449–82.

Fishman, C. (2006). *The Wal-Mart Effect: How the world's most powerful company really works and how it's transforming the American economy*. London: Penguin.

Fletcher, J. (2004). The paradox of postheroic leadership: an essay on gender, power and transformational change. *Leadership Quarterly*, 15(5), 647–61.

Flynn, F. (2006). How much is it worth to you? Subjective evaluations of help in organizations. In B. Staw (ed.) *Research in Organizational Behaviour: an annual series of analytical essays and critical reviews*. Oxford: JAI Press, 133–74.

Fombrun, C. (1996). *Reputation: realizing value from the corporate image*. Boston, MA: Harvard Business School Press.

Gerstner, L. (2003). *Who Says Elephants Can't Dance?* London: HarperCollins.

Gill, R. (2006). *Theory and Practice of Leadership*. London: Sage.

Grint, K. (2005). Problems, problems, problems: social construct of leadership. *Human Relations* 58(11), 1467–94.

Groon, P. (2002). Distributed leadership as a unit of analysis. *The Leadership Quarterly*, 13, 423–51.

Guthey, E., Clark, T., and Jackson, B. (2009). *Demystifying Business Celebrity*. Oxford: Routledge.

Hatch, M. J., and Schultz, M. (2009). From corporate to enterprise branding. *Organizational Dynamics*, April–June, 38(2), 117–30.

Hatch, M. J., and Schultz, M. (2008). *Taking Brand Initiative: how companies can align strategy, culture and identity through corporate branding*. San Francisco: Jossey Bass.

Hayward, M., Rindova, V., and Pollock, T. (2004). Believing one's own press: the causes and consequences of CEO celebrity. *Strategic Management Journal*, 25(7): 637–53.

Higgs, M. (2009). The good, the bad and the ugly: leadership and narcissism. *Journal of Change Management*, 9(2), 165–78.

Hodges. J., and Martin, G. (forthcoming) Branding leadership: can it work in theory and practice to resolve the integration-responsiveness problems facing multinational enterprises?

Hofstede, G. (1998). Identifying organizational subcultures: an empirical approach. *Journal of Management Studies*, 35(1), January, 1–12.

Hogan, R., and Hogan, J. (2001). Assessing leadership: a view from the dark side. *International Journal of Selection and Assessment*, 9, 40–51.

Hogan, R., and Kaiser, R.B. (2005). What we know about leadership. *Review of General Psychology*, 9, 169–80.

Hogg, M. A. (2001). Social identification, group prototypicality and emergent leadership. In M.A. Hogg and D.J. Terry (eds), *Social Identity Processes in Organizational Contexts* (pp. 197–21). Philadelphia, PA: Psychology Press.

House, R., Hanges, P., Javidan, M., Dorfman, P., and Gupta, V. (2004). *Culture, Leadership, and Organizations: The GLOBE study of 62 cultures*. Thousand Oaks, CA: Sage Publications.

Hunter, S. T., Bedell-Avers, K. E., and Mumford, M. D. (2007). The typical leadership study: assumptions, implications, and potential remedies. *The Leadership Quarterly*, 18, 435–46.

Jackson, B., and Guthey, E. (2006). Putting the visual into the social construction of leadership. In J. R. Meindl and B. Shamir (eds), *Follower-centred Perspective on Leadership* (pp. 167–86). Greenwich: Information Age Publishing.

Keegan, W., and Green, M. (2005). *Global Marketing*. London: Pearson/Prentice Hall.

Kellerman, B. (2008). *Followership: how followers are creating change and changing leaders*. Boston, MA: Harvard Business Press.

Kellerman, B. (2004). *Bad leadership: what it is, how it happens and why it matters*. Boston, MA: Harvard Business School Press.

Kets de Vries, M. F. R. (1993). *Leaders, Fools and Imposters: essays on the psychology of leadership*. San Francisco, CA: Jossey-Bass.

Kets de Vries, M. F. R. (2001). *Struggling with the Demon: perspectives on individual and organizational irrationality*. Madison, CT: International Universities Press.

Khurana, R. (2002). The curse of the superstar CEO. *Harvard Business Review*, September, 60–66.

Kitchen, P., and Laurence, A. (2003). Corporate reputation: an eight country analysis. *Corporate Reputation Review*, 6, 103–17.

Larsson, L. (2007). Public trust in the PR industry and its actors. *Journal of Communication Management*, 11(3), 222–34.

Larsson, R., Brousseau, K., Driver, M., Holmqvist, M., Tarnovskaya, V., Bengtsson, K., and Sandström, P. (2003). International growth through cooperation: Brand-driven strategies, leadership, and career development in Sweden. *Academy of Management Executive*, 10795545, 17, 1 (February).

Lawler, W., and Porras, J. (2006). *Built to Change*. San Francisco: Jossey-Bass,

Liker, J., and Hoseus, M. (2008). *Toyota Culture: the heart and soul of the Toyota way*. New York: McGraw-Hill.

Lord, R. G., and Brown, D. J. (2004). *Leadership Processes and Follower Self-identity*. Mahwah, NJ: Erlbaum.

Luthans, F., and Avolio, B. (2003). Authentic leadership: a positive developmental approach. In K. Cameron, J. Dutton, and R. Quinn (eds), *Positive Organizational Scholarship: foundations of a new discipline* (pp. 241–58). San Francisco, CA: Berrett-Koehler.

Maccoby, M. (2004). Narcissistic leaders – the incredible pros. *Harvard Business Review*, 78(1), 68–79.

Manz, C., and Sim, H. (1991). Superleadership: Beyond the myth of heroic leadership. *Organizational Dynamics*, 19(4), 18–35.

Martin, G. (2009). *Web 2.0 and Human Resource Management: groundswell or hype*. London: Butterworth-Heinemann.

Martin, G., and Hetrick, S. (2009). Employer branding in international organizations: the case of Finco. In P.S. Sparrow (ed.), *Handbook of International Human Resource Management: Integrating people, process and contexts*. Oxford: Wiley-Blackwell.

Martin, G., and Hetrick, S. (2006). *Corporate Reputations, Branding and People Management*. London: Butterworth-Heinemann.

Martin, G., Reddington, M., and Alexander, H. (2008). *Technology, Outsourcing and Transforming HR*. London: Butterworth-Heinemann.

McDonald, W., and Keegan, W. (2002). *Marketing Plans that Work*. 2nd edition. Woodburn, MA: Butterworth-Heinemann.

Meindl, J. R., Erlich, S. B., and Dukerich, J. M. (1985). The romance of leadership. *Administrative Science Quarterly*, 30: 78–102.

Mintzberg, H. (2004). *Managers not MBAs*. Harlow, UK: Financial Times/Prentice Hall.

Morris, A., Brotheridge, C., and Ubranski, J. (2005). Bringing humility to leadership: antecedents and consequences of leader humility. *Human Relations*, 58(10), 1323–50.

Mintzberg, H. (2009). Rebuilding companies as communities. *Harvard Business Review*, July/August, 87(7/8), 140–3.

Munshi, N., Oke, A., Puranam, P., Stafylarkis, M., Towells, S., Moeslin, K., and Neely, A. (2005). *Leadership for Innovation: summary report for an AIM management research forum in cooperation with the Chartered Institute of Management*. London: AIM.

O'Neal, M. (2002). Coming up roses in a downcast year. *New York Times*, December 29, Section 3, p. 1.

O'Toole, J., and Warren, B. (2009). What's needed next: a culture of candor. *Harvard Business Review*, 87, June (6), 54–61.

Patzelt, H., zu Knyphausen-Aufseß, D., and Nikol, P. (2008). Top management teams, business models, and performance of biotechnology ventures: an upper echelon perspective. *British Journal of Management*, 19: 205–22.

Pearce, C. L. (2004). The future of leadership, combining vertical and shared leadership to transform knowledge work. *Academy of Management Executive*, 18(1), 47–57.

Pfeffer, J., and Sutton, R. (2006). *Hard Facts, Dangerous Half-Truths, and Total Nonsense: profiting from evidence-based management*. Boston, MA: Harvard Business School Press.

Porras, J., Lawler, E III, and Worley, C. (2006). *Built to Change: How to achieve organizational effectiveness*. London: Jossey Bass.

Price, K. N., Gioia, D. A., and Corley, K. (2008). Reconciling scattered images: managing disparate organizational expressions and impressions. *Journal of Management Inquiry*, 17: 173–85.

Rindova, V., Pollock, T., and Hayward, M. (2006). Celebrity firms: the social construction of market popularity. *Academy of Management Review*, 31(1): 50–71.

Roberts, J. (2004). *The Modern Firm: organizational design for performance and growth*. Oxford: Oxford University Press.

Rojek, C. (2001). *Celebrity*. New York: Reaktion Books.

Rosenzweig, P. (2007). *The Halo Effect and the Eight Other Business Delusions That Deceive Manager*. New York: Simon and Schuster Ltd.

Stile, P., Trevor, J., Paauwe, J., Farndale, E., Wright, P., Morris, S., Stahl, G., and Bjorkman, I. (2006). *Best Practices and Key Themes in Global Human Resource Management: project report*. Available at www.jbs.com.ac.uk/research/subjectgroups/downloads/ghrra_reports.pdg.

Tichy, N. M., and Devanna, M. A. (1990). *The Transformational Leader*. 2nd edition. New York: Wiley.

Ulrich, D., Smallwood, N., and Sweetman, K. (2009). *The Leadership Code: five rules to lead by*. Boston, MA: Harvard Business Press.

Ulrich, D., and Smallwood, N. (2007). *Leadership Brand: developing customer-focused leaders to drive performance and build lasting value*. Boston, MA: Harvard Business School Press.

Van Riel, C. (1999). *Corporate Communications*. Upper Saddle River, NJ: Prentice Hall.

Vogel, C. (2006). A field guide to narcissism. *Psychology Today*, 39(1), 68–74.

Wade, J., Porac, J., Pollock, T., and Griffin, S. (2006). The burden of celebrity: the impact of CEO certification contests on CEO pay and performance. *Academy of Management Journal*, 49(4), 643–60.

Walsh, K., and Gordon, J. R. (2008). Creating an individual work identity. *Human Resource Management Review*, 18: 46–61.

Worcester, R. (2009). Reflections on corporate reputations. *Management Decision*, 47 (4), 573–89.

10 *The Role of the News Media in Corporate Reputation Management*

CRAIG E. CARROLL

Introduction

The news media can exert a great deal of influence on corporate reputation (Chen and Meindl, 1991; Fombrun and Shanley, 1990). Corporations depend on what the news media report about them because the media are the main legitimate source of information asymmetry reduction for many stakeholders (McWilliams and Siegel, 2001; Siegel and Vitaliano, 2001), who might not have any direct interaction with the corporation (Deephouse, 2000, p. 1098). Moreover, the media are not only "vehicles for advertising and mirrors of reality reflecting firms' actions," they also are "active agents shaping information through editorials and feature articles" (Fombrun and Shanley, 1990, p. 240), thus having the power to influence the opinions of many stakeholders, as a long series of research in mass communication studies indicates (e.g., Ader, 1995; Behr and Iyengar, 1985; McCombs and Shaw, 1972). Freeman (1984) captured the important influence that the mass media can have on corporate behavior when he noted that "little stirs the anger in an executive more than an unfair story in the press" (p. 22).

Fombrun and van Riel (2003) share an old French saying: "to live well, live in hiding." Many companies act as if they believe it. They have no contact with the outside world unless a crisis occurs. This is a poor strategy in a time when our views of the world outside of our own lived experience are shaped by images in our head provided by the mass media (Lippmann, 1922; McCombs, 2004). Stakeholders demand transparency and insist on knowing what you do not tell. There are enough reporters whose goal is to discover and reveal it.

The question is, does news coverage about firms help them in any way? This chapter examines the role of the news media in corporate reputation management. First, the chapter will identify how news coverage about firms and corporate reputation are both multi-dimensional concepts. News coverage does not have uniform effects on corporate reputation because there are multiple types, forms, frames, and topics surrounding news coverage. Likewise, there are multiple dimensions to reputation, and news coverage relates more to its individual components than its aggregated nature. The second section then explores the question of what starting point organizations should use in building a media relations program for reputation management: should they start from an organization response with a set of goals, objectives, and key messages, or from a working knowledge of how the news media operate?

We can begin with a simple question about whether familiarity breeds contempt or favor. The research results indicate favor. Brooks et al. (2003) investigated whether familiarity can lead to both positive and negative views of corporations and whether the view held depends on the type of elicitation. They found a positive relationship between a firm's familiarity and its reputation: companies that are better known are associated more with positive features than negative ones. McCorkindale (2008) also found that the more familiar respondents were with a company using the Roper Corporate Reputation Scorecard, the more positively they rated the company's reputation. Similar effects were found for each of six industries examined: automotive, consumer packaged goods, entertainment, financial, pharmaceutical, and technology. The Reputation Institute (Fombrun and Riel, 2003) reports similar results—the more familiar the public is with a firm, the better the public rates it.

It is not true, however, that "there's no such thing as bad publicity." The results are not the same for visibility. Figure 10.1 explores the link between negative visibility and reputation. In the United States, Cisco and Johnson & Johnson score nearly 100 percent of their nominations for positive visibility, whereas Firestone, ExxonMobil, and Philip Morris are nominated entirely for their negative visibility. The results confirm that strong reputations result only from positive visibility and there are no reputational benefits to be had from negative visibility.

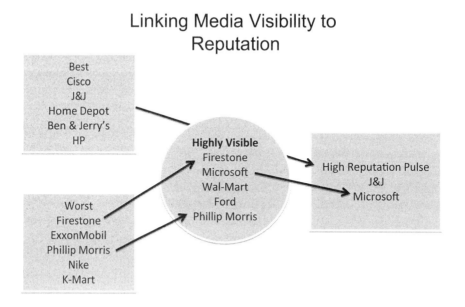

Figure 10.1 The link between negative visibility and corporate reputation

Note: Adapted from Fombrun and van Riel (2003)

Figure 10.2 is a visual representation of a study conducted by the Reputation Institute (Fombrun and van Riel, 2003) that focused strictly on the relationship between negative visibility and reputation. Fombrun and van Riel (2003) found that companies with more than 50 percent negative visibility developed substantially lower reputation ratings. Negative visibility creates reputational risk; when companies experience rising negative visibility, they are increasingly at risk of suffering reputational decline, and the threat of negative financial consequence looms closer. This analysis suggests that regularly tracking positive and negative ratings can help companies anticipate problems. The next section explores three ways that companies face reputational risks through the news media: through media visibility, media favorability, and media associations.

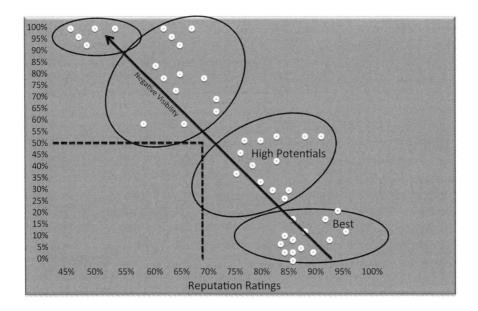

Figure 10.2 The relationship between negative visibility and corporate reputation

Note: Adapted from Fombrun and van Riel (2003)

Overall Model

This section explores the multiple relationships that news coverage has with corporate reputation. The results for the effects of the news media on corporate reputation are mixed when reputation is measured as a global variable (Fombrun and Shanley, 1990; Kiousis et al., 2007; Meijer and Kleinnijenhuis, 2006b). One explanation for the mixed findings is that previous research has failed to break corporate reputation into its relative dimensions. Several authors in the past have attempted to break corporate reputation down into a series of attributes, such as executive leadership, products and services, financial performance, workplace issues and corporate social responsibility. These can be seen as components of one dimension of reputation (attributes), but there are two others: public prominence and public esteem. Together, corporate reputation has multiple dimensions:

public prominence, *public esteem*, and a *series of attributes* or qualities tied to the firm. With these ideas in mind, this section argues—based on previous research showing that effects of the news media are not uniform (Einwiller et al., 2009)—that the news media's effects for each of these three corporate reputation dimensions are slightly different. In particular, this section reviews how a firm's media visibility relates more to its public prominence, a firm's media favorability relates more to its public esteem, and a firm's media attributes relates more to the its substantive reputation. Each of these ideas will be described in more detail. Some may notice how these classifications fit conveniently within agenda-setting theory and priming theory applied to firms (Carroll and McCombs, 2003).

RELATIONSHIP BETWEEN FIRMS' MEDIA VISIBILITY AND PUBLIC PROMINENCE

The first way the news media may influence corporate reputation is through the relationship between media visibility and firms' public prominence. *Media visibility* refers both to media attention—"[the] media awareness of an object, usually gauged by the sheer volume of stories or space dedicated to topics in newspapers, television news and so on" (Kiousis, 2004, p. 74)—and to media prominence—"the positioning of a story within a media text to communicate its importance" (Kiousis, 2004, p. 74)—that is, the placement of the story, its size, the pictures or other visual devices used and so on (Williams, 1985). A firm's public prominence is the degree to which it receives large-scale collective recognition, public attention, and salience in the minds of stakeholders (Rindova et al., 2005). It involves the sorting out of one firm amidst a sea of firms competing for attention. For firms to acquire reputation, the public must first think about them (Carroll and McCombs, 2003). Adapting Cohen's (1963) well-known dictum concerning the media and politics to the study of firms, Carroll and McCombs (2003) argued that while the news media may not be successful in telling the public *what* to think about a specific firm, they often succeed in telling the public *which* firms to think about. This level of "thinking about" is a firm's public prominence (Stocking, 1984). A firm's public prominence differs from its familiarity in that firms may be publicly prominent even though individuals may not be personally familiar with them. When people lack first-hand knowledge of a firm and thus are operating under conditions of uncertainty, they rely on others, such as the news media, for data, even if most of the data they receive are general, nonspecific impressions. Carroll (in press) found that an organization's media salience relates to its prominence in the minds of the public, rather than *directly* to its reputation. That study used secondary data from the Annual RQ 1999 and 2000 originally analyzed by Gardberg and Fombrun (2002), in which a random sample of the US population nominated firms as having the best or worst reputation. These 30 companies accounted for almost 90 percent of all the US nominations (Gardberg and Fombrun, 2002, p. 385). Taking into account each firm's existing level of public prominence, advertising expenditures, and wire-issued press releases, Carroll (in press) found that the change in the firm's media salience contributed to the firm's rise or fall in prominence in the subsequent year. Rindova et al. (2005) found that higher degrees of public prominence afforded firms the ability to charge premium prices for their products and services.

RELATIONSHIP BETWEEN FIRMS' MEDIA FAVORABILITY AND PUBLIC ESTEEM

The second way the news media may affect corporate reputation is through the relationship between media favorability and firms' organizational public esteem. A firm's media favorability refers to "the overall evaluation of a firm presented in the media resulting from the stream of media stories about the firm" (Deephouse, 2000, p. 1097). Organizational public esteem is the degree to which the public likes, trusts, admires, and respects an organization (Carroll, 2009). Organizational public esteem is a fundamental concern for corporate reputation management because it is concerned with earning respect (Hon, 1997; Y. Kim, 2001). Without a base level of trust, admiration, and respect, individuals lack sufficient incentives to consider relationships with organizations, whether through employment, investing, product consumption, or social causes.

The most prevalent theoretical perspective for the relationship between firms' media favorability and firms' public esteem is attribute agenda setting (Carroll, 2009; Carroll and McCombs, 2003). Using this theory, McCombs and others (e.g., Ghanem, 1997; McCombs et al., 2000; McCombs, Shaw, and Weaver, 1997) articulated two dimensions of attributes: cognitive and affective. Our focus in this section is on the affective dimension because it conveys the concept "media favorability" (Deephouse, 2000). Specifics about the cognitive dimension will be described in the next section. Assessments of the affective dimension recognize that news stories and public survey responses convey not only descriptions of objects but also feelings and tone about the objects described (McCombs and Ghanem, 2001; McCombs, Llamas et al., 1997; McCombs, et al., 2000). McCombs, Llamas et al. (1997) found a close correspondence between the affective descriptions of candidate attributes and the audience's descriptions of those candidates during the 1996 Spanish general election. Others have reported similar results (Becker and McCombs, 1978; Golan and Wanta, 2001; Kiousis et al., 1999; Weaver et al., 1981).

Research by Austin et al. (2007), however, suggests important differences between how researchers and audiences evaluate media favorability. Using attribute affective priming (K. Kim and McCombs, 2007; S. H. Kim et al., 2002), Carroll (2009) specified another dimension of media favorability that may relate to firms' public esteem—news articles' overall evaluative tone. This form of tone is a firm's *peripheral* media favorability. A firm's peripheral media favorability is "the overall evaluative tone accumulating from a stream of media stories where a firm is mentioned, yet is independent of how the focal firm is portrayed relative to the content" (Carroll, 2009, p. 6). This evaluative tone, adjacent to how the firm is evaluated, provides cues that audiences use to judge the report's portrayal of the firm (Carroll, 2009; K. Kim and McCombs, 2007; S. H. Kim, et al., 2002). Through this process of attribute priming, the news media's overall evaluative tone (Sheafer, 2007) may prime the public's attitudes and opinions, regardless of how a firm embedded within the article is portrayed. On a broad level, attribute priming research suggests that the news media establish standards that audiences employ to judge a firm. These "standards" emerge from the tone in the symbolic environment surrounding an object which provides cues for its interpretation. The association between the information and another topic need not be explicit; nor does the audience necessarily need to infer the association as intentional.

As for the effect of a news article's evaluative tone on an object embedded in its content to which the tone may not pertain, Carroll (2009) argued that the real power comes from the news media's cumulative tone that builds up over time in articles where the firm's name is present. For example, if the evaluative tone of a stream of news articles where an object is mentioned is negative, the negative evaluative tone can transfer over and become associated with the object even if the object itself is not the target of the negative tone. That is, increased evaluative tone salience surrounding the mention of a firm over a stream of articles has been shown to correspond to the audiences' evaluation of the firm with the same tone, even if the evaluative tone is not directed explicitly or intentionally toward the firm. Thus, if a stream of articles where a firm is mentioned contains 80 percent negative content unrelated to the firm, audiences may still derive negative affect about the firm from the stream of articles, even if the remaining 20 percent of content was positive and specifically about the firm. Firms' peripheral tone is best assessed through computer-aided text analysis programs that rely on standardized dictionaries, such as DICTION (Hart, 1985, 2001; Hart and Carroll, 2008). Carroll (2009) found a relationship between firms' focal media favorability and their public esteem for respondents with more knowledge of the firms' attributes and between firms' peripheral media favorability and their public esteem for respondents having little to no knowledge about the firms' attributes.

RELATIONSHIP BETWEEN MEDIA ASSOCIATIONS AND FIRMS' SUBSTANTIVE REPUTATIONS

A third way that the news media may influences corporate reputation is through the relationship between media associations and the public's perceptions of specific attributes or qualities in the context of the firm. Firms receive news coverage on a variety of news topics—as many topics as there are possibilities for a firm's reputation to develop. Carroll and McCombs (2003) relied on the reputation attributes assessed by Fombrun et al. (2000). Fombrun (1998) reviewed the attributes rated and ranked by a variety of media rankings and social monitors. Using attribute agenda-setting theory, Carroll and McCombs (2003) proposed that a firm's news coverage related to specific reputation topics (e.g., social responsibility, products and services, and financial performance) should correspond to the public's assessments of those particular dimensions. Wry et al. (2006) went further, using the term "substantive media reputation" and identifying how firms could be categorized into strategic cognitive groups based upon their shared news coverage related to certain attributes. Wry et al. found that firms could be classified by their substantive media reputations reflecting different cognitive strategic groups. They also found that firms classified according to these different substantive media reputations varied in their degrees of media favorability.

Far more research is needed on the relationship between media associations and firms' attributes. At present, analyses proceed two in one of two ways: by examining attributes within the context of a specific firm or by examining firms within the context of a specific attribute. For attributes within the context of a specific firm, the sample size of firms is much smaller—usually a case study or an experiment examining only one or two firms. Another example would be league tables that pull out attributes within the context of a firm. For example, examining the eight attributes of *Fortune*'s Most Admired Companies to see which attributes are rated higher or lower for any given firm. For firms within the context of attributes, the sample size is much larger; an example is *Business Week*'s World's Most Innovative Companies, where the top 50 firms are all rated similarly on the attribute of innovation. Attribute agenda setting and attribute priming may raise some interesting prospects for the study of corporate reputation in the context of cognitive attributes and associations. Attribute agenda setting may provide more descriptive or prescriptive power for media audiences with more familiarity with the firm. Using attribute agenda setting and issue ownership for a select group of eight organizations, Meijer and Kleinnijenhuis (2006a), found that the more news coverage the organizations received about specific attributes, the more the public matched those attributes to those firms. The attributes studied were specific to the firms rather than from a drawn list. In contrast, Ragas and Roberts (2009) found that for the Chipotle restaurant chain, the more news coverage there was for corporate social responsibility (CSR) activities, the more an online community of brand loyalists dissociated the attribute from the firm's reputation. Thus, already there are mixed results that call for additional research and exploration.

Thus far we have reviewed the importance of the media for the development of corporate reputation. In the next section, we will describe how firms can respond strategically to manage their reputations through media relations programs.

Media Relations Response

Having some basic idea of the different ways that media exposure can affect corporate reputation, it is time to think of what sort of response an organization should make in light of these views. There are at least two basic starting points: one is from the standpoint of the organization; the other is from the standpoint of the news media. In the end, for a successful media relations program, both elements are necessary. The question is simply a matter of which one comes first. The answer may lie in whether one has more working knowledge of how the news media operate first or whether one has more organizational experience. Given that the first generation of public relations practitioners were often former journalists, it makes sense that former journalists-turned-communication practitioners are more likely to start with a working knowledge of the press, while those with less knowledge may start more from the goals and objectives for media relations established by the organization.

A RESPONSE STARTING WITH THE ORGANIZATION

An organization focus entails starting with the senior level management team to develop a series of objectives for a single story or for a media relations program—preferably the latter, because it is more beneficial to the organization in the long run. Nevertheless, every media relations program begins with the placement of its first story. Responding to a request for an interview or a quote will be dealt with later in this chapter.

Carroll et al. (2010) offered five types of key messages that you can attempt to deliver through the news media: those pertaining to *information dissemination, raison d'être, categorical placement, resource management,* and *social relevance.* The first type of key message pertains to *information dissemination*, which can either be about education (the what) or mobilization (the how). Educational key messages are those that involve issues you want to teach the public about. The public may not know about your message or may simply take it for granted. The emphasis here is on teaching and learning new information that may ultimately change the public's awareness, attitude, or behavior. You may be trying to educate the public about your organization, some larger issue facing public debate (i.e., issues management), or simply what your point of view is on some public matter. Key messages about mobilization deal with logistical details, such as what, when, where, and how to get involved. Mobilization messages primarily concern events where you want the public to become involved: how or where to purchase a new product or service, how the public can help in the event of a crisis.

A second type of key message pertains to the organization's *raison d'être* (Carroll et al., 2010). These messages deal with the mission and organizational identity of the organization, attributes the organization deems are central, enduring, and distinctive about the itself (Albert and Whetten, 1985), claims about "who we are" and "what we are about."

Carroll et al. (2010) suggest that a third type of key message, *categorical placement*, helps to place an organization within cultural crowd of similar organizations, and then uniquely distinguish the organization against others sharing the same categorical placement. Key messages with categorical placement help to serve three functions: boundary setting, positioning, and linking. Boundary setting refers the setting of limits or parameters that help to define the outer edges of an organization and the juxtaposing of a chosen category against others for contextualization. Carroll et al. (2010) give examples of boundary setting: a nonprofit organization, the Council of State Governments, claims a "non-partisan" status in order to "encourage political participation" of both Democrats and Republicans, thus avoiding being categorized as a "partisan" organization; another nonprofit, Junior Achievement, describes itself as committed to "market-based economics" and entrepreneurship, which clearly eliminates socialism as a goal. The second function of categorical placement is to position the organization vis-à-vis competitors or other similar organizations (Carroll et al., 2010). This may be signified by words such as *leading, first, best, largest, only, oldest*, and so on. For example, the American Cancer Society claims to be the "largest source of private, nonprofit cancer research." The American Symphony Orchestra claims to be the "leading nonprofit orchestra"; the Arthritis Foundation claims to be the "most accurate source of information about arthritis." The third function of categorical placement is linking, which can occur through coupling or through decoupling. With this kind of placement, organizations attempt to establish ties to other organizations, such as their partnerships and alliances. It can also function to link the organization to the larger environment such as shared values held within the larger (national) culture.

A fourth type of key message pertains to organizational resource management. Carroll et al. (2010) identified two types of resource management messages, those about organizational survival and those about organizational stewardship. These equate to how organizations make money and how they spend them. Key messages such as these cover organizational strategy and financial performance, but also how they use their resources wisely by investing in their employees, take care of the environment, or give to charities. A good example here would be the Red Cross explaining how it uses the money it receives from donations and accounting for where the funds go.

The last type of key message pertains to *social relevance* (Carroll et al., 2010). This is where organizations demonstrate their service or value to their publics—the benefits, for instance, of their products or service. This category can also be used for issues management where organizations attempt to explain some larger purpose by the views they advance, or how their causes help society in some particular way.

The key message types developed by Carroll et al. (2010) are not mutually exclusive and they are not exhaustive. The classifications are not pure, and organizations may attempt to "blend" or "synthesize" these key message types into something more useful for themselves. Nevertheless, they are a useful starting point for thinking about the types of messages to convey to the news media for the goal of the media's dissemination to the public.

Evaluating key messages can be done in two ways. The first is by evaluating the degree of key message integrity present in news articles published about the organization. This is where most evaluation work occurs. The basic idea, following agenda-setting theory, is that if the news media cover the story, the key concepts will be translated and understood by your key publics. This is problematic for a number of reasons (foremost that it presumes your key publics pick up messages from the media and adopt them as mindless "automatons"), yet it is the simplest and least obtrusive form of evaluation. The second form of evaluation is with your key publics. This can be done by focus groups, interviews, or survey data. It's essentially asking them their degree of knowledge, recall, understanding, or acceptance of the key message.

After developing your key messages, you must be concerned with how to best reach your key publics. This chapter presumes that you have already made the decision to focus on the news media, although this is not the only way of reaching the public. Never lose sight that your end goal is building relationships with your end publics, and that the news media are an intervening public you must work through and with.

A RESPONSE STARTING WITH KNOWLEDGE OF THE NEWS MEDIA

A media focus entails starting with some understanding of how the news media operate, the types of stories they publish, and a thorough understanding how journalists think.

In order reach your publics through the media, you must understand something about the way the news media operate, which will then help you to think like a journalist. The key things to keep in mind are the convergence of the media, public, and corporate agendas; the concepts of news values and newsworthiness; and the multiple identities of the news media.

Convergence of the media, public, and corporate agendas

The following Venn diagram from Smith (2009) describes the relationship between the key messages an organization wants to communicate (the corporate agenda), what the media publish (the media agenda), and what the public is interested in (the public agenda). This Venn diagram serves as a useful model for understanding the different ways of communicating key messages (see Figure 10.3): here "A" represents the news media as a gatekeeper, "B" represents the audience (or public agenda), and "C" represents the firm. The area of overlap labeled "AB" is information not involving the organization that is of interest both to the media and to the key public. This is an area of little concern for the organization, but it may be worth knowing something about. The overlap region labeled "BC" is information that of interest to the company and to the audiences, but that does not fit the news values of the media, thus meaning it makes little sense to contact the media about it. Most novices in media relations make the mistake of calling the media or preparing news releases containing this category of information. Perhaps the goal is to funnel this information through the news media taking advantage of the news media's third party endorsement (see overleaf). If so, the information needs to repackaged or reframed; otherwise, forego the news media's third party endorsement and relinquish the information to advertising channels.

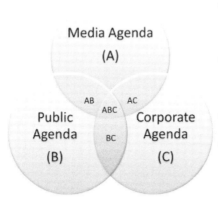

News is about the audience (ABC)

Media Agenda

(A)

AB   AC
ABC
Public   Corporate
Agenda   BC   Agenda
(B)   (C)

- **AB** information not involving the organization that is of interest both to the media and to the key public.
- **BC** non-newsworthy information better shared through advertising unless it can be repackaged/reframed.
- **AC** newsworthy information about the organization.
- **ABC** Information about the organization that is of interest both to the news media and to key publics.

Figure 10.3 The interrelationship between the media agenda, public agenda, and corporate agenda

The area of overlap labeled AC is newsworthy information about the organization, but it may not fit the particular audience that the journalists serve, in which case, it is better to find the news medium that has this audience in mind. Simply because you think something is newsworthy does not automatically mean that it is.

News values and newsworthiness

How newsworthy a potential story is depends on whether you can answer "yes" to any of the questions below, and the more of them you can say "yes" to the better. Companies can relate better to the media by understanding these elements of news. Sometimes you can call and ask to find out whether it serves the needs of the journalist's audience, but the best professionals have done the research necessary to know the answer to this ahead of time. Guth and Marsh (2007) offer these questions for helping to decide whether your story idea is newsworthy:

1. Does the story affect a large portion of the reporter's audience? While a story about new technology may generate interest in Silicon Valley, it may not have the same weight in a town not as wired into the internet.
2. Is it happening now, or is about to happen? Timeliness is at the heart of news. People want to know "the latest" or "what's happening next."
3. Is the story unusual for the reporter's audience? Is it the first, the biggest, or the only one of its kind? People are interested in the novel and unique.
4. Is the story relevant to the reporter's audience? Does it address the audience's self-interests? Does it touch their hearts?

5. Does it involve someone the reporter's audience knows? People are attracted to celebrities—even though the definition of a celebrity can vary from one location to another.

The multiple identities of the news media

The third major factor you need to understand about the news media is how they operate. The news media are not monolithic; like other target publics, they can be segmented into smaller publics, whether by the size of the audience they serve (*local, regional, national,* or *international*), the scope of that audience (mass circulation or specialized), or the medium they use (*newspaper, radio, television, magazine,* or *the internet*). As a result, reporters generally respond to messages defined by their segmentation.

Guth and Marsh (2007) offer useful ways to segment the media: by their deadlines, their competitive edge, the special challenges of their medium, and the amount of lead time they all require.

Deadlines

The different types of news media differ fundamentally by the deadlines they adhere to, so you must know something about their deadlines. For newspapers, you must first know whether the newspaper is a morning paper or an afternoon paper. The deadlines for most

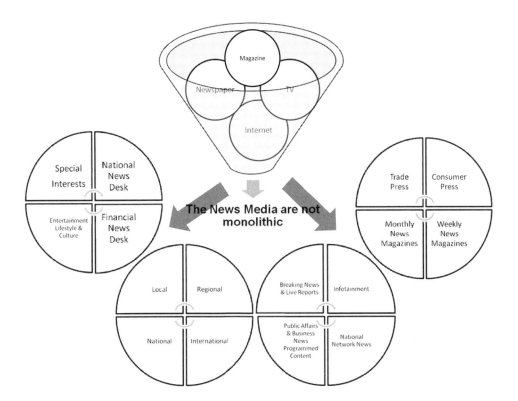

Figure 10.4 The news media are not monolithic

morning papers are around midnight, while they are late morning for most afternoon papers. For magazines, the deadlines depend on whether the magazine is published once a week or once a month; to determine their deadlines, simply call them. For radio news stories, the morning and afternoon commuter traffic times are the most important; these deadlines can be early in the morning 4 or 5am for reaching the early morning show, or a few days ahead if it is a human interest story. Television, like radio, is capable of reporting breaking news anytime. Early and late evening news broadcasts are most important. Then finally, internet news may have deadlines 24 hours a day, seven days a week, so it is simply a matter of finding out when they expect the story to go live. Having no knowledge of, or failing to respect, the working deadlines under which the news media operate is one of the surest ways of getting relationships with the media off to a bad start.

Competitive edge

Guth and Marsh (2007) offer a second way that news media differ: by their competitive edge. In addition to knowing deadlines, you must have some understanding of each news media format's competitive edge when compared to the other formats. Newspapers are usually better staffed than other forms of news media; they are often the most important news outlet in the market, setting the agenda for the other media. In addition, newspapers are the most likely to take an editorial stand. Magazines, on the other hand, cannot compete in the area of daily breaking news coverage, but excel in longer feature and analytical reporting. Radio has the special advantage of being a portable medium, reaching listeners in their cars, where other media cannot. Radio offers minimal logistics for reporters, and also provides a quick capsule on the news. Television, on the other hand, is the most dramatic because of sight and sound dynamics; this is where most people get their news. Finally, the Internet brings together pictures, video, sound, and text, and has a global reach.

Challenges associated with the medium

A third way news media differ from one another that you must understand when attempting to work with them has to do with the challenges associated with each medium. These challenges may affect which type of medium you pursue for story placement. Guth and Marsh (2007) observe that daily newspapers require journalists gain quick access to details for in-depth reporting of breaking news stories, as well as pictures and artwork to illustrate stories. Magazines, too, require thorough research, and their high-quality printing requirements add additional attention to artwork, photography, and design. Radio, on the other hand, requires tight writing, meaning the emphasis should be on short sound bites. Natural sound effects and music aid in telling stories, if they can be developed fast enough. Television requires compelling pictures, and this often drives which stories are selected. This format is not well suited for stories with significant detail. Finally, internet news requires the combined talents of a reporter, editor, designer, and programmer. With constant deadline pressure, accuracy is critical and requires more attention due to the speed of production.

Lead time

The last major issue affecting which media type to pursue is the amount of lead time the media need in their production. Guth and Marsh (2007) recommend that for newspapers you give about a week's notice for routine information, a day or several hours for important news, and less than an hour for major on-deadline news. News releases can be submitted at any time, but Sunday and Monday often find less competition for space because weekends traditionally are slow news days. Newspapers are also lightly staffed on most weekends. On the other hand, newspapers have more pages because of increased advertising. Magazines require a much greater lead time for information: two months for monthly magazines. Weekly news magazines have a much shorter lead time, but they seldom take information from public relations sources. For radio, give about a week's notice for routine information and for upcoming events that reporters might cover, with important news being handled up to news time. Breaking news may be covered live. Other live coverage may be planned with a lead time of a week or longer. Talk shows and other programs with guests may require several weeks or months to schedule. Finally, for the internet, provide up to a week's notice for routine information and for events that reporters might cover, with important news being handled up to news time. Breaking news may be covered live. Talk shows and programs with guests may require several weeks to schedule.

Working through the news media is not without its organizational costs. The organization must expend considerable time, energy, and resources in adapting its message for the news media's audience through the writing of the news release, including the production costs associated with subsidies. Yet bearing these costs is what makes a source more valuable to the media, because using such materials reduces the costs to the news media of developing them on their own. At the same time, however, there is no guarantee that the news media will use the subsidies developed by firms.

Should firms circumvent or work through the media?

The primary assumption of this chapter is that organizations are interested in building those relationships through the news media, but rarely is this always the case. Another path is open to organizations, but it is not recommended for dealing with news that organizations want communicated with the general public. This path is to circumvent the news media altogether. There are a couple of reasons that companies may circumvent the news media by taking their news directly to the public. First, during times of crisis, organizations are encouraged to "steal thunder" by releasing their information straight to the public before the news media has had a chance to report on the story (Arpan and Pompper, 2003). We have little research examining whether organizations can or should release their information to the public during times of routine or non-crisis states. Some claim that with the general distrust towards the media, or the anti-media bias, organizations are better off making their information available straight to the public. These issues become more pronounced in light of the second reason that companies may take their news directly to the public: they can. It used to be that that working through the news media was the only game in town; organizations did not have access to a wide range of channels and new technologies that now exist since the creation of the internet.

The Media as a Third-party Endorsement

The media's third-party endorsement is often cited as a reason that many firms employ public relations techniques instead of advertising. The third-party endorsement is a concept dealing with the degree of credence audiences give to information in a news report. Such reports receive credence because they come from a source sufficiently dissociated from the subject of the report, and one who has no stake in how audiences interpret the information.

> Institutions depend for their viability and survival upon the knowledge and at least tacit consent of third parties that are not directly involved in the particular interaction the institution regulates…. [W]hat those involved in an institutional interaction can and cannot expect from each other is itself expected by third parties or outside observers. (Offe 1993, cited in Lammers and Barbour, 2006, p. 360)

Hallahan (1999b) proposed the idea that the media implicitly endorse the topics they cover to agenda-setting theory and the news media's status conferral role (cf. Lazarsfeld and Merton, 1971). Hallahan (1999b) noted, however, that the idea of journalists' intentionally endorsing the topics they cover is in conflict with journalists' professional standards, and in fact, there is "little research evidence that people actually believe journalists have endorsed a product when they run a story" (Hunt and Grunig, 1994, p. 383). Hallahan (1999b) suggested an alternate characterization of endorsement: that audiences infer endorsements from the media, if nothing more than believing that some firms are more worth knowing about than others. The view taken in the present study is that even if audiences do not infer a third-party endorsement, sources defer to the news media in ascribing this role.

Hallahan (1999a) argued that different sets of conventions, rules, or contracts, apply between the message producer and audience for different media genres: Under the reality contract for news, audiences believe information is real, important, and could affect their lives. Under the advertising contract, a message sponsor's persuasive intent is understood and dictates that audiences scrutinize messages differently.

Despite widespread anecdotal acceptance in the field, the third-party endorsement has been the subject of little empirical research. What research has been done indicates that receiving firms' news from the media, rather than from advertising, leads to enhanced learning and recall among audiences (Cameron, 1994; Hallahan, 1999b), greater believability (Schwarz et al., 1986), and more positive attitudes (Salmon et al., 1985; Straughan et al., 1996). Research on the topic has focused on evaluating the effectiveness of advertising as opposed to news coverage but has not investigated whether it is better for firms to release news to the public directly or to rely on subsidies to the news media.

Summary

This chapter has explored the role of the news media in corporate reputation management. The basic argument is that the relationship between the news media and corporate reputation is fairly complex and is comprised of multiple dimensions. The news media are not monolithic, and the types of coverage that the news media give to firms are not uniform. Moreover, news attention can be conceptualized in a number of different ways that relate to corporate reputation differently. At the same time, corporate reputation is also multi-dimensional. Previous research has classified corporate reputation according to a number of different traits or attributes. This chapter introduced another classification scheme that helps to explain how the news media relate to corporate reputation. These dimensions of corporate reputation are public prominence, public esteem, and public associations.

In response to the news media, organizations are encouraged to build relationships with them. Indeed, media relations may even be viewed as a form of corporate social responsibility in which firms do more than simply manage their reputations: they demonstrate the commitments they have to society through their openness and transparence, particularly on matters of public interest, determined from the point of view of the public rather than just from the point of view of the firm.

The chapter identified two particular ways that organizations can respond to the news media. The first is from an organizational starting point of identifying key messages for which the organization wants to be known. The second is to begin with a working knowledge of how the news media work and then develop an organizational response based on this working knowledge. Organizations always have the choice of circumventing the news media. For many smaller organizations, this is the only choice they have, because the "news hole" for media coverage is not large enough to give equal treatment to all firms. For firms that do have the choice, however, recognizing and ascribing to the media the power of the third party endorsement may confer additional elements of legitimation.

References

Ader, C. R. (1995). A longitudinal study of agenda setting for the issue of environmental pollution. *Journalism and Mass Communication Quarterly, 72*(2), 300–311.

Arpan, L. M., and Pompper, D. (2003). Stormy weather: Testing "Stealing thunder" as a crisis communication strategy to improve communication flow between organizations and journalists. *Public Relations Review, 29,* 291–308.

Austin, E. W., Pinkleton, B. E., Hust, S. J. T., and Coral-Reaume Miller, A. (2007). The locus of message meaning: Differences between trained coders and untrained message recipients in the analysis of alcoholic beverage advertising. *Communication Methods and Measures, 1*(2), 92–111.

Becker, L. B., and McCombs, M. E. (1978). The role of the press in determining voter reactions to presidential primaries. *Human Communication Research, 4*(4), 301–307.

Behr, R., and Iyengar, S. (1985). Television news, real-world cues and changes in the public agenda. *Public Opinion Quarterly, 58*(1), 479–508.

Brooks, M. E., Highhouse, S., Russell, S. S., and Mohr, D. C. (2003). Familiarity, ambivalence, and firm reputation: Is corporate fame a double-edged sword? *Journal of Applied Psychology, 88*(5), 904–14.

Cameron, G. T. (1994). Does publicity outperform advertising? An experimental test of the third-party endorsement. *Journal of Public Relations Research, 6*(3), 185–207.

Carroll, C. E. (2009). The relationship between firms' media favorability and public esteem. *Public Relations Journal, 4*(4), 1–32.

Carroll, C. E. (in press). Corporate Reputation and the News Media in the United States. In C. E. Carroll (ed.), *Corporate Reputation and the News Media: Agenda-setting within business news in developed, emerging, and frontier markets*. New York: Routledge Press.

Carroll, C. E., Huang, N. C. L., and Weberling, B. (2010). *Conceptualizing Key Messages for Public Relations Evaluation: Case studies of non-profit organizations*. Paper presented at the 14th International Public Relations Conference. Miami, FL.

Carroll, C. E., and McCombs, M. E. (2003). Agenda-setting effects of business news on the public's images and opinions about major corporations. *Corporate Reputation Review, 6*(1), 36–46.

Chen, C. C., and Meindl, J. R. (1991). The construction of leadership images in the popular press: The case of Donald Burr and People Express. *Administrative Science Quarterly, 36*(4), 521–51.

Cohen, B. C. (1963). *The Press and Foreign Policy*. Princeton, NJ: Princeton University Press.

Deephouse, D. L. (2000). Media reputation as a strategic resource: An integration of mass communication and resource-based theories. *Journal of Management, 26*(6), 1091–112.

Einwiller, S., Carroll, C. E., and Korn, K. (2009). Under what conditions do the news media influence corporate reputation? The roles of media systems dependency and need for orientation. *Corporate Reputation Review, 12*(4), 1–17.

Fombrun, C. J. (1998). Indices of corporate reputation: An analysis of media rankings and social monitors' ratings. *Corporate Reputation Review, 1*(4), 327–40.

Fombrun, C. J., Gardberg, N. A., and Sever, J. M. (2000). The Reputation Quotient: A multi-stakeholder measure of corporate reputation. *Journal of Brand Management, 7*(4), 241–55.

Fombrun, C. J., and van Riel, C. B. M. (2003). *Fame and Fortune: How successful companies build winning reputations*. London: Financial Times Prentice Hall.

Fombrun, C. J., and Shanley, M. (1990). What's in a name? Reputation building and corporate strategy. *Academy of Management Journal, 33*(2), 233–58.

Freeman, E. R. (1984). *Strategic Management: A Stakeholder Approach*. Boston, MA: Pitman/Ballinger.

Gardberg, N. A., and Fombrun, C. J. (2002). USA: For better or worse – the most media visible American corporate reputations. *Corporate Reputation Review, 4*(4), 385–91.

Ghanem, S. I. (1997). Filling in the tapestry: The second level of agenda-setting. In M. E. McCombs, D. L. Shaw and D. H. Weaver (eds), *Communication and Democracy: Exploring the intellectual frontiers in agenda-setting theory* (pp. 3–14). Mahwah, NJ: Lawrence Erlbaum Associates.

Golan, G., and Wanta, W. (2001). Second-level agenda setting in the New Hampshire primary: A comparison of coverage in three newspapers and public perceptions of candidates. *Journalism and Mass Communication Quarterly, 78*(2), 247–59.

Guth, D. W., and Marsh, C. (2007). *Adventures in Public Relations: Case studies and critical thinking*. Boston, MA: Pearson/Allyn and Bacon.

Hallahan, K. (1999a). Content class as a contextual cue in the cognitive processing of publicity versus advertising. *Journal of Public Relations Research, 11*(4), 293–320.

Hallahan, K. (1999b). No, Virginia, it's not true what they say about publicity's "implied third-party endorsement" effect. *Public Relations Review, 25*(3), 331.

Hart, R. P. (1985). Systematic analysis of political discourse: The development of DICTION. In K. Sanders and D. Nimmo (eds), *Political Communication Yearbook: 1984* (pp. 97–134). Carbondale, IL: Southern Illinois Press.

Hart, R. P. (2001). Redeveloping DICTION: Theoretical considerations. In M. West (ed.), *Theory, Method and Practice of Computer Content Analysis*. (pp. 43–60). New York: Ablex.

Hart, R. P., and Carroll, C. E. (2008). DICTION (Software). In L. M. Given (ed), *The Sage Encyclopedia of Qualitative Research Methods* (pp. 215–16). Thousand Oaks, CA: Sage Publications.

Hon, L. C. (1997). What have you done for me lately? Exploring effectiveness in public relations. *Journal of Public Relations Research, 9*, 1–30.

Hunt, T., and Grunig, J. E. (1994). *Public Relations Techniques*. Fort Worth, TX: Harcourt Brace College Publishers.

Kim, K., and McCombs, M. E. (2007). News story descriptions and the public's opinions of political candidates. *Journalism and Mass Communication Quarterly, 84*(2), 299–314.

Kim, S. H., Scheufele, D. A., and Shanahan, J. (2002). Think about it this way: Attribute agenda-setting function of the press and the public's evaluation of a local issue. *Journalism and Mass Communication Quarterly, 79*(1), 7–25.

Kim, Y. (2001). Measuring the economic value of public relations. *Journal of Public Relations Research, 13*(1), 3–26.

Kiousis, S. (2004). Explicating media salience: A factor analysis of New York Times issue coverage during the 2000 U.S. presidential election. *Journal of Communication, 54*(1), 71–87.

Kiousis, S., Bantimaroudis, P., and Ban, H. (1999). Candidate image attributes: Experiments on the substantive dimension of second-level agenda setting. *Communication Research, 26*(4), 414–28.

Kiousis, S., Popescu, C., and Mitrook, M. A. (2007). Understanding influence on corporate reputation: An examination of public relations efforts, media coverage, public opinion, and financial performance from an agenda-building and agenda-setting perspective. *Journal of Public Relations Research, 19*(2), 147–65.

Lammers, J. C., and Barbour, J. B. (2006). An institutional theory of organizational communication. *Communication Theory, 16*(3), 356–77.

Lazarsfeld, P. F., and Merton, R. K. (1971). Mass communication, popular taste and organized social action. In W. Schramm and D. F. Roberts (eds), *The Process and Effects of Mass Communication* (pp. 554–78). Urbana, IL: University of Illinois Press.

Lippmann, W. (1922). *Public Opinion*. New York: Harcourt, Brace and Company.

McCombs, M. E. (2004). *Setting the Agenda: The mass media and public opinion*. Cambridge, UK: Polity Press.

McCorkindale, T. M. (2008). Does familiarity breed contempt? Analyses of the relationship among corporate familiarity, corporate reputation, corporate citizenship, and corporate personality on corporate equity. *Public Relations Review, 34*(4), 392–5.

McCombs, M. E., and Ghanem, S. I. (2001). The convergence of agenda setting and framing. In S. D. Reese, O. H. Gandy, Jr. and A. E. Grant (eds), *Framing Public Life: perspectives on the media and our understandings of the social world* (Vol. 67–82). Mahwah, NJ: Lawrence Erlbaum Publishers.

McCombs, M. E., Llamas, J. P., Lopez-Escobar, E., and Rey, F. (1997). Candidate images in Spanish elections: Second level agenda-setting effects. *Journalism and Mass Communication Quarterly, 74*(4), 703–13.

McCombs, M. E., Lopez-Escobar, E., and Llamas, J. P. (2000). Setting the agenda of attributes in the 1996 Spanish general election. *Journal of Communication, 50*(2), 77–92.

McCombs, M. E., and Shaw, D. L. (1972). The agenda-setting function of the mass media. *Public Opinion Quarterly, 36*, 176–87.

McCombs, M. E., Shaw, D. L., and Weaver, D. H. (1997). *Communication and Democracy: Exploring the intellectual frontiers in agenda-setting*. Mahwah, NJ: Lawrence Erlbaum Associates.

McWilliams, A., and Siegel, D. (2001). Corporate social responsibility: A theory of the firm perspective. *Academy of Management Review, 26*(1), 117–27.

Meijer, M.-M., and Kleinnijenhuis, J. (2006a). The effects of issue news on corporate reputation: Applying the theories of agenda setting and issue ownership in the field of business communication. *Journal of Communication, 56*(4), 543–59.

Meijer, M.-M., and Kleinnijenhuis, J. (2006b). News and corporate reputation: Empirical findings from The Netherlands. *Public Relations Review, 32*(4), 341–8.

Ragas, M. W., and Roberts, M. S. (2009). Agenda setting and agenda melding in an age of horizontal and vertical media: A new theoretical lens for virtual brand communities. *Journalism and Mass Communication Quarterly, 86*(1), 45–64.

Rindova, V. P., Williamson, I. O., Petkova, A. P., and Sever, J. M. (2005). Being good or being known: An empirical examination of the dimensions, antecedents, and consequences of organizational reputation. *The Academy of Management Journal, 48*(6), 1033–49.

Salmon, C. T., Reid, L. N., Pokrywcznski, J., and Willett, W. (1985). The effectiveness of advocacy advertising relative to news coverage. *Communication Research, 12*, 546–67.

Schwarz, N., Kumpf, M., and Bussman, W. (1986). Resistance to persuasion as a consequence of influence attempts in advertising and non-advertising communications. *Psychology: A Quarterly Journal of Human Behavior, 23*(2–3), 72–6.

Sheafer, T. (2007). How to evaluate it: The role of story-evaluative tone in agenda setting and priming. *Journal of Communication, 57*(1), 21–39.

Siegel, D. S., and Vitaliano, D. F. (2001). An empirical analysis of the strategic use of corporate social responsibility. *Journal of Economics and Management Strategy, 16*(3), 773–92.

Smith, R. D. (2009). *Strategic Planning for Public Relations* (Vol. 3). New York, NY: Routledge.

Stocking, S. H. (1984). Effect of public relations efforts on media visibility of organizations. *Journalism Quarterly, 62*(2), 358–66, 450.

Straughan, D., Bleske, G. L., and Zhao, X. (1996). Modeling format and source effects of an advocacy message. *Journalism and Mass Communication Quarterly, 73*(1), 135–46.

Weaver, D. H., Graber, D. A., McCombs, M. E., and Eyal, C. H. (1981). *Media Agenda Setting in a Presidential Election: Issues, images, and interest.* New York, NY: Praeger.

Williams, J., W. (1985). Agenda setting for the civil rights issue. *Public Opinion Quarterly, 45*, 376–83.

Wry, T., Deephouse, D. L., and McNamara, G. (2006). Substantive and evaluative media reputations among and within cognitive strategic groups. *Corporate Reputation Review, 9*(4), 225–42.

11 *The Impact of Web 2.0 and Enterprise 2.0 on Corporate Reputation: Benefits Problems and Prospects*

MARTIN REDDINGTON AND HELEN FRANCIS

Introduction

The emergent nature of the family of social media technologies often collectively labelled as 'Web 2.0' is generating significant interest amongst academics and practitioners in respect of the potential impacts associated with people management and corporate reputation (Birkinshaw and Pass, 2008; Martin et al., 2009; Withers et al., 2010).

The central premise is that these technologies help to build and improve employee communication and engagement through a process in which employees have greater control over relevant information, a greater participation in the organisation, a sense of corporate identity, and a deeper and more timely understanding of the needs of the business, e.g. through web-based portals. In turn, the hoped-for outcomes are higher levels of organisational identification and engagement and a superior employer brand and corporate reputation (Martin, 2009; Martin and Hetrick, 2006; Parry et al., 2007; Rosethorn, 2009).

However, there are a number of cautionary observations and findings that question this central premise. For example, the Chartered Institute of Personnel and Development or CIPD (2009) highlighted an incident involving the misuse of social networking site, Facebook, which had severe repercussions for Virgin Atlantic, a UK-based airline. The misconduct related to claims by passengers that staff had used a Facebook site to criticise safety standards in the airline and to call passengers 'chavs', which is a disparaging British middle-class characterisation of certain working-class groups as 'tasteless, pallid, Burberry-wearing, jewellery-encrusted' people (Maconie, 2007, p. 47). The disciplinary hearing concluded that the crew's misbehaviour had brought the airline into disrepute and that passengers who paid the salaries of staff had been insulted. The comments about safety standards related to claims that 'the planes were full of cockroaches' and allegations that 'the airline's jet engines were replaced four times in one year'.

The BBC website on 31 October 2008 reported the following statement from a senior Virgin representative:

> It is impossible for these cabin crew members to uphold [our] high standards of customer service ... if they hold these views ...

> [There] is a time and a place for Facebook ... There is no justification for it to be used as a sounding board for staff of any company to criticise the very passengers who ultimately pay their salaries ... We have numerous internal channels for our staff to feed back legitimate and appropriate issues relating to the company.

This example begins to surface the potential difficulties for corporate reputation associated with the liberalisation of 'employee voice' in the 'uncontrolled' space of the external web. Organisations have responded to this risk by developing so-called Enterprise 2.0 applications (McAfee, 2006) – effectively bringing Web 2.0 behind organisational firewalls to reap the benefits of participation and collaboration but minimising the risks of openness and user-control.

The nature and extent of the interrelated implications for corporate reputation of using Enterprise 2.0 are now examined in more detail by reviewing illustrations from our own research in the public and private sector.

HR Strategies Incorporating Web 2.0

Building on the introduction, the emergence of Web 2.0 and Enterprise 2.0 has stimulated considerable discussion about the potential opportunities and challenges presented by these technologies and how human resource management (HRM) can play an important role in guiding their adoption to improve business performance (CIPD, 2009; Withers et al., 2010).

Indeed, notwithstanding the Virgin Atlantic example, HR professionals can assist transformation at work by helping implement these social media technologies to provide the basis for more effective collaboration and knowledge sharing, more effective two-way communication with employees, and by giving employees interesting and authentic alternatives to the traditional ways of expressing their opinions and ideas – improved employee voice (Birkinshaw and Pass, 2008; Martin et al., 2009). This is seen to be an increasingly important way of creating a participative culture, in which employees across the organisation can help shape appropriate workable arrangements to respond to the competing challenges faced by their organisations (Singapore Institute of Management 2009).

Critically, our reflections on the literature reveal that the tensions underlying these challenges, shown illustratively in Figure 11.1, create activation triggers – stimuli that encourage or compel a response and which shape emergence of new *HR strategies*. These reflect how employees are treated and managed and what role they play in the overall success of the business. This perspective allows for contextualisation and more specific levels of action within an organization.

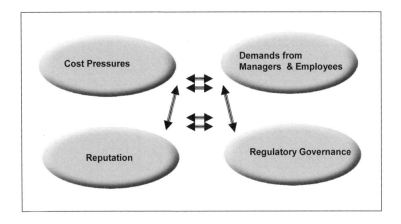

Figure 11.1 Diverse and competing challenges – some organisational-level tensions

The Outputs of Web 2.0 for Human Resource Management

One of the main benefits of Web 2.0 is in providing the opportunity for organisations to change their business models (McAfee, 2006; Tredinnick, 2006) because it helps improve and extend knowledge sharing and collaboration among employees, suppliers, contractors, and new and existing customers. It can also involve existing and potential customers in product design and rating of existing offerings, and to increase their reach to new generations of customers (see McKinsey, 2008).

Extending this argument to HRM, just as organisations are using Web 2.0 to create new business models, we believe that this family of social media can help HR professionals create value for employees, potential employees and other stakeholders in the extended organisation in developing a new or at least complementary architectures for collaboration, participation and facilitating employee voice and conversations for change. Perhaps a good way of elaborating this message is to draw on the ideas of Li and Bernoff (2008) who discuss five strategies for tapping into the 'groundswell', a term they use to describe stakeholder participation and collaboration which is driving the adoption of Web 2.0. The focus of their book is on customer and supplier groundswell with only one chapter devoted specifically to employees. However, all five of the strategies are relevant to creating internal groundswell (see Table 11.1).

Note: To assist the reader, a glossary of terms used to describe different applications of Web 2.0 is shown in Appendix 1 to this chapter.

Table 11.1   Adding strategic value: applications to HR and people management

Strategies for adding value through Web 2.0 to HRM and people management	Applications to key functions in HR and people management
More effective listening to understand employees and other internal stakeholders through richer social media research.	*Employee engagement* Promoting the use of employee blogs and online discussion forums to raise issues which are important to employees, so surfacing authentic employee voice rather than responses to attitude surveys. Good examples are the use of employee blogging in Microsoft (Walker Rettberg, 2008), in some of the research on the positive application of employee blogs by James Richards (2007) and the use of discussion forums.
Talking to employees and others by increasing the reach and richness of messages and learning using Web 2.0.	*Learning* Using corporate blogs and RSS feeds to help people learn about important and up-to-date knowledge of matters that are relevant to them. IBM is a good example, but unions too are beginning to use blogs in interesting ways to open communications with members (see Richards, 2007). *Employee Communications* Using corporate blogs and social networking sites to keep employees and partner organisations up to date with key areas of company business.
Motivating and energising employees and others by building on the enthusiasm of key influencers and using the power of word of mouth to spread the message/medium.	*Employee motivation and managing psychological contracts* Tapping into and engaging with enthusiastic employee bloggers and contributors to media sharing sites about your organisations to demonstrate you are listening and acting on what is being discussed on the 'street' about the organisation. *Recruitment* Use the power of these online opinion-formers to 'virally' market positive messages about the organisation for recruitment purposes. Research shows that the opinions of users of products and services in the consumer field are the most trusted source of knowledge among potential consumers. Bloggers and comments on blogs are also trusted as a source of information. Social networking has become an important media for both of these activities. *Impacting on employer brands* Participate in and encourage online communities which discuss your employer brand.

Table 11.1 *Concluded*

Strategies for adding value through Web 2.0 to HRM and people management	Applications to key functions in HR and people management
Supporting employees and others by using web 2.0 tools to help them support each other.	*Knowledge creation and knowledge sharing* Knowledge creation and learning are two of the most important ways in which social media can be used, especially where employees and partner organisations are geographically dispersed. The use of wikis, which draw on the 'wisdom of crowds' (Surowiecki, 2004; Tapscott and Williams, 2008), is an extremely important example of social media being used to great effect to create collective knowledge and help contributors and readers learn at the same time. *Promoting work–life balance* Just as some organisations have set up online self-help to support users through technical problems, such as Dell, others are beginning to use discussion forums to help support employees in managing their careers and work–life balance.
Reaching out to employees and other stakeholders to participate in innovation in people management and HR policy and process design.	*Employer Branding and Value Creation* One of the key issues in developing corporate values and employer brands is authenticity. Currently most organisations take a top-down approach to this, sometimes consulting employees about decisions that have already been taken but often lack authenticity with employees, particularly those remote from head office locations. Some organisations have begun to use discussion forums to surface the values, attitudes and opinions that 'really matter to staff' before taking such decisions. *Designing rewards systems and benefits* Increasingly organisations are incorporating customers into the design of new products using Web 2.0 tools.

Based on Li and Bernoff (2008).

Note: The 'wisdom of crowds' thesis, which underpins applications such as Wikipedia (Tapscott and Williams, 2008), states that collective intelligence by groups often results in better decision-making than could be made by any individual.

It is clear that HR professionals need to keep abreast of these developments and gain the knowledge and confidence to help shape the approach to Web 2.0 adoption.

In our case examples from the public and private sectors, the tensions arising from the need for enterprise and greater shareholder value, within an atmosphere of financial austerity and increasing regulation, feature prominently as the activation triggers to promote the use of Web 2.0 technologies. One of our cases introduces a new model that we have been developing to link HR strategies with organisational outcomes. The other case is more vignette in style but in our view provides a useful and practical perspective on the deployment of Web 2.0 and Enterprise 2.0 to promote transformation of working practices.

Case Study 1: AEGON UK

AEGON UK is one of the leading providers of life and pensions and investment products in the UK. It has consistently followed a strategy which has been concerned with a real focus on the customer and their need for financial solutions that fit their differing situations, whilst ensuring the business operated in markets in which there was a strong return, thus helping to build a strong and reliable brand.

The current financial turbulence has created a range of competing challenges and tensions which have brought into sharper focus the need to attend to a range of commercial and social outcomes that shape its corporate reputation. Amongst these tensions are the need to create new, innovative products and services which receive favour with customers and shareholders, while at the same time demonstrating compliance with increasingly stringent financial regulation.

In March 2009, under the sponsorship of Martin Glover, Head of Corporate HR and Organisational Effectiveness, a project was initiated to review AEGON's Employee Value Proposition (EVP). This initiative was designed to enhance the organisation's ability to achieve its corporate reputation aims.

As Martin states:

The organisation had many initiatives underway to improve various aspects of its operational effectiveness, such as investment in new HR and customer service management processes and systems, but we appreciated that in transforming the culture of the business through more innovative people management practices and securing higher levels of employee engagement then we would considerably boost our potential to realise our corporate aims – both financial and social.

Our approach to this was a close examination of the Employee Value Proposition and how this would help us, both short term as we face unprecedented challenges created through the financial turbulence in global markets and ever increasing financial regulation, and long term as we seek to establish a sustainable, highly respected corporate reputation.

METHOD

The research into the impact of EVP on corporate reputation was carried out during 2009 and 2010 and comprised a multi-stage approach. This was underpinned by a model developed by us that is grounded within current literature on the subject and our own practical experience and research into HRM-based change and corporate reputation. The model shown in Figure 11.2 depicts a 'line of sight' between the adopted HR strategies of an organisation, and commercial and social outcomes. The particular focus illustrated in this case concerns an examination of the EVP architecture, and the role of Enterprise 2.0 technologies in shaping this.

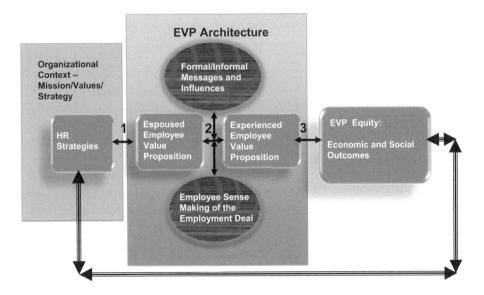

Figure 11.2 HR strategies, EVP architectures, EVP equity and commercial and social outcomes

The notion of a 'line of sight' model provides simplification and coherence to what is in practice a dynamic and complex process. It is designed to advance new perspectives in accessible ways that resonate with practitioners, and to provide a platform for more complex theory building currently being undertaken by the authors.

By creating added value for managers and employees through more effective leadership, policies and enhanced people management practices in the form of an EVP, HR can claim to create competitive advantage and align the function more closely with business/ corporate strategy and the longer-term branding and reputational aims of organisations. However, the challenge facing organisations is not, in our view, whether they should justify the development and articulation of an EVP or whether it has strategic potential, but how to deploy and adopt it in a way that creates value to different stakeholders.

To address this challenge, our work is primarily concerned with elaborating recent research which supports overall theoretical frameworks for EVP adoption and its associated outcomes. This is borne from the recognition that there continues to be a lack of recent research in this area, although some notable exceptions are Heger (2007), Martin (2009), Martin and Hetrick (2006) and Rosethorne (2009). It is our intention here to explain the essence of our model and to provide a context which illustrates the role of Web 2.0 within the research. Our future work in this area will provide a more detailed description of the model enriched by a subsequent phase of data capture and analysis.

EVP ARCHITECTURE©

The *EVP architecture* shapes and is shaped by HR strategies and working practices of the organisation (Relationship 1). Our use of the term accommodates a broad notion which incorporates not only what we would traditionally consider as elements of an *employment deal*, which typically means *pay and benefits, leadership etc.*, but also how these EVP components are constructed and interpreted by different stakeholders.

We make the point that how the EVP design process is managed and communicated by change leaders has an important shaping influence upon the design of these components. The ability to create a framework for action that has relevance, and can be understood and accepted across different interest groups, is central to the process. Pivotal to this ability is the persuasive/political dimension of language which is a powerful medium in the hands of top managers aimed at persuading employees to adapt to constant change (Musson and Cohen, 1999; Kelemen 2000).

Accepting this action-oriented role of language, we present a dynamic view of the construction of EVP architectures that is always open to re-articulation and change. The concept of EVP can be seen as an attempt by employers to define the 'psychological contract' in terms of the value or 'deal' an employee derives from his employment in an organisation, linking this to a corporate personality or identity that both employees and customers will identify with (Martin, 2009; Martin and Hetrick, 2006; Rosethorn, 2009). Interest in EVP has mostly flourished within the practitioner literature, promoted by recruitment consultancies as part of the 'war for talent'. Academic interest in this trend is fairly recent and there is a paucity of research as to how firms are currently developing their underlying value propositions, nor the kind of processes that can be cited as examples of good practice (Backhaus and Tikoo, 2004; Heger, 2007).

Drawing on the underlying concept of the psychological contract (Conway and Briner, 2009; Cullinane and Dundon, 2006; Rousseau, 2003) and associated work surrounding employee engagement (MacLeod and Clarke, 2009; Wefald and Downey, 2009), we observe that there appears to be a 'natural link' between emergent concepts of EVP, employee engagement and various organisational outcomes which is compelling enough for a growing investment being made in employer branding and employee engagement strategies (MacLeod and Clarke, 2009; Wong et al., 2009).

Our synthesis of the literature, combined with our research and practice in the field of brand and corporate reputation allows us to elaborate features of the EVP architecture, shown in Figure 11.3.

The *Espoused EVP* represents the formal articulation of the 'deal on offer' by the organisation and is the 'autobiographical account' of the EVP, projected and promoted by the top management team. This embodies the unique and differentiating promise a business makes to its employees and potential candidates and the reciprocal obligations placed on them.

The *Experienced EVP* (shown as Relationship 2 in Figure 11.2) represents the perceived 'deal on offer' by organisational members and is effectively the 'biographical account' of the EVP.

The *EVP Attributes* are inducements and contributions informed by a synthesis of the relevant literature and published research associated with the components of 'the deal' (Dawley et al., 2008; Francis 2003, 2006, 2007; Heger, 2007; Martin, 2009; Martin and Hetrick, 2006; Withers et al., 2010).

The moderating elements (shown in Figure 11.2) reflect the changing and dynamic nature of EVP in its varying organisational contexts. These comprise formal and informal interactions and how they are perceived to promote and support the Espoused EVP. Formal interactions can take the form of public relations/internal communications systems/Web 2.0, advertising and customer relationship management programmes.

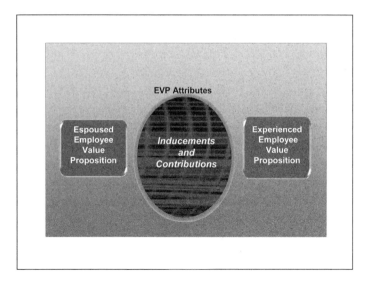

Figure 11.3 EVP attributes (adapted from Francis and Reddington, forthcoming)

Informal interactions can relate to the day-to-day influence of co-workers, managers and leaders and how they are perceived to 'live' the Espoused EVP. This can also be described as 'perception of organisational support' which concerns the overall levels of helpful social interaction available on the job. Other informal interactions may take the form of knowledge of customer feedback – e.g. social conversations and access to customer testaments on the internet.

In terms of application, organisations can engage with this model at a different point. Some may already have technology applications and tools, such as Web 2.0, in place to help re-architect and re-articulate an EVP, whereas other organisations may be engaging with these more advanced technologies for the first time, as HR seeks to become a more strategic partner (Withers et al., 2010).

Collectively these elements of the EVP architecture are described by us as an 'EVP Wheel©', is embedded in the following methodology (see Francis and Reddington, forthcoming, for fuller explanation):

- Position Statements that define six features of EVP (described as 'EVP Wheel Segments') – namely Customer Service, Participation and Collaboration, Reputation, Reward and Recognition, Learning and Innovation, Performance.
- Each segment represents a bundle of contextualised leadership and people management practices and the Position Statements are designed to stimulate conversations about these practices across three levels – strategic, managerial and operational – consistent with the notion of multilayered 'conversations for change' developed by Francis (2003, 2006, 2007).
- Web 2.0 portal technology which acts as an engagement tool to facilitate a 'democratic architecture' for conversation and its subsequent thematic analysis.
- Survey Items which provide a statistical perspective on the perceived intent and implementation of the policies and practices in respect of each of the defined segments of the EVP wheel.

- Survey items which explicitly include tensions that arise across all segments, such as 'perceived organisational support' (Dawley et al., 2008) and those identified in 'conversations for change'.

In addition, our model accommodates an EVP Personality© dimension, which gives expression to the EVP in the form of human characteristics.

This overall approach allows the collection and interpretation of both qualitative and quantitative data, with the intention of using both types in a way that seeks to enrich the quality of the other.

EVP EQUITY©

The EVP architecture will frame perceptions of the relative satisfaction and perceived value of EVP equity (shown as Relationship 3 in Figure 11.2). This is a measure of the relative value of the Experienced EVP as experienced by organisational members and is expressed in the form of commercial and social outcomes. Typically, these would include financial measures of interest to shareholders and regulators, customer experience measures, brand affinity, loyalty and differentiation, corporate social responsibility, and employee measures such as enhanced well-being, attrition and engagement.

DATA CAPTURE

The data capture was organised through two complementary channels. The first of these comprised a series of workshops, to which members of AEGON's senior management group (SMG) were invited. They were tasked with inspecting a range of proposed EVP position statements, which had been agreed with the project sponsor, and invited to comment on them with a view to creating an initial *Espoused EVP* for subsequent release to the wider organisation.

An Enterprise 2.0 portal, made available through AEGON's own Microsoft SharePoint© application, allowed the creation of a virtual 'walled garden' to facilitate online discussion by the SMG, enabling this community to extend and amplify their contributions beyond the workshops. All comments could be viewed by each member of the community and the identities of the participants were disclosed.

The use of Enterprise 2.0 represented a radical departure for AEGON in an attempt to encourage knowledge sharing and participation in this high priority project, which Martin Glover, the EVP project sponsor, fully acknowledged.

Very careful consideration was given to the use of SharePoint for this exercise. It was vital to get this right because it would impact the credibility of the project. The intention was to assess the level of engagement by the SMG in the knowledge that we would use Enterprise 2.0 portal technology as a major element of the 'big conversation' with our wider organisation at a later date. This would be an opportunity to engage our employees in discussions about the architecture of our EVP – effectively to test how well the initial espoused EVP lands with our people. So we were learning a great deal about ourselves and our appetite to adopt new technologies in support of achieving our project objectives. For example, it was apparent that some members of the SMG did not participate actively in the virtual discussions. However, those that did were able to enrich the commentary.

RESULTS

In Table 11.2 we set out themed examples of the types of comments deposited on the Enterprise 2.0 portal, aligned with the EVP segments.

Table 11.2 Researcher and senior management group comments on EVP attributes

EVP segment	Extracts of main themes (researcher perspectives)	Senior management group comments
Learning and Innovation	The need to encourage innovation and enterprise. The importance of correctly managing the tensions implied in fostering collaboration. The importance of considering individual development and career progression.	*Need to be more innovative, need to encourage people to take responsibility to create value. Work on collaboration, but don't constrain individual genius by forcing collaboration. Individuals may have to 'give up something' (e.g. control, power) to do this! Organisation should provide more flexible approaches to career progression/working patterns etc. to increase the choices available to employees.*
Reward and Recognition	Transparent linkage of performance management outcomes and reward, ensuring consistency and fairness. Flexibility to manage a work–life balance in others successfully. Importance of reward and recognition in attracting talent. The value of flexible, devolved reward strategies.	*Consistency of approach in paying performance related bonus ... Pay and benefits should be a fair reflection of employees' contribution. Work–life balance, yes, needs to be better defined and understood ... But concerns about recognizing discretionary effort conflicting with work–life balance e.g. encouraging 'workaholics'. If we want to be the best, we need the best people – if we pay 'fair value' then by definition we need to be above average. Often employees will see their self 'worth' being more intrinsic than being affected by monetary value, so recognition is vital.*
Reputation	Current mismatch between expectations and working experience. The need to celebrate CSR but also to broaden the scope of related activity. The importance of being perceived as competent by customers.	*We need compelling statements about how global professionals can contribute to the business/brand. [In some cases] Promises made and expectations raised are not matching the employee work experience and may damage the brand. Celebrate CSR internally and externally - not enough (of this). For me the message is about having fully rounded people playing a part in society. Needs to be more than current focus on charity. Competence. At the heart of what we need to be perceived as, if we want people to trust us with their money.*

Table 11.2 *Concluded*

EVP segment	Extracts of main themes (researcher perspectives)	Senior management group comments
Participation and Collaboration	Importance of employee voice within an open, honest culture. Importance of giving people empowerment and influence. Tension between influence and inaction.	*Increase informality to encourage more participation, openness and culture change ... and we really do need to listen and act on the feedback. Needs the mechanisms for people to be able to participate and influence the agenda. Disproportionate importance given to negative comments. Often, getting more participation generates a list of potential problems which leads to inaction.*
Performance	The need to increase accountability and agility. The need to improve the general standard, consistency and effectiveness of performance management. The need to make tougher, faster decisions.	*Need this (EVP attribute) to promote a more agile environment with greater accountability and sense of contribution. Ensure we act consistently and equitably in managing performance. Be ruthless with poor performance and reward high performers. Make things simpler in terms of making decisions and get things done ... being prepared to stand up ... and to achieve best commercial outcomes.*
Customer Service	The importance of technical proficiency of customer service staff. Recognition of the need for more empowerment and enterprise.	*... We need to continue to deliver technical expertise, competency in what we do ... In our sector, we are all competing to offer best customer experience; relying on our people to deliver. We need to be less risk averse and give our people more empowerment to deliver superior service.*

It was apparent to us that the SMG participants had contributed some very powerful views about the EVP, which informed an understanding about aspects of its current state and matters that needed attention going forward as part of the re-architecting and re-articulation of the EVP.

This was combined with other data from the workshop sessions and EVP Personality results to provide a more comprehensive overview of the SMG's perception of 'current state' EVP and identification of areas for improvement. These other data sources will feature in our future work.

The results provide examples of the interconnectedness of the EVP segments, e.g. Learning and Innovation and Customer Service share the theme of enterprise. Collectively, the data highlight a joined-up view of the nature and scope of challenges and tensions inherent in re-architecting the EVP with the clear aim of enhancing emergent EVP equity expressed as a range of commercial and social outcomes. In particular, the tensions that we identify and depict as 'compliance vs enterprise' and 'business driven vs employee driven' were given a level of exposure that had not been possible to detect with AEGON's previous survey architecture. This relied primarily upon statistically derived data which failed to capture the dynamic, conversational elements that shape the very nature of EVP, and the inherent tensions underpinning this.

As previously stated, our approach to EVP data capture seeks to address these limitations by embracing a combination of quantitative and qualitative data.

Furthermore, our approach recognises that people management tensions are poorly conceptualised in mainstream accounts of corporate reputation and branding, which typically adopt a very unitarist view of organisational life. Analysts typically shy away from addressing dilemmas associated with the need to maintain control and seek commitment from workers, and there is a need for more skilled and pragmatic approaches to managing these at the workplace (Francis, 2006).

At the time of writing, preparations are being made to undertake the next phase of the project, which will allow the initial Espoused EVP to be revealed to the wider organisation, to stimulate a conversation and evaluate reaction.

Notwithstanding the earlier comments about less-than-enthusiastic engagement with the Enterprise 2.0 portal technology by some SMG members, Martin Glover could identify added significance for the EVP project in general and the use of Enterprise 2.0 in particular:

The 2009 financial results announced on 25 February 2010 revealed that our market is changing, with events such as pensions reform and new solvency regulation creating a very different operating landscape. We need to ensure that AEGON is ready to compete in the new environment. Improving our customer service, creating compelling products and building an agile and responsive business will be our priorities. This goes hand-in-hand with building a powerful and sustainable EVP.

In addition, I believe that the appropriate use of Enterprise 2.0 will be an important component in supporting the cultural transformation necessary to bring about these goals.

Case Study 2: PPMA

The Public Sector Personnel Managers' Association (PPMA) serves and represents the professional interests of members working across the HR/OD professions within the UK public sector. The Association, formerly known as SOCPO, influences and contributes to the development of public policy and legislation in this respect, constantly advocating the need for higher standards of people management and development to further enhance the delivery of public services.

In June 2008, the membership of the PPMA expressed a wish to access Web 2.0 technologies as a means to share knowledge and enhance opportunities to find solutions to the challenges faced in their respective organisations by tapping into a broader base of expertise. This initiated the development of the 'MyTHRU' portal under the leadership of Martin Rayson, the PPMA's Lead Officer of its HR Transformation Network.

THE DEVELOPMENT OF THE 'MYTHRU' PORTAL

The fundamental thinking behind the development of the portal originated from the primary need to find innovative ways to assist the PPMA membership actively to consider whether their HR function was meeting the needs of their organisations and the extent to which they might need to change to do so. It was evident from earlier consultation exercises that members' knowledge, understanding and capacity to put in place a transformation programme were highly variable. In particular, the following needs were identified:

- More information on HR transformation as a whole and specific aspects of it, as well as HR's role in delivering change.
- Practical tools that people can use to enable them to take forward a transformation programme.
- Support mechanisms, where members can seek advice, enter into the debate about what works and what does not work and potentially work together on difference aspects of transformation.

As Martin Rayson explains:

The PPMA was tasked with demonstrating its ability to respond to the members' request for more immediate access to knowledge and opportunities for collaboration, to help address the increasing pressures being faced by the public sector as we move into a highly challenging period, described by many as 'unprecedented austerity'.

The success of the MyTHRU portal will have a direct bearing on the corporate reputation of the PPMA and enhance the value of membership. For this reason, it has assumed a central component of our emerging business strategy for the next two years.

One of us has had significant involvement as an expert advisor to the PPMA and in that capacity as a contributor to the portal architecture. This architecture has been adapted to reflect the interests of the PPMA members, which is both the transformation of HR, and the role of HR in transforming organisations. Indeed, it is our view that in the context of the challenges facing the public sector, this latter point is the most significant issue for the HR community. A view echoed by Martin Rayson:

The public sector is facing an unprecedented challenge of responding to increased customer demands with significantly reduced resources. Public sector organisations will have to change to survive and prosper. Change will impact on business models and ways of working. The people implications will be huge and HR needs to be at the heart of that change process.

This is a prime opportunity to utilize the portal to capture the imagination of our members by provoking 'A Big Debate' on the future of public sector organisations and the role of HR in re-shaping them.

THE MYTHRU PORTAL ARCHITECTURE

The portal architecture has been designed around two main components:

The first is an overall HR transformation 'road map' which provides a step-by-step guide to undertaking a transformation programme. This road map has been informed by PPMA members and a range of expert opinions, and has a variety of tools linked to it.

The second main component is relevant to 'HR as Transformation Agent', embodied within the Big Debate. This is designed as a discussion zone where debate can be stimulated and questions can be posed and answered by PPMA members and other approved parties. Illustrative questions to pump-prime the debate are shown in Box 11.1.

BOX 11.1: START-UP QUESTIONS FOR THE BIG DEBATE

- What will our organisations look like in the future?
- What are the implications of the change?
- What does HR need to adapt to play its part in driving change?
- How do public sector services truly transform, rather than being a trimmed down version of what we currently have?
- What legal obstacles might be an impediment to public sector reform and what legislative frameworks could be out in place to enable such transformation?
- How will public sector leadership need to change to deliver transformed services?
- How can professional silos and tribalism be addressed to deliver a new public sector culture of *Total Place*?
- How do HR professionals enable true transformation of public sector services?

Note: *Total Place* is an exercise to explore the extent of the resources deployed by public services in a particular geographical area and through an exercise termed 'deep diving' how those resources are deployed to address the needs of a particular client group and the impact they have.

Bridging the two components is a series of 'How to Guides' on key topics, written by identified experts in their fields and we have been invited to make a contribution to this series. One of the guides written by us can be accessed at: http://www.martinreddington.com/managing-technology-and-process.

All the guides seek to provide academically robust and practical insights into different facets of HR transformation and OD, supported by good case study evidence.

A screen shot of the home page of the MyTHRU portal illustrating these features is shown in Figure 11.4.

Figure 11.4 Illustrative screen shot of MyTHRU portal (courtesy of PPMA and MyTHRU)

CONTENT ANALYSIS

The ensuing discussions and associated content will be regarded as research data and the PPMA has granted exclusive permission for Edinburgh Napier University to conduct thematic analysis. The idea is that such treatment will liberate new insights into the nature of the virtual conversations provoked by the Big Debate questions and others that arise in the process.

This approach is consistent with a founding principle of the portal architecture, namely a governance structure that establishes and maintains appropriate safeguards for the user community. As Martin Rayson explains:

> *It is vital that all users know that their activities in the portal take place within an environment of trust and integrity. Our members must feel secure that they are in charge of their own user experience and in control of which features they use and which sources of information or support they choose to engage with, whether other public sector colleagues, sponsors or subject*

matter experts. As such, all entrants into the portal will be validated against PPMA criteria. In keeping with this, we see collaboration with Edinburgh Napier as an important strand of our effort to demonstrate high levels of professionalism and integrity in managing our data analysis.

DELIVERING THE MYTHRU PORTAL

The roll out of the portal is being performed in a sequential, phased way. Initially, a number of English regional launch events, also known as 'soft launches' and hosted by KPMG, allowed a group of approximately 50 PPMA members from different public sector organisations to comment on the portal architecture and to discuss their observations with PPMA officers and expert authors of the 'How To' guides.

The primary feedback from these events concerned the need for the portal content to remain relevant and refreshed if high levels of utilisation were to be encouraged.

The next phases are scheduled for late March 2010 at the PPMA National Conference and then a full launch to all PPMA members in the autumn.

Reflecting on progress to date and the forthcoming roll out schedule, Martin remarked:

The recent soft launches of the MyTHRU portal, which we completed in early March 2010, have produced some helpful feedback. The theme of HR transformation is still strong but more and more of our members are reporting to me that HR is facing increasing demands to play a pivotal role in the wider organizational transformations necessary to respond to the turbulent operating environment.

This is creating a 'pull' effect for the MyTHRU portal to take on an expanded form to incorporate a broader spectrum of 'expert' information – effectively an expansion of our knowledge store – and greater access to sources of collaborative support.

This portal is based on the principles that we can learn from each other and we can learn together. Collaboration must be the way forward for the public sector and this portal supports collaboration amongst the HR community. Its success is directly linked to our reputational standing in the eyes of our members, expert authors and other interested parties.

Discussion

These cases reveal a range of outcomes of interest to us as we reflect on the benefits, problems and prospects of Web 2.0 and Enterprise 2.0 in relation to corporate reputation.

In the case of AEGON, as previously stated, our EVP model was derived from our knowledge of the literature in this emerging field and our practical knowledge and experience in the field of brand and corporate reputation. It can be used as a starting point for a framework for analysing data on EVP and corporate reputation and normatively as a guide to practitioners who are embarking on this process for the first time.

However, having reflected on the evidence in this case, we feel that the development of the model itself would benefit from further research providing a deeper and broader coverage of cases, in particular exposing the similarities and differences in perception of EVP architecture in a variety of contextual settings. Indeed, we referred earlier to the lack of well-researched evidence of the linkage between EVP and commercial and social outcomes known to influence corporate reputation, which our study has attempted to address.

In the case of the PPMA, we are able to see how the public sector is engaging with social mediation technologies to promote innovation and to help find ways through one of the most challenging periods in decades. The link with corporate reputation is very clear; if the MyTHRU portal project has enduring success, it will enhance the organisation's standing significantly. Our opportunity as researchers to become immersed in the capture and analysis of public-sector-wide debate is immensely exciting and will inform future publications and potentially government policy.

Overall, we are able to observe that perhaps more than most managerial functions, HR professionals need to be aware of the opportunities and challenges presented by Web 2.0 and Enterprise 2.0 and its appropriate and effective application. HR professionals can assist transformation at work by helping implement these social media technologies to provide the basis for more effective collaboration and knowledge sharing, more effective two-way communication with employees, and by giving employees interesting and authentic alternatives to the traditional ways of expressing their opinions and ideas – improved employee voice.

But beyond this in our view, is the opportunity for social media technologies to re-architect and re-articulate 'conversations for change', leading to the embedding of behaviours that support high performance working practices and the consequential impact on corporate reputation.

References

Backhaus, K. and Tikoo, S. (2004) Conceptualizing and researching employer branding. *Career Development International*, 9, 5, 501–17

Birkinshaw, J. and Pass, S. (2008) *Innovations in the Workplace: how are organisations responding to generation Y employees and Web 2.0 technologies?* London: Chartered Institute of Personnel and Development.

Chartered Institute of Personnel and Development (2009) *Web 2.0 and Human Resource Management: groundswell or hype?* Research into Practice Report. London: CIPD.

Conway, N. and Briner, R. B. (2009) Fifty years of psychological contract research: what do we know and what are the main challenges? *International Review of Industrial and Organizational Psychology*, 21, 71–131.

Cullinane, N. and Dundon, T. (2006) The psychological contract: a critical review. *International Journal of Management Reviews*, 113–29.

Dawley, D., Andrews, M. C. and Bucklew, N. S. (2008) Mentoring, supervisor support, and perceived organizational support: what matters most? *Leadership and Organization Development Journal*, 29, 3, 235–47.

Eisenberg, B., Kilduff, C., Burleigh, S. and Wilson, K. (2001) *The Role of the Value Proposition and Employment Branding in Retaining Top Talent*. Alexandria, VA: Society for Human Resource Management.

Francis, H. and Reddington, M. (forthcoming) Reframing the Employee Value Proposition in Francis, H. and Reddington, M. (eds) *Organisational Effectiveness: the dynamic new agenda for HR and OD*. CIPD: London.

Francis, H. (2003) Teamworking: meanings and contradictions in the management of change. *Human Resource Management Journal*, 13, 3, 71–90.

Francis, H. (2006) A critical discourse perspective on managers' experiences of HRM. *Qualitative Research in Organizations and Management: An International Journal*, 1, 2, 65–82.

Francis, H. (2007) Discursive struggle and the ambiguous world of HRD. *Advances in Developing Human Resources*, 9, 1, 83–96.

Heger, B. K. (2007) Linking the employment value proposition (EVP) to employee engagement and business outcomes: preliminary findings from a linkage research pilot study. *Organization Development Journal*, 25, 2, 121–32.

Keleman, M. (2000) Too much or too little ambiguity: the language of total quality management, *Journal of Management Studies*, 37, 4, 484–97.

Li, C. and Bernoff, J. (2008) *Groundswell: winning in a world transformed by social technologies*. Boston, MA: Harvard Business Press.

MacLeod, D. and Clarke, N. (2009) *Engaging for Success: enhancing performance through engagement*. London: Department for Business, Innovation and Skills.

Maconie, S. (2007) *Pies and Prejudice: in search of the north*. London: Ebury Press.

McAfee, A. P. (2006) Enterprise 2.0: the dawn of a new collaboration. *Sloan Management Review*, 47, 3, 21–8.

Martin, G. (2009) Employer branding and corporate reputation management: a model and some evidence. In C. L. Cooper and R. Burke (eds), *The Peak Performing Organization*. London and New York: Routledge.

Martin, G. and Hetrick, S. (2006) *Corporate Reputations, Branding and Managing People: a strategic approach to HR*. Oxford: Butterworth Heinemann.

Martin, G., Reddington, M., Kneafsey, M. and Sloman, M. (2009) Scenarios and strategies for Web 2.0. *Education and Training*, 51, 5/6, 370–80.

McKinsey (2008) Building the Web 2.0 enterprise: a McKinsey global survey. *McKinsey Quarterly*. Available at: http://www.mckinseyquarterly.com/PDFDownload.aspx?L2=16&L3=16&ar=1913, accessed 25 February 2010.

Musson, G. and Cohen, L. (1999) Understanding language processes, a neglected skill in the management curriculum. *Management Learning*, 30, 1, 27–42.

Parry, E., Tyson, S., Selbie, D. and Leighton, R. (2007) *HR and Technology: impact and advantages*. London: Chartered Institute of Personnel and Development.

Richards, J. (2007) Unmediated workplace images from the internet: an investigation of work blogging. Paper presented to the 25th Annual Labour Process Conference, University of Amsterdam, 2–4 April.

Rosethorn, H. (2009) *The Employer Brand: keeping faith with the deal*. Farnham: Gower.

Rousseau, D. (2003) Extending the psychology of the psychological contract: a reply to 'putting psychology back into psychological contracts'. *Journal of Management Inquiry*, 12, 229.

Singapore Institute of Management (2009) How types of organisational cultures contribute in shaping learning organisations. Research report.

Surowiecki, J. (2004) *The Wisdom of Crowds*. London: Little Brown Publishing.

Tapscott, D. and Williams, A. (2008) *Wikinomics: how mass collaboration changes everything*. 2nd edn. London: Atlantic Books.

Tredinnick , L. (2006) Web 2.0 and business: a pointer to the intranets of the future. *Business Information Review*, 23, 228–35.

Walker Rettberg, J. (2008) *Blogging*. Cambridge, UK: Polity Press.

Withers, M., Williamson, M. and Reddington, M. (2010) *Transforming HR: creating value through people*. Oxford: Butterworth Heinemann.

Wefald, A and Downey, R. G. (2009) Job engagement in organisations: fad, fashion, or folders? *Journal of Organisational Behaviour*, 30, 141–5.

Wong, W., Albert, A., Huggett, M. and Sullivan, J. (2009) *Quality People Management for Quality Outcomes: the future of HR review of evidence on people management*. Work Foundation report, August.

Appendix 1: A Glossary of Terms

Aggregation	Collecting information from various sources and displaying it together in customisable formats, such as on a website (e.g. pulling news data in from a source and displaying it on your own website) or a desktop or browser-based aggregator which can manage several 'social networking' or 'social bookmarking' sites, blogs, RSS fees, various types of media and other content from one location and allow these various types of data to be easily accessed, used or shared.
Avatar	3D characters created to represent themselves and/or reflect an identity they want to portray, in a video-games and virtual worlds, such as Second Life.
Blog	A blog (a web log) is a website, usually maintained by an individual, with regular entries which are commonly displayed in reverse chronological order. Many blogs provide commentary or news on a particular subject; others function as more personal online diaries. A typical blog combines text, images, and links to other blogs, web pages, and other media related to its topic as well as the ability for readers to leave comments. http://en.wikipedia.org/wiki/Blog
Browser	A browser is an application that allows users to display web pages and files on the web through an internet connection. There are a number of widely used browsers such as Internet Explorer, Firefox, Opera, Safari, Chrome.
del.icio.us	A social bookmarking website which is designed to allow you to store and share your bookmarks on the web instead of inside your browser. Bookmarks are organised by 'tags' which are searchable keywords assigned by users. http://del.icio.us/about/ See also 'tagging', 'social bookmarking'
Digital native	A person raised in a technological environment, who accepts that environment as the norm. This person often has grown up surrounded by digital devices, such as MP3 players and cell phones, and regularly uses these devices to interact with other people and the outside world. http://www.digitalnative.org/wiki/Glossary#Digital_Native
Discussion forum	An application that allows users to post original messages and replies on a website. Forums are often divided into topics and conversational 'threads' which allow users to follow conversations on certain topics.

Disruptive technologies	'Disruptive technology' is a term coined by Harvard Business School professor Clayton M. Christensen to describe a new technology that unexpectedly displaces an established technology. This is contrasted with 'sustaining technology' which relies on incremental improvements to an already established technology. http://whatis.techtarget.com/definition/0,,sid9_gci945822,00.html
Enterprise 2.0	Enterprise social software, also known as Enterprise 2.0, is a term describing social software used in 'enterprise' (business) contexts. It includes social and networked modifications to company intranets and other classic software platforms used by large companies to organise their communication. http://en.wikipedia.org/wiki/Enterprise_social_software
Facebook	Facebook is a free-access social networking website. Users can post messages for their friends to see, and update their personal profile to notify friends about themselves. http://en.wikipedia.org/wiki/Facebook and http://www.facebook.com See also 'social networking'
Firewall	A system designed to prevent unauthorised access to or from a private network, using either hardware or software, or a combination of both. Firewalls are frequently used to prevent unauthorised internet users from accessing private networks connected to the internet, especially intranets. All messages entering or leaving the intranet pass through the firewall, which examines each message and blocks those that do not meet the specified security criteria. http://www.webopedia.com/TERM/f/firewall.html
Flickr	Flickr is an online photo management and sharing website. Users can add comments, notes and 'tags' to photos to create their own ways of viewing, searching for and sharing them. http://www.flickr.com/ See also 'tagging'
Hit	The retrieval of any item, like a page or a graphic, from a web server, also called a 'page hit'. Alternatively, any time a piece of data matches criteria you set, e. g. each of the matches from a Yahoo or any other search engine search is called a hit. http://www.webopedia.com/TERM/H/hit.html
Information aggregation	Information aggregation is a service that collects relevant information from multiple sources for easy access and to help users to effectively access the growing amount of information on the web. http://digital.mit.edu/research/papers/106%20SMadnick,%20Siegel%20Information%20Aggregation.pdf. See also 'mashups'
Instant messaging	Instant messaging (IM) and chat are technologies that facilitate near real-time text-based communication between two or more participants over a network. Some IM systems allow users to use webcams and microphones so that users can have a real-time conversation. http://en.wikipedia.org/wiki/Instant_messaging

Internet architecture	The internet is a meta-network, a constantly changing collection of thousands of individual networks intercommunicating with a common protocol, TCP/IP, which is designed to connect any two networks despite any differences in internal hardware, software and technical design. http://www.livinginternet.com/i/iw_arch.htm
Mashups	Mashups are web applications that combine data from more than one source into a single integrated tool, thereby creating a new and distinct web service that was not originally provided by either source. These web applications are always composed of three parts: • The content provider or source of the data. • The mashup site itself – the web application which provides the new service using different data sources that are not owned by it. • The client web browser which is the user interface of the mashup. http://en.wikipedia.org/wiki/Mashup_(web_application_hybrid)
Massively multiplayer online game (MMOG or MMO)	MMOGs are video games which are capable of supporting hundreds or thousands of players simultaneously. By necessity, they are played on the internet, and feature at least one persistent virtual world. http://en.wikipedia.org/wiki/Massively_multiplayer_online_game
Media sharing	Media sharing occurs in online social networks and digital communities where users can aggregate, upload, compress, host and distribute images, text, applications, videos, audio, games and new media. It is the process of sending, posting or linking to media on a website or blog. As media are shared they take on a variety of different contexts and meanings as they are uploaded to different online 'places', tagged and/or commented upon and shared and possibly changed in various ways. http://en.wikipedia.org/wiki/Media_sharing
Metadata	Metadata is 'data about data'. http://en.wikipedia.org/wiki/Metadata Metadata is structured data which describes the characteristics of a resource. It shares many similar characteristics to the cataloguing that takes place in libraries, museums and archives. A metadata record consists of a number of pre-defined elements representing specific attributes of a resource, and each element can have one or more values. http://www.library.uq.edu.au/iad/ctmeta4.html
MySpace	MySpace is an online social networking community that lets you meet your friends' friends and in which you can share photos, journals and interests with your growing network of mutual friends. www.myspace.com See also 'social networking'

Net or V(irtual) Generation	The Net or Virtual Generation is made up of people from multiple demographic age groups who make social connections online – through virtual worlds, in video games, as bloggers, in social networks or through posting and reading user-generated content at e-commerce sites like Amazon.com. http://www.pcworld.com/article/id,139748-c,researchreports/article.html Don Tapscott describes the Net Generation as having the following characteristics: • they are able to multitask • they have little tolerance for delays, expecting web pages to load quickly, responses to e-mail immediately, etc. • they prefer to be interactive – they want to be users, not just viewers or listeners. http://academictech.doit.wisc.edu/resources/products/netgen/index.htm
Network effects	The core description of a network effect is when a good or service has more value the more that other people have it too. Examples include e-mail, instant messaging, the blogosphere, and even the web itself. Various authors have tried to describe the raw potential of network effects in computer networks, including Robert Metcalf, David Reed and Odlyzko and Tilly. Whichever formulation you believe is right, the result is clear: At even an early point, the cumulative value of a large number of connected users goes exponentially off the charts. http://web2.socialcomputingmagazine.com/web_20s_real_secret_sauce_network_effects.htm
Open source	Open source is a development methodology for software that harnesses the power of distributed peer review and transparency of process. Programming code for open source software is freely available and this code can be redistributed and modified and must adhere to open source principles regarding licensing. http://www.opensource.org/
Podcasting	Podcasting is delivering audio content to iPods and other portable media players on demand, so that it can be listened to at the user's convenience. The main benefit of podcasting is that listeners can sync content to their media player and take it with them to listen whenever they want to. http://www.podcastingnews.com/articles/What_is_Podcasting.html
Remixing	Remixing describes the customisation of web pages created by others and/or data provided by others for reuse on another web page. Extracting and combining samples of content to create a new output. The term was originally used in music but is now also applied to video and other content. http://www.rossdawsonblog.com/weblog/archives/2007/05/launching_the_w.html See also 'information aggregation' and 'mashup'

Reputation management software	Reputation management software gathers ratings for people, companies, and information sources. Reputation management software can create a track record for each user that acts as an incentive for them to exhibit good behaviour and make them accountable for their actions. This is important because it adds elements of expectation and possible repercussions that can affect future interactions. http://www.moyak.com/researcher/resume/papers/reputation.html
RSS feeds	Really Simple Syndication (RSS) is a lightweight XML format designed for sharing headlines and other web content. It provides a wimple way to quickly view rapidly changing content such as news headlines, blog entries or podcasts. http://www.webreference.com/authoring/languages/xml/rss/intro/ See also 'web feed'
Second Life	Second Life is an internet-based 3D virtual world created by its residents. In the online world, residents can explore, socialise and communicate as well as create and trade items in a virtual martketplace using a virtual unit of currency, the Linden Dollar. http://secondlife.com/ See also 'virtual worlds'
SlideShare	SlideShare is an online community for sharing presentations. Users upload presentations to share their ideas, connect with others, and generate leads for their businesses. Presentations can be tagged, downloaded, or embedded in other websites or blogs. Slides can also be shared privately to facilitate collaboration.
Social bookmarking	Social bookmarking is a method for internet users to store, organise, search, and manage bookmarks of web pages on the internet with the help of metadata. Most social bookmark services encourage users to organise their bookmarks with informal tags instead of the traditional browser-based system of folders. http://en.wikipedia.org/wiki/Social_bookmarking
Social networking	Social networking is a phenomena defined by linking people to each other in some way, in this case using the internet to form communities and build networks. These communities or networks may be based around anything, geographical location, shared schools or employers, shared interests or hobbies, etc. or may be designed to allow 'new' networks for develop for making new online 'friends' or creating new professional connections. http://www.topicguru.net/?c1=webmaster&c2=glossary
Social software	Social software is used to build online social networks. Most services are primarily web-based and provide a collection of various ways for users to interact, such as chat, messaging, e-mail, video, voice chat, file sharing, blogging, discussion groups, and so on. http://en.wikipedia.org/wiki/Social_network_service
Streaming media or video streaming	Streaming media is streaming video with sound. With streaming video or streaming media, a web user does not have to wait to download a large file before seeing the video or hearing the sound. Instead, the media is sent in a continuous stream and is played as it arrives. http://searchunifiedcommunications.techtarget.com/sDefinition/0,,sid186_gci213055,00.html

Tagging	A tag is a (relevant) keyword or term associated with or assigned to a piece of information (e.g. a picture, a blog entry, a bookmark etc.), describing the item and enabling keyword-based classification and search of information. Tags are usually chosen by item author/creator or by its consumer/viewers/community. http://en.wikipedia.org/wiki/Tag_(metadata)
Viral marketing	Viral marketing describes any strategy that encourages individuals to pass on a marketing message to others, creating the potential for exponential growth in the message's exposure and influence. Like viruses, such strategies take advantage of rapid multiplication to explode the message to thousands, to millions. Off the internet, viral marketing has been referred to as 'word-of-mouth' or 'creating a buzz' but on the internet it's called 'viral marketing'. Viral marketing is often characterised by giving away some sort of product or service, allowing for effortless transfer to others, exploiting common motivations and behaviours, utilising existing communication networks and others' resources. http://www.wilsonweb.com/wmt5/viral-principles.htm
Virtual learning environment	A virtual learning environment (VLE) is a software system designed to support teaching and learning in an educational setting. A VLE will normally work over the internet and provide a connection of tools such as those for assessment, communication, uploading of content, return of students' work, peer assessment, administration of student groups, collecting and organising student grades, questionnaires, tracking tools, wikis, blogs, RSS and 3D virtual learning spaces, etc. While originally created for distance education, VLEs are now often used to supplement the face-to-face classroom as well to add more flexibility to learning. http://en.wikipedia.org/wiki/Virtual_learning_environment
Virtual worlds	A virtual world is a computer-based simulated environment intended for its users to inhabit and interact via avatars which are usually depicted as textual, two-dimensional, or three-dimensional graphical representations. The computer accesses a computer-simulated world and presents perceptual stimuli to the user, who in turn can manipulate elements of the modelled world. Communication between users has ranged from text, graphical icons, visual gesture, sound, and rarely, forms using touch and balance senses. http://en.wikipedia.org/wiki/Virtual_world See Second Life
Web services	Web services are pieces of a software program or web site that are exposed for third party systems to interact with, often providing a question/answer dialogue. For example, web services allow any website to ask an airline if a flight is delayed and receive an answer back that can be displayed in any format. http://www.tocquigny.com/knowledge/the_semantic_web/
Web feed	A web feed (or news feed) is a data format used for providing users with frequently updated content. Content distributors syndicate a web feed, thereby allowing users to subscribe to it. http://en.wikipedia.org/wiki/web_feed

widgets	A generic term for the part of a GUI (graphical user interface) that allows the user to interface with the application and operating system. Widgets display information and invite the user to act in a number of ways. Typical widgets include buttons, dialog boxes, pop-up windows, pull-down menus, icons, scroll bars, forms, etc. http://www.webopedia.com/TERM/w/widget.htm
Wiki	A Wiki is a piece of server software that allows users to freely create and edit web page content using any web browser. A Wiki supports hyperlinks and has simple text syntax for creating new pages and crosslinks between internal pages on the fly. A Wiki is unusual among group communication mechanisms in that it allows the organisation of contributions to be edited in addition to the content itself. http://www.wiki.org/wiki.cgi?WhatIsWiki
Wikipedia	Wikipedia is a free, multilingual, open content encyclopaedia project operated by the non-profit Wikimedia Foundation. Its name is a blend of the words wiki (a technology for creating collaborative websites) and encyclopaedia. Launched in 2001 by Jimmy Wales and Larry Sanger, it is the largest, fastest-growing and most popular general reference work currently available on the internet. http://en.wikipedia.org/wiki/Wikipedia
XML	Extensible Markup Language (XML) is a markup language like HTML. It was designed to transport and store data, with a focus on what data is. HTML was designed to display data, with a focus on how data looks. http://www.w3schools.com/XML/xml_whatis.asp
YouTube	YouTube is the online video sharing website. YouTube allows people to easily upload and share video clips on www.YouTube.com and across the internet through websites, mobile devices, blogs, and e-mail. Videos in YouTube can be commented upon, shared, tagged and turned into playlists. http://youtube.com/

Source: CIPD, 2009

12 Re-creating Reputation Through Authentic Interaction: Using Social Media to Connect with Individual Stakeholders

CELIA V. HARQUAIL

The closer you get to someone, something, some brand, some organization ... the harder it is to demonize it, objectify it or hate it. So, if you want to not be hated, open up. Let people in. Engage. Interact.

Seth Godin

Social media are creating opportunities for organizations to demonstrate "who they really are" to any stakeholder with a vested interest in the organization's behavior. Organizations are now able to create a larger volume of more targeted, one-to-one impressions on individual stakeholders, thus influencing their reputation in the eyes of these stakeholders. However, social media allow for something more than an increase in impressions; they allow for an entirely new quality of impressions—impressions that can be experienced as authentic. Social media provide exponentially more opportunities for an organization and its stakeholders to interact, to create dialogues and to establish relationships. These dialogues and relationships, in turn, allow stakeholders to assess the authenticity of an organization and feel confident about their perceptions of who the organization really is. By using social media to facilitate relationships between stakeholders and the organization, organizations can establish their messages as more trustworthy and themselves as more authentic, in ways that ultimately contribute to the organization's reputation.

Even though social media are tools designed to support interpersonal relationships and not relationships between individuals and organizations, organizations are finding ways to represent their collective self on social media to establish something closer to an interpersonal relationship with individual stakeholders. These social media relationships, unlike the organization-public relationships that reputation scholars have emphasized in the past (e.g., Hon and Grunig, 1999), have a person-to-person component that allows stakeholders to assess the authenticity of their interaction with the organization, and then to project this authenticity onto the organization as a whole. When an organization's communication is perceived as authentic, stakeholders will feel more confident about their perception of the organization and they will be more willing to trust the way that the organization presents itself.

By definition, an organization's stakeholders are individuals and groups who stand to be affected by that organization's behavior. Stakeholders may contribute, either voluntarily or involuntarily, to the organization's capacity, and the organization's actions may either benefit or cost the stakeholders in some way (Post et al., 2002). Stakeholders believe that the organization's actions will affect them, and they want in return to influence how the organization acts. However, the power disparity between organizations and individual stakeholders, as well as stakeholder groups, often makes it difficult for stakeholders to influence the organization.

The interests and priorities of the organization and its stakeholders may not always be aligned; there is often a gap between the interests of the organization and the interests of any stakeholder. With regard to the organization's reputation, the gap may be as simple as the difference between how the organization wants to be seen (its desired image; Brown et al., 2006) and how its stakeholders actually perceive the organization. Reputation management strategies, and organizational communications more generally, are designed to close this gap. Reputation management strategies range from efforts to convince stakeholders to adopt the organization's desired image, to engaging in conversation that develops mutual understanding of each other's positions, to collaborating on mutually satisfying solution that dissolves the gap.

The goal of this chapter is to offer a rationale for reorienting how we think about organizational reputation to focus more attention on creating relationships between the organization and individual stakeholders. The chapter opens by describing what it means to consider how an organization's reputation is constantly being re-created with each unique impression on an individual stakeholder. Focusing attention on an individual's ongoing construal of an organization's reputation helps us anticipate why authentic communication matters and where social media can have the biggest impact on organizational reputation. Next, we identify opportunities that social media present, based on their technological features and by the usage norms that these features encourage, for creating something closer to a two-way, symmetrical communication (e.g., Grunig, 2001) between the organization and individual stakeholders. We consider how interactive, constant, public, and easily shared communication encourages dialogue and shifts power towards individual stakeholders. These technical features and the relationships dynamics that they support make authentic interaction possible.

However, what makes authentic communication likely is social presence (Biocca et al., 2003) as we consider in the third section. Social presence, a participant's "humanness" in an online interaction, lets us display cues that we need to assess the authenticity of our communication with each other. The tactics that organizations use to establish their social presence online can either frustrate or enhance authentic communication, to the degree that these social presence tactics allow the organization and the individual stakeholder closer to each other through understanding and adjustment. Moreover, social presence allows the organization to demonstrate "who it is". Finally, we conclude by recommending both internal and outwardly focused adjustments to an organization's reputation management approach.

What We Should Emphasize About Reputation to Anticipate the Impact of Social Media

WHY RE-CREATING REPUTATION?

I use the term *re-creating* reputation to emphasize how reputation is constantly being influenced by new perceptions of an organization's behavior. The organization's behavior creates data that individual stakeholders use to construe their perceptions of the organization's character and thus its reputation. Individuals create and revise their perceptions of an organization each time they experience the organization directly by interacting with it, or indirectly through information shared by other stakeholders (Bromley, 1993; Bruning and Ledingham, 2000; Grunig and Hung, 2002). At any moment, one's perception of the organization can change—reputation can shift, be spoiled or be polished, by some interaction. Each interaction, whether directly experienced or indirectly shared, creates a perception by the stakeholder, as the organization's behavior enacts and demonstrates its character for the stakeholder. And, each interaction demonstrates to the stakeholder how willing the organization is to consider stakeholders' concerns as it makes decisions and moves to close the gap between them. Each discrete perception influences the stakeholder's overall construal of the organization's reputation, and so the organization's reputation is constantly re-created.

WHY AUTHENTIC?

Stakeholders are not naive about the importance to organizations of developing positive reputations. It is clear that a positive reputation nets an organization goodwill and competitive advantage (Fombrun and Rindova, 2000; Kowalczyk and Pawlish, 2002), and stakeholders know that organizations are always working to make themselves look as much like their desired corporate image as possible. Stakeholders also distrust organizations more than they trust them (Edelman, 2009). Thus, stakeholders are inclined to be cautious about what to believe about an organization, and so they look for ways to determine whether what they are told about an organization is true.

When individuals construe the reputation of an organization, we implicitly and explicitly consider whether the organization seems authentic: What does the organization claim about itself? Are the organization's claims honest, credible, and trustworthy? Is the organization acting as it says it will? Is the organization really what it claims to be? (Corley and Harrison, 2009; Kelleher and Miller, 2006). Stakeholders assess the organization not only through its general behavior, but also through the ways we experience the organization when we interact with it. Because we cannot know whether or not the organization is authentic (Gilmore and Pine, 2007), we must consider instead whether it is communicating authentically with us. From our assessment of whether the organization is authentic in its interactions with us we extrapolate our assessment of the organization's authenticity.

The perceived authenticity of an organization's communication matters, because stakeholders are skeptical about the degree to which an organization's communication reflects something close to the truth of a situation. Stakeholders do not want to base their assessments of an organization's reputation on untrustworthy information. And, the authenticity of the organization itself matters, because stakeholders will not trust an inauthentic organization to behave according to its claims and promises, regardless of what those promises are. Without authentic information about what the organization claims, and without a sense that the organization is striving to behave according to its claims, stakeholders will conclude that the organization's reputational claims are untrustworthy and that the organization itself is untrustworthy.

It is not easy to assess the authenticity of an organization's communication. Instead of a single, definitive test for authenticity, there is an array of accepted and often unexamined criteria through which we assess the authenticity of what is communicated to us (Showkeir and Showkeir, 2008) (see Table 12.1). These characteristics include: being accurate and factually correct; dealing with the core issues and information; telling the whole story, including the meanings and implications of the issue in question; providing information when it is known; responding to what the other party has said; and not contradicting one's own words or actions. These criteria reflect both an expectation of adaptability and responsiveness to the particular situation and conversation and, simultaneously, an expectation of consistency and truthfulness. What people look for is communication from another party that is responsible to their own particular needs and contributions, and yet still retains its own integrity and internally coherent. We want the other party's communication to us to be flexible enough to mesh with what we are adding, but consistent enough to stay anchored to what they actually believe and can do.

Traditional forms of public relations and reputation management, with their "thrust and parry" dynamic, are largely an exchange of monologues where the organization has more power than the stakeholders to control the overall communication. In these asymmetrical, monologue-driven communication efforts, it is not hard for an organization to represent its motives, values, and even its actual actions in self-serving ways (Coupland and Brown, 2004). When the organization's communication includes reference to the stakeholders' concerns, these concerns are presented from the organization's perspective and quite often differ from how stakeholders would describe the concerns themselves.

Knowing that the information shared by the organization is carefully crafted and spun, audiences struggle to assess whether the organization's claims about its priorities and motivation are backed up by other claims and actions. We assume that this communication serves the organization's interests, and we are justifiably suspicious of its truth-value and authenticity. And, because monologues make it difficult if not impossible for audiences to clarify, test and confirm what the organization supposedly means to say, we have few ways to assess whether the organization is communicating authentically.

Table 12.1 Characteristics of authentic communication

Relevant	Taking into account and making connections with the interests of the parties involved
Specific	Being specific to that situation and its uniqueness, not being rote
Personal	Perceived as relevant to and customize-able by individual stakeholders
Fundamental	Dealing with the core or essential issues and information
Clear	Using language that is appropriate and understandable for those involved, explaining technical terms, organizing and illustrating the information logically and understandably
Timely	Providing information when it is known, leaving sufficient time for response prior to decisions or actions
Consistent	Not opposing or contradicting your own or your organization's other words or actions
Accessible	Making information, relevant sources and opportunities for discussion easily available to all parties
Responsive to feedback	Engaging in two-way communication, seeking others' views and concerns and allowing those concerns to influence the organization's actions
Comprehensive	Telling the whole story, including the meanings and implications of the issue in question
Empathic	Showing respect, concern and compassion for the circumstances, attitudes, beliefs and feelings of other parties
Truthful	Being accurate and factually correct
Straightforward	Being free of unnecessary hyperbole
Respectful	For individuals, institutions and contexts
Inspiring	To us, to our clients and their stakeholders
Trustworthy	Credible to advocates and detractors alike

(Bishop, 2003; Kelleher and Miller, 2006; Gilmore and Pine, 2007; Showkeir and Showkeir, 2008)

WHY INTERACTION?

Interaction between the organization and stakeholders makes it possible for stakeholders to assess the organization's authenticity, because interactions make dialogue possible. Through dialogue with an organization, an individual stakeholder can clarify, test and confirm what the organization is trying to communicate, and begin to assess whether the organization is authentic. But even more important to authenticity is that dialogue is necessary for creating mutual understanding, the kind of understanding required to bridge any gaps between the organization's interests and the stakeholder's interests. In addition, the interactive features and social presence capabilities facilitated by social media allow stakeholders and organizational representatives to create relationships. These relationships allow stakeholders ongoing opportunities to assess the authenticity of the organization's communication and its overall character while allowing the organization to demonstrate a concern for the stakeholder.

Reputation scholars have already taken a "relational approach" towards understanding the relationships between the organization and its important publics (e.g., Bruning et al., 2004; Grunig, 2001; Grunig et al., 2002). This relational approach has adopted concepts used to analyze interpersonal relationships and applied them as a metaphor for understanding the qualities of the outcome interdependence between the organization and stakeholder groups. However, social media allow us to use concept of interpersonal relationships in a more direct, less metaphoric way, so that we consider the role of a real interpersonal relationship between an organization's representative and an individual stakeholder.

WHY SOCIAL MEDIA?

Social media create opportunities for more interaction and for a different quality of interaction between stakeholders and the organization because the technologies of social media support direct interaction—dialogue—between stakeholders and the organization. Through social media, organizations and individuals can create relationships that, in turn, lead towards more authentic communication.

Reputation scholars and practitioners have long advocated for a two-way, symmetrical communication model (Grunig, 2001), where organization-stakeholder communication serves a joint or collective interest with adjustments by all parties. However, in practice this model is more idealized than evidenced (Grunig et al., 2002). Organizations have only been able to create two-way relationships occasionally, with a small set of "critical stakeholders" (Mitchell et al., 1997) and not more broadly with any stakeholder. The one-way, asymmetrical model has predominated not because organizations lacked the interest to become more interactive or to create genuine relationships with individual stakeholders, but because organizations lacked the tools to make this kind of interaction widely efficient and effective. Social media put this ideal model of a symmetrical, two-way relationships within reach of organizations and individual stakeholders.

Recognizing The Opportunities of Social Media

FEATURES OF SOCIAL MEDIA TOOLS

Each social media tool has its own combination of characteristics—text, audio, visual, video, synchronous, asynchronous—that shape its intended communication purpose (Howard, 2009). Social media can be used to inform, entertain, educate, schedule, converse, resolve conflict, and make decisions. Social media tools include public community networks like Facebook, publishing platforms like blogs, public micro-blogging sites like Twitter, rating sites and complaint sites, community and membership sites like Ning, and more. All social media facilitate a finer grained approach to interacting with individual stakeholders than do traditional media. Instead of taking a broad-brush, broadcasting approach by treating individual stakeholders as part of larger publics, social media make it possible for each individual stakeholder to engage more directly with the organization (Paine and Kowlaski, 2008).

While each social media platform has specific features based on the type of communication and kind of users it is built to facilitate, all of these platforms have some features in common. These features include the technical scaffolding for: (1) user interactivity, (2) constant streaming of public, accessible, and searchable conversations, and (3) easy sharing beyond immediate participants. These features, taken together, make it possible for organizations to create relatively more symmetrical, two-way communications with individual stakeholders.

SOCIAL MEDIA ARE DESIGNED FOR INTERACTIVITY, WHICH IS ESSENTIAL TO DIALOGUE

Probably the most important feature of social media is the one we take most for granted, the fact that all social media are designed to create and facilitate direct, interactive communication between two or more individuals. Social media platforms are not only tools for sending messages out but are also tools for receiving messages—they are two-way by design. Moreover, social media platforms link messages to the content that triggered them, keeping each message as part of its specific conversation. This linked, contextual interaction, where ideas are exchanged, shared, and responded to by each party, is what makes mutual understanding possible (McGuire, 1989, 2001). By definition, dialogue is based on listening to one another's concerns and exhibiting a willingness to make changes in understanding as a result of having listened.

Although social media interactions are two-way dialogues, these dialogues may not be symmetrical in terms of the power dynamic that surrounds them. However, the normative expectation on social media that any message will receive a response of some kind does help to put more power in the hands of the individual stakeholder. Consider too that a "response" on social media means more than being sent an automatically generated, prepackaged bit of information. Instead, a response is information that is specifically tailored to what the stakeholder actually said. Stakeholders using social media expect to have unscripted, situation-specific interactive dialogue with the organization (Kelleher and Miller, 2006). The organization is expected to adjust its response to adapt to the needs of the stakeholder. This expectation of responsiveness pushes the dialogue between the individual and the organization's representative closer to the criteria of authentic communication.

Our expectations about responsiveness on social media are so strong that most people simply assume that organizations and their representatives will be accessible to them online. By their very adoption of social media tools, organizations are seen as signaling that they want to engage with individual stakeholders (Paine and Kowalski, 2008). (Many early adaptors acquired some goodwill from these efforts.) In contrast, not being available on social media is taken to suggest that the organization does not care about communicating with all stakeholders, or worse that the organization is afraid to be accessible by stakeholders, perhaps because it has something to hide.

SOCIAL MEDIA ESTABLISH A CONSTANT STREAM OF PUBLIC, ACCESSIBLE, AND SEARCHABLE CONVERSATIONS BETWEEN THE ORGANIZATION AND INDIVIDUAL STAKEHOLDERS

The multitude of interactions between an organization's representatives and each individual stakeholder on social media are visible, searchable and sharable, not only in real time but also historically. The visibility of these conversations makes it possible for individuals to hold organizations accountable for what they say. This means that one dialogue can be seen, referred to and influenced by many other dialogues and in turn can influence an infinite number of individual stakeholders. And, because interactions over time and across stakeholders can be searched and aggregated, individuals can create a large database from which to determine the organization's reputation.

Individuals can use the online archive of interactions to analyze the history of an issue and assess how the organization engaged with others about that situation. Active stakeholders can view previous dialogues about an issue, or dialogues with the same representative, or dialogues between other stakeholders and the organization, and educate themselves on the organization's position before they even engage with the organization themselves. Interested individuals who are not directly engaging with the organization are influenced by reading these public dialogues. And, although they are not conversing themselves, these "active lurkers" (Takahashi et al., 2007) use this new knowledge in other situations. They actively propagate the information by sharing it with others who may then revise their perceptions of the organization.

Publicly available, real-time and historic dialogue between individuals and the organization also documents any explanations the organization has proffered and any promises it has made. This documentation allows individual stakeholders and the organization to hold each other accountable for previous actions and future plans. Earlier explanations and commitments made elsewhere can be used to support or challenge what goes on in their own interaction. Because what has been said and done before, and what is going on in a current interaction, are now visible to others, participants are more motivated to keep their word, to be reasonable, and to make the dialogue work. Ultimately, this public availability acts as trust safeguard (Akerlof, 1970), because it discourages organizations from contradicting themselves or from saying one thing and doing another across audiences and over time.

The openness and public availability of an organization's communication on social media is not the same as organizational transparency. Organizational transparency is the degree to which an organization's actions, decision-making processes, decision criteria and data are hidden or displayed (Scoble and Israel, 2006; Rawlins, 2009). Social media interactions do reveal some of an organization's internal processes and information, so organizations that use social media are relatively more transparent than organizations that do not use social media. However, organizations still have control over how much and what types of information are laid bare on social media and elsewhere online. The organization still controls what information is available, where it is available, and how it is presented. When it is made available through channels other than social media, the organization's information is still framed, formatted, shaped and presented in ways that suit the interests of the organization. Sometimes transparent information is not all that different from broadcasted monologues in its structure and content. The big difference is that the information is not pushed out, but rather made available for stakeholders to come and look.

Transparency is often equated with authenticity (e.g., Rawlins, 2009), but transparency is only a tactic for allowing authenticity to be demonstrated or assessed. Transparency makes it possible for organizations to show that they act as they say they will and point out the substance that supports their claims. And, transparency gives stakeholders a chance to investigate issues, and match up some claims and some behaviors to see whether these align, thus getting a sense of how authentic the organization is. But, an organization can be more or less transparent and still be inauthentic, if the organization's claims and actions do not align.

Social media make it so easy for individuals to share information about their interaction with an organization that the power dynamics of the relationship shift towards the individual, making communication somewhat more symmetrical. Any stakeholder's interaction on social media has the potential to influence the perceptions of an infinite number of other individual stakeholders and thus have an exponential impact on an organization's reputation. Because searchable archives make individual interactions visible to others, the individual stakeholders have the potential to influence others' perceptions if their interaction with the organization captures other people's attention. And, if the interaction seems to the stakeholder to be important data, the stakeholder can send a copy of this compelling information out to members of her network, who send that information out into their own networks. Because the organization has no control over the stakeholder's sharing behavior, and because sharing is so easy for the individual stakeholder, the power dynamics of the interaction shift slightly and importantly towards the stakeholder. The stakeholder, and not the organization, gets to decide whether or not the interaction is worthy of being communicated broadly, potentially to influence other stakeholders.

When individuals receive copies of an interaction or some other information through their social networks, this information often has additional implied importance. First, it has been sent by a personal connection who has made this information important simply by deeming it worthy of sharing. Second, the information often is received in a more direct, less distanced way. Members of a network often experience digital copies of interactions vicariously, taking the perspective of the network member over the perspective of the organization. Third, when the interaction itself is shared, it is experienced as legitimate data and not gossip or even legitimate word of mouth. Finally, if the shared interaction is emotionally compelling (quite likely for a "viral" message), it will have a stronger impact on the recipient's perceptions.

An organization cannot predict which individual stakeholders are likely to have interactions they feel need to be promoted to their own networks. And, an organization cannot predict which interactions are more likely to "go viral." Thus, every stakeholder could potentially become a "critical stakeholder" (Mitchell et al., 1997) able to influence many others' perceptions of the organization. And, any mishandled or especially promising interaction could potentially "go viral," making every interaction important. The possibility that any one interaction could become disproportionally influential across an infinite network of individuals acts as another trust safeguard by motivating organizations to treat each interaction and individual stakeholder with some care and respect.

Taken together, the features of interactivity, publicness, and easy sharing on social media make two-way symmetrical communication possible. They provide enough information about the organization's behavior and shift enough power towards the individual stakeholder that the organization is (relatively) more accountable for communicating in an honest, even candid manner. However, these features do not by themselves make the communication between the organization and the individual authentic. Authenticity requires us to go beyond exchanging and sharing information; authenticity requires us to demonstrate that we are influencing, understanding, adapting to and connecting with each other. And, social media can help us demonstrate authenticity through the way they enable social presence.

Social Presence and Authentic Communication

SOCIAL MEDIA ARE DESIGNED TO MAXIMIZE THE SOCIAL PRESENCE OF EACH PARTICIPANT, AND A SOCIAL PRESENCE ALLOWS US TO CONVEY AND ASSESS AUTHENTICITY

Social presence is the perception that there is another person, another human being, on the other side of a computer-mediated interaction (Biocca et al., 2003). The two sets of criteria for assessing social presence, psychological engagement and behavioral interdependence, are the very activities that close the gap between others and ourselves. And, they map very closely onto the criteria for authentic communication.

To tell whether we are interacting with another human being and not a robot, we look at the interaction partner's social presence. We assess the social presence of an interaction partner by his or her demonstrations of psychological engagement and behavioral interdependence. We demonstrate psychological engagement when we show that we are paying attention, are emotionally involved, and are working to comprehend what the other party is trying to convey. When an online participant is attending to us, is acknowledging or sharing our emotion, and is reflecting that he or she understands what we are trying to say, we experience that party as making an effort to close the emotional and cognitive space between us.

We demonstrate behavioral interdependence when we show that our next step depends on what the other party has just said or done. We do more than follow a script or a recipe. Instead, we make more unique adjustments to provide what the other party wants and needs in the dialogue. When an online participant responds directly to what we have just said, or adjusts his or her behavior to accommodate ours, we experience that party as making an effort to close the behavioral space between us. Working together, demonstrations of psychological engagement and behavioral interdependence create a sense of social presence. And, the very same psychological engagement and behavioral interdependence are what is necessary for individuals and organizations to reach agreement and to influence each other.

The particular medium, the design of the digital interface, and the kind of interaction permitted all constrain how much a real individual can demonstrate social presence and how much a computer, robot or script can simulate social presence. Social media are designed to make it possible for people in computer-mediated relationships to display and deliver as much information about themselves to each other. A myriad of what seem to be small design features, like time stamps, avatars, topic tagging, geotagging, flagging, searching, visual customizations, sharing and gifting, and displaying common network connections, not to mention the ways that information can be linked and triangulated across various social media, are built into social media precisely so that participants can display cues that they are socially present.

With social media, the very same features that convey humanness and sensitivity also expose automation and inflexibility. This creates a challenge for organizations, since organizations must find ways to fit themselves into media designed for individuals and demonstrate social presence. How can organizations take all these little features, designed to display the attributes of individuals, and adapt them to display attributes of their collective entity? And, how can organizations participate on these media in ways that demonstrate sensitivity and flexibility?

Organizations have struggled to find ways to use social media to interact with individual stakeholders in ways that demonstrate and generate psychological engagement and behavioral interdependence (Kelleher and Miller, 2006). Strategies have run the gamut from hyper-sophisticated automation (e.g., "live" chat) to human representatives reading from scripts and following decision trees (e.g., call centers), to having individual employees with discretion over their own actions represent the organization online (e.g., brandividuals; Harquail, 2009).

An organization's presence on social media is difficult to automate. In an automated interaction, the individual is limited to a predetermined set of possible inquiries to which the organization's software program returns a pre-scripted response. By design, there is no opportunity for the stakeholder to feel listened to, to feel understood, and to feel influential in the automated interaction. When organizations assign an employee to interact online, but require that employee to adhere to a predetermined set of responses as they interact with an individual stakeholder, both the employee and the stakeholder can become frustrated by their inability to establish mutual social presence. The employee, pressed to stay on the predetermined message, is prohibited from actually responding to the individual's concerns to close the gap between the stakeholder and the organization. Individual stakeholders, looking for understanding and problem-solving action, see only the organization's unwillingness to engage. Neither automated nor tightly scripted employees can render the organization as socially present. Instead of a real relationship, the stakeholder and the organization enact what is called a parasocial relationship, one based on a "simulacrum of conversational give and take" (Horton and Wohl, 1956, p. 215) rather than a real dialogue.

Organizational Representatives as Translators and Mediators

Given the limitations of automated and tightly scripted communication, nearly all organizations active on social media are experimenting with giving individual employees the authority to represent the organization in dialogues with individual stakeholders (Harquail, 2009). This authority permits representatives to translate the organization's general priorities, values and decisions into the language and the specific situation of the individual stakeholder and to mediate between the interests of the organization and the stakeholder. Individual stakeholders, for their part, assume that because the representative knows more about the organization and has a more intimate understanding of the organization, the representative is able to craft a more accurate interpretation of a situation and a more specific response to it. Thus, the translated communication of the organization, directly conveyed by the representative, not only feels more responsive but also is more responsive to the stakeholder's concern.

An organization's representative also mediates between the interests of the organization and the interests of the stakeholder, to help bridge the gap between their positions and develop their understanding of each other. To be effective mediators, representatives have to demonstrate that they understand the stakeholder's concern, that they have listened carefully, that they can find mutuality, balance power, reduce conflicts and work toward change in concert with the stakeholder. The moves that the representative makes, the concessions, agreements, interpretations, and so on that the representative negotiates with the stakeholder, feel more trustworthy.

Stakeholders evaluate the qualities of the representative's interaction with them and with other stakeholders. Stakeholders watch how the representative manages the dialogue, evaluates criteria and makes decisions, responds to concerns of other stakeholders, and extends apologies. From the representative's behavior, stakeholders draw conclusions about how the organization approaches its interactions and resolves concerns with stakeholders. This "process reputation" (Mahon and Wartick, 2003) reflects stakeholders' perceptions of how the organization works through issues to close the gaps between the organization's position and those of other stakeholders. Organizations can develop process reputations for handling issues effectively or ineffectively, in a trustworthy manner or a manipulative one, and so this process reputation influences how we interpret and trust other kinds of information the organization is communicating.

Individual Representatives as Relational Proxies for the Organization

In powerful yet less explicit way, individual stakeholders may also treat the representative as though he or she were the organization. When this happens, a representative fills the role of the organization's relational proxy (Ackerlof, 1970). A relational proxy is an intermediary whose own features stand in for those of the party it represents. The features of the organization's human representative become the data from which the individual makes inferences about the organization. The representative's behavior is understood to reflect some amalgam of the representative's own personal attributes and the attributes of the organization.

As a representative participates in a relationship with the stakeholder, the stakeholder infers characteristics about the organization from the way that the representative manages their relationship. The stakeholder transfers the qualities of the interpersonal experiences and connections made with the representative to the organization as an entity. The social presence created by the representative, and all the attributes that go with it, become attributed to the organization. The stakeholder experiences his or her relationship with the representative as a relationship with the organization itself. If the stakeholder experiences the representative as authentic, he or she will attribute this authenticity to the organization as well.

Having employees represent the organization works best when the employees are out front, with a name and a personality. Employees can work behind the scenes, using the organization's name, symbol, icon, character or avatar that represents the organization while the employee speaks or writes the voice of behind the name or symbol (Coupland and Brown, 2004; Harquail, 2009). However, when organizations use an unnamed, anonymous person to act "as" the organization, this practice can be off-putting to social media users, simply because it violates the person-to-person norms of social media. Social media users know that there is an employee behind the organization's logo, working the mouse and the keyboard. When the employee is hidden, unnamed, and without a unique voice, there may not be quite enough social presence to make it easy for the employee and the stakeholder to create a relationship. Moreover, when an anonymous employee represents the organization, we wonder what each or both might be hiding.

The representative reduces the asymmetry in the relationship by serving as both a target and a source of emotional connection and behavioral interdependence. The connection between the organization's representative and the individual stakeholder is created using the representative's personal self-expression. The representative's personality, self-disclosure, and personal communication style help to establish her or him as a person, attracts the stakeholder's attention and helps the stakeholder establish an interpersonal connection with the representative (Harquail, 2009). By engaging with the representative, stakeholders may begin to develop a sense of intimacy, a sense of commitment to the relationship, and a sense of familiarity (Bromley, 1993; Grunig and Hung, 2002). Although these connections are created between two individuals, they are simultaneously experienced as being with the organization as an entity. Granted, this relationship with the organization is mediated by the representative, but it is a significant improvement on the impersonal "relationship" created through other, less socially present tactics.

One interesting feature of the way that stakeholders use representatives as relational proxies is that stakeholders do not assume that statements, decisions or behaviors that obviously communicate the organization's point of view are necessarily suspect, untrustworthy or inauthentic (Howard, 2008). This is because, in part, stakeholders assess the representative's behavior towards them as individuals, determine whether the representative is trustworthy and authentic in their interpersonal relationship, and then transfer that assessment to the information itself. So even if the information serves the organization, if it is conveyed within authentic communication, it is treated as authentic information.

Having representatives available on social media invites stakeholders to engage with the organization by making engagement seem worthwhile. Stakeholders will only engage with organizations if they can expect that their engagement will make a difference and will help close the gap between their interests and those of the organization. And, when individual stakeholders make an effort to engage in active communication with an organization these stakeholders are also more likely to cultivate their relationship with an organization over time (Rhee, 2004; Youngmeyer, 2002). If organizations can encourage stakeholders to make an initial effort to engage, representatives can develop relationships in which they can show themselves, and thus the organization, to be truthful, sincere, honest, open with all necessary information, and responsive to stakeholders' expressed concerns (Beal and Straus, 2008; Coupland and Brown, 2004, Rawlins, 2009).

Challenges and Recommendations for Organizations

The opportunities to build dialogue and relationships with individual stakeholders through a constant stream of social media interactions hold great potential for organizations that want to create strong, positive reputations. Some social media experts suggest that authentic interaction is blossoming in social media, while others point to a growing cooptation of the original interpersonal support of social media by commercial interests (Rawlins, 2009; Scoble and Israel, 2006). Neither direction is inevitable. However, if organizations want to take full advantage of the possibilities of social media, they must make the choice to experiment with how best to represent themselves on social media.

It is now possible to create authentic relationships with stakeholders, but organizations need to reorient their energies, reset their priorities, and get ready to challenge themselves to act more authentically. Here are a few very basic recommendations, largely towards refocusing the organization's reputation management energy.

EXTERNALLY FOCUSED CHALLENGES

1. Organizations will need to learn how to develop specifically interpersonal relationships, shifting from an emphasis on informing stakeholders to an emphasis on connecting with them. They will need to develop skills and systems for the intermediary steps of relationship building such as listening, engaging (Paine and Kowalski, 2008), negotiating and collaborating with individual stakeholders.

2. Organizations will need to shift from a focus on controlling the message to a focus on creating connections and relationships. Organizations should pay close attention to what they continue to control, with an emphasis on the qualities of the processes they use to invite, understand, and assist in resolving stakeholder concerns.

3. Organizations should pay as much (if not dramatically more) attention to ongoing, small, distributed interactions as they do to the larger-scale, discreet initiatives that are traditionally part of reputation management and corporate relations programs. Given that the impact of each corporate response, each byte of outreach and each interaction with a stakeholder over social media can potentially be magnified if it is shared across social networks, organizations need to take all of these interactions seriously. Even interactions that seem repetitive and banal have the potential to influence perceptions of the organization. To support these distributed interactions, organizations must develop internal systems to address technology development, information sharing, and employee training, as well as systems for collating and funneling information from these interactions to develop organizational improvement plans.

4. Corporate reputation strategies should recognize that although there will always be a need for targeted communications that fit particular stakeholder niches and for reputation-crafting initiatives appropriate to particular markets and social arenas, social media will not necessarily conform to or respect the boundaries between stakeholder groups. (Consider how a simple Google search by a customer with a service problem can turn up information on corporate social responsibility, product development, recruiting, and even executive compensation.) In between a "one size fits all" reputation and a "made-to-measure" niche reputation is a mass customization model, where many adjustments can be made at the margins to fit the specific need, while the core remains consistent. Organizations should support these more distinctive and targeted desired images with a common, authentic interactional character that reflects the organization's core values and is responsive to all kinds of stakeholders.

5. Similarly, employee representatives in different parts of the organization should draw on a shared set of relational principles so that the tone of interactions across all areas and stakeholder groups reflects the organization's core values. Authentic communication should be a goal regardless of the niche.

6. The organization's claims need to be backed up not only in a particular interaction but also through follow-up actions. For example, telling a customer "We're here to help, we'll send a technician" can assuage a customer's concern, but only a service call that actually fixes the problem will make that statement authentic.

7. Similarly, organizations need to realize that stakeholders will not be fooled by an organization with friendly representatives that resolve an immediate situation while the organization-wide systems that continue to cause similar problems remain unchanged. An authentic response to an issue closes that particular gap not only for that individual stakeholder but also for all similar stakeholders.

INTERNALLY FOCUSED CHALLENGES

1. Organizations must make it easier for individual representatives to translate the organizations' position in each specific interaction with a stakeholder. Representatives will need to develop a deep understanding of the organization, its priorities, capabilities and limitations, before they can represent the organization effectively on line. To make this knowledge possible, organizations will need to open themselves up to a full range of employees, sharing information and clearly communicating values and priorities internally. Organizations must discover where their boundaries are, in terms of what representatives can discuss and what they can offer to stakeholders.

2. Organizations will need to clarify and describe the collective "voice" that should express the organization. In order for the organization to have a coherent "voice," all members representing the organization will need to become expert at understanding the organization and have ways to align their understanding with those of other representatives. Organizations will want to consider internal activities like workshops on how to use media tools as well as internal experiences that help people know what the organization would like spread as its desired image.

3. Organizations must help representatives give good process, not only by making sure that representatives have the information they need, but also making sure that representatives have the authority they need to interpret the organization's position, propose action to resolve the situation and to respond to stakeholders in good faith. And, organizations will need to back up the commitments of their representatives, by taking action internally and developing systems to support the commitments that their representatives make on their behalf.

4. Organizations must incorporate the feedback and the learning from interactions with stakeholders, so that they don't appear to be tinkering at the margins with superficial, temporary resolutions. They need to be seen as actively trying to incorporate internally what they are learning in a comprehensive and strategic way. Consider the example of Comcast, the US-based telecom company. Comcast has a dicey reputation for bad service, dysfunctional equipment, and high prices, but it is also considered to be a role model for how to use the social media platform Twitter. Yet, many stakeholders raised concerns when Comcast's CEO claimed that the organization's participation on Twitter had changed Comcast's corporate culture. Too many stakeholders saw a gap between the solicitous interaction online and the actual poor telecom service that Comcast delivered. However, Comcast's customer service EVP was able to point to several initiatives that had recently been built into their system to monitor service

quality, and direct stakeholders to their website to see public tracking data that demonstrated Comcast's ongoing service improvements.

For Future Discussion

For reputation scholars and practitioners, there are several broad implications of recognizing that social media can help organizations make direct relationships with individual stakeholders, who themselves can be powerful influencers of an organization's reputation. First, these new opportunities make it all the more important that we understand reputation-building as a process that depends upon an individual stakeholder's experience of an organization, and may also depend on a individual employee's ability to represent their organization online. This may be particularly challenging to those of us who take a more broadcast, public, collective, or entity-level approach to conceptualizing stakeholders (e.g., as groups reached through public communication), the organization (e.g., as an unnamed entity rather than as represented by an individual), and/or the relationship between them.

Second, we need to expand our research on the relational nature of corporate reputation (Bruning et al., 2004; Ledingham, 2009). In perhaps a roundabout way, we might return to the original understanding of the relationship between an individual stakeholder and an organization as something more like an interpersonal relationship, with relatively less emphasis on outcome interdependence. We might also explore the dynamics of stakeholders using employees as relational proxies for the organization. Reputation scholars and practitioners will want to think along the lines of interpersonal relationship maintenance strategies (e.g., Stafford and Canary, 1991; Wright, 2004) and consider how organizations can demonstrate a commitment to a relationship, while participating in a way that demonstrates characteristics of authentic communication.

Third, we need to investigate, understand, and explain how users experience organizations online as authentic or not. This will require interdisciplinary collaboration, since the research on computer-mediated relationships (in computer science and engineering) is so distant from research on corporate reputation (in strategy, and marketing communications). Moreover, social media features are evolving rapidly. For example, in the fall of 2009 alone Twitter introduced three new features intended to help organizations use their service. Right now, so much seems novel that it is unclear what kinds of situations will become common. Likely there are several types of positive and problematic situations that have not yet occurred as stakeholders, organizations and their representatives interact on social media, and so best practices have yet to be established. As situations become more typical, we will get a better sense of what issues to prioritize in our research and practice.

Finally, organizations will need to think longer term about how far to take the processes of establishing interactive relationships with stakeholders. Embracing social media seems full of opportunity, and it is. Yet, to embrace social media fully, organizations will need to change the ways that they think about stakeholder relationships, about employees' authority to speak on the organization's behalf, about an organization's willingness to listen, about organization's respect for and acknowledgement of individuals as important stakeholders, and more. This larger dialogue is not about how to use tools and link platforms to spread messages, but is instead about building authentic relationships that generate trust between and mutual opportunities for organizations and their stakeholders, so that positive reputations can be honestly earned.

References

Akerlof, G. A. (1970). The market for "lemons": Quality uncertainty and the market mechanism. *The Quarterly Journal of Economics*, 488–500.

Beal, A., and Strauss, J. (2008). *Radically Transparent: Monitoring and managing reputations*. New York: Sybex/Wiley.

Biocca, F., Harms, C., and Burgoon, J. (2003). Toward a more robust theory and measure of social presence: Review and suggested criteria. *Presence: Teleoperators and Virtual Environments, 12*(5), 456–80.

Bishop, B. (2003). When the truth isn't enough: Authenticity in public relations. *The Strategist 9*(4): 2–5.

Bromley, D. B. (1993). *Reputation, Image, and Impression Management*. Chichester, UK: John Wiley and Sons.

Bruning, S. D. (2002). Relationship building as a retention strategy: Linking relationship attitudes and satisfaction evaluations to behavioral outcomes. *Public Relations Review, 28*(1), 39.

Bruning, S. D., Castle, J. D., and Schrepfer, E. (2004). Building relationships between organizations and publics: Examining the linkage between organization public relationships, evaluations or satisfaction, and behavioral intent. *Communication Studies, 55*(3), 435–46.

Bruning, S. D., and Ledingham, J. A. (2000). Perceptions of relationships and evaluations of satisfaction: An exploration of interaction. *Public Relations Review, 26*(1), 85.

Brown T. J., Dacin P. A., Pratt M. G., and Whetten D. A. (2006). Identity, intended image, construed image, and reputation: An interdisciplinary framework and suggested terminology. *Journal of Academy of Marketing Science, 34*(2): 99–106.

Corley, K., and Harrison, S. (2009). Finding the positive in organizational identity change. In L. M. Roberts and J. Dutton (eds), *Exploring Positive Identities and Organizations: Building a Theoretical and Research Foundation* (pp. 361–84). New York, NY: Taylor and Francis Press.

Coupland, C., and Brown, A. D. (2004). Constructing organizational identities on the web: A case study of Royal Dutch/Shell. *Journal of Management Studies, 41*(8): 1325–47.

Edelman (2009). Edelman Trust Barometer 2009. January. Retrieved from http://www.edelman.com/trust/2009/

Fombrun, C. J., and Rindova, V. P. (2000). The road to transparency: Reputation management at Royal Dutch Shell. In M. Schultz, M. J. Hatch, and M. H. Larsen (eds), *The Expressive Organization: Linking identity, reputation, and the corporate brand* (pp. 77–96). Oxford, UK: Oxford University Press.

Gilmore, J., and Pine, J. (2007). *Authenticity: What consumers really want*. Boston, MA: Harvard Business School Press.

Godin, S. (2009). Demonization. Retrieved December 1, 2009 from http://sethgodin.typepad.com/seths_blog/2009/03/demonization.html.

Grunig, J. E. (2001). Two-way symmetrical public relations: Past, present, and future. In R. L. Heath (ed.), *Handbook of Public Relations* (pp. 11–32). Thousand Oaks, CA: Sage.

Grunig, L. A., Grunig, J. E., and Dozier, D. M. (2002). *Excellent Public Relations and Effective Organizations: A study of communication management in three countries*. Mahwah, NJ: Lawrence Erlbaum Associates.

Grunig, J. E., and Huang, Y. H. (2000). From organizational effectiveness to relationship indicators: Antecedents of relationships, public relations strategies, and relationship outcomes. In J. A. Ledingham and S. D. Bruning (eds), *Public Relations as Relationship Management: A relational approach to the study and practice of public relations* (pp. 23–53). Mahwah, NJ: Lawrence Erlbaum Associates.

Grunig, J. E., and Huang, Y. (2000). From organization effectiveness to relationship indicators: Antecedents of relationships, public relations strategies, and relationship outcomes. In J. A. Ledingham and S. D. Bruning (eds), *Public Relations as Relationship Management* (pp. 23–53). Mahwah, NJ: Lawrence Erlbaum Associates.

Grunig, J. E., and Hung, C-J. F. (2002). *The effect of relationships on reputation and reputation on relationships: A cognitive, behavioral study.* Paper presented at the PRSA Educator's Academy 5th Annual International, Interdisciplinary Public Relations Research Conference, Miami, Florida.

Harquail, Celia V. (2009). *The Rise of the Brandividual: Rendering organizational authenticity through social media.* Proceedings of the 13th International Conference on Corporate Reputation, Brand, Identity and Competitiveness. Amsterdam, May.

Hon, L., and Grunig, J. (1999). Guidelines for measuring relationships in public relations. Retrieved November 17, 2009, from http://www.instituteforpr.org/index.php/IPR/research_single/guidelines_measuring_relationships/282

Howard, R. G. (2008). The Vernacular Web of participatory media. *Critical Studies in Media Communication, 25*(5), 490–513.

Horton, D., and Wohl, R. (1956). Mass communication and parasocial interaction: Observations on intimacy at a distance. *Psychiatry, 19*, 215–29.

Kelleher, T., and Miller, B. M. (2006). Organizational blogs and the human voice: Relational strategies and relational outcomes. *Journal of Computer-Mediated Communication, 11*(2), 17–32.

Kowalczyk, S. J., and Pawlish, M. J. (2002). Corporate branding through external perception of organizational culture. *Corporate Reputation Review, 5*(2–3), 159–74.

Ledingham, J. A. (2009). A chronology of organization-stakeholder relationships with recommendations concerning practitioner adoption of the relational perspective. *Journal of Promotion Management, 14*(3&4), 243–62.

Ledingham, J. A., and Bruning, S. D. (2000a). A longitudinal study of organization-public relationship dimensions: Defining the role of communication in the practice of relationship management. In J. A. Ledingham and S. D. Bruning (eds), *Public Relations as Relationship Management* (pp. 55–69). Mahwah, NJ: Lawrence Erlbaum Associates.

Mahon, J. F., and Wartick, S. L. (2003). Dealing with stakeholders: How reputation, credibility and framing influence the game. *Corporate Reputation Review, 6*(1), 19–35.

McGuire, W. (1989). Theoretical foundations of campaigns. In Ronald E. Rice and Charles K. Atkin (eds), *Public Communication Campaigns* (pp. 43–65). Thousand Oaks, CA: Sage.

McGuire, W. (2001). Input and output variables currently promising for constructing persuasive communications. In R. E. Rice and C. K. Atkin (eds), *Public Communication Campaigns* (3rd. ed., pp. 22–48). Thousand Oaks, CA: Sage.

Mitchell, R. K., Agle, B. R., and Wood, D. J. (1997). Toward a theory of stakeholder identification and salience: Defining the principle of who or what really counts. *Academy of Management Review, 22*(4), 853–86.

Rawlins, B. (2009). Give the emperor a mirror: Toward developing a stakeholder measurement of organizational transparency. *Journal of Public Relations Research, 21*(1), 71–99.

Scoble, R., and Israel, S. (2006). *Naked Conversations: How blogs are changing the way businesses talk with customers.* Hoboken, NJ: John Wiley and Sons.

Showkeir, J., and Showkeir, M. (2008). *Authentic Conversations: Moving from manipulation to truth and commitment*. San Francisco, CA: Berrett-Koehler.

Paine, K. D., and Kowalski, P. (2008). *Are We Engaged Yet? A framework for measuring engagement in social media*. Proceedings from the 11th International Public Relations Research Conference, Coral Gables, Florida.

Post, J. E., Preston, L. E., and Sachs, S. (2002). *Redefining the Corporation: Stakeholder management and organizational wealth*. Palo Alto, CA: Stanford University Press.

Rhee, Y. (2002). Global public relations: A cross-cultural study of the Excellence theory in South Korea. *Journal of Public Relations Research, 14*(3), 159–84.

Rhee, Y. (2004). *The Employee-Public-Organization Chain in Relationship Management: A case study of a government organization*. Gainesville, FL: The Institute for Public Relations.

Rubin, R. B., and McHugh, M. P. (1987). Development of parasocial interaction relationships. *Journal of Broadcasting and Electronic Media, 31*, 279–92.

Spears, R., Postmes, T., Lea, M., and Wolbert, A. (2002). When are net effects gross products? The power of influence and the influence of power in computer-mediated communication. *Journal of Social Issues*, 58(1), 91–107.

Stafford, L., and Canary, D. J. (1991). Maintenance strategies and romantic relationship type, gender, and relational characteristics. *Journal of Social and Personal Relationships, 8*, 217–42.

Takahashi, M., Fujimoto, N., and Yamasaki, N. (2007). Active lurking: Enhancing the value of in-house online activities through the related practices around the online communities. MIT Sloan School of Management Working Paper 4646-07.

Wright, K. B. (2004). On-line relational maintenance strategies and perceptions of partners within exclusively Internet-based and primarily Internet-based relationships. *Communication Studies*, 55 (2), 239–53.

Youngmeyer, D. R. (2002). *Measuring Organization-public Relationships: The case of a university department of communication and its undergraduate student public*. Paper presented at the Educators' Academy, Public Relations Society of America International Conference, November 16–19, San Francisco.

PART IV

Reputation Recovery

13 *Corporate Governance and Corporate Reputation: A Disaster Story*

THOMAS CLARKE

Introduction

It is often commented that it may take a company generations to acquire a solid corporate reputation and only seconds to lose it. One of the fastest ways to lose a corporate reputation is enduring a disaster in corporate governance. The scale and contagion of the recent global financial crisis has starkly confirmed this, however episodic crisis and frequent corporate governance failures have punctuated the development of the market system (Clarke 2007).

There are many explanations for the recent sustained and intense interest in corporate governance including the growth of international capital markets, the scale of the multinationals, the increasing proportion of individual wealth held in securities with the development of vast investment institutions, and the dawning awareness that if these investments are to be secure there must be effective monitoring and higher standards of corporate governance. Finally there is:

> *a general trend in society, facilitated by new technology and driven by social awareness, towards developing greater openness, transparency and disclosure. Yet the most widespread reason for the heightened interest in corporate governance is the now general sense that corporations cast a long shadow, and they must be governed responsibly if they are to benefit the economy and society. It is likely the present significance will continue to develop, as James Wolfensohn, the former President of the World Bank, put it, 'The proper governance of companies will become as crucial to the world economy as the proper governing of countries.' (Economist 2 January 1999, p. 38)*

This explains the sustained international effort to improve governance and disclosure. Good information is a prerequisite for any well-functioning market. It is the responsibility of company boards of directors to disclose any information that is market sensitive as soon as it is available. The alternative is a certain descent into secrecy, insider trading, and market manipulation. This chapter begins with a brief review of the attempts to reform corporate governance and disclosure, and an outline of the intermediaries who monitor and report on corporate governance. Recent celebrated corporate governance disasters are then analysed, where corporate reputation was fatally wounded by irresponsible behaviour and practices. Finally the causes and consequences of the global financial crisis will be examined, and conclusions drawn on the lessons for corporate reputation.

Corporate Governance Intermediaries

Efforts have been made since the origins of the joint-stock company and associated investment and governance systems to redress the evident weaknesses that each system periodically exposed. All systems of corporate governance are punctuated, to a lesser or greater extent by periodic failures as well as notable successes. Problems of accountability, transparency, fairness and openness of governance and finance have persisted widely, though expressed in different ways in different governance systems. Successive attempts to enhance the independence and accountability of company directors, to improve disclosure and to make equity markets more transparent have yielded results, but new problems and issues have inevitably arisen as old abuses have been eliminated. For example the disaffection with the entrenched managerialism of poorly performing US corporations in the early 1980s led to a revival of the market for corporate control: the threat of takeover it was thought would discipline managers, and replace those managers who could not realize the true value of corporate assets (Walsh and Seward 1990; Goldstein 2000; Davis 1991). What began as a revitalizing force ultimately resulted in the use of junk bonds in overpriced and reckless financing deals that disrupted corporations rather than stimulating them.

Periodic crisis has inevitably led to insistent calls for better regulation of corporate governance.

The Cadbury Report in the UK in 1992 proved a watershed in the international movement to improve corporate governance. Called at the instigation of the London Stock Exchange as a result of a series of large bankruptcies of companies that had recently received favourable audit reports (including Robert Maxwell's Mirror Group, Polly Peck and the Bank of Credit and Commerce International), Cadbury set out a code of best practice that was subsequently emulated by countries world-wide as part of their stock exchange listing requirements (Aguilera and Cuervo-Cazurra 2004). Central to the code was the division of responsibilities at the head of the company, with independent non-executive directors responsible for the audit committee, and remuneration of senior executives, and the board reporting on the effectiveness of internal financial controls and verifying the business as a going concern. Companies were left with a choice whether to comply with the guidelines or to offer an explanation to the market as to the reason for their divergence.

These principles represented an important step forward in restoring a sense of the responsibility and accountability of boards and directors, however this was only effective and meaningful in the context of the efficacy of wider institutional disciplines, and the work of other reputational intermediaries in corporate governance. Hence the independence and accountability of boards of directors requires the reinforcement of the duty of disclosure policed by effective regulators and well-functioning legal systems.

In addition market transparency, well-run stock exchanges with effective restrictions on market manipulation and competent securities analysts and financial journalists are necessary. Finally the engaged and capable practice of a range of professional intermediaries is required including independent accountants and auditors, sophisticated lawyers and bankers, and active external monitoring agencies (Black 2000).

Despite the apparently increasing rigour of the extensive monitoring and disciplinary mechanisms of corporate governance, all of the methods available have limitations that have created the possibility for executives, who are determined to do so, readily to escape effective monitoring, at least for significant periods of time, until poor performance cannot be concealed any longer. Bebchuk and Fried (2005) reveal how successive efforts to incentivise senior executives by linking their pay to performance and aligning their interests to shareholders with stock options, can either be manipulated, or reward managers when equity markets are inflated rather than corporate performance improving. Similarly transparency can be camouflaged and board committees unduly influenced. Finally executives have built defences against the market for corporate control, and ensured they benefit whatever occurs (Table 13.1). The difficulties experienced in exercising effective governance with regard to managerial activity, combined with the inevitable cycle of market growth and recession, and the tendency for ambitious strategies to come adrift when tested by a sudden collapse in the market, provokes recurring problems and periodic crises in corporate governance (MacAvoy and Millstein 2004; Roe 2005; Aglietta and Reberioux 2005).

Table 13.1 How efficient are the various methods of controlling managers?

Device	Rationale	Limits
Incentive pay		
Indexing wage on performance	Aligning managers' and rank-and-file workers' interests	Possible manipulation of performance by managers
Bonus linked to profit	Aligning managers' interests and firm strategy	
Stock options	Aligning CEO interest with shareholders' wealth	Still a major gap between CEO and shareholders' interests
Attribution of stock of the company	Aligning CEO interest with shareholders' wealth	Loosely correlated with CEO strategy and large benefits during financial bubble
Transparency		
Public disclosure of CEO's remuneration	Trigger outrage from shareholders and institutional investors	Camouflage tactic by managers in spite of statements in favour of transparency

Table 13.1 *Concluded*

Remuneration setting		
Creation of an independent remuneration committee	Prevent self-determination of remuneration by CEOs	The CEO may largely control the committee
Large number of independent members of the board	Prevent excessive remuneration by the detriment of shareholders	The income of members may depend on their generosity to the manager
Survey by consultant firms of CEO remuneration	Set an objective benchmark	The reference to average or median remuneration induces spillover and excessive pay increases
Market for corporate governance		
Firing of CEOs	Incentive to commitment	Exceptional configuration in the past
Threat of takeover	Puts a limit on CEO opportunism	Golden parachute for losers CEO income may increase even if shareholders suffer value destruction

Source: Inspired by Bebchuk and Fried (2003)

Active and Passive Boards

ACTIVE BOARDS

The ideal portrayal of the company board is as an active, deliberative and decisive forum for the business: 'Boards of directors collectively determine, through the decisions they make, the fate of the corporation … The principal work of a board of directors is to make decisions' (Leblanc and Gillies 2005, p. 24). Certainly the extensive portfolio of significant board activities encompassing succession planning, budgeting, strategy, risk management, compliance, disclosure, and corporate social and environmental responsibility suggest a very full agenda. However boards are inevitably part-time (due firstly to the necessary extensive external other commitments of directors that enhance the potential contribution they may make to the company; and to the fact that boards that begin to become nearly full-time inevitably stray into operational management, often losing their sense of objectivity and detachment in the process). Therefore board work tends to be concentrated in very intensive short periods of time. (Since board papers will normally be circulated well in advance of meetings though, the amount of time spent on individual preparation by directors may far exceed the time actually spent at board meetings.)

However Carter and Lorsch (2004, p. 22) citing an Egon Zhender (2000) survey suggest 'The "average" directors in North America and Europe dedicate around 100 hours or even less to their task (including time spent outside meetings on their own, gathering and reviewing information), with an average seven meetings a year.' Other consultancy surveys suggest slightly more hours of engagement on the part of the typical non-executive, though the tradition in most countries in the majority of companies is that being a non-executive board director is a very part-time commitment (which explains why some non-executives felt free to acquire a string of company directorships, together with an even larger number of board positions on public, educational, voluntary or artistic bodies).

The weight of recent legislation is beginning to change these practices somewhat. The growing importance attributed to the work of board committees, the increasing emphasis on internal financial controls and risk management, the heightened sense of legal liability, the more conscious expectation for non-executives to at least be knowledgeable about the company strategy, and the new emphasis on director development, performance and assessment will have all taken their toll on any inclination on the part of non-executive directors towards a minimal commitment. It is likely today that being a non-executive member of an active and engaged board of directors might involve at least double the amount of time formerly thought necessary (which explains the emphasis in most codes of practice, and often also in large company director contracts, on a reasonable limit to the number of other non-executive director positions an individual may hold).

Of course the extent of non-executive involvement, and the intensity of the commitment called for, together with the resulting stress, is greatly amplified when the responsibilities of the position are put to the test in times of crisis. Such periods of corporate crisis may last a few days, or can stretch into months or years. (One large company in Australia reported 83 board meetings in a single year during a prolonged crisis which involved corporate restructuring, divestment, adopting a new financial structure, and setting out on an entirely new strategic direction. In this case the company was conveyed from the brink of disaster (a humiliating takeover by a rival of the shell of the company), to a renewed growth and respect in the market).

PASSIVE BOARDS

There is much evidence that in the past boards of directors enjoyed a fairly passive existence, carrying out their duties, if at all, in a largely nominal way (Mace 1971; Lorsch and MacIver 1989). In the United States for example for much of the twentieth century it was accepted in many companies that the CEO would select and control the board: even if new directors wish to make an independent contribution, over time they learn passivity is what is expected: 'To initiate discussions where the boardroom culture has historically involved directors listening to management presentations, reacting primarily for the purposes of approving management initiatives, risks being viewed as obstructionist. The director who questions management and disrupts the carefully scheduled agenda will almost certainly receive feedback, either directly or non-verbally, that such interruptions are unwelcome' (Dalton and Dalton 2005, p. 96).

The growing prosperity of the US economy in the middle decades of the last century encouraged the sense that all was well in the corporate world, and the best thing boards could do was offer unqualified support to their management. But this complacency was briefly dispelled when Penn Central the largest railway company in the country collapsed in 1970. Louis Cabot, a Harvard professor, gave a graphic account of the role of the board in the doomed company:

I served for one fateful year on the board of Penn Central. The education was fast, brutal and highly practical. Even today the lawsuits are not settled and that education has cost me several times more than the price of a Harvard Business School tuition. At each Penn Central directors' meeting, which only lasted one and a half hours, we were presented with long lists of relatively small capital expenditures to approve, we were shown sketchy financial reports which were rarely discussed in any detail. The reports were not designed to be revealing, and we were asked not to take them away from the meeting. We always had an oral report by the Chief Executive Officer promising better results next month which never came true. (Cadbury 2002, p. 7)

As Cadbury (2002, p. 7) indicates Cabot 'did all the right things as an outside director, including writing a letter to the chairman to say that this was no way to run a business. But before any of the letters had even been answered, Penn Central had collapsed and Louis Cabot was being sued along with the other directors. What is clear from his vivid description of board meetings at Penn Central is that the board simply failed to do its job. It was both uninformed and misinformed and it exercised no control over the CEO.' The ensuing SEC enquiry into the misreporting of earnings and collapse of Penn State company, published an official report fiercely critical of the board's shortcomings and emphasized the need for board independence and for vigilant outside directors 'the somnolent Penn Central board...was typical of most giant corporations' boards in the post-war period' (Millstein 1998, p. 14)

The fact that even the most prestigious companies had dysfunctional boards is illustrated by Bill Wyman's sense as a long serving board member of General Motors until 1999 of the 'inactivity and passivity that had plagued GM board for many years.' Wyman insisted:

I was proud to serve on the GM board but we operated in a very passive manner. We were invited to join the board by the CEO, and rarely met alone to share our thoughts on the company's progress and, more particularly, on the performance of the CEO and management. The board endorsed the annual plans and long range strategies, but any role in developing or refining those plans was small. Board meetings were crowded with presentations, but with little time allotted for discussion. Carter and Lorsch (2004, p. 6)

The consistent attempt to marginalize boards by management, and the underestimation of the significance of their duties, was shattered by the fall-out from the Enron debacle, and the new zeal associated with the enforcement of the Sarbanes-Oxley Act. Replacing rank complacency was the zealous enforcement of compliance. The sea change affecting one director was reported in the *Wall Street Journal* (21 June 2004). 'Having served on the board of public companies since 1993, she has watched the culture of boardrooms change from golf games, cigars and fancy dinners, to meetings that begin at 6am and intense pressure to submerge oneself in ever-changing accounting and governance regulations.' There was certainly good reason for a dramatic change in board behaviour, since whatever may have gone before, the most spectacular case of a passive board was undoubtedly Enron with the most appalling consequences.

The Enron Board: Asleep at the Wheel?

On 2 December 2001, Enron Corporation, the seventh largest publicly traded corporation in the United States, declared bankruptcy. The shock waves caused by this catastrophic corporate collapse transformed the corporate governance environment not simply in America, but throughout the rest of the world. It took many years of Congressional inquiry, SEC investigation, and courtroom trials to bring the senior Enron executives, Chairman Kenneth Lay, CEO Jeffrey Skilling and CFO Andrew Fastow to justice. But the Enron board of directors was also directly responsible for this disaster.

The Special Investigation Committee set up by the Enron board itself under the chairmanship of William Powers issued a report on 1 February 2002 concluding 'The Board of Directors of Enron failed ... in its oversight duties ... with ... serious consequences for Enron, its employees and shareholders..While the primary responsibility for the financial reporting abuses ... lies with Management ... those abuses could and should have been prevented or detected at an earlier time had the Board been more aggressive and vigilant' (2002, pp. 22, 24). The US Senate Committee on Governmental Affairs report on *The Role of Directors in Enron's Collapse* (2002) is more damning:

> All of the Board members interviewed...were well aware of and supported Enron's intense focus on its credit rating, cash flow, and debt burden. All were familiar with the company's 'asset-lite' strategy and actions taken by Enron to move billions of dollars in assets off its balance sheet to separate but affiliated companies. All knew that, to accomplish its objectives, Enron has been relying increasingly on complicated transactions with multiple special purpose entities, hedges, derivatives, swaps, forward contracts, prepared contracts, and other forms of structured finance. While there is no empirical data on the extent to which U.S. public companies use these devices it appears that few companies outside of investment banks use them as extensively as Enron. At Enron, they became dominant: at its peak, the company apparently had between $15 and $20 billion involved in hundreds of structured finance transaction. (2002, p. 8)

The Senate investigation could not substantiate claims from Enron directors that they challenged management or asked tough questions:

> Instead the investigation found a Board that routinely relied on Enron management and Andersen representations with little or no effort to verify the information provided, that readily approved new business ventures and complex transactions, and that exercised weak oversight of company operations. The investigations also identified a number of financial ties between Board members and Enron which, collectively, raise questions about Board members independence and willingness to challenge management. (2002, p. 14)

The Senate inquiry identified more than a dozen red flags that should have caused the Enron board to ask hard questions. 'Those red flags were not heeded. In too many instances, by going along with questionable practices, and relying on management and auditor representations ...' (2002, p. 59).

The US Senate investigations made the following findings with respect to the role of the Enron board of directors in Enron's collapse and bankruptcy:

Fiduciary Failure

> The Enron Board failed to safeguard Enron shareholders...by allowing Enron to engage in high risk accounting, inappropriate conflict of interest transactions, extensive undisclosed off-the-books activities, and excessive executive compensation.

High Risk Accounting

The Board of Directors knowingly allowed Enron to engage in high risk accounting practices.

Inappropriate Conflicts of Interest

Despite clear conflicts of interest, the Enron Board of Directors approved an unprecedented arrangement allowing Enron's Chief Financial Officer to establish and operate the LJM private equity funds which transacted business with Enron and profited at Enron's expense.

Extensive Undisclosed Off-The-Books Activity

The Enron Board of Directors knowingly allowed Enron to conduct billions of dollars in off-the-books activity to make its financial condition appear better than it was and failed to ensure adequate public disclosure of material off-the-books liabilities that contributed to Enron's collapse.

Excessive Compensation

The Enron Board approved excessive compensation for company executives, failed to monitor the cumulative cash drain caused by Enron's 2000 annual bonus and performance unit pans, and failed to monitor or halt abuse by Board Chairman and Chief Executive Officer Kenneth Lay of a company-financed, multi-million dollar, personal credit line.

Lack of Independence

The independence of the Enron Board was compromised by financial ties between the company and certain board members. The Board also failed to ensure the independence of the company's auditor, allowing Andersen to provide internal audit and consulting services while serving as Enron's outside auditor. (2002, p. 3)

The conclusion of the Senate Inquiry's investigation into the Enron board's complicity in the downfall of the company was withering:

The failure of any Enron Board member to accept any degree of personal responsibility for Enron's collapse is a telling indicator of the Board's failure to recognize its fiduciary obligations to set the company's overall strategic direction, oversee management, and ensure responsible financial reporting … The Enron Board failed to provide the prudent oversight and checks and balances that its fiduciary obligation required and a company like Enron needed. By failing to provide sufficient oversight and restraint to stop management excess, the Enron Board contributed to the company's collapse and bears a share of the responsibility for it. (2002, pp. 14, 59)

The WorldCom Board: Going Through the Motions

If the stance of the Enron board could best be described as supine, the performance of the board of WorldCom, the even larger bankruptcy that immediately followed Enron, was just as abysmal in the apparent failure to fulfil competently any of the duties that the board was supposed to carry out. As the report prepared for the District Court of New York stated:

> While it is not clear that the independent directors could have discovered the fraud, WorldCom's board didn't do many things that might have prevented or limited the tragedy. For example, the board does not appear to have been adequately involved with the Company and its personnel. On average the board met quarterly, and the meetings were largely filled with formal presentations to the directors and other routine exercises, including CEO Ebber's opening prayer. These relatively infrequent meetings did not involve substantial amounts of time. Even meetings that were intended to review significant issues such as multibillion dollar acquisitions seem to have been concluded in a perfunctory manner. This was sufficient for blind ratification of actions, but not sufficient for informed, independent decision making. The Audit Committee most vividly exemplified the board's inadequate time commitment … The Audit Committee spent as little as six hours per year in overseeing the activities of a company with more than $30 billion in revenue, while the WorldCom Compensation Committee met as often as 17 times per year. This level of activity was consistent with 'going through the motions' rather than developing a thorough understanding of the accounting policies, internal controls and audit programs in use by the Company… It does not appear that either the Company's internal audit department or the Audit Committee perceived the widespread serious weaknesses in the Company's internal controls over external financial reporting. (Breeden 2003, pp. 30–32)

The WorldCom board did nothing to restrain the CEO Bernie Ebber's wildest commercial adventures, even though by all accounts Ebbers did not have the background, experience or training to lead such a large corporation:

> The lack of time commitment was not the board's worst failing. Despite having a separate Chairman of the Board and independent members, the board did not act like it was in control of the Company's overall direction. Rather than making clear that Ebbers served at the pleasure of the Board, and establishing reasonable standards of oversight and accountability, the board deferred at every turn to Ebbers. Ebbers controlled the board's agenda, the timing and scope of board review of transactions, awards of compensation, and the structure of management. He ran the Company with an iron control, and the board did not establish itself as an independent force within the Company. The Chairman of the Board did not have a defined role of substance, did not have control of the board's agenda, did not run the meetings and did not act as a meaningful restraint on Ebbers …WorldCom met the formal standards, and yet the board did not take action to limit Ebbers' power. Formalities were usually observed, and yet no director said 'no' when the Ebbers loans of $408 million came before the Board, no director said 'no' to grants of massive volumes of stock options, and no director appears to have questioned Ebbers' competence and fitness to serve as CEO until the disaster was unavoidable. (Breeden 2003, pp. 33–5)

The WorldCom board was dazzled by the meteoric growth of the company, and seduced by the apparent wealth this strategy generated, and did not perform the most minimal duties of accountability as a result. In the post-Enron era of heightened corporate governance compliance, nobody suspected that the rapid recovery of markets would be followed by an even more spectacular collapse.

The Global Financial Crisis

THE SECOND WALL STREET CRASH

The apparent ascendancy of Anglo-American markets and governance institutions was profoundly questioned by the scale and contagion of the 2008 global financial crisis. The crisis was initiated by falling house prices and rising mortgage default rates in the highly inflated US housing market. A severe credit crisis developed through 2007 into 2008 as financial institutions became fearful of the potential scale of the sub-prime mortgages concealed in the securities they had bought. As a result banks refused to lend to each other because of increased counter-party risk that other banks might default. A solvency crisis ensued as banks were slow to admit to the great holes in their accounts the sub-prime mortgages had caused (partly because they were themselves unaware of the seriousness of the problem), and the difficulty in raising capital to restore their balance sheets. As an increasing number of financial institutions collapsed in the US, UK and Europe, successive government efforts to rescue individual institutions, and to offer general support for the financial system, did not succeed in restoring confidence as markets continued in free-fall.

Financial insecurity rapidly became contagious internationally as fears of a global economic recession became widespread and stock markets around the world crashed. This financial crisis was larger in scale than any crisis since the 1930s Great Depression, involving losses estimated in October 2008 by the IMF as potentially $1,400 billion dollars, eclipsing earlier crises in Asia, Japan and the US. Martin Wolf was quick to realize the implications of the crisis, as he put it in the *Financial Times* (5 September 2007):

> *We are living through the first crisis of the brave new world of securitised financial markets. It is too early to tell how economically important the upheaval will prove. But nobody can doubt its significance for the financial system. Its origins lie with credit expansion and financial innovations in the US itself. It cannot be blamed on 'crony capitalism' in peripheral economies, but rather on responsibility in the core of the world economy.*

ORIGINS OF THE CRISIS

In the cyclical way markets work, the origins of the 2008 financial crisis may be found in the solutions to the previous market crisis. The US Federal Reserve under the sage Alan Greenspan responded to the collapse of confidence caused by the dot-com disaster and Enron failures in 2001/2002 by reducing US interest rates to 1 per cent, their lowest in 45 years, flooding the market with cheap credit to jump-start the economy back into life. US business did recover faster than expected, but the cheap credit had washed into the financial services and housing sectors producing the largest speculative bubbles ever witnessed in the American economy (Fleckenstein 2008; Einhorn 2008).

The scene was set by the 1999 dismantling of the 1932 Glass-Steagall Act which had separated commercial banking from investment banking and insurance services, opening the way for a consolidation of the vastly expanding and increasingly competitive US financial services industry. Phillips (2008, p. 5) describes this as a 'burgeoning debt and credit complex': 'Vendors of credit cards, issuers of mortgages and bonds, architects of asset-backed securities and structured investment vehicles – occupied the leading edge. The behemoth financial conglomerates, Citigroup, JP Morgan Chase et al, were liberated in 1999 for the first time since the 1930s to marshal banking, insurance, securities, and real estate under a single, vaulting institutional roof.'

In this newly emboldened finance sector the name of the game was *leverage* – the capacity to access vast amounts of credit cheaply to take over businesses and to do deals. Wall Street investment banks and hedge funds flourished with their new found access to cheap credit. Exotic financial instruments were devised and marketed internationally: futures, options and swaps evolved into collateralized debt obligations (CDOs), credit default swaps (CDSs), and many other acronyms, all of which packaged vast amounts of debt to be traded on the securities markets. Abandoning their traditional financial conservatism banks looked beyond taking deposits and lending to the new businesses of wealth management, and eagerly adopted new instruments and business models. As the IMF put it:

> Banking systems in the major countries have gone through a process of disintermediation – that is, a greater share of financial intermediation is now taking place through tradable securities (rather than bank loans and deposits) … Banks have increasingly moved financial risks (especially credit risks) off their balance sheets and into securities markets – for example, by pooling and converting assets into tradable securities and entering into interest rate swaps and other derivatives transactions – in response both to regulatory incentives such as capital requirements and to internal incentives to improve risk-adjusted returns on capital for shareholders and to be more competitive … Securitization makes the pricing and allocation of capital more efficient because changes in financial risks are reflected much more quickly in asset prices and flows than on bank balance sheets. The downside is that markets have become more volatile, and this volatility could pose a threat to financial stability. (2002, p. 3)

MASTERS OF THE UNIVERSE

Each financial boom is associated not only with reckless risk-taking and wildly inflated rewards, but an indulgent culture proclaiming the new Masters of the Universe (Galbraith 1993). Tom Wolfe coined this phrase (based on a children's comic book) for financial *parvenus* in the middle of the 1987 boom in his book *The Bonfire of the Vanities*. (Oliver Stone's iconic movie *Wall Street* set in this period was supposed to be about crime and punishment on Wall Street, but Michael Douglas playing the ruthless magnate Gordon Gekko, who won an Oscar for his 'Greed is Good' speech, now cannot have breakfast in New York without being approached by young men saying it was seeing the movie that made them want to become Wall Street traders.) The hubris returned a decade later with the NASDAQ boom, and the posturing of the executives of Enron, WorldCom and other companies who in strenuous self-promotion declared they were leading the best companies in the world, before they ran out of funds and then ran out of hype as they faced the courts. With the recovery of US financial markets after the Enron debacle, the explosion of financial innovation gave the world a new breed of Masters of the Universe in the derivatives dealers and hedge fund managers who manipulated trillions of dollars, while charging immense fees. This long financial boom of recent years saw the culture of financial excess permeate through swathes of the rich industrial countries as people were encouraged to live on debt.

Symptomatic of the humiliating fall from assumed greatness was the end of Lehman Brothers, an 158-year-old Wall Street institution forced into bankruptcy by an incapacity to face reality. Lehman's had failed before in 1984, selling itself to American Express at a discount price (Auletta 1986). The chairman at the time, Lewis L. Glucksman said, 'We never made a culture where people were concerned with the firm and not just each other. We had a level of greed here and personal selfishness that was disgraceful' (*New York Times*, 19 January 1986). Later Richard S. Fuld became chief executive, returning Lehman back to being an independent bank in 1994. Lehman's was the fourth largest investment bank on Wall Street and was a self-proclaimed 'innovator in global finance'.

As the Wall Street investment banks stumbled, Fuld had dinner with Henry Paulson in April 2008 and came away thinking Lehman's had a 'huge brand' with the US Treasury. The announcement of a first quarter 2008 loss of US$2.8 million and a larger second quarter loss of $3.9 billion exposed the weaknesses in Lehman's position. As Fuld cast about for a white knight to invest in the firm in the US, Europe and among Asian sovereign wealth funds, Lehman's was publicly presenting a rosy view of its future. After the company collapsed three separate federal investigations began into the conduct of Lehman's in the final months, and Fuld was hauled in front of the US Congress House of Representatives oversight committee. Democratic congressman John Sarbanes referring to a June 2008 statement in which Fuld insisted the company's liquidity was strong said, 'Either he has lost all perspective and is completely clueless or he is quite savvy and deceiving people' (*Financial Times; New York Times* 6 October 2008).

But nobody imagined the scale of the tragedy that befell Wall Street's leading investment banks. 'Wall Street: RIP,' pronounced *The New York Times* (28 September 2008). 'A world of big egos. A world where people love to roll the dice with borrowed money, of tightwire trading, propelled by computers ... that world is largely coming to an end.' Replacing the triumphal past was disillusion and disorientation: 'Enthusiasm was gone from Wall Street yesterday, replaced by a febrile uncertainty and a foreboding that 2008 might turn into 1929' (*The Times Online*, 1 October 2008).

REGULATION AND GOVERNANCE

While the accumulated cost of the global financial crisis was being realized the commitment to establish a new international financial regulatory framework increased. The general market assistance and specific rescue packages for individual financial institutions amounted to almost $11 trillion worldwide by October 2008. With the international financial community still in a state of profound shock, and heavily dependent upon state aid, any protests about the dangers of over-regulation were muted. Adair Turner head of the Financial Services Authority (FSA) in the UK (responsible for regulating financial institutions) commented:

If a year and a half ago, the FSA had wanted higher capital adequacy, more information on liquidity, had said it was worried about the business models at Bradford & Bingley and Northern Rock, and had wanted to ask questions about remuneration, the fact is that we would have been strongly criticised for harming the competitiveness of the City of London, red tape, and over regulation. We are now in a different environment. We shouldn't regulate for its own sake, but over-regulation and red tape has been used as a polemical bludgeon. We have probably been over-deferential to that rhetoric. (Guardian, 16 October 2008).

However the question is, will the deference of regulators return when financial markets recover, and financial institutions and markets are free again to pursue their self-interest? An early indication of how entrenched the irresponsibility of the financial sector had become was the astonishing news that the surviving US financial institutions were preparing to pay 2008 end-of-year executive bonuses approximately equivalent to the billions of dollars of aid they had just received from Congress. While the US economy was collapsing around them, and the US public were becoming increasingly concerned how they might survive a severe recession, the executives of major banks seemed focused primarily on maintaining their bonuses (Clarke 2009, 2010).

Conclusions

The catalogue of corporate disasters in recent decades does not inspire confidence that corporate reputations will recover early, or prove durable. Investment dollars will continue to pour into corporate equities and bonds, since there is little place else for them to go. But trust is effectively shattered, and deep doubts will continue regarding the stability of markets, the reputation of many corporations, and the integrity of executives. Winning back trust by throwing money at public relations consultants, and a return to CEOs soaring rhetoric is unlikely to win hearts and minds. Hubris is likely to be dismissed with the disbelief it fully deserves.

The route to restoring corporate reputations will be a hard and long road for business people to travel. A closer and more open relationship with regulators is now inevitable. Much greater and more effective engagement with shareholders and stakeholders will be required. The demand will be for disclosure and transparency to be continuous and accurate. Boards of directors themselves will be subject to much greater scrutiny and evaluation. CEOs and other executives will find reward will be much more closely geared to performance. Companies will be expected to live up to their promises, and the mechanisms of public monitoring will be applied to ensure they do so.

References

Aglietta, M. and A. Rebérioux (2005) *Corporate Governance Adrift: A Critique of Shareholder Value.* Cheltenham: Edward Elgar.

Aguilera, R. V. and A. Cuervo-Cazurra (2004) Codes of Good Governance Worldwide: What is the Trigger? *Organization Studies* 25(3): 415–43.

Auletta, K. (1986) *Greed and Glory on Wall Street: The Fall of the House of Lehman.* New York: Random House.

Bebchuk, L.A. and Fried, J.M. (2005) *Pay Without Performance: Overview of the Issues.* Harvard Law School Discussion Paper No 528. Boston, MA: Harvard University.

Breeden, R.C. (2003) *Restoring Trust.* Report on Corporate Governance For the Future of MCI, Inc., to The Hon. Jed. S. Rakoff, The United States District Court, For the Southern District of New York. Available at http://fl1.findlaw.com/news.findlaw.com/hdocs/docs/worldcom/corpgov82603rpt.pdf (accessed 7 January 2011).

Black, B. (2000). *Political Determinants of Corporate Governance.* Oxford: Oxford University Press.

Cadbury, A. (2002) *Corporate Governance and Chairmanship.* Oxford: Oxford University Press.

Carter, C.C. and Lorsch, J.W. (2004) *Back to the Drawing Board: Designing Corporate Boards for a Complex World.* Boston, MA: Harvard Business School Press.

Clarke, T. (2007) *International Corporate Governance.* London and New York: Routledge.

Clarke, T. (2009) *European Corporate Governance.* London and New York: Routledge.

Clarke, T. (2010) *Recurring Crises in Anglo-American Corporate Governance, Contributions to Political Economy.* Oxford: Oxford University Press.

Dalton, C.M. and Dalton D.R. (2005) Boards of Directors: Utilising Empirical Evidence in Developing Practical Prescriptions. *British Journal of Management*, 16, 91–7.

Davis, G. F. (1991) Agents without Principles? The Spread of the Poison Pill through the Intercorporate Network. *Administrative Science Quarterly*, 36(4), 583–613.

Einhorn, D. (2008) *Fooling Some of the People All of the Time: A Long Short Story.* Hoboken, NJ: Wiley.

Fleckenstein, F. (2008) *Greenspan's Bubbles: The Age of Ignorance at the Federal Reserve.* New York: McGraw Hill.

Galbraith, J.K. (1993) *A Short History of Financial Euphoria.* London: Penguin.

Goldstein, D. (2000) Hostile Takeovers As Corporate Governance? Evidence from the 1980s. *Review of Political Economy*, 12 (4): 381–402.

IMF (2002) *The Globalisation of Finance and Development.* Washington, DC: IMF.

Leblanc, R. and Gillies, J. (2005) *Inside the Boardroom.* New York: Wiley.

Lorsch, J.W. and MacIver, E. (1989) *Pawns or Potentates: The Reality of America's Corporate Boards.* Boston, MA: Harvard Business School Press.

MacAvoy, P. W. and I. M. Millstein (2004) *The Recurrent Crisis in Corporate Governance.* Stanford, AA: Stanford Business Books.

Mace, M.L. (1971) *Directors: Myth and Reality.* Boston, MA: Harvard University Press.

Millstein, I. (1998) *The Evolution of Corporate Governance in the United States.* Geneva: World Economic Forum.

Phillips, K. (2008) *Reckless Finance Bad Money: Reckless Finance, Failed Politics, and the Global Crisis of American Capitalism.* New York: Viking Books.

Roe, M.J. (2005) The Inevitable Instability of American Corporate Governance. In Lorsch, J., Berlowitz, L. and Zelleke, A. (eds), *Restoring Trust in American Business.* Cambridge, MA: MIT Press.

Stiglitz, J. (2010) *Freefall: America, Free Markets, and the Sinking of the World Economy.* New York: W. W. Norton and Company.

Walsh, J. P. and Seward, J. K. (1990) On the Efficiency of Internal and External Corporate Control Mechanisms. *The Academy of Management Review*, 15(3): 421–58.

14 *Corporate Rebranding*

DALE MILLER AND BILL MERRILEES

Corporate rebranding is an emerging domain of academic research and practitioner interest. Corporate rebranding has a major contribution to make to reinvigorating and enhancing corporate reputation. We contend that corporate rebranding can be relevant to firms, public sector agencies and not-for-profit organisations.

The apparent scope of rebranding in industry and trade publications spans many facets including brand renewal, repositioning, makeover, and reinvention (Merrilees and Miller, 2008, p. 357). An early academic paper on rebranding was Berry's (1988) summary of Ogilvy & Mather's brand revitalisation programme. A common trigger for revitalising brands is under-performance (Kapferer, 1997). Renaming is sometimes classed as rebranding, but changing a name without changing any component of the brand essence or brand associations, is really only that – a change of name, as we discuss further.

Corporate rebranding stands in contrast to corporate branding, which refers to the initial coherent articulation of the corporate brand and can occur at any time. Corporate rebranding refers to the disjunction or change between an initially formulated corporate brand and a new formulation. The scope of corporate rebranding therefore potentially affects all aspects of an organisation's strategy and operations.

This chapter examines corporate rebranding in several ways. First, we discuss a model of corporate rebranding drawing on six central principles. Second, we canvass the literature on corporate rebranding to set the scene, noting that it appears in three main areas, namely corporate business, cities and not-for-profit rebranding. Third, we address defensive corporate rebranding for brands that have been in decline, neglected or for brands that have experienced brand damage. Fourth, we apply corporate rebranding proactively, for organisations, which want to shift their brand strategically. Next, we consider the potential to incorporate sustainability into corporate rebranding. Finally, practical lessons for managers undertaking corporate rebranding are given.

A Model of Corporate Rebranding

To understand corporate rebranding both conceptually and practically we start with a model of rebranding, which the authors developed in part from the literature and in part from case research. Merrilees and Miller (2008) present an integrated articulation of corporate rebranding theory with three phases, which they extend with a conceptualisation of six principles of corporate rebranding. They found case research supported the principles.

The three phases are (1) re-visioning the corporate brand, (2) achieving stakeholder buy-in to the revised corporate brand, and (3) corporate rebranding strategy implementation. Each phase is potentially complex, and must be synergistic with the other phases. A holistic and strategic approach to corporate rebranding is in fact a prerequisite. Poor practice, for example, sees firms rushing in to change colours or logos without addressing the other significant phases. The outcome at best is a superficial change. Strategic management underpins each phase, meaning that ongoing performance management and evaluation are built-in to the processes.

PHASE 1: RE-VISIONING THE CORPORATE BRAND

The re-visioning process can be complex and depends on the factors precipitating the re-visioning. Some factors could be moving to new locations, mergers and acquisitions, or a major change in strategy direction. These factors could be thought of as drivers or triggers (e.g. Lomax and Mador, 2006). There may be some latent brand concepts that the revised brand will address explicitly. Articulating authenticity, corporate social responsibility or brand heritage may be important in the revised brand. The actual process will depend on the scale of the organisation. For example, a relatively small local community organisation may be able to consult directly with staff, customers, the board of directors and local authorities, in a series of workshops and consultations, whereas a larger, more geographically dispersed firm may need to develop more extensive and creative opportunities for interactive input to the re-visioning.

PHASE 2: ACHIEVING STAKEHOLDER BUY-IN TO THE REVISED CORPORATE BRAND

In the corporate branding literature, most of the discussion about stakeholders is on internal stakeholders, predominantly employees. This focus, while very important, underestimates the extent of stakeholders in corporate rebranding. Suppliers and customers are significant stakeholder groups, whether in business-to-business (B2B) or business-to-consumer (B2C) contexts. Depending on the organisation type, community groups may be significant stakeholders. During this phase, companies try to develop stakeholder commitment to the revised brand. With internal stakeholders, the genuine inclusion of staff in planning proposed changes, and the training of employees for changes (which occurs in Phase 3), are just two ways to engage staff in the revised corporate brand. Indeed, successful engagement of the internal stakeholders can position them constructively as what can be called 'brand warriors'.

PHASE 3: CORPORATE REBRANDING STRATEGY IMPLEMENTATION

As with many strategy initiatives, well-planned and well-executed implementation is crucial for success. In the implementation phase, managing internal and external communications is vital. The essence of this phase is to align the revised corporate brand and the functional and experiential components of the brand. For example, in a retail corporate rebranding context, the re-visioned brand would be reflected in components such as store design (infrastructure, layout, merchandise spatial planning, and visual merchandising), in external and in-store promotion, pricing, product assortment and packing, and store locations. Staff service can support the brand, and the specific terms and conditions of the employment arrangements, and human resource management policies and practices can reinforce the firm's brand values to the employees.

Moving to the principles of corporate rebranding, which mesh with the three phases, Table 14.1 summarises the Merrilees and Miller (2008) findings, and demonstrates the complexity of corporate rebranding. The key to successful corporate rebranding is a systematic and integrated approach that spans the entire organisation and its stakeholders, and embraces performance management.

Table 14.1   Principles for corporate rebranding

Principle 1: Brand re-vision Designing a suitable brand vision for the corporate rebrand should balance the need to continue to satisfy the core ideology of the corporate brand and yet progress the corporate brand so that it remains relevant to contemporary conditions.
Principle 2: Retention of core brand values Successful corporate rebranding may require retaining at least some core or peripheral brand concepts to build a bridge from the existing corporate brand to the revised corporate brand.
Principle 3: Possible new market segments Successful corporate rebranding may require meeting the needs of new market segments relative to the segments supporting the existing corporate brand.
Principle 4: Brand orientation A company applying a high level of brand orientation through communication, training, other human resource management strategies, and internal marketing is more likely to have effective corporate rebranding.
Principle 5: Alignment of Brand Elements A company having a high level of integration and coordination of all aspects of the marketing mix and human resource management, with each brand element aligned to the corporate brand concept in its corporate rebranding strategy implementation, is more likely to have effective corporate rebranding.
Principle 6: Stakeholder awareness Promotion is needed to make stakeholders aware of the revised brand, with possible additional benefits if non-mass media, such as public relations, are included in the promotion mix.

(Adapted from Merrilees and Miller, 2008, Table II, p. 546)

Principle 1, brand re-vision, reveals one of the paradoxes of corporate rebranding. That is, how does an organisation keep its core brand values and yet move forward? The explanation is that the vision and substance of the corporate brand must be revitalised rather than merely changing the visual manifestations of the brand like colours and logos. Unfortunately, many firms considering a corporate rebrand start with discussing for example desirable colours or a cute new name, rather than grappling with the current and desired brand vision and strategy. Principle 5 manages the specifics of colour and visual representation of the brand.

As Principle 2 suggests, success is likely if the *core values* from the existing brand continue to the revised brand. That is, the organisation's competitive advantages are linked mainly to the core brand values, which can be classed as intellectual property or intangible capabilities. To be able to rebrand successfully, the organisation must first fully recognise and understand its core brand values, capabilities and competitive advantages. However, the retention of peripheral values as part of a universal offering may be less critical.

Part of the re-visioning as shown by Principle 3 will include consideration of market segments. Do we retain all current market segments, or delete some? Do we add market segments? Managing a change of market segments will require specific attention to Principles 5 and 6 for managing stakeholder buy-in, and to Principle 4 to ensure internal stakeholders understand any revision of segments. New segments could be more time-constrained, or more price sensitive, or have similar product needs, but different service needs.

Principle 4 highlights the role of brand orientation in rebranding. If the organisation has a strong, very identifiable corporate brand, compelling resonance with employees and suppliers especially is highly likely. The chief executive officer (CEO) has the demanding role of being the overarching brand champion. The communication among senior managers, who are in effect brand ambassadors, is often facilitated by cross-functional responsibilities, moderating any silo effects in the rebranding process. Thus, the rebranding process is not just the role of the marketing function, or the branding management function, or the corporate communications function; it is a whole-of-organisation process.

Principle 5 invokes the need for integration and co-ordination of all aspects of the marketing mix. The word 'all' is informative. That is, it is no superficial consideration of product, place, price and promotion, but a comprehensive in-depth examination of how each brand element is aligned to the corporate brand concept in its corporate rebranding strategy implementation. In part, this is the principle that guides any changes to the visual representation of the brand. If there are multiple market segments, the alignment of brand elements and co-ordination of the marketing mix is even more complex and sophisticated.

Principle 6 advocates stakeholder awareness. An integrated communication strategy could concentrate for example on print, radio and the organisation's website. Here the promising work on eCRM (electronic Customer Relationship Marketing) can offer guidance on building trust and brand loyalty (e.g. Merrilees and Fry, 2002, 2003). During the early phases of implementation, messages can bring together the familiarity of the past with the new brand values. Emerging work suggests that multiple stakeholders may have multiple corporate brand meanings (Merrilees and Miller, 2010). Further research could examine this prospect theoretically and in practice. In the interim, organisations with multiple market segments and other stakeholders should consider to what extent different stakeholders may have different meanings for the corporate brand, and how that possibility could affect the integration and co-ordination of the marketing mix overall (Principle 5).

Overall, the six-principle framework indicates the scope of issues that brand champions and brand ambassadors can address and some of the tools that can be used when embarking on corporate rebranding. The application of the framework presumes a strategic management approach, and associated organisational capabilities.

Corporate Rebranding Studies

Using the Merrilees and Miller (2008) nomenclature, *corporate rebranding* refers to the disjunction or variation between an initially formulated corporate brand and a new formulation, whereas *corporate branding* refers to the initial coherent articulation of the corporate brand. The corporate branding literature has increased significantly over the past decade. However, the focus of this chapter is on corporate rebranding, where few academic studies explicitly discuss corporate rebranding, and tend to be case studies rather than conceptualisations.

Despite the frequency of corporate rebranding in practice, academic studies remain scarce (Lomax and Mador, 2006; Stuart and Muzellec, 2004); however, this 'significant phenomenon ... merits academic attention' (Muzellec and Lambkin, 2006, p. 804). Understandably, the majority of published academic articles on rebranding are in the corporate business sector. The next most frequent explicit use of corporate rebranding frameworks is in city and place branding, where the city brand is framed as a corporate brand, and recently some researchers are examining not-for-profit organisations in the context of corporate rebranding. Is there a single model of corporate rebranding that is viable across sectors, or does each sector require a different rebranding conceptualisation? To explore answers to that question we first examine the corporate rebranding literature by industry, to identify similarities and differences.

FOR-PROFIT INDUSTRY REBRANDING STUDIES

The business media frequently reports the rebranding of businesses. However, the extent of the discussion and activities often focuses on renaming, with little more substance to the so-called rebranding than cosmetic changes. Such a name change can occur in response to image factors, especially in the case of mergers and acquisitions. In contrast, and more pertinent to this chapter, are the emerging academic studies on rebranding businesses (for-profit), where the scope of the changes is much more extensive than a mere renaming.

Table 14.2 summarises selected studies of organisations particularly businesses where rebranding has been attempted. The reported studies range from France Télécom and Canadian Tire, to Accenture and Shell Retail Forecourts, all major firms, as well as the much smaller and local firm, The Olde Hide House. The latter case reinforces the possibility that corporate rebranding can be relevant to small firms too, a perspective rarely discussed. In general, the results reported in the studies suggest that overall businesses recognise the three phases (corporate brand re-visioning, achieving stakeholder buy-in, and corporate rebranding strategy implementation). However, in some specific studies, activities consistent with each principle are quite patchy on the one hand, but on the other, taken collectively across the studies, the principles are covered.

Table 14.2 Evaluation of business (for-profit) studies against the principles of corporate rebranding

Examples of Studies	Principle						Outcomes
	1 Brand re-vision	2 Retain core values	3 New market segments	4 Brand orientation	5 Align brand elements	6 Promotion to stakeholders	
Merrilees & Miller, 2008 *Olde Hide House* Canada	☑ Trigger was development of additional store in different location. Change from a destination slogan to powerful new vision: 'the authority on leather goods'	☑ Retained authenticity Authority on leather over time; continues with quality, sourcing, service and wider presence (two locations). peripheral values changed to heritage (Acton), modern (Toronto)	☑ Added new segment which had broadly similar product needs, but different service needs	☑ High CEO-led	☑	☑ Extensive internal promotion External promotion to existing and new segments	*Successful rebranding; probable brand morphing*
Gotsi et al., 2007 Gotsi et al., 2008 *TECLI* (pseudonym) Two studies of the one firm, looking at various aspects of rebranding, categorised by authors as revolutionary rebranding	☑ Drivers of rebranding included ownership changes, growth by acquisitions. Shift in focus from location-specific, telecom focused to 'young, integrated and innovative communications company' (p.346) Pressure to rebrand before stock market floatation	?Unclear in their effort to completely change the firm's image and positioning, they seem to have departed from the firm's heritage and identity to such an extent that they have alienated stakeholders	?Unclear Implicit because of shift in focus	?Unclear	☒ Poor investment of time and resources by executives Poor engagement with employees New name determined by executives with little staff involvement very poor planning of implementation	☑ Some attempt make but top-down approach to staff	*Unsuccessful rebranding because of the highhanded and possibly paternalistic approach to the stakeholders Poor re-visioning, failure to retain sufficient of the existing core values, failure to develop brand orientation and thus inability to achieve stakeholder buy-in, ineffective implementation*

Table 14.2   Continued

Examples of Studies ✎	1 Brand re-vision	2 Retain core values	3 New market segments	4 Brand orientation	5 Align brand elements	6 Promotion to stakeholders	Outcomes
			Principle				
Kaikati, 2003; *Accenture* Time bounded rebranding resulting from decision of international arbitrator that a name change was essential to the division of the two businesses. The change of name had to take effect from 01 January 2001	☑ Precipitated by the splitting of Andersen Consulting from Andersen Worldwide Renaming to Accenture based on internal "brandstorming" consultations	☑ Yes, but disconnect from Andersen Consulting	☒	☑ Led by top management Used 55 rebranding teams worldwide	☑ New name, new logo to reflect new name – extensive research to ensure integration. Use of 'teaser ads' leading up to the change Aligned internal and external messages Sponsorship of major sporting events	☑ Business-to business rebranding advertising Non-traditional releases to the press New website	*Successful corporate rebranding*
Melewar et al., 2005 *France Télécom* New visual identity launched in 2000	☑ Changing business strategy. Used consultants who responded to visual identity brief: 'branding to promote close relations' *Emphasis on visual identity, with some discussion of core values and aims*	? Unclear Decided to retain name Defined core values and aims	? Unclear *Implicit because of changing nature of the telecom industry*	☑ Launched by CEO	☑ Focus on visuals including colour schemes, logo, type font; also new signage in retail outlets. *Emphasis seems to have been on promotion, with no discussion on product, pricing or distribution the other three elements of the marketing mix.*	☑ External launch via press conference with demonstrations of applications of new visual identity, including model of a France Télécom branch	*The study discusses the need to measure the outcomes more effectively.* *Does not discuss brand equity valuation*

Table 14.2   Continued

Examples of Studies ✏	Principle						Outcomes
	1 Brand re-vision	2 Retain core values	3 New market segments	4 Brand orientation	5 Align brand elements	6 Promotion to stakeholders	
Merrilees, 2005 *Canadian Tire* Case study of rebranding by major Canadian mass merchandise retailer	☑ Extensive research by small team to develop new market position	☑ Brand heritage, Brand as icon	☑	☑ Major success factor for the rebranding process Brand leadership by company president. Recognition of multiple internal stakeholders. Vendor briefings	☑ Well integrated marketing communications. Co-managing multiple purposes of IMC. Co-ordination of all elements of marketing mix. More positive instore-experiences	☑ Launch of revitalized brand. President gave a public luncheon presentation to multiple stakeholder groups	*Internal and external evaluations in the study indicate successful corporate rebranding*
Lomax & Mador, 2006 7 UK Based organisations, which rebranded. Importance of project management, implementation planning and allowing enough time Two strands of Rebranding: 1. project management, resources 2. brand development, stakeholder engagement	?Unclear External & internal factors may be triggers Importance of internal and external stakeholder consultation Clarification of mission, values through internal and external consultation	☒	? Unclear Consider (in)congruence of stakeholder perceptions and organisational values. *By inference would need to consider segments if there were issues here.*	☒	Project management approach: consider using specialists to help	☑	Evaluation of objectives and monitoring stakeholder responses important because of costs Most changed name Developed a typology of branding choices

Table 14.2   Concluded

Examples of Studies	Principle						Outcomes
	1 Brand re-vision	2 Retain core values	3 New market segments	4 Brand orientation	5 Align brand elements	6 Promotion to stakeholders	
Muzellec & Lambkin, 2006 166 rebranded companies Focus on renaming Also two case studies 1. rebranding to erase negative brand equity (Telecom Eiram to ericom) 2. rebranding to transfer brand equity (Eircell to Vodafone Ireland)	☑ Rationale for rebranding Precipitating factors and drivers: Change in ownership structure (33% acquisitions; 20% spin offs) Change in corporate strategy Change in competitive position (17.5% image related problems) Change in external environment	☒	☒	☑	☑ Concentration on name and marketing aesthetics	☑Customer brand images primarily based on encounters with employees, therefore must convince internal stakeholders to act w consistently with the brand. *Emphasis on the importance of the internal stakeholders.*	*Corporate rebranding hierarchy*
Boyle, 2002 Rebranding of *Shell Retail's* forecourts in 1990s Linked with business format franchising. The study reveals multiple problems, and even when the forecourts reverted to company owned outlet, the attempt at rebranding did not bring about positive brand equity.	?Unclear	☒	☒ Aimed to attract customers for fuel *and* for convenience times	☑ Intense training and support through the franchise arrangements	☑ Sub-branded the forecourts as Shell Select Store redesign *Only partially aligned*	?Unclear	*Generally unsuccessful* *Negative factors included: the business, also lack of recognition of customer needs.* *lack of quality assurance across geographically dispersed locations.* *Arguably, they did not understand the rebranding process*

Key:　☑ = yes, covered in this study　　☒ = no, not addressed specifically　　? = unclear; *Commentary notes in italics*

One significant point arising in the studies is the identification of triggers for or drivers of, corporate rebranding. Lomax and Mador (2006) found that both internal and external triggers could stimulate corporate rebranding. Their research embraced a pilot study of company names changes, followed by a qualitative study of seven companies, which changed their names, and their brand vision. The rebranding precipitating factors were changes in ownership structure, in corporate strategy, in the external environment or in competitive positioning. Similar drivers emerged in the Muzellec and Lambkin (2006) study of 166 companies that rebranded, where the focus was on renaming.

Most of the studies are less clear about how and what processes contributed to achieving the brand re-vision. The studies of TELCI (pseudonym) illustrate this concern (Gotsi and Andriopoulos, 2007; Gotsi et al., 2008). The rebranding was categorised as revolutionary, where the triggers involved ownership changes, growth by acquisitions, and a significant shift in focus from a location specific telecom to a 'young, integrated and innovative communications company' (Gotsi and Andriopoulos, 2007, p. 346). The timing of the rebranding resulted from pressure to rebrand prior to stock market flotation. The rebranding was unsuccessful because of the highhanded and possibly paternalistic approach to the stakeholders. Assessing this case against the principles, it is evident that the principles of corporate rebranding were addressed inadequately. Poor re-visioning, failure to retain sufficient of the existing core values, failure to develop brand orientation and thus the inability to achieve stakeholder buy-in culminated in ineffective implementation.

One aspect of the re-visioning process is to determine how to satisfy the core ideology of the corporate brand, while revitalising it. Stakeholder consultations are one process, which can aid in these decisions. Some internal stakeholders (e.g. staff) and external stakeholders (e.g. customers) were consulted in rebranding processes that the Lomax and Mador (2006) study examined. However, none of the firms had a comprehensive stakeholder consultation process.

France Télécom's brand re-vision resulted from changing business strategy (Melewar et al., 2005), where consultants responded to a visual identity brief to promote close relations through branding. The emphasis was on visual identity, retaining the existing name and defining core values and aims. New market segments were implicit giving the changing nature of the telecom industry; brand orientation was evident, for example, with the launch of the rebranding by the CEO. Alignment of the brand elements emphasised promotion. There was no discussion of adjustments to the brand elements of product, pricing or distribution. Given the implicit shift in markets, presumably some adjustment was made to product offerings to create consistency with the revised strategy. The promotion to external stakeholders was predominantly through a press conference with demonstrations of applications of the new visual identity, including a model of a France Télécom branch, the latter of which suggests that the brand element alignment was probably more extensive than reported.

Furthermore, while the principles are presented in a logical sequence (Table 14.1), clearly from time to time, an iterative not linear approach between the principles will be necessary for their successful application during the three phases of corporate rebranding. Overall, the for-profit industry studies reinforce the nature of the phases of corporate rebranding, and collectively demonstrate aspects of the principles. In addition, the studies do not appear to suggest any additional principles.

CITY REBRANDING STUDIES

Increasingly corporate branding is adopted as a suitable framework for analysing city brands (Kavaratzis, 2005; Merrilees et al., 2009). Even in city branding studies that do not acknowledge a corporate branding framework, there is often a tacit understanding that the latter framework applies. The connection to corporate branding is self-evident. Cities are an entity and the aim of city branding studies is to examine the whole-of-entity branding. The stakeholders may vary from tourists, residents or businesses, but the attention to the whole of the entity remains, thus corporate branding is relevant.

Much of the city branding literature is about revitalising the city brand, thus the relevance of corporate rebranding. A majority of the city rebranding literature focuses on the front end of the corporate rebranding process, namely *re-visioning* of the city brand. A 'white knight' industry is often selected to revitalise a city brand. The 'white knight' takes several forms of a new vision of the city: greater emphasis on innovation, tourism, culture or revitalised retailing. An innovative city (creative city) is a growing favourite, in cities like Manchester, Barcelona or Singapore (Daniels and Bryson, 2002; Sim et al., 2003). Secondly, rejuvenating the tourism industry is another favourite city rebranding strategy. Five declining industrial British cities were revitalised with various tourist strategies (Bramwell and Rawding, 1994). Thirdly, adding a new cultural dimension is also popular in city rebranding strategies, with the classic examples including Glasgow and more recently the Guggenheim Museum in Bilbao, Spain (Evans, 2003; Garcia, 2004). Finally, a fourth popular route to city brand revitalisation is urban renewal or urban regeneration, especially applicable to inner-city redevelopment of slum or derelict areas in large cities like New York. Retailing is a common choice of application for this approach (Doyle, 2004; Mitchell and Kirkup, 2003; Rex and Blair, 2003).

The four popular approaches to revitalising a city brand have extrinsic appeal. If parts of a city brand are in decline or in ruin then, scope exists to repair it with a shiny new brand component – thus the 'white knight' rescue analogy.

In terms of the six principles outlined, the current emphasis in city rebranding is on Principle 3, meeting new needs of a new segment. The new segments could be newly attracted IT firms, tourists, culture-seekers or a new breed of shoppers. Therefore, consistency with Principle 3 is ostensibly achieved.

However, Principles 1 and 2 seem to be missing from consideration or at least downplayed in developing the re-vision of the city brand. For example, were all of the five declining industrial cities in the Bramwell and Rawding (1994) study conducive to tourism solutions? Was there any factoring of the initial core corporate values? In this instance, the past seems to have been abandoned in a desperate move to create a future position. A more sophisticated approach could have embraced the retention of some core or peripheral brand concepts, to develop a strong link from the existing corporate brand to the revised corporate (city) brand.

Apart from Principle 3, the only other principle attracting much attention in the city rebranding literature is Principle 4 where brand orientation is achieved through communication, training and internal marketing, and thus creating overall co-ordination among stakeholders and stakeholder corporate brand buy-in. For example, in their study of getting stakeholder co-ordination for rebranding the Birmingham City brand, Virgo and de Chernatony (2006) explain how the Delphi technique could be adapted to create a Delphic Brand Vision Model, to help develop brand buy-in. The reported conclusions indicated that the model worked as an effective consultation method for bringing together future vision, brand purpose and brand values, that is, creating a corporate brand vision.

Implementation issues, represented by Principles 5 and 6, also receive little attention in city rebranding studies. Some research in progress about the brand of the City of Burlington (Ontario, Canada) by the authors indicates that considerable importance is given to developing style manuals, logos and sign ways to achieve a consistent look of a revised city brand. Thus integrating and coordinating the marketing mix, together with explicit promotion using non-mass media, including public relations to stakeholders, are the effective means of implementing the revised corporate brand.

In summary, city rebranding studies focus most on the front-end re-vision of the new city brand phase and least on the implementation of the new city brand. Of the six principles of corporate rebranding enunciated in this chapter, Principles 3 and 4, dominate attention. Therefore, scope exists for a more comprehensive approach to city rebranding where all the principles of corporate rebranding are brought into play.

NOT-FOR-PROFIT REBRANDING STUDIES

In many countries, not-for-profit brands as a sector are very important, as much as a quarter of gross national product. Yet, compared to for-profit brands, academic studies are few. Part of the problem is the attitudes in the sector. Managers in the not-for-profit sector often associate branding with commercial ventures and not applicable to their own sector. Research by Stride and Lee (2007) shows the narrow way senior not-for-profit communications staff conceptualise their corporate brand. There is limited attention to differentiation from competitors and even awareness-raising has limited connection to the needs of supporters or the external audience. Often the brand is simply a crude tangible visual identity, with limited attempt to explore intangible dimensions. Gradually such conservative attitudes are changing. Consequently more studies are appearing on not-for-profit branding.

Given the limited understanding of corporate brands held by not-for-profit organisations, it is unsurprising that many initial attempts in corporate rebranding are modest, with simple changes to logo or the name (Khan and Ede, 2009). Even minor rebranding changes of this nature require strong leadership and internal culture. Another driver to corporate rebranding, especially for more major changes, is the use of external consultants, as a substitute for the lack of internal capabilities (Khan and Ede, 2009). The main barriers to corporate rebranding by not-for-profit organisations identified by Khan and Ede (2009) include the lack of an ambitious re-vision of the brand (Principle 1 in the six-part framework of corporate rebranding) and the resistance from employees (Principle 4). Limited budgets may also limit the effectiveness of the rebranding by not-for-profit organisations.

Charities provide a contrasting cluster within not-for-profit rebranding studies. A more positive perspective on the front-end re-visioning of charities rebranding is expressed in Hankinson (2000) and Hankinson and Lomax (2006) who interpret charity rebranding changes as a fundamental re-evaluation of the charity's function and values. Hankinson and Lomax (2006) refer to the three rebranding studies of the charities NSPCC, Crisis and Help the Aged (Dixon, 1997; Lindsay and Murphy, 1996; Mazur, 2003). The Crisis rebranding moved its organisational positioning from the very specific seasonal needs of the homeless to a broader year-round positioning. The Help the Aged rebranding provided greater clarity and a more relevant set of brand values. Principles 1 and 2 become strengths in the charity rebranding cases.

Hankinson and Lomax (2006) examine the role of staff in charity rebranding. They show that for rebranding UK charities, there were sizable pockets of staff who felt they were not engaged with the rebranding process. Their survey shows that in terms of the rebranding giving staff more knowledge about the new brand positioning, staff were neutral. In terms of the rebranding making staff feel more involved and motivated, negative views prevailed. The most negative aspect of all was the impact of rebranding on staff behaviours, especially with respect to the training received.

Keller et al. (2010) assess the situation for the back-end, implementation phase for charity rebranding for the American operations of the YMCA, Red Cross and The Salvation Army. Their assessment is negative, with the main failings being inconsistent projection of positioning and the inability to develop emotional appeals to stakeholders based on universally shared values.

In terms of the six principles of rebranding, a mixed assessment emerges depending on whether general not-for-profit or charity not-for-profit organisations are the focus. The studies by Stride and Lee (2007), and Khan and Ede (2009), paint a dismal picture of general not-for-profit rebranding efforts. Both studies indicate that not-for-profit organisations are struggling with *all* six principles. That is, all three phases of corporate rebranding, namely corporate brand re-vision, getting stakeholder buy-in and implementing the revised corporate brand are weak. Such disarray may reflect a timid approach to both marketing and branding practices more generally, associated with restrictive and narrow interpretations of advertising and visual identity. In particular, not-for-profit organisations struggle with reformulating an appropriate corporate brand re-vision (Principles 1 and 2). External consultants can help overcome this barrier in some cases, but the organisations still face potential resistance from stakeholders at this point.

Studies of charity rebranding efforts contrast to the general not-for-profit situation. In particular, the evidence to date is relatively complimentary in terms of charities rebranding their organisations based on their brand values and their positioning. A strong front-end is a powerful and positive way to initiate corporate rebranding, with Principles 1 and 2 strongly endorsed. Why is there a contrast between general and charity not-for-profit organisations in terms of the front-end stage of corporate rebranding? One explanation is that the contrast simply reflects the particular cases studied. However, we conjecture that charities operate in a very competitive environment, competing aggressively with many other charities, evident in frequent telemarketing and advertising appeals. Hence, charities have to hone their corporate branding skills to survive, probably more so than other not-for-profit organisations.

In terms of the middle (Principle 4) and back-end phases (Principles 5 and 6) of corporate rebranding, the evidence is less positive for charities. There is some indication that charities have not been very successful in getting buy-in from staff to the revised corporate brand (Hankinson and Lomax, 2006). Further, there is some evidence of limitations in the implementation of the corporate rebranding.

TOWARDS A SINGLE VIABLE MODEL ACROSS INDUSTRY CONTEXTS

The previous industry studies assess corporate rebranding cases in three different contexts: for-profit corporate rebranding, city rebranding, and not-for-profit rebranding. Each context is examined through the lens of the Three-Phases (re-vision of the corporate brand; achieving stakeholder buy-in to the revised corporate brand; corporate rebranding strategy implementation) and the Six Principles framework for corporate rebranding (Principles 1-3 apply to Phase 1; Principle 4 applies to Phase 2 and Principles 5–6 apply to Phase 3).

In broad terms, the corporate rebranding framework works well in elucidating corporate rebranding issues across the three contexts. The Three-Phase, Six-Principle framework appears useful as a conceptual basis to evaluate corporate rebranding cases and to guide future activities. Not all of the cases covered all three phases or all six principles. However, the framework is adequate to assess the particular phases and principles covered.

Within the perspective of the corporate rebranding framework, certain differences emerge in the pattern of results across the three industry contexts. Generally, the for-profit corporate rebranding cases achieve a higher level of effectiveness, in terms of greater achievement of the six principles. Such an outcome is not surprising, with for-profit organisations having greater and more sophisticated marketing and management resources.

In contrast, city rebranding and not-for-profit rebranding cases are generally ineffective, despite the pressing social need for reform. There are patches of success, such as Principles 3 and 4 in the city rebranding context and Principles 1 and 2 in the charity not-for-profit rebranding context. However, the overall corporate rebranding scorecard is bleak in the city rebranding and not-for-profit rebranding contexts. The conceptual framework given here is sufficient to illuminate the nature of the problems in previous corporate rebranding exercises. Further, the framework equally indicates the requirements for future changes in corporate rebranding. Therefore, the conceptual framework is both diagnostic and prescriptive to guide future corporate rebranding efforts in these two sectors.

Defensive and Reactive Corporate Rebranding

From time to time, certain corporate brands come under stress, necessitating corporate rebranding as defensive or reactive responses. Three main types of negativity or stress are discussed, namely *corporate brands in decline, neglect of corporate brands* and *damaged brands*. In these situations, corporate rebranding offers a framework for a systematic approach for dealing with the complex and confronting challenge of how to revive the corporate brand.

For greater impact, corporate brands in decline are discussed in the context of city brands, as exemplar cases. However, there are many cases of commercial, for-profit corporate brands in decline. For example, the American retailer F. W. Woolworth went bankrupt after a long-term decline in dollar revenue. Although there were minor attempts to rebrand the company, the company was unable to rebrand sufficiently to save itself, despite having a billion dollars of sales at the time of bankruptcy. Similarly, neglected corporate brands are discussed in terms of not-for-profit organisations, as an exemplar illustration. Finally, damaged brands are discussed in terms of commercial, for-profit organisations. However, all types of organisations are subject to possible damage and thus the potential need for damage control rebranding efforts.

CHALLENGES OF REVITALISING CORPORATE BRANDS IN DECLINE: CITY BRANDS AS EXEMPLAR EXAMPLES

Most of the city rebranding literature focuses on different means of overcoming negative perceptions of a city brand through repositioning of the brand (Trueman et al., 2007). Interestingly, few of the articles probe the reasons for the decline in the city brand, save for the obvious causes such as declining industrial demand for the cases of industrial cities. However, we contend that another explanation of declining city brands is the sheer difficulty of managing city corporate brands. The difficulties include the absence of a clear brand owner, disparate stakeholder groups (in particular, commercial versus social interest groups), not-for-profit characteristics and complexity (covering a very broad suite of activities from retailing, education, leisure and recreation to parks and gardens). And, while managing city brands is difficult enough, managing *changes* in city brands is even more difficult.

Our initial analysis of city rebranding research indicates that Principles 1 and 2 of our corporate rebranding framework are not sufficiently considered in city rebranding exercises. Our analysis concludes that new segments, such as tourists or culture seekers, are often the focus of the new city re-vision brand (consistent with Principle 3), but the new elements are not properly integrated into the existing core values of the city brand (thereby violating Principles 1 and 2). Thus, a common risk across the four types of city brand revitalisation reviewed is that the future (revised) corporate brand becomes fragmented. It is as if the latest fad (say, one of the four main types of city rebranding, such as tourism or innovation) is simply loosely-stapled to the existing city brand, with a resultant lack of cohesion.

A similar pattern seems to derive in the studies of Trueman et al. (2007) and Bennett and Savani (2003). In their study of the City of Bradford, Trueman et al. (2007) attribute many of the negative perceptions that residents have of the city to the 'silo mentality' of different neighbourhoods – a fortress mentality where locals feel comfortable within the precinct, but uncomfortable in relating to other precincts. The diversity of geographical interest groups makes it hard to fuse into a coherent city brand vision in the first instance and equally difficult to evolve that city brand. Principles 1 and 2 are difficult to achieve because of the conflicting interests of the stakeholder groups. The city planners may have inadvertently exacerbated the problem, by favouring the rural environment image at the expense of the metropolis. Trueman et al. (2007) suggest a solution based on unifying the city's corridors through visual design. While agreeing that more consistent visual design will partially help (consistent with Principle 5), more constructive city rebranding requires attention to the fundamentals of a unified and collaborative city brand re-vision that integrates all stakeholders.

In their cross-national study of city rebranding in three localities (London, Copenhagen and Boston), Bennett and Savani (2009) assess that the major problem in city rebranding stems from multiple stakeholder conflicts, particularly between commercial and community groups. The city rebranding seems to exacerbate conflict and issues that were already present before the rebranding. Failure of city management to address

Principles 1 and 2 carries through to the difficulty of getting stakeholder buy-in (Principle 4), both contributing to inconsistent city brand communications (Principle 5). The conflict problems persisted despite some offsetting positives, such as well-working, cross-functional, multi-discipline teams implementing the rebranding. The lack of integrated marketing communications across the three countries was observed by Bennett and Savani (2009), attributed in part to the distortion of communication messages to appease different stakeholder groups.

In summary, the common tendency of city brands to decline may reflect changing demand patterns and the sheer difficulty in managing city brands. Rectifying the problem of declining city brands through city rebranding seems to offer an opportunity for a stronger approach. However, to date, the expected benefits of city rebranding are often ephemeral or not fully realised. The limitation of city rebranding efforts so far, is evident in terms of the six-Principle framework of corporate rebranding. The main problem of many city rebranding attempts often rests in the *front-end* city-brand re-vision phase, in particular issues relating to Principles 1 and 2. Many new visions of a city brand have appeal in that they represent the latest fad of innovation or tourism for example, and appease most interest groups. However, the 'white knight' solution actually underperforms because of poor corporate rebranding design. In practice, the new re-vision of the city brand is not well integrated to the existing core values of the city brand. Nor does the new re-vision adequately address the different needs of multiple stakeholders. These two failures make it difficult to obtain full stakeholder buy-in and consistent and sustainable implementation.

The challenges to city rebranding, as enunciated, are considerable. Nearly all of the studies of city rebranding indicate that the challenges remain unresolved. Unless our articulated concerns about inadequate front-end planning of city rebranding are dealt with comprehensively, then future efforts at revitalising city brands are similarly likely to be unsuccessful.

CHALLENGES OF REVITALISING CORPORATE BRANDS THAT ARE NEGLECTED OR UNDER-FULFILLED: NOT-FOR-PROFIT BRANDS AS EXEMPLAR EXAMPLES

Not-for-profit corporate brands often suffer from neglect because of short-term imperatives (solving today's crisis or emergency) and the domination of social over commercial, profit objectives despite the necessity to be economically viable. Potentially this problem applies to both general and charity forms of not-for-profit organisations, though less so to charities because of the competitive nature of this type of organisations.

Unfortunately, management attitudes or competing problems force many not-for-profit brands into neglect despite the corporate rebranding potential. The brand equity associated with corporate brands includes both pecuniary and non-pecuniary (social) benefits. To the extent that not-for-profit brands fail to reach their full potential, then both the monetary and social benefits will be less than optimal. That is, failure to develop the corporate brand of a not-for-profit organisation implies a failure to maximise the social benefits to the organisation's constituents.

The considerable potential for not-for-profit corporate rebranding stems especially from the vital importance of *values* to the core corporate brand values of most such organisations. That is, values such as helping the needy and community care are powerful emotional core values for an organisation and resonate well with most audiences. Powerful core values are an excellent way of developing a corporate brand, providing that they can be harnessed correctly and purposively. Charities are adopting a values-based approach to core corporate brand values to a certain extent (Dixon, 1997; Hankinson, 2000; Lindsay and Murphy, 1996; Mazur, 2003; Saxton, 1994), but the application is less so in general not-for-profit organisations (for an exception see Sullivan Mort et al., 2007).

Despite the huge upside to not-for-profit corporate rebranding, linked to the emotional power of values-based core values, in reality the conservative attitudes can inhibit such organisations. General not-for-profit organisations are the most disadvantaged in terms of all three phases of corporate rebranding. Neglect of the corporate brand is greatest for this category of organisation. Managers of general not-for-profit have a duty of care to do more about extracting value from their corporate brand. Management education or consultants could be part of the answer. Alternatively, continuing neglect implies a breach of their duty of care, with our stern suggestion that the relevant CEOs and managers should be dismissed and replaced by more corporate-branding savvy managers.

In terms of charities, there is more recognition of the value of corporate branding and the need for corporate rebranding. Consequently, the front-end phase of corporate rebranding is generally executed reasonably well. Unfortunately, charities are weak in the middle and last phases of corporate rebranding – getting staff buy-in (Principle 4) and implementing the new or revised corporate brand (Principles 5 and 6). Challenges to charity corporate rebranding will remain until Principles 4–6 are met.

CHALLENGES OF REVITALISING CORPORATE BRANDS THAT ARE DAMAGED

The exemplar example of corrective rebranding to fix a damaged brand is the Coca-Cola case in the 1980s. Based on weak market research (taste tests rather than whole of branding comparisons) Coke changed the taste of its Classic Coke brand. Consumers reacted negatively and Coca-Cola was forced to re-introduce the original formula. This is an example of bad brand management, a surprise because Coca-Cola consistently ranks in the top three corporate brands worldwide. In this case, the rebranding was a flagship product brand, not strictly a corporate brand. However, arguably, mismanagement of the flagship product (one of the brand elements) damaged the corporate brand. If a world brand leader has this problem, what hope do the others have? Similar cases arose with Cadbury and Kraft, where initiatives to change a flagship product brand had to be reversed in response to negative consumer backlash.

Again, there may be other initiatives of the company, that on the surface, in the minds of the managers appear positive, but could have unintended consequences. For example, Muzellec and Lambkin (2006) raise the possibility that an inappropriate merger may cause damage by destroying brand equity.

The fashion brand Burberry went into damage control after several years of mismanagement allowed chaos to appear in its corporate brand management. Corporate rebranding by a new management team tightened product design, culled inappropriate distribution members and focused advertising (Moore and Birtwistle, 2004). This example indicates that corporate rebranding to fix damage necessitates that all three phases of corporate branding are addressed and integrated. As a caveat to this advice, it should be noted that few of the for-profit cases in Table 14.2 are about damaged brands, probably because of the difficulty of researchers to access the relevant information. Additional research is needed before can make definite conclusions about the appropriate corporate rebranding requirements to repair damage.

Proactive Corporate Rebranding

Defensive corporate rebranding suggests that the organisation is forced to deal with a problem or crisis, not necessarily of its making. On the other hand, proactive corporate rebranding indicates that the organisation is taking action 'ahead of any immediate need' to do so. Given the dynamic nature of the world of business, all organisations need to adapt their corporate brand from time to time. Excessive frequency of change to the corporate brand is costly and unwise strategically, as it would create confusion in the marketplace. However, it makes sense to undertake at least moderate (proactive) changes to the corporate brand every two to three years.

Many of the for-profit cases of corporate rebranding in Table 14.2 were triggered proactively. In other words, it is quite normal for commercial, for-profit firms to undertake corporate brand changes. The evidence in Table 14.2 suggests that proactive corporate rebrands are managed effectively, with most cases effecting change that is consistent with nearly all of the Six Principles. The positive evidence should encourage other firms to seriously consider corporate rebranding, using the Six Principle framework as a tool to assist with such change.

The Canadian Tire case in Merrilees (2005) is a case in point. The company had been performing fairly well, but there were competition clouds forming, with formidable competitors such as Walmart and Home Depot. Notwithstanding, the Canadian Tire corporate brand had considerable cachet, providing a unique combination of products closely linked into Canadian heritage. A new, young, female marketing manager emerged with product branding experience and immediately became the corporate brand champion. It took about six months to get this new role accepted by the mature, male-dominated, conservative executive team. As a comment on dynamics, this experience indicates that corporate brand changes are rarely instantaneous. It also took considerable time to get the potential changes in the corporate brand accepted by other stakeholders, including the dealers and the advertising team. A very positive force was the innovative market research that helped identify the new direction (re-vision) for the corporate brand – it was possible to develop new corporate brand values that resonated with the lifestyle of its customers and Canadian heritage generally. In summary, all three phases and all six principles (in hindsight, because the model was not available at the time of the corporate rebranding) were incorporated appropriately into the new corporate brand.

Sustainability and Corporate Rebranding

A new perspective on corporate rebranding is the infusion of the corporate brand with sustainability features. In the past, having a sustainable business might have referred to having a viable ongoing business. However, the current context for sustainable businesses includes economic, environmental, sustainability and social responsibility pressures from diverse stakeholders. A broader conception of sustainable business is one which is not only viable, but which also embraces a widening scope of sustainability elements and strongly integrates those elements into the corporate brand and strategy. Examples of firms responding to these pressures with revised corporate strategies and brand re-visioning include firms like the world's three largest retailers (Walmart, Carrefour and Tesco). For example, Tesco has rebranded incrementally to inculcate sustainability into many facets of its strategy, and thus its services, buildings and store designs, product offerings and distribution channels (see Tesco, 2010; Tesco plc, 2010). Many firms responding to the external contextual pressures set up separate corporate social responsibility and sustainability functions. In contrast, and as an exemplar, Tesco has taken a more holistic and strategic approach by integrating these domains, inculcating them throughout the business and engaging actively with stakeholders (including staff, customers and suppliers) (Tesco plc, 2009). Clearly, all the principles of corporate rebranding are identifiable in the case of Tesco.

Similarly, both Carrefour and Walmart are developing and implementing sustainable elements in their corporate brands. Carrefour's approach to sustainability and its corporate brand appears more overt and integrated (Carrefour, 2009), than Walmart, where nevertheless 'part of Walmart's ongoing mission [is] to be a more sustainable company' (Walmart, 2010). Walmart addresses ethical practices and sustainability separately on its website, but intuitively these spheres intersect in both corporate strategy and in practice. The gradual nature of the inclusion of sustainability elements into the corporate brand indicates the dynamic nature of corporate rebranding in some situations. Unquestionably, firms embarking on corporate rebranding with a sustainability focus can benefit from embracing the phases and principles of corporate rebranding to help them to develop a holistic and systematic approach to this complex yet vital process.

Lessons for Managing Corporate Rebranding in Practice

Arguably, in all principles, the firms in many of the cases could amplify their efforts. For example, within brand orientation, the corporate culture could be developed to reflect and embrace that brand orientation. Further research is needed to understand better the culture-brand orientation nexus. Does culture need to change before strengthening the extent of brand orientation and introducing a revamped corporate brand or can the change in corporate brand be used as a tool to change the culture? In addition to culture, should more attention be paid to policies, procedures and rules? What is the role of human resource management as part of internal support for the brand and for internal stakeholder buy-in?

When aligning brand elements, a much more holistic approach together with detailed specifications, could strengthen the implementation of this principle. Integrated marketing communication is mooted as a possible tool that has been under-utilised in past corporate rebranding efforts.

Throughout the rebranding process, stakeholder recognition and substantial stakeholder involvement can underpin successful corporate rebranding. How to do this is not fully clear, but many firms make little effort. Therefore, simply making an effort is a superior strategy, with upside scope to discover best practices ahead of others.

Finally, techniques for project management and performance management systems can guide the application of the phases and principles of corporate rebranding. Such techniques help manage the process effectively and efficiently and enable evaluation of outcomes.

Conclusions and Future Directions for Corporate Rebranding

The chapter outlines the exciting developments in recent corporate rebranding. Just a few dozen studies pertain to the domain of literature. There is clearly much more to ascertain. Our interpretation of the literature is moderated through the lens of a particular conceptual framework, albeit a fairly broad and flexible one. Alternative conceptualisations may paint a different picture. Three major challenges emerge from this chapter.

The first challenge is to reach a consensus as to an appropriate conceptual framework for corporate rebranding. At this stage, the authors have argued for a Three-Phase, Six-Principle framework. Evidence suggests that the conceptual framework is robust across industry contexts (for-profit, cities and not-for-profit) and across strategic triggers for change (defensive versus proactive). Other studies are desirable, to reinforce this framework, modify it or replace it with a superior conceptualisation.

A second challenge that stands out is to make corporate rebranding work in the not-for-profit sector. The evidence indicates a dismal track record of past corporate rebranding efforts here. Our main recommendation is for not-for-profit organisations to use systematically our Six-Principle model, together with an appreciation of why previous efforts have failed.

A final challenge is a willingness of researchers to explore alternative methods to study corporate rebranding. We have structured some suggestions below.

Case studies dominate the corporate rebranding literature. Given the complexity and idiosyncratic nature of rebranding such domination is appropriate. Our main recommendation is that case studies should continue to prevail in future research. The proviso is that they are framed in terms of one or more conceptual frameworks, such as the Three-Phase, Six-Principle framework of corporate rebranding presented in this chapter. Conceptual framing of future studies facilitates progress to a generalisable model, with appropriate situation specific components as needed.

Within the realm of case studies, we recommend the sometime use of comparative case studies. That is, two or three purposeful cases can be compared, with an assessment of the contrasting behaviour between the cases. Comparative case analysis is an especially good way of evolving theory.

A variation of case analysis is to study particular cases over time; that is, longitudinally. An advantage of this approach is that dynamic aspects of the case are identifiable. For example, some phases may be slower or faster than expected, with scope to explore the reasons for this variability as a guide for other companies. A longitudinal case study can explore in depth the positive and negative forces of change. How did the parties achieve consensus or general agreement on a particular matter?

A further suggestion is the potential use of action research. Action research occurs when the researcher is active in the actual corporate rebranding exercise. Often there is limited opportunity for the researcher to do this, with their involvement usually starting after the event is completed. In some cases, commercial-in-confidence restrictions would prevent the presence of academic researchers during the corporate rebranding process. However, one situation where action research is especially useful is the not-for-profit area. Academic researchers can in essence be consultants, interacting with the managers, to guide the corporate rebranding process. There may be less commercial sensitivity issues in not-for-profit organisations. Moreover, our assessment above indicates that such organisations are in desperate need for outside help, with nearly all cases indicating major problems with previous attempts at corporate rebranding.

In conclusion, corporate rebranding offers significant promise as a framework for managing the organisation's brand, especially in terms of strategic brand change. All industry sectors have an opportunity to engage in corporate rebranding. The analysis above suggests that it does not matter whether change is imposed from the outside or initiated internally. Ideally, the best time for an organisation to undertake a corporate rebrand is when times are good, with the rebranding helping to maintain the momentum.

References

Bennett, R., and Savani, S. (2003). The rebranding of city places: an international comparative investigation. *International Public Management Review, 4*(2), 70–87.

Berry, N. (1988). Revitalizing brands. *Journal of Consumer Marketing, 5*(3), 15–20.

Boyle, E. (2002). The failure of business format franchising in British forecourt retailing: a case study of the rebranding of Shell Retail's forecourts. *International Journal of Retail and Distribution Management, 30*(5), 251–63.

Bramwell, B., and Rawding, L. (1994). Tourism marketing organizations in industrial cities: Organizations, objectives and urban governance. *Tourism Management, 15*(6), 425–34.

Carrefour (2009). *Annual Report 2009*. Available at http://www.carrefour.com/static/cdc/carrefour_minisite-ra-en_2009//, accessed 11 January 2010.

Daniels, P., and Bryson, J. (2002). Manufacturing services and service manufacturing knowledge-based cities and changing form of production. *Urban Studies, 39*(5–6), 977–91.

Dixon, M. (1997). Small and medium-sized charities need a strong brand too: crisis' experience. *Journal of Nonprofit and Voluntary Sector Marketing, 2*(1), 52–7.

Doyle, S. (2004). Urban regeneration in New York: gardens and grocers. *International Journal of Retail and Distribution Management, 32*(12): 582–6.

Evans, G. (2003). Hard branding the cultural city – from Prado to Prada. *International Journal of Urban and Regional Research, 27*(2), 417–40.

Garcia, B. (2004). Cultural policy and urban regeneration in Western European cities: lessons from experience, prospects for the future. *Local Economy, 19*(4): 312–26.

Gotsi, M., and Andriopoulos, C. (2007). Understanding the pitfalls in the corporate rebranding process. *Corporate Communications: An International Journal, 12*(4), 341–55.

Gotsi, M., Andriopoulos, C., and Wilson, A. (2008). Corporate re-branding: is cultural alignment the weakest link? *Management Decision, 46*(1), 46–57.

Hankinson, P. (2000). Brand orientation in charity organisations: qualitative research into key charity sectors. *International Journal of Nonprofit and Voluntary Sector Marketing, 5*(207–19).

Hankinson, P., and Lomax, W. (2006). The effects of re-branding large UK charities on staff knowledge, attitudes and behaviour. *International Journal of Nonprofit Voluntary Sector Marketing, 11*(3), 193–207.

Kaikati, J. (2003). Lessons from Accenture's 3Rs: rebranding, restructuring and repositioning. *Journal of Product and Brand Management, 12*(7), 477–90.

Kapferer, J.-N. (1997). *Strategic Brand Management: Creating and Sustaining Brand Equity Long Term*. London: Kogan Page.

Kavaratzis, M. (2005). Place branding: a review of trends and conceptual models. *The Marketing Review, 5*, 329–42.

Keller, E. W., Dato-on, M. C., and Shaw, D. (2010). NPO branding: preliminary lessons from major players. *International Journal of Nonprofit and Voluntary Sector Marketing,* 15 (2, May): 105–21.

Khan, H., and Ede, D. (2009). Now do not-for-profit SMEs attempt to develop a strong brand in an increasingly saturated market? *Journal of Small Business and Enterprise Development, 16*(2), 335–54.

Lindsay, G., and Murphy, A. (1996). NSPCC: marketing the 'solution' not the 'problem'. *Journal of Marketing Management, 12*, 707–18.

Lomax, W., and Mador, M. (2006). Corporate re-branding: from normative models to knowledge management. *Journal of Brand Management, 14*(1/2), 82–95.

Mazur, L. (2003). Celebrating old age. *Marketing Business*, April, 5.

Melewar, T. C., Hussey, G., and Srivoravilai, N. (2005). Corporate visual identity: the re-branding of France Télécom. *Journal of Brand Management, 12*(5), 379–94.

Merrilees, B. (2005). Radical brand evolution: a case-based framework. *Journal of Advertising Research, 45*(2) (June), 201–10.

Merrilees, B., and Fry, M.-L. (2002). Corporate branding: a framework for e-retailers. *Corporate Reputation Review, 5*(2 and 3), 213–25.

Merrilees, B., and Fry, M.-L. (2003). E-trust: the influence of perceived interactivity on e-retailing users. *Marketing Intelligence and Planning, 21*(2), 123–128.

Merrilees, B., and Miller, D. (2008). Principles of corporate rebranding. *European Journal of Marketing, 42*(5/6), 537–52.

Merrilees, B., and Miller, D. (2010), Brand morphing across Wal-Mart customer segments. *Journal of Business Research, 63*(11), 1129–1134.

Merrilees, B., Miller, D., and Herington, C. (2009). Antecedents of residents' city brand attitudes. *Journal of Business Research, 62*(3), 362–7.

Mitchell, A., and Kirkup, M. (2003). Retail development and urban regeneration: a case study of Castle Vale. *International Journal of Retail and Distribution Management, 31*(9): 451–8.

Moore, C., and Birtwistle, G. (2004). The Burberry business model: creating an international luxury fashion brand. *International Journal of Retail and Distribution Management, 32*(8), 412–22.

Muzellec, L., and Lambkin, M. (2006). Corporate rebranding: destroying, transferring or creating brand equity? *European Journal of Marketing 40*(7/8), 803–24.

Rex, D., and Blair, A. (2003). Unjust des(s)erts: Food retailing and neighbourhood health in Sandwell. *International Journal of Retailing and Distribution Management, 31*(9): 459–65.

Saxton, J. (1994) A strong brand comes from strong beliefs and values. *Journal of Brand Management,* 2 (4): 211–20.

Sim, L., Ong, A., Agarval, A., Parsa, A., and Keivani R. (2003). Singapore's competitiveness as a global city: development strategy, institutions and business environment. *Cities, 20*(2): 115–27.

Stride, H., and Lee, S. (2007). No logo? No way. Branding in the non-profit sector. *Journal of Marketing Management, 23*(1–2), 107–22.

Stuart, H., and Muzellec, L. (2004). Corporate makeovers: can a hyena be rebranded? *Journal of Brand Management, 11*(6), 472–82.

Sullivan Mort, G., Weerawardena, J. and Williamson, B. (2007). Branding in the nonprofit context: the case of Surf Life Saving Australia. *Australasian Marketing Journal 15*(2), 108–19.

Tesco (2010). Tesco. Available at http://www.tesco.com/

Tesco plc (2009). *Corporate Responsibility Report.* Available at http://www.tescoplc.com/plc/corporate_responsibility_09/

Tesco plc (2010). Tesco plc. Available at http://www.tescoplc.com/

Trueman, M., Cornelius, N., and Killingbeck-Widdup, A. (2007). Urban corridors and the lost city: overcoming negative perceptions to reposition city brands. *Journal of Brand Management, 15*(1), 20–31.

Virgo, B., and de Chernatony, L. (2006). Delphic brand visioning to align stakeholder buy-in to the City of Birmingham brand. *Journal of Brand Management, 13*(6), 379–92.

Walmart (2010). Sustainability. Available at http://walmartstores.com/Sustainability/

15 *Repairing Damages to Reputations: A Relational and Behavioral Perspective*[1]

MOOWEON RHEE AND ROBIN J. HADWICK

Introduction

Corporate reputation is a firm's unique property that has been established and experienced by insiders and evaluated by outsiders over time (Fombrun, 1996; Podolny, 1993). Abundant research in economics and management has shown that while reputation is intangible it is of great value to the firm and firms are required to pay close attention to the successful building and management of their reputations. Working from the premise that a good reputation is an asset,[2] there are also an increasing number of studies that analyze the impact of a damaged reputation on a firm and steps a firm could take to repair the damage (Dukerich and Carter, 2000; Rhee and Haunschild, 2006; Rhee and Valdez, 2009). In particular, the difficulty of repairing reputational damage can greatly differ depending on various contextual factors. The goal of this chapter is to create a greater understanding of how those factors impact the heterogeneity of this difficulty.

Studies in various business disciplines, including economics, marketing, and management, have focused on the significant implications of a good reputation for firm performance and behaviors (see Barnett et al., 2006; Rhee and Valdez, 2009, pp. 147–50 for a review). Economic research has focused on the importance of reputation to financial performance of firms. For example, studies in economics have found that a good reputation gives a firm the ability to charge a premium (Shapiro, 1983) and provides a stronger contract negotiating position (Banerjee and Duflo, 2000) and protection against market entrants (Milgrom and Roberts, 1982). This link between reputation and financial performance implies that there are potential negative financial consequences to reputation damage.

---

1   This work was supported by the National Research Foundation of Korea Grant funded by the Korean Government (NRF-2010-330-B00100).

2   Haunschild et al. (2009) and Rhee and Haunschild (2006) provide exceptions showing that a good reputation can be a liability in some contexts.

Marketing is closely related to reputation in both research and practice through the concept of brand image, as exemplified in the website of a marketing firm stating, "The brand of a company is really its reputation. Just like a personal reputation, a brand's reputation is formed based on the behaviors and actions of the company (or person), and how those behaviors and actions are perceived" (www.mpdailyfix.com/2008). Marketing research has shown that a good brand image can positively impact distribution channels (Anderson and Weitz, 1992), vendor relationships (Ganesan, 1994) and pricing strategies (Banks et al., 2002). These finding suggest that such positive impacts can be reversed when a good brand suffers reputational damage.

There is a richness of research in management and sociology, which attempts to examine less explored constructs and positive roles of a good reputation. A striking development can be particularly found in the notion of third-party effects where a firm's reputation is constructed and influenced by the reputation of other firms tied to the focal firm. Podolny (1993) presents a theoretical ground for such spillover processes of reputation in the market, which has been followed by a series of empirical evidence for various economic benefits from the third-party effects (see Podolny, 2005, for an extensive review), including enhanced ability to raise funds (Shane and Cable, 2002), to hire and retain superior employees (Gatewood et al., 1993), and to select joint venture partners (Dollinger et al., 1997). This stream of research makes it possible to suspect that the processes of reputation damage and repair are also subject to such third-party effects.

As shown in our brief review of prior reputation research above, the scholarly focus has, in large part, been on the antecedents and consequences reputation across multiple disciplines. However, less attention has been paid to the evolutionary nature of reputation and particularly to the fact that reputation will suffer damage and require repair throughout the life of the firm (Rhee and Valdez, 2009) although the theoretical foundations underlying the previous studies already involve insights into the dynamic nature of firm reputation. Rhee and Valdez (2009) aim to fill this void by offering a research model that calls for examining a set of contextual variables that leads to variations in reputation repair activities taken in response to a reputation-damaging event: the positive versus negative dimensions of reputation, the relevance of positive reputation to the a damaging event, organizational age, the diversity of the markets served by the organization, and the impact of third parties such as watchdog agencies and the mass media. Their model proposes that those factors influence stakeholders' perception of a firm's capability to repair reputation and the external visibility of the reputation-damaging event, which in turn affect the difficulty in repairing damaged reputations.

In this chapter, we seek to extend Rhee and Valdez's (2009) model for a more holistic understanding of reputation repair processes in the aftermath of a reputation-damaging event. While their model addresses the structural and environmental facets of reputation repair in that it considers the reputation-dimensional, organizational, and inter-organizational contexts as main factors that produce different extents of challenges in reputation repair, this chapter attempts to complement the model by exploring relational and strategic components essential for a reputation repair process. More specifically, we propose that the theoretical underpinnings in the existing studies of trust management and crisis management should also serve as critical assets for identifying the underlying mechanisms of reputation repair challenges. Trust and distrust has been studied at various levels and dimensions of analysis across multiple disciplines (Lewicki and Bunker, 1996; Lewicki et al., 1998; Zucker, 1986), and reputation repair can be approached from the perspective of repairing trust relationships (Blois, 1999; Dirks et al., 2009; Gillespie and Dietz, 2009). Reputation repair is also conceptualized as a part of corporate crisis management (Tucker and Melewar, 2005), so the existing research on various managerial steps and tactics in response to corporate crisis can help shed light on addressing different challenges in reputation repair (Coombs, 1998; Elsbach and Kramer, 1996).

In the following sections, we begin with a review of the existing literature in those two research arenas along with their possible implications for reputation repair studies, and then extend the literature to help present a set of research agenda that provides for a more fruitful model that we will call "Repairing Damage to Reputation." The purpose of our model is not to introduce a complete, independent model but to enrich the current work on reputation repair, particularly the model proposed by Rhee and Valdez (2009).

Background Literature and Potential Links to Reputation Repair Studies

TRUST

The scholarly study of the construct of trust is well worn (Deutsch, 1958), multi-faceted (Dirks et al., 2009), and multi-disciplinary (Lewicki et al., 1998; Rousseau et al., 1998; Zucker, 1986). An emerging treatment of trust is to link it to organizational reputation: corporate reputation emerges because of the trust of various market audiences in a firm's behavior and performance and vice versa (Caruana and Chircop, 2000; Fombrun, 1996; Lane and Bachmann, 2000; Swift, 2001). Recently, the link between trust and reputation has become more prominent due to the growth of virtual relationships between market actors, which intensifies information asymmetry between the transacting parties (Corritore et al., 2003; Grabner-Kraeuter, 2002; Tan and Thoen, 2000). The coupling of reputation and trust thus naturally implies the pairing of reputation damage and trust violation (Swift, 2001) in that damages to a firm's reputation takes place in the process whereby the firm lose trustworthiness. Thus, an understating of the reputation repair process can benefit from the emerging literature on trust repair (e.g., Kim, P.H., et al., 2009; Tomlinson and Mayer, 2009) and it can be proposed that challenges in trust repair inform challenges in reputation repair.

While acknowledging diverse conceptualizations of trust, Rousseau et al. (1998) define trust as "a psychological state comprising the intention to accept vulnerability based on positive expectations of the intentions or behaviors of another" (p. 395). This definition suggests that there is a multi-dimensional nature of trust, including a future orientation ("intent" and "expectations"), a level of perception versus reality ("psychological state" and "expectations"), a relational position ("of another"), a directional positioning ("accept vulnerability")[3] and a level of uncertainty ("expectations or intentions"). While complex, this approach to trust can help present a more integrative analytical tool to examine a trust repair process and a reputation repair process (Tomlinson and Mayer, 2009). For

---

3   While trust often takes the form of reciprocity rather than directional positioning (Nowak and Sigmund, 2000), the notion of reciprocity is less pertinent to corporate reputation given the asymmetric relationships between the firm and the market audience.

example, when stakeholders' trust in a firm is violated and its reputation is damaged, the firm may have to address various aspects of trust/reputation repair by bringing up such questions as how the trust-violating and reputation-damaging event would affect each of those dimensions of trust (e.g., what would be the impact of the event on the current relationship between perception and reality?).

The distinctive constructs of "trust" and "trustworthiness" also provide useful insights into the analysis of challenges in reputation repair. Trustworthiness is a quality displayed by an organization, which engenders and enables others' trust in the organization (Barney and Hansen, 1994; Blois, 1999). In other words, trust characterizes interorganizational relationships and trustworthiness is a descriptor of organizational behavior. Trust is not a compilation of acts, rather it is an internalized belief in the reliability of the compilation, while acts that one performs can be judged as trustworthy or untrustworthy (or somewhere in between). For example, a market audience would trust a firm's particular action along the trustworthy–untrustworthy continuum. Thus, the distinction between trust and trustworthiness suggests that when a trust-violating or reputation-damaging event occurs, a firm may need to engage in two separate repair processes. One process involves buffering the damages to the extent to which market audience has trusted the firm, i.e., has relied on the trustworthiness of the firm. The other repairing process would be affected by the properties possessed by the object of trustworthiness, e.g., the extent to which an organizational dimension that has been trusted is vulnerable to damages.

The communication and diffusion channels through which trust is formed in a community are another arena that informs the ways in which a damaged trust is repaired. Although many existing studies of trust have focused primarily on the formation of trust in dyads, trust typically develops between actors "who are embedded in a complex web of existing and potential relationships" (Ferrin et al., 2006, p. 870), where trustors and trustees are usually interlinked via third parties. The third party effects are materialized through various structural configurations such as network structures (i.e., social interaction with third parties) and structural equivalence (i.e., equivalent relationships with potential third parties) (Burt and Knez, 1995, 1996; Ferrin et al., 2006). Moreover, the trust formed based on a third party effect is considered a major construct of reputation (Burt, 2005; Hosmer, 1995; Podolny, 2005; Rindova et al., 2005), so it is natural to suspect that a reputation repair process is also not independent of such third party effects (Rhee and Valdez, 2009). However, there may be a notable difference in the role of third parties between reputation formation and reputation repair. While the formation of a good reputation requires long-lasting consistent contributions of third parties (Deephouse and Carter, 2005; Podolny, 2005; Washington and Zajac, 2005), a reputation repair process may be vulnerable to somewhat capricious assessments of third parties in response to a reputation-damaging event (Rhee and Haunschild, 2006).

Given the various potential ways in which the existing literature about trust can have relevance to studies of reputation repair as we selectively reviewed above, a review of the theoretical frameworks presented to study trust repair will provide a more direct understanding of the challenges in reputation repair. We introduce three representative frameworks of trust repair with a discussion on their applicability to research conducted on reputation repair. They present neither the complete picture of trust repair nor the perfect fit with the study of reputation repair. Our main purpose is to provide a guiding reference that exemplifies how the study of trust repair can extend, if not in total, to the study of reputation repair.

Drawing upon Goffman's (1967) work on interaction rituals, Ren and G present a causal model of effective relationship restoration, which particula a conceptualization of which restoration mechanisms increase the effectiven relationship restoration. While their model focuses on the restoration of relationshi the individual level (e.g., person-to-person conflict), it still holds value for the restoratio of relationships between an organization and its stakeholder groups. For example, the restoration mechanisms suggested in their model, such as accounts, apologies, demonstrations of concerns, and penance, are also widely accepted in the reputation repair process. Thus, it would be imperative to examine various roles of those mechanisms in repairing damaged reputations: e.g., (1) how does a firm manage the stakeholders' perceptions of the firm's reputation-damaging events through accounts?; (2) is the timing of a firm's apology about the event important in restoring its relationship with stakeholders?; (3) which signaling effects can be obtained through a firm's demonstration of concern for the stakeholders' needs and interests?; and what types of penance would be necessary for rebuilding relationships with the suffered parties? Ren and Gray's (2009) model also makes a unique contribution to the reputation repair literature by indicating that challenges in reputation repair will vary across different cultural environments. For example, given that individualists tend to blame individual, rather than situational, factors for a negative event (Morris and Peng, 1994), one can speculate that firms operating in an individualistic culture are required to deliver restoration mechanisms to their stakeholders via more direct and open communications. In contrast, market audiences in collectivistic cultures are more likely to blame social contexts, so "external" explanations through more indirect channels, such as appealing to third parties, will be more effective reputation repair tactics (Ting-Toomey, 1999).

Similarly, Lewicki and Bunker (1996) present four steps for repairing trust: recognizing and acknowledging the occurrence of a violation, determining the nature of the violation, admitting the destructiveness of the act, and accepting responsibility. However, they propose that the capacity to implement those steps varies depending on the type and magnitude of trust violation. In particular, "the more the trust violation creates significant challenges to the 'integrity' of the relationship," "the less likely that trust can be effectively rebuilt and restored" (p. 136). The integrity of the relationship is defined by the bases of trust, such that damages to the integrity of trust, hence challenges to the repair of trust, also may be differentiated by the very bases upon which trust is built. In "calculus-based trust," which Sheppard and Tuchinsky (1996) identify as deterrence-based trust, trust is maintained to the extent that clear measures and punishments exist to prevent trust-violating actions. Thus, trust can be effectively repaired as long as the violator of trust can accommodate such measures and punishments for their action and engage in renegotiations based on new contracts. However, "knowledge-based trust" and "identification-based trust" are grounded in generalized expectancy and emotional obligations, making trust repair far more problematic because violations of these forms of trust present a direct threat to the victim's long-standing judgments and commitments. In a similar vein, one can suggest that a firm's challenges in reputation repair also vary across different components of its reputation. For example, damages to reputations based on economic or legal contracts and credibility (Diamond, 1991; Ely and Valimaki, 2003) may be much more difficult to repair than those to reputations constructed from public

legitimacy bestowed on a firm (Podolny, 2005; Turban and
ton and Zajac, 2005).[4]

's (2009) model of trust repair invites Weiner's (1986) causal
that causal attributions of a negative outcome shed light on
which "trustworthiness" is repaired and eventually "trust" is
above regarding a possible distinction between trustworthiness
causal attribution theory, actors evaluate the causes of an
..uibution dimensions: "locus of causality" determines whether the
...us external or internal, thus ascribing blame; "controllability" is the degree to which
the trustee has control over the outcome; and "stability" indicates the static or dynamic
nature of the causes. Drawing upon these attribution dimensions, Tomlinson and Mayer
(2009) propose that damaged perceptions of trustworthiness, comprising the trustee's
ability, benevolence and integrity, are more likely to be repaired by demonstrating that
the causes of negative outcomes were driven by external factors, unstable internal factors,
or uncontrollable abilities. Indeed, the causal ascription of a reputation-damaging event
can be also represented by different combinations of the three attribution dimensions:
e.g., an airline accident owing to unexpected bad weather can be reported as having
internal, unstable, and uncontrollable causes whereas an accident due to a repeated control
tower mistake can be attributed to internal, stable, and controllable causes (Haunschild
and Sullivan, 2002; Reason, 1997). Then, analogous to Tomlinson and Mayer (2009),
reputation researchers would be interested in investigating how different combinations
of attribution dimensions result in variance of challenges to reputation repair.

CRISIS MANAGEMENT

Research in crisis management also offers a wealth of studies that can serve abundant
research ideas and practical implications for the study of reputation repair as managing
damaged reputations address a firm's behavior in times of trouble or "crisis" (Pearson
and Clair, 1998; Rhee and Valdez, 2009; Tucker and Melewar, 2005).[5] Like the literature
in trust, the research subject of crisis management spans several disciplines, including
psychology, management, marketing, and specifically, public relations (Ashcroft, 1997;
Coombs, 2001; Horsley and Barker, 2002; Marra, 1998). While a well-studied stream
of research approaches the relationship between reputation and crisis management in
terms of whether and how reputation can help a firm in times of crisis (Coombs, 1999;
Coombs and Holladay, 2006; Morley, 1998; Rhee, 2009; Rhee and Haunschild, 2006), in
this chapter we address the reverse scenario by looking at how various elements in crisis
management may impact challenges facing a firm that attempts to repair its damaged
reputation.

The label "crisis" is used to cover an almost unlimited scope of events with a wide
range of outcomes, thus allowing a broad definition of crisis. Pearson and Clair (1998)
describe organizational crises as "a low-probability, high-impact event that threatens
the viability of the organization and is characterized by ambiguity of cause, effect, and

---

4   The opposite prediction is also possible when we consider a different mechanism underlying reputation formation
(see our discussion in the next section).

5   Indeed, there are considerable research overlaps between crisis management and trust repair. However, we recognize
and discuss the distinctive features of crisis management in relation to its implications for reputation repair in this
section.

means of resolution, as well as by a belief that decisions must be made swiftly" (p. 60). Crisis management can thus be naturally defined as a planned effort by organizational members (often with a group of external stakeholders) to effectively manage those crises. What makes reputation repair a part of crisis management is the finding that numerous examples of a firm's crises usually involves damages to its reputations. For example, in their guide to managing corporate crises, Mitroff et al. (1996) assess the effectiveness of Exxon's handling of the Valdez incident and Johnson & Johnson's management of Tylenol tampering from the perspective of how successfully the firms recovered (or not) their damaged reputations. Effective crisis management reduces the impact of reputational damage and even improves or reinforces a firm's reputation while failure in crisis management leads a firm to suffer long-lasting negative repercussions of the damaged reputations.

Based on interviews with more than 500 individuals in more than 200 firms who had crisis management responsibility, as well as nationwide surveys of America's largest companies, the University of Southern California's Center for Crisis Management developed a framework that integrated four major issues in each component of crisis management: crisis types, time phases, organizational systems, and critical stakeholders (Pearson and Mitroff, 1993; Mitroff et al., 1996). The type of crisis is differentiated along two dimensions, "technical/economic" versus "human/social" origins or natures and "normal" versus "aberrant/severe" causes. The greater challenges in crisis management due to severe, rather than normal, events have been well documented in prior studies. For example, severe auto product recalls are shown to give greater damages, hence greater challenges in crisis management and reputation repair, to a firm than non-severe recalls (Hoffer et al., 1994; Rhee and Haunschild, 2006). However, studies of the challenges from technical/economic origins relative to those from human/social origins appear to require more complicated research designs because (1) this dimension is mixed with the dimension of internal–external causes discussed in the previous section (Tomlinson and Mayer, 2009) (i.e., technical and human origins can be attributed to internal causes while economic and social origins can be attributed to external causes); and (2) many studies have experienced major problems in identifying the origins of crises or reputation-damaging events, thus making it difficult to estimate the relative challenges in managing each type of origins, as shown by numerous research on aviation accidents (Haunschild and Sullivan, 2002; Mahler and Casamayou, 2009; Morris and Moore, 2000; Perrow, 1984; Vaughan, 1996, 1997).

The phases through which most crises pass include various activities, from preparation (e.g., warning and prevention), through response and recovery, to organizational learning (Fink, 1986; Hale et al., 2005). Various findings from the research on each phase, especially on the phase of response and recovery, would provide the most practical and managerial implications for the containment of damages to reputations and the subsequent reputation repair. Preparation for a crisis is seemingly unrelated to a reputation repair process, but the greater amount of crisis preparation can facilitate the process of response and recovery, as demonstrated in Johnson & Johnson's effective handling of the Tylenol tampering crisis (Haywood, 2002). In particular, a well-designed preparation for product or technical defects in high-risk industries encourage firms to engage in proactive, not defensive, responses to a crisis, making its recovery efforts more effective (Reason, 1997; Vaughan, 1996). However, most firms are equipped with less than the necessary preparation for potential crises and reputation-damaging events. For example, among the firms surveyed by Augustine (1995), only half of them had designed active steps to prepare for crises. While there might be diverse reasons for a firm's unpreparedness for crises, a notable reason is found to be the mindset that "our firm is protected from future crises," which can be attributed to the properties of the firm, the technical and social environments, and prior history of crises (Pearson and Mitroff, 1993). Indeed, such a mindset was confirmed by our informal interviews with corporate managers stating: "Excellent, well-managed companies don't have crises"; "Crisis management is a luxury"; and "Each crisis is so unique that it is not possible to prepare for them." Thus, reputation repair studies may benefit from the investigations into which internal and external contexts create this kind of organizational mindset, making reputation repair more challenging when a reputation-damaging event does occur.

For the phase of response and recovery,[6] numerous managerial steps have been suggested in several practice-oriented articles (e.g., Augustine, 1995; Mitroff et al., 1987; Pearson and Mitroff, 1993). In particular, a variety of measures tailored for responding to reputation damaging vents and recovering damaged reputations are also increasingly discussed in the reputation literature (e.g., Haywood, 2002; Tucker and Melewar, 2005). A remarkable practice that is adopted by a growing number of American firms is to put a standing crisis management team in place that is entitled to accomplish those measures when a reputation-damaging event occurs. For instance, the crisis management program in SABMiller is charged with designing predetermined procedures to deal with crisis situations and monitor potential or actual threats to its brands and reputation (Chaloner and Brotzen, 2002). Moreover, such a team is assigned to act as the leader of response and recovery by analyzing various scenarios of reputation-damaging processes and planning relevant responses (Kash and Darling, 1998).

The phases of response and recovery in crisis management probably have the most direct, practical relevance to the implementation of reputation repair as it encompasses a wide range of specific action rules geared to successfully cope with a crisis that occurred. For example, Hale et al. (2005) present behavioral guides along the four sub-steps of crises responses: observation, interpretation, choice, and dissemination. During the observation step, it is critical to gather and identify extensive and correct information on the event of crisis. While firms recognize the importance of immediate responses to a crisis (Kash and Darling, 1998), the intense time pressure may impede the appropriate search efforts (Beatty and Smith, 1987; March and Simon, 1958; Ordonez and Benson, 1997; Vermeir and Van Kenhove, 2005). Interpretation seeks to ensure complete and accurate assessment of the crisis based on the information collected. The choice step involves intensive internal communications among the members of crisis management team, who consider possible options for action and agree upon a decision while facing ambiguity and time pressure (Weick and Sutcliffe, 2002). Finally, that decision must then be communicated outwardly to two different groups: one is the group that needs to implement the crisis response plan and the other is the public. The internal communication of the plan will be critical to the immediate success of the recovery, including reputation repair, while mistakes in the communication to the public will have serious and long term repercussions. Hale et al. (2005) warn against treating those four steps of response as a linear process and introduce the "Spiral Crisis Response Communication Model," which allows each of the four steps

---

6   Crisis response and crisis recovery are defined as two separate phases in the literature (Fink, 1986), but they often involve the same actions and lack a clear boundary (Hale et al., 2005).

to be continually revisited, while maintaining the general flow of activities discussed previously.

A firm's communication to the public is particularly imperative to a reputation repair process as it directly concerns the recovery of public images (Benoit, 1995). If a firm does not engage its stakeholders in the aftermath of a reputation-damaging event in a way that is acceptable to them, the firm will suffer reputational damages for a long time: e.g., if the stakeholders believe the firm is trying to control opinion, it can backfire. In addition, cultural/institutional environments or socio-technical factors may also impose some challenges to the public communication process. For example, the anti-corporate sentiment and the populist nature of the internet have increased the difficulty of clearly disseminating the crisis response plan to the public (Tucker and Melewar, 2005). The type and speed of communication and the accuracy of information disseminated also partly determine the performance of a firm's recovery effort (Horsley and Barker, 2002; Hunter et al., 2008). In particular, due to the paucity of research on the psychological impacts of crises despite its importance in crisis management, special attention needs to be devoted to the notion of "psychological service" (Butcher and Hatcher, 1988) in communicating with the public, which addresses victims' emotional needs following a crisis by appealing to effective communication strategies. This theme is especially imperative in that it can further offer many promising research topics related to the roles of emotions in reputation management in general and reputation repair in particular (Choi and Lin, 2009; Coombs, 2007; Coombs and Holladay, 2005).

The learning phase is not the core part of crisis management but it receives growing scholarly attention as successful learning from crisis experience is found to help a firm reduce its subsequent rate of crises. A better understanding of a crisis through experiential and (sometimes vicarious) learning will add clarity to crisis management and to the planning of preventing the future occurrences of the similar types of crises. Thus, this phase may make a substantial contribution to a crisis management in the long run. However, many organizations do not learn from crisis experience (e.g., the *Columbia* accident repeats the same problems as the *Challenger* accident; Mahler and Casamayou, 2009), and the literature on learning from errors and failures have explored the contexts under which organizations may learn from a crisis (e.g., Baum and Dahlin, 2007; Haunschild and Rhee, 2004; Kim, J.Y., et al., 2009; Kim, J., and Miner, 2007). Interestingly, Rhee and his colleagues (Rhee, 2009; Rhee and Haunschild, 2006; Rhee and Valdez, 2009) suggest that reputation itself constructs a context that facilitates or impedes learning from a reputation-damaging event.

The role of organizational systems, which Pearson and Mitroff (1993) and (Mitroff et al., 1996) suggest as the third key issue in crisis management, can be approached from the view of how various components of an organizational system tend to cause a crisis, help prevent the crisis, and aid in the recovery process. There have been many models that present the essential ingredients of organizational systems (see Scott and Davis, 2007, for a review), and reputation studies may benefit from exploring the possible consequences of each element for challenges to reputation repair. For example, drawing on Nadler and Tushman's congruence framework (1997), one can examine the impact that a firm's environment (e.g., cultural and social), strategy (e.g., cost-leadership, differentiation, and focus; Porter, 1980), technology, human resource practice, organizational structure (e.g., functional and product), organizational culture, and leadership have on the ways in which crisis management or a reputation repair process is facilitated or impeded.

Finally, the question of which stakeholder groups were impacted by a crisis and which stakeholder groups will respond should be addressed in the study of crisis management and reputation repair (Carroll and Buchholtz, 2008; Coombs, 2000; Pearson and Clair, 1998). Given the multi-dimensionality of reputation, a reputation-damaging event relates to a particular dimension (Rhee and Valdez, 2009), so stakeholders hurt by the event will be different depending on the dimensions affected by the event. Thus, researchers may be interested in examining the correspondences between reputational dimensions/ reputation-damaging events and stakeholder groups, the coverage of stakeholder groups impacted by the event, and communication relevant to each stakeholder group (Buysse and Verbeke, 2003; Fombrun et al., 2000; Ray, 1999; Ulmer, 2001).

A Sample of Research Agenda on Reputation Repair

Building upon our discussion on the various potential contributions of the literature on trust and crisis management to the study of reputation repair, we attempt to present a research model that we hope one can utilize and extend for their own studies of reputation repair. As stated earlier, the model presented here is not a complete model and in particular, it is an extension of Rhee and Valdez's (2009) model of "repairing damages to reputations." While their model focuses on the contextual factors underlying the heterogeneity of challenges in reputation repair, our model adds more action- and relation-oriented factors through the intuitions drawn from the previous research into trust and crisis management. Since reputation repair studies are still at an embryonic stage, the establishment of a reputation repair research model should take a step-wise approach, whereby any remaining research agenda needs to be incorporated in the subsequent efforts to complete the model. Thus, our discussion on trust and crisis management and their implications for reputation repair in preceding sections is selectively adapted to our model, so future studies need to make the model more fruitful by accommodating other parts of the discussion.

Our model focuses on three areas where we connect the notions of trust and crisis management to challenges in reputation repair. First, we propose that the multi-dimensional nature of trust affects the difficulty of reputation repair. Second, we benefit from the existing frameworks of rebuilding trust following a trust violating event to estimate the level of difficulty in reputation repair. Third, we substantiate the relationship between crisis management and reputation repair by looking at how activities along the phases of preparation, response, and communication surrounding a crisis can determine the difficulty in repairing damaged reputations.

From Rousseau et al.'s (1998) definition of trust discussed above, we find that the constructs of reputation and reputation repair intertwined with the various dimensions of trust, especially future orientation, perception (versus reality), directional positioning, and a level of uncertainty. We suggest that certain properties in each of those dimensions affect the ease or difficulty with which a firm faces its reputation repair activities. First, consider the *future orientation* of trust. A firm's reputation formed by the stakeholders' trust in the firm is built on its past behaviors and performance and pays present dividends, but it is in its future expectations that its greatest advantages reside. Most benefits attributed to a firm's good reputation, such as low costs and premium price, is based on the expectation that the firm will continue to perform well in the future. That is, current reputation building activities enhance market expectations on a firm's behavior and performance, generating greater future rents (Tadelis, 1999; Weigelt and Camerer, 1988). This suggests that the future orientation also matters in reputation repair as a firm's reputation-damaging event is perceived to fall short of the expectations a market audience has regarding the firm's actions related to the event. Given the expectancy violation effects (Burgoon and LePoire, 1993), therefore, one can propose that a greater expectation stemming from a firm's good reputation renders its reputation-damaging event more severe (Jones and Skarlicki, 2005; Rhee and Haunschild, 2006), thus making it more difficult for the firm to weather the crisis. However, when we consider *uncertainty* surrounding a trust relationship, it would also be possible to predict the opposite direction. Under the context of information asymmetry between a firm and its market audience, the firm's reputation serves as a signal of its trustworthiness and in particular, legitimacy, loyalty, third-party endorsements, popularity, and familiarity attached to a good reputation (Podolny, 2005; Rao, 1994; Rindova et al., 2006; Stuart et al., 1999; Whetten and Mackey, 2002) corroborate the positive roles of a good reputation under a high level of uncertain environments (Podolny, 1994, 2001). Thus, a firm's good reputation may form an important buffer against a reputation-damaging event (Cleeren et al., 2008), thus making it less challenging for the firm to overcome the crisis.

As trust represents a level of psychological state, a firm's reputation is viewed as the stakeholders' perceptions of the firm's performance and behaviors (Fombrun et al., 2000; Weiss et al., 1999). Researchers have been concerned about investigating the extent to which such perceptions are decoupled from the actual behaviors and performance (Benjamin and Podolny, 1999; Washington and Zajac, 2005). For example, regarding the evaluations of product quality, there is a relatively small discrepancy between perceived quality and actual quality in manufacturing industries (e.g., automotive) but a much larger discrepancy exists in professional services (e.g., hospitals and schools) (Podolny and Hsu, 2003). A good reputation that has been tightly coupled with a firm's actual qualities would be drastically affected by a reputation-damaging event because the event directly concerns the construct of the firm's reputation (e.g., Toyota's product recalls). In contrast, firms which have a reputation that is loosely coupled with actual qualities will be less vulnerable to a reputation-damaging event since the event may not be perceived to hurt the elements buttressing their reputations (e.g., poor quality paper authored by an HBS professor). Thus, one can suspect that the former case leads to a more challenging reputation repair process than the latter case.

The directional nature of trust relationship suggests that the trustor allows himself to be vulnerable to a breach of trust by the trustee and to reconcile himself to potential negative repercussions following the breach (Kim, P.H., et al., 2009). A firm's reputation also implies this directional nature in the relationship between the firm (trustee) and its market audience (trustor). We speculate, however, that a market audience's tolerance of potential or actual breaches of trust by a firm would not take a uniform path and will vary across different institutional and cultural environments. For example, given the different conceptualization of corporate responsibility along the political and ideological variations (Hart, 2005; Scherer and Palazzo, 2007), market audience in a socialist society (e.g., European socialism or welfare capitalism), where corporate social responsibility and citizenship are strongly emphasized, will be less tolerant of a firm's trust violating acts, but a market audience in a liberal capitalist society (e.g., American individual capitalism) may be more lenient with unethical behaviors driven by managerial greed for financial gains or profits. The East Asian business systems embedded in the "Confucian capitalism" (Chai and Rhee, 2010; Wilkinson, 1996; Yao, 2002) appears to produce mixed predictions: while their collectivistic and egalitarian approaches to business transactions and social welfare will lead a market audience to be unforgiving of a firm's trust violating acts, the state-led market coordination and its isomorphic diffusion at the societal level may help persuade the public to accept a firm's reputation-damaging event as inevitable for the achievement of the state's long-term goals. As suggested in this example, the political and ideological dimensions need to be considered to better understand variance in challenges in reputation repair at the societal level.

As briefly discussed above, intuitions from the model of trust repair also help generate an important research agenda for the study of reputation repair. In our model, we intend to introduce a couple of guiding examples in which the trust repair model can be utilized for the creation of research questions on reputation repair. Let us first revisit Tomlinson and Mayer's (2009) framework that synthesizes Mayer et al.'s (1995) model of repairing trustworthiness with Weiner's (1986) causal attribution theory. Applying this model to reputation repair studies, one can infer that if a reputation-damaging event occurs, which lessens the market audience' regard for a firm's ability, benevolence, or integrity, the market audience usually evaluates the event through three attribution dimensions. First, the audience asks whether the event was caused internally or externally. At this stage, researchers may be interested in testing a hypothesis: internally caused reputation-damaging events make it more difficult for a firm to repair damaged reputations than externally caused events. If the event is perceived to have internal causes, the market audience may raise a following question of whether the firm had control over the situation surrounding the reputation-damaging event. A possible hypothesis for this question would be that a damaged reputation is more likely to be repaired if the event is perceived to be beyond the firm's control, particularly when the reputation is related to firm's ability rather than benevolence or integrity. Finally, the market audience will consider whether the instance of a reputation-damaging event was a stable or unstable circumstance. To the extent that the market audience sees the event as one time incident rather than repeated, chronic one, damages to reputation will be more readily repaired.

Lewicki and Bunker's (1996) four-step model of trust repair also offers various informative foundations for research on reputation repair. In addition to our previous discussion on the possible variance in reputation repair challenges due to different elements comprising a reputation, their model suggests that various tactics across those four phases have different levels of efficacy in repairing damaged reputations. For example, Kim, P.H., et al.'s (2004) experimental study on the effects of apology versus denial for repairing trust drives us to propose an analogous hypothesis on reputation repair that a firm's damaged reputation will be more successfully repaired when the firm apologizes for a reputation-damaging event concerning matters of the firm's competence but denies culpability for a event concerning matters of the firm's integrity. Kim, P.H., et al.'s (2006) further study on the interaction effects between the type of trust violation (competence vs. integrity) and the type of apology leads to an additional hypothesis that a damaged reputation is more likely to be repaired when the firm apologizes with an internal attribution when the reputation-damaging event affects the firm's reputation for competence, but apologizes with an external attribution when the event affects the firm's reputation for integrity. Because a firm's justification, excuse, and denial following a reputation-damaging event are explicitly included in its public statements, researchers can benefit from content analyses to decode and quantify different types of such communication tactics, which will aid in testing many important hypotheses on their effects on the performance of reputation repair.

Finally, similar to the literature on the phases of trust restoration, research on various steps in crisis management (Fink, 1986; Hale et al., 2005) also encourages one to design useful research models for the study of reputation repair.[7] For example, the literature in crisis management strongly suggests the importance of a firm's immediate, yet informed response to a crisis or a reputation-damaging event under the intensive time pressure and high ambiguity. A series of studies presented by Meyer and his colleagues (Meyer, 1982; Meyer et al., 1990; Meyer et al., 2005) on organizational adaptations and learning find several organizational variables that help a firm successfully adapt to environmental jolts. Given the possible conceptualization of a reputation-damaging event as a form of an environmental jolt, we can propose a set of hypotheses exploring organizational properties that allow better responses and adaptations to the occurrence of a reputation-damaging event. The "law of requisite variety" (Ashby, 1956) suggests that for a firm to successfully accommodate an unforeseen outcome, it needs to maintain as much variety and flexibility within itself as the disturbance induced by the outcome. Thus, it is possible to propose that a firm with a greater level of internal variety and flexibilities will face less difficulty in repairing a damaged reputation. Based on this research proposition, numerous hypotheses can be derived that reflect the differing levels of difficulty in achieving reputation repair.

A variety of organizational variables can affect the reputation repair task, which is presumed to be mediated by internal variety or flexibility, and examples of such variables would include: structure—organic structure is more likely to facilitate timely response to a reputation-damaging event than a tightly coordinated structure (Adler et al., 1999; Jennings and Seaman, 1994; Puranam et al., 2006); technology—the extent to which advanced IT is adopted will be positively related to the ease with which organizational members can respond to a reputation-damaging event in a concerted way (Kane and Alavi, 2007); strategy—a reputation repair is more effectively managed through an autonomous strategy process than an induced strategy process (Burgelman, 1991); culture—"adaptive" organizational culture helps facilitate a reputation repair process (O'Reilly and Chatman, 1996); demographic diversity—the knowledge and experience diversity of members in a firm's crisis management team leads the firm to prepare for an extensive set of risk scenarios following a reputation-damaging event (Beckman, 2006; Taylor and Greve, 2006); and communication systems—a strong horizontal communication system vis-à-vis top-down communication in a firm helps reduce the rate of errors in its reputation repair process (Kim, T., and Rhee, 2009).

The literature on learning from crisis management experience or failure (Miner et al., 1999; Sitkin, 1992; Stern, 1997) presents another important arena where an abundant set of hypotheses on reputation repair can emerge. While positing that cumulative experience in reputation-damaging events reduce the difficulty with which a firm copes with subsequent events, researchers may seek to explore various properties of experience that enhance or dampen such learning effects. For example, studies on the learning

---

7   In fact, the most direct implications of crisis management for reputation repair can be found in studies of crisis management strategies, including impression management, symbolic communication strategies, and stigma management strategies. An intensive discussion on those implications appears in Rhee and Valdez (2009, pp. 163–5).

effects across different types of approaches to crisis or failure (e.g., Haunschild and Rhee, 2004; Kim, L., 1998) suggest that a defensive experience in reputation repair is less likely to produce learning effects than a proactive experience, thus making subsequent experiences more challenging. Findings from the study of learning from others' crises and failure experiences (e.g., Baum and Dahlin, 2007; Kim, J., and Miner, 2007) lead us to propose that reputation-damaging events and reputation repair processes experienced by a firm's reference groups or competitors provide a set of guiding routines and practices beneficial to the focal firm's reputation repair. Studies by Haunschild and Sullivan (2002) and Kim, J.Y., et al. (2009) highlight the possibility that a firm's successful reputation repair may require optimal levels of volume and diversity in its previous reputation repair experience.

Conclusion and Discussion

This chapter has examined how intuitions from two related research fields, trust and crisis management, can help explain the reputation repair processes following a reputation-damaging event and present a set of important research agenda centered on the factors which produce variance in the difficulty of reputation repair. More specifically, for a more integrative model, we have sought to complement Rhee and Valdez's (2009) structural approaches to reputation repair challenges by adding relational and behavioral perspectives. We believe that our work contributes to the reputation literature in three unique ways.

First, while the study of reputation has grown in the past several years, reputation repair research has not received much attention. While an understanding of reputation repair is impossible without an understanding of reputation building, the two reputational processes have distinct traits, elements, and dynamics. We hope that our presentation of a set of research agenda for the study of challenges in reputation repair is pioneering, not only inducing empirical tests for our propositions but also furthering scholarly efforts to investigate different aspects of reputation repair.

Second, we have directed attention to less explored links between trust restoration/ crisis management and reputation repair. The process of repairing a firm's damaged reputation is not independent of the process of restoring the lost trust a market audience has in a firm, and it should also be regarded as the central part of a firm's crisis management system. It is somewhat surprising to observe, however, that few attempts have been made to create such links. We have demonstrated some substantive ways in which research on reputation repair could be fruitful by benefiting from the literature on trust and crisis management, which would hopefully be reinforced by subsequent studies.

Third, this chapter offers valuable managerial and practical insights. Given the growing importance of corporate social responsibility in both domestic and global markets, managers should ensure that their firms are equipped with a series of systematic practices and routines in preparation for a reputation-damaging event. This article may provide managers with some useful guides on how they can manage reputation-damaging events with less difficulty when they face greater reputation repair challenges.

Certainly, this chapter constitutes just one step in a long journey of reputation repair studies. While we have added to the Rhee and Valdez's (2009) model of reputation repair, the integrate model still remains incomplete. Our research agenda on reputation repair from the relational and behavioral perspective is also indicative, rather than conclusive. To point out a few remaining gaps: although the relational and behavioral factors in reputation repair is incorporated into Rhee and Valdez's (2009) model of structural and contextual factors, the relationships between those two types of factors were not examined (e.g., mutually reinforcing); despite its critical roles in the performance of reputation repair, the effects of different stakeholder groups (insider vs. outside groups) on challenges in reputation repair were not discussed; we are still unclear whether the goal of reputation repair is to re-establish initial reputations or build a new reputation; and we did not differentiate among the reputation-damaging events (e.g., based on severity) whereby our model is based on the assumption that challenges in reputation repair does not vary with the nature of events. We leave this research task to future reputation studies.

Finally, we hope that future researchers convert our theoretical suggestions and propositions to testable forms of hypotheses and operationalize our key constructs for empirical analyses. However, a firm's reputation repair process is not usually publicized and its key elements are not easily quantifiable. Thus, an intensive qualitative study, such as direct observation of a whole reputation repair process following a reputation-damaging event in a firm's crisis management team, needs to be conducted to supplement or corroborate evidence from possible quantitative analyses. We suggest that research methodologies for the study of reputation repair should be also informed by those that have been established in the study of trust (restoration) and crisis management.

References

Adler, P. S., Goldoftas, B., and Levine, D. I. 1999. Flexibility versus efficiency? A case study of model changeovers in the Toyota production system. *Organization Science*, 10: 43–68.

Anderson, E. W., and Weitz, B. 1992. The use of pledges to build and sustain commitment in distribution channels. *Journal of Marketing Research,* 29: 18–34.

Ashby, W. R. 1956. *An Introduction to Cybernetics*. London: Chapman Hall Ltd.

Ashcroft, L. 1997. Crisis management-public relations. *Journal of Managerial Psychology,* 12: 325–32.

Augustine, N. R. 1995. Business crisis: Guaranteed preventatives – and what to do after they fail. *Executive Speeches*, 9: 28–42.

Banerjee, A.,and Duflo, E. 2000. Reputation effects and the limits of contracting: A study of the Indian software industry. *Quarterly Journal of Economics*, 115: 989–1015.

Banks, D. T., Hutchinson, J. W., and Meyer, R. J. 2002. Reputation in marketing channels: Repeated transactions bargaining with two-sided uncertainty. *Marketing Science*, 21: 252–72.

Barnett, M. L., Jermier J. M., and Lafferty, B. A. 2006. Corporate reputation: The definitional landscape. *Corporate Reputation Review*, 9: 26–38.

Barney, J. B., and Hansen, M. H. 1994. Trustworthiness as a source of competitive advantage. *Strategic Management Journal*, 15: 175–90.

Baum, J. A. C., and Dahlin, K. B. 2007. Aspirational performance and railroads' patterns of learning from train wrecks and crashes. *Organization Science*, 18: 368–85.

Beatty, S. E., and Smith, S. M. 1987. External search effort: An investigation across several product categories. *Journal of Consumer Research*, 14: 83–95.

Beckman, C. M. 2006. The influence of founding team company affiliations on firm behavior. *Academy of Management Journal*, 49: 741–58.

Benjamin, B. A., and Podolny, J. M. 1999. Status, quality and social order in the California wine industry. *Administrative Science Quarterly*, 44: 563–89.

Benoit, W. L. 1995. *Accounts, Excuses and Apologies: A Theory of Image Restoration*. Albany, NY: State University of New York Press.

Blois, K. J. 1999. Trust in business to business relationships: An evaluation of its status. *Journal of Management Studies*, 36: 197–215.

Burgelmen, R. A. 1991. Intraorganizational ecology of strategy making and organizational adaptation: Theory and field research. *Organization Science*, 2: 239–62.

Burgoon, J. K., and LePoire, B. A. 1993. Effects of communication expectancies, actual communication, and expectancy disconfirmation on evaluations of communicators and their communication behavior. *Human Communication Research*, 20: 67–96.

Burt, R. S. 2005. *Brokerage and Closure: An Introduction to Social Capital*. Oxford: Oxford University Press.

Burt, R. S., and Knez, M., 1995. *Trust in Organizations*. Thousand Oaks, CA: Sage.

Burt, R. S., and Knez, M. 1996. Trust and third party gossip, in R. M. Kramer and T. R. Tyler (eds) *Trust in Organizations: Frontiers or Theory and Research* (pp. 68–89). Thousand Oaks, CA: Sage.

Butcher, J. N., and Hatcher, C. 1988. The neglected entity in air disaster planning: Psychological services. *American Psychologist*, 43: 724–9.

Buysse, K., and Verbeke, A. 2003. Proactive environmental strategies: A stakeholder management perspective. *Strategic Management Journal*, 24: 453–70.

Carroll, A. B., and Buchholtz, A. K. 2008. *Business and Society: Ethics and Stakeholder Management*. Florence, KY: Cengage Learning.

Caruana, A., and Chircop, S. 2000. Measuring corporate reputation: A case example. *Corporate Reputation Review*, 3: 43–57.

Chai, S.-K., and Rhee, M. 2010. Confucian capitalism and the paradox of closure and structural holes in East Asian firms. *Management and Organization Review*, 6: 5–29.

Chaloner, N., and Brotzen, D. 2002. How SABMiller protects its biggest asset – its reputation. *Strategic Communication Management*, 6: 12–16.

Cleeren, K., Dekimpe, M. G., and Helsen, K. 2008. Weathering product-harm crises. *Journal of the Academy of Marketing*, 36: 262–70.

Choi, Y., and Lin, Y.-H. 2009. Consumer responses to Mattel product recalls posted on online bulletin boards: Exploring two types of emotion. *Journal of Public Relations Research*, 21: 198–207.

Coombs, W. T. 1998. An analytic framework for crisis situations: Better responses from a better understanding of the situation. *Journal of Public Relations Research*, 10: 177–91.

Coombs, W. T. 1999. *Ongoing Crisis Communication: Planning Managing and Responding*. Thousand Oaks, CA: Sage.

Coombs, W. T. 2000. Crisis management: The advantages of a relational perspective, in Ledingham, J. A. and Bruning, S. D. (eds) *Public Relations as Relationship Management*, Mahwah, NJ: Lawrence Erlbaum Associates, Inc.

Coombs, W. T. 2001. Interpersonal communication and public relations, in Heath, R. L. (ed.) *Handbook of Public Relations*, Thousand Oaks, CA: Sage.

Coombs, W. T. 2007. *Ongoing Crisis Communication: Planning, Managing and Responding*. Sage: Thousand Oaks, CA.

Coombs, W. T., and Holladay, S. J. 2006. Unpacking the halo effect: Reputation and crisis management. *Journal of Communication Management*, 10: 123–37.

Corritore, C. L., Kracher, B., and Wiedenbeck, S. 2003. On-line trust: Concepts, evolving themes, a model. *International Journal of Human-Computer Studies*, 58: 737–58.

Deephouse, D. L., and Carter, S. M. 2005. An examination of differences between organizational legitimacy and organizational reputation. *Journal of Management Studies*, 42: 329–60.

Deutsch, M. 1958. Trust and suspicion. *Journal of Conflict Resolution*, 2: 265–79.

Diamond, D. W. 1991. Monitoring and reputation: The choice between bank loans and directly placed debt. *Journal of Political Economy*, 99: 689–721.

Dirks, K. T., Lewicki, R. J., and Zaheer, A. 2009. Repairing relationships within and between organizations: Building a conceptual foundation. *Academy of Management Review*, 34: 68–84.

Dollinger, M. J., Golden, P. A., and Saxton, T. 1997. The effect of reputation on the decision to joint venture. *Strategic Management Journal*, 18: 127–40.

Dukerich, J. M. ,and Carter, S. M. 2000. Distorted image and reputation repair, in Schultz, M., Hatch, M. J., and Larsen, M. H. (eds) *The Expressive Organization: Linking Identity, Reputation and the Corporate Brand*. Oxford: Oxford University Press.

Elsbach, K. D. and Kramer, R. M. 1996. Members' responses to organizational identity threats: Encountering and countering the business wee rankings. *Administrative Science Quarterly*, 41: 442–76.

Ely, J., and Valimaki, J. 2003. Bad reputation. *Quarterly Journal of Economics*, 118: 785–814.

Fink, S. 1986. *Crisis Management: Planning for the Inevitable*. New York: American Management Association.

Ferrin, D. L., Dirks, K. T., and Shah, Pri P. 2006. Direct and indirect effects of third-party relationships on interpersonal trust. *Journal of Applied Psychology*, 91: 870–83.

Fombrun, C. 1996. *Reputation, Realizing Value from the Corporate Image*. Boston, MA: Harvard Business School Press.

Fombrun, C., Gardberg, N. A., and Sever, J. M. 2000. The reputation quotient: A multi-stakeholder measure of corporate reputation. *Journal of Brand Management*, 7: 241–55.

Ganeson, S. 1994. Determinants of long-term orientation in buyer-seller relationships. *Journal of Marketing*, 58: 1–19.

Gatewood, R. D., Gowan, M. A.,and Lautenschlager, G. J. 1993. Corporate image, recruitment image and initial job choice decisions. *Academy of Management Journal*, 36: 414–27.

Gillespie, N., and Dietz, G. 2009. Trust repair after an organization-level trust failure. *Academy of Management Review*, 34: 127–45.

Goffman, E. 1967. *Interaction Ritual: Essays on Face-to-face Behavior*. Garden City, NY: Anchor Books.

Grabner-Kreuter, S. 2002. The role of consumers' trust in online-shopping. *Journal of Business Ethics*, 39: 43–50.

Hale, J. E., Dulek, R. E., and Hale, D. P. 2005. Crisis response communication challenges: Building theory from qualitative data. *Journal of Business Communication*, 42: 112–34.

Hart, S. 2005. *Capitalism at the Crossroads: the Unlimited Business Opportunities in Solving the World's Most Difficult Problems*. Philadelphia: Wharton School Publishing.

Haunschild, P., Chandler, D., Rhee, M., and Beckman, C. M. 2009. Is good reputation always good? Asymmetric status homophily and interfirm network structure. Presented at the Insead Network Conference.

Haunschild, P., and Rhee, M. 2004. The role of volition in organizational learning: The case of automotive product recalls. *Management Science*, 50: 1545–60.

Haunschild, P. and Sullivan, B. N. 2002. Learning from complexity: Effects of prior accidents and incidents on airlines' learning. *Administrative Science Quarterly*, 47: 609–43.

Hayward, R. 2002. *Manage Your Reputation*. London: Kogan Page.

Hoffer, G. E., Pruitt, S. W., and Reilly, R. J. 1994. When recalls matter: Factors affecting owner response to automotive recalls. *Journal of Consumer Affairs*, 28: 96–106.

Horsley, J. S., and Barker, R. T. 2002. Toward a synthesis model for crisis communication in the public sector. *Journal of Business and Technical Communication*, 16: 406–41.

Hosmer, L. T. 1995. Trust: The connecting link between organizational theory and philosophical ethics. *Academy of Management Review*, 20: 379–403.

Hunter, M. L., Le Menestrel, M., and de Bettignies, H.-C. 2008. Beyond control: Crisis strategies and stakeholder media in the Danone boycott of 2001. *Corporate Reputation Review*, 11: 335–50.

Jennings, D. F., and Seamen, S. L. 1994. High and low levels of organizational adaptation: An empirical analysis of strategy, structure, and performance. *Strategic Management Journal*, 15: 459–75.

Jones, D. A., and Skarlicki, D. P. 2005. The effects of overhearing peers discuss an authority's fairness reputation on reactions to subsequent treatment. *Journal of Applied Psychology*, 90: 363–72.

Kane, G. C., and Alavi, M. 2007. Information technology and organizational learning: An investigation of exploration and exploitation processes. *Organization Science*, 18: 796–812.

Kash, T. J., and Darling, J. R. 1998. Crisis management: prevention, diagnosis and intervention. *Leadership and Organization Development Journal*, 19: 179–86.

Kelley, H. H. 1973. The process of causal attribution. *American Psychologist*, 28: 107–28.

Kim, J., and Miner, A. S. 2007. Vicarious learning from the failures and near-failures of others: Evidence from the U. S. commercial banking industry. *Academy of Management Journal*, 50: 687–714.

Kim, J. Y., Kim, J. Y. J., and Miner, A. S. 2009. Organizational learning from extreme performance experience: The impact of success and recovery experience. *Organization Science*, 20: 958–78.

Kim, L. 1998. Crisis construction and organizational learning: Capability building in catching up at Hyundai Motors. *Organization Science*, 9: 506–21.

Kim, P. H., Dirks, K. T, Cooper, C. D., and Ferrin, D. L. 2006. When more blame is better than less: The implications of internal vs. external attributions for the repair of trust after a competence- vs. integrity-based trust violation. *Organization Behavior and Human Decision Processes*, 99: 49–65.

Kim, P. H., Dirks, K. T., and Cooper, C. D. 2009. The repair of trust: A dynamic bilateral perspective and multilevel conceptualization. *Academy of Management Review*, 34: 401–22.

Kim, P. H., Ferrin, D. L., Cooper, C. D., and Dirks, K. T. 2004. Removing the shadow of suspicion: The effects of apology versus denial for repairing competence- versus integrity-based trust violations. *Journal of Applied Psychology*, 89: 104–18.

Kim, T., and Rhee, M. 2009. Exploration and exploitation: Internal variety and environmental dynamism. *Strategic Organization*, 7: 11–41.

Lane, C., and Bachman, R. 2000. *Trust Between and Within Organizations: Conceptual issues and empirical applications*. Oxford: Oxford Press.

Lewicki, R. J. and Bunker, B. B. 1996. Building and maintaining trust in work relationships. *Trust in organizations: Frontiers of theory and research* (pp. 114–39). Thousand Oaks, CA: Sage.

Lewicki, R. J., McAllister, D. J., and Bies, R. J. 1998. Trust and distrust: New relationships and realities. *Academy of Management Review*, 23: 438–58.

Mahler , J. G.,and Casamayou, M. H. 2009: *Organizational Learning at NASA: The Challenger and Columbia accidents*. Washington, D C: Georgetown University Press.

March J. G. and Simon, H. A. 1958. *Organizations*. New York: John Wiley.

Marra, F. J. 1998. Crisis communication plans: Poor predictors of excellent crisis public relations. *Public Relations Review*, 24: 461–74.

Mayer, R. C., Davis, J. H., and Schoorman, F. D. 1995. An integrative model of organizational trust. *Academy of Management Review*, 20: 709–34.

Meyer, A. D. 1982. Adapting to environmental jolts. *Administrative Science Quarterly*, 27: 515–37.

Meyer, A. D., Brooks, G. R., and Goes, J. B. 1990. Environmental jolts and industry revolutions: Organizational responses to discontinuous change. *Strategic Management Journal*, 11: 93–110.

Meyer, A. D., Gaba, V., and Colwell, K. A. 2005. Organizing far from equilibrium: Nonlinear change in organizational fields. *Organization Science*, 16: 456–73.

Milgrom, P. and Roberts, J. 1982. Predation, reputation and entry deterrence. *Journal of Economic Theory*, 27: 253–79.

Miner, A. S., Kim, J.-Y., Holzinger, I. W., and Haunschild, P. R. 1999. Fruits of failure: Organizational failure and population level learning. *Advances in Strategic Management*, 16: 187–220.

Mitroff, I. I., Pearson, C. M., and Harrigan, L. K. 1996. *The Essential Guide to Managing Corporate Crises. A step-by-step handbook for surviving major catastrophes.* New York: Oxford University Press.

Mitroff, I. I., Shrivastava, P., and Udwadia, F. C. 1987. Effective crisis management. *Academy of Management Executive*, 1: 283–92.

Morley, M. 1998. *How to Manage Your Global Reputation.* Basingstoke, UK: Macmillan.

Morris, M. W., and Moore, P. C. 2000. The lessons we (don't) learn: Counterfactual thinking and organizational accountability after a close call. *Administrative Science Quarterly*, 45: 737–65.

Morris, M. W., and Peng, K. 1994. Culture and cause: American and Chinese attributions for social and physical events. *Journal of Personality and Social Psychology*, 67: 949–71.

Nadler, T. A., and Tushman, M. L. 1997. *Competing by Design: The power of organizational architecture.* New York: Oxford University Press.

Nowak, M. A. and Sigmund, K. 2000. Cooperation versus competition. *Financial Analyst Journal*, 56: 13–22.

Ordonez, L., and Benson, L. 1997. Decision under time pressure: How time constraint affects risky decision making. *Organizational Behavior and Human Decision Making Processes*, 71: 121–41.

O'Reilly, C. A., and Chatman, J. A. 1996. Culture as social control: Corporations, cults, and commitment, in Cummings, L. L., and Staw, B. M. (eds) *Research in Organizational Behavior.* Stamford, CT: JAI Press.

Pearson, C. M., and Mitroff, I. I. 1993. From crisis prone to crisis prepared: A framework for crisis management. *Academy of Management Executive*, 7: 48–59.

Pearson, C. M., and Clair J. A. 1998. Reframing crisis management. *The Academy of Management Review*, 23: 59–77.

Perrow, C. 1984. *Normal Accidents: Living with high-risk technologies.* New York: Basic Books.

Podolny, J. M. 1993. A status-based model of market competition. *American Journal of Sociology*, 98: 829–72.

Podolny, J. M. 1994. Market uncertainty and the social character of economic exchange. *Administrative Science Quarterly*, 39: 458–83.

Podolny, J. M. 2001. Networks as the pipes and prisms of the market. *American Journal of Sociology*, 107: 33–60.

Podolny, J. M. 2005. *Status Signals: A sociological study of market competition.* Princeton, NJ: Princeton University Press.

Podolny , J. M., and Hsu, G. 2003. Quality, exchange and Knightian uncertainty. *Research in the Sociology of Organizations*, 20: 77–103.

Porter, M.E. 1980. *Competitive Strategy.* New York: Free Press

Puranam, P., Singh, B. C., and Zollo, H. 2006. Due diligence failure as a signal detection problem. *Strategic Organization*, 4: 319–48.

Rao, H. 1994. The social construction of reputation: Certification contests, legitimation, and the survival of organizations in the American automobile industry, 1895–1912. *Strategic Management Journal*, 15 (Special Winter Issue): 29–44.

Ray, S. J. 1999. *Strategic Communication in Crisis Management Lessons from the Airline Industry*. Westport, CT: Quorum.

Reason, J. 1997. *Managing the Risks of Organizational Accidents*. Aldershot, UK: Ashgate.

Ren, H., and Gray, B. 2009. Repairing relationship conflict: How violation types and culture influence the effectiveness of restoration rituals. *Academy of Management Review*, 34: 105–26.

Rhee, M. 2009. Does reputation contribute to reducing organizational errors? A learning approach. *Journal of Management Studies*, 46: 676–703.

Rhee, M., and Haunschild, P. 2006. The liability of a good reputation: A study of product recalls in the U.S. automobile industry. *Organization Science*, 17: 101–17.

Rhee, M., and Valdez, M. E. 2009. Contextual factors surrounding reputation damage with potential implications for reputation repair. *Academy of Management Review*, 34(1): 146–68.

Rindova, V. P., Pollock, T. G., and Haywood, M. L. A. 2006. Celebrity firms: The social construction of market popularity. *Academy of Management Review*, 31(1): 50–71.

Rindova, V. P., Williamson, I.O., Petkova, A. P., and Sever, J. M. 2005. Being good or being known: An empirical examination of the dimensions, antecedents, and consequences of organizational reputation. *Academy of Management Journal*, 48: 1033–49.

Rousseau, D. M., Sitkin, S. B., Burt, R. S., and Camerer, C. 1998. Not so different after all: A cross-discipline view of trust. *Academy of Management Review*, 23: 393–404.

Scherer, A. G., and Palazzo, G. 2007. Toward a political conception of corporate responsibility – business and society seen from a Habermasian perspective. *Academy of Management Review*, 32: 1096–120.

Scott, W. R., and Davis, G. F. 2007. *Organizations and Organizing: Rational, natural, and open system perspectives*. Upper Saddle River, NJ: Pearson Prentice Hall.

Shane, S., and Cable, D. 2002. Network ties, reputation and the financing of new ventures. *Management Science*, 48: 364–81.

Shapiro, C. 1983. Premiums for high quality products as returns to reputations. *Quarterly Journal of Economics*, 98: 659–79.

Sheppard, B. H., and Tuchinsky, M. 1996. Micro O.B. and the network organization, in Kramer, R. M., and Tyler, T. R. (eds) *Trust in Organizations: Frontiers in theory and research* (pp. 140–64). Thousand Oaks, CA: Sage.

Sitkin, S. 1992. Learning Through Failure: The strategy of small losses. *Research in Organizational Behavior*, 14: 231–66.

Snyder, C. R., and Higgins, R. L. 1988. Excuses: Their effective role in negotiation of reality. *Psychological Bulletin*, 104: 23–35.

Stern, E. 1997. Crisis and learning: A conceptual balance sheet. *Journal of Contingencies and Crisis Management*, 5: 69–86.

Stuart, T. E., Hoang, H., and Hybels, R. 1999. Interorganizational endorsements and the performance of entrepreneurial ventures. *Administrative Science Quarterly*, 44: 315–49.

Swift, T. 2001. Trust, reputation and corporate accountability to stakeholders. *Business Ethics*, 10: 16–26.

Tadelis, S. 1999. What's in a name? Reputation as a tradeable asset. *The American Economic Review*, 89: 548–63.

Tan, Y.-H., and Thoen, W. 2000. Toward a generic model of trust for electronic commerce. *International Journal of Electronic Commerce*, 5: 61–74.

Taylor, A., and Greve, H. 2006. Superman or the fantastic four? Knowledge combination and experience in innovative teams. *Academy of Management Journal*, 49: 723–40.

Ting-Toomey, S. 1999. *Communicating across Cultures*. New York: The Guilford Press.

Tomlinson, E. C. and Mayer, R. C. 2009. The role of causal attribution dimensions in trust repair. *Academy of Management Review*, 34(1): 85–104.

Tucker, L., and Melewar, T. C. 2005. Corporate reputation and crisis management: The threat and manageability of anti-corporatism. *Corporate Reputation Review*, 7: 377–87.

Turban, D. B., and Greening, D. W. 1997. Corporate social performance and organizational attractiveness to prospective employees. *Academy of Management Journal*, 40: 658–73.

Ulmer, R. R. 2001. Effective crisis management through established stakeholder relationships. *Management Communication Quarterly*, 14: 590–615.

Vaughan, D. 1996. *The Challenger Launch Decision: Risky technology, culture, and deviance at NASA*. Chicago, IL: The University of Chicago Press.

Vaughan, D. 1997. The trickle-down effect: Policy decision, risky work and the Challenger tragedy. *California Management Review*, 39: 80–102.

Vermeir, I., and Van Kenhove, P. 2005. The influence of need for closure and perceived time pressure on search effort for price and promotional information in a grocery shopping context. *Psychology and Marketing*, 22: 71–95.

Washington, M., and Zajac, E. J. 2005. Status evolution and composition: Theory and evidence. *Academy of Management Journal*, 48: 282–96.

Weick, K. E., and Sutcliffe, K. M. 2002. *Managing the Unexpected: Assuring high performance in an age of complexity*, Hoboken, NJ: Wiley.

Weigelt, K., and Camerer, C. 1988. Reputation and corporate strategy: A review of recent theory and applications. *Strategic Management Journal*, 9: 443–54.

Weiner, B. 1986. *An Attributional Model of Motivation and Emotion*. New York: Springer-Verlag.

Weiss, A. M., Anderson, E., and MacInnis, D. J. 1999. Reputation management as a motivation for sales structure decisions. *Journal of Marketing*, 63: 74–89.

Whetten, D. A., and Mackey, A. 2002. A social actor conception of organizational identity and its implications for the study of organizational reputation. *Business and Society*, 41: 393–414.

Wilkinson, B. 1996. Culture, institutions and business in East Asia. *Organization Studies*, 17: 421–47.

Yao, S. G. 2002. *Translation and the Languages of Modernism: Gender, politics, language*. New York: Palgrave Macmillan.

Zucker, L. G. 1986. Production of trust: Institutional sources of economic structure, 1840–1920. *Research in Organizational Behavior*, 8: 53–111.

Index

If you have found this book useful you may be interested in other titles from Gower

An HR Guide to Workplace Fraud and Criminal Behaviour:
Recognition, Prevention and Management
Michael J. Comer and Timothy E. Stephens
Hardback: 978-0-566-08555-0

Brand Risk:
Adding Risk Literacy to Brand Management
David Abrahams
Hardback: 978-0-566-08724-0
e-book: 978-0-7546-8890-7

Crime and Corruption in Organizations:
Why It Occurs and What To Do About It
Edited by
Ronald J. Burke, Edward C. Tomlinson and Cary L. Cooper
Hardback: 978-0-566-08981-7
e-book: 978-1-4094-1260-1

Estimating Risk:
A Management Approach
Andy Garlick
Hardback: 978-0-566-08776-9

GOWER

Risk Strategies:
Dialling Up Optimum Firm Risk
Les Coleman
Hardback: 978-0-566-08938-1
e-book: 978-0-566-08939-8

Risky Business:
Psychological, Physical and Financial Costs
of High Risk Behavior in Organizations
Edited by
Professor Ronald J. Burke and Professor Cary L. Cooper
Hardback: 978-0-566-08915-2
e-book: 978-1-4094-0553-5

Safety Culture:
Assessing and Changing the Behaviour of Organisations
John Bernard Taylor
Hardback: 978-1-4094-0127-8
e-book: 978-1-4094-0128-5

Terrorism, the Worker and the City:
Simulations and Security in a Time of Terror
Luke Howie
Hardback: 978-0-566-08889-6
e-book: 978-0-566-09250-3

Visit **www.gowerpublishing.com** and

- search the entire catalogue of Gower books in print
- order titles online at 10% discount
- take advantage of special offers
- sign up for our monthly e-mail update service
- download free sample chapters from all recent titles
- download or order our catalogue